Instructor's Manual and Media Guide

to accompany

Educational Psychology
Windows on Classrooms

Sixth Edition

Paul Eggen
University of North Florida

Don Kauchak
University of Utah

PEARSON

Merrill
Prentice Hall

Upper Saddle River, New Jersey
Columbus, Ohio

Pearson Prentice Hall™ is a trademark of Pearson Education, Inc.
Pearson® is a registered trademark of Pearson plc
Prentice Hall® is a registered trademark of Pearson Education, Inc.
Merrill® is a registered trademark of Pearson Education, Inc.

Instructors of classes using Eggen & Kauchak, *Educational Psychology: Windows on Classrooms, Sixth Edition,*
may reproduce material from the instructor's manual and media guide for classroom use.

10 9 8 7 6 5 4 3 2 1

ISBN: 0-13-110889-1

TABLE OF CONTENTS

TRANSPARENCY LIST

TRANSPARENCY MASTER LIST

TO THE INSTRUCTOR

Welcome to the sixth edition of this text! In preparing the Instructor's Manual (IM) for the sixth edition of *Educational Psychology: Windows on Classrooms*, we've tried to further streamline the presentation outline, so you can use it even more efficiently than was possible in earlier editions. We've also continued to increase number of teaching ideas and have added some additional support materials. We hope you and your students find these changes helpful.

New to This Edition

Seven *new* features in the package for *Educational Psychology: Windows on Classrooms* (6th ed.) are designed to make your teaching more effective and efficient. They are:

■ **"Looking Through Classroom Windows" Video.** This video includes 12 classroom lessons, each of which is either an opening or a closing chapter case study in the text. The videos allow you to have the students both read the written transcript of the lesson and see the lesson itself, which will allow richer discussions of the lesson and the topic that is taught. The videos are described in detail in the media guide that is included as part of this manual.

■ **New chapter: "Constructing Understanding."** This chapter expands the coverage of cognitive learning theory with emphasis on knowledge construction and the implications it has for teaching and assessment.

■ **New chapter: "Motivation in the Classroom."** This chapter translates theories of motivation into practical suggestions for classroom practice.

■ **New chapter: "Assessment Through Standardized Testing."** This chapter extends the assessment theme of the text to include a detailed discussion of standardized testing and issues involved in the emphasis on standardized testing.

■ **Assessment Theme.** Each chapter includes a section examining the role of assessment related to the chapter's topics.

■ **Instructional Strategies.** Each major topic in every chapter includes an instructional strategies section that offers specific applications of the topic in classrooms.

■ **Expanded Companion Website.** The book's companion website at www.prenhall.com/eggen has been significantly expanded and improved. It now includes:
  ● *Practice Quiz* and *Essay Questions* that provide self-assessments and feedback to help students study for quizzes and exams.
  ● Brief video clips (referenced in the margins of textbook pages) in the *Classrooms on the Web* module, which illustrate key educational psychology concepts. (An example is on page 7 of the text, and each chapter has one or more of the clips.)
  ● Feedback for Constructed-Response Questions and Document-Based Analysis (found in the book's closing case studies) in the *Practice for PRAXIS™* module.
  ● *Online Cases* that provide students with additional practice in applying knowledge to genuine classroom episodes.
  ● *Online Portfolio Activities* that contribute to the creation of a teaching portfolio.
  ● *Additional Content,* which provides supplementary information that goes beyond the scope of the content presented in the text.
  ● *Web Links* that take students to selected educational psychology sites on the Web.

Using the Instructor's Manual

The *Instructor's Manual* is organized into five sections each of which was designed to provide you with strategies to model effective instruction.

- **Teaching Suggestions**. Teaching suggestions are general suggestions for teaching your course, together with the rationale for each suggestion. They are designed to help you "practice what you preach." We emphasize that they are merely "suggestions." You are the best judge of what will produce the most learning in your students.

- **Suggested Projects**. The *Suggested Projects* offer ideas for student activities, one or more of which you may choose to assign your students.

- **Observing in Classrooms**. If you have a field component attached to your course, or you have access to schools, you may want your students to complete some of the field activities outlined in this section. Guidelines are presented in this section to inform your students of appropriate protocol when making school visits.

- **Transparency Masters**. The transparency masters (**TM**) referred to the chapter-by-chapter outlines are located in this final section of the IM.

- **Chapter-by-Chapter Guides**. The chapter-by-chapter guides are set up as follows:

Chapter Overview	The overview provides you with a short summary of the major concepts in each chapter.
Chapter Objectives	The objectives describe the important learning outcomes for each chapter.
Transparencies	A list of transparencies designed to be used with the chapter is included. The transparencies exist in a combination of color and black and white. They are identified by chapter and number, e.g., T 2.1 is the first transparency on the list for Chapter 2.
Transparency Masters	The transparency masters include a number of problems, questions, and activities designed to enrich your instruction and increase your students' depth of understanding. The transparency masters are listed by chapter and number, e.g., TM 2.1 is the first transparency master on the list for Chapter 2. The transparency masters are located in a separate section near the end of this Instructor's Manual. They are written in large type and only need to be copied onto an acetate.
Videos	Suggestions for using the new *Looking Through Classroom Videos* as well as the other videos that accompany the book.
Chapter Outline	The chapter outline includes all the headings for all sections of the chapter.
Presentation Outline	The presentation outline provides a number of teaching strategies. Teaching suggestions are identified with the symbol ■.

Enrichment information is included in some of the outlines. This includes information that is *related* to topics covered in the text, *but the information itself isn't included in the text*. It is offered to allow you to enrich the topic you present if you should choose to do so. This supplementary material is boxed in this IM.

Discussion Starters

Discussion starters are questions designed to stimulate student thinking in a more analytical and integrative way. Discussion starters can be used for large or small group activities or given to students as take-home assignments.

Background Readings

Outside sources were chosen to help you better prepare for the teaching of each chapter. Some references included in this list are also references in the chapters themselves; some are not. All are annotated to assist you in a selection process.

Constructed Response and Document-Based Analysis Feedback

This section provides you with feedback for the *Constructed Response* and *Document-Based Analysis* questions that are written in a format that parallels the PRAXIS™ exam. The questions appear at the end of every chapter.

Classroom Exercises

The classroom exercises ask your students to further apply the information they're studying to new situations. They can be used as in-class activities or homework. Feedback for each of these exercises is included in this IM. (Students do not have access to the feedback unless you choose to share it with them.)

Features of the Text

A number of features in the text have been designed to make the content more meaningful and applicable to the real world of teaching. The use of these features is supported in ancillary materials and in particular through the Presentation Outlines in the IM, the Videos and Video Guide, and the Student Study Guide.

- **Beginning-of-Chapter Case**. Each chapter in the text begins with a case study taken from an actual classroom. The case is integrated with the chapter content, and in several instances, dialogue from the case is inserted into the discussion to further illustrate the topic.

- **End-of-Chapter Case and Practice for PRAXIS™** . Each chapter also ends with a case that asks your students to apply their understanding of the chapter content to a new situation. The application questions parallel the format used in the PRAXIS™ exam.

- **Examples and Vignettes**. Each chapter includes several short classroom examples vignettes that further illustrate chapter content.

- **Margin Questions**. The questions in the margins of all the chapters ask students to think critically to immediately apply their understanding of the content to new situations. In addition, margin notes integrate content from one chapter to another. All margin notes are sequentially numbered within each chapter. The numbers align with margin note answers in the Student Study Guide.

Additional Ancillaries

- **Test Bank.** The comprehensive test bank, available in Windows and MacIntosh formats, includes about 1700 test items from which you can develop your examinations. Test items include true-false, lower- and higher-level multiple-choice questions, and essay items. Most of the test items require higher-level responses from students. A printed version of the test bank is also available.

- **Media Guide**. The media guide includes detailed descriptions of the media that accompany the text together with suggestions for use. It is included in this manual.

- **Transparencies**. Over 100 transparencies presented in both acetate form and as PowerPoint slides are available to support your learning activities. Suggestions for using the transparencies are included presentation outlines.

- **Transparency Masters**. The transparency masters are organized by chapter and appear in this manual beginning on page xxx.. Many of the masters are in the form of exercises that can be used as class activities.

- **Student Study Guide.** The *Student Study Guide* includes 1) feedback for the margin questions in one-to-one correspondence with the numbers in the text, 2) additional *application exercises*, and 3) *self-help quizzes*; all are designed to put students into active learning roles to construct a deeper understanding of educational psychology.

- **Companion Website.** The expanded website was described in the "New to this Edition" section.

- **CD-ROM.** All available print ancillaries for *Educational Psychology: Windows on Classrooms, the fifth edition*, are also available on the accompanying CD-ROM. Unique access to the Presentation Outlines from the Instructor's Manual will enable you to link to the transparencies and transparency masters allowing you to customize your lectures and present them electronically, if you wish.

We hope you find these materials useful. If you have any questions or comments about information in the text, this Instructor's Manual, or any of the other supporting materials, please feel free to call or email either of us at any time. Our phone numbers and email addresses are:

Paul Eggen   (904) 620-2764, peggen@unf.edu
Don Kauchak (801) 587-7995, kauchak@ed.utah.edu.

We would be pleased to talk to you or hear from you. Good luck in your teaching!

TEACHING SUGGESTIONS

Suggestion	Rationale	Text Reference
If your classes aren't so large that the effort is prohibitive, try to learn students' names	Knowing their names is a form of personalization which promotes a sense of belonging in the students and demonstrates caring.	Chapter 11
Begin your classes on time, and have your materials prepared and ready.	Effective teachers maximize their time available for instruction.	Chapter 13
Establish routines for turning in and collecting materials and other procedural activities.	Experts teachers have as many of their procedures routinized as possible. These routines contribute to organized classrooms and maximize time available for learning.	Chapter 13
Begin your lessons with a problem, question, or some other attention getter. (Suggestions are offered in the presentation outlines.)	Attention is the beginning point for information processing. Attention getters can induce curiosity, which is one characteristic of intrinsically motivating activities.	Chapter 7 Chapter 11 Chapter 13
Present problems and questions, and have students work in teams to solve them.	Group work capitalizes on socially shared cognition. Well organized groupwork is consistent with constructivist views of learning and student-centered approaches to instruction.	Chapter 2 Chapter 8 Chapter 13
When conducting groupwork, specify a relatively short time limit to work, and require the groups to turn in a product (usually a written response).	When students are involved in groupwork, they are usually in a more active role than they are during whole-group activities. The characteristics of effectively conducted groupwork include: clear directions, a specific and relatively short time limit, and a product.	Chapter 8
Give frequent, announced assessments. Make major assessments cumulative. Return assessments and discuss frequently missed items.	Frequent assessment is associated with increased achievement. Giving assessments and returning and discussing items provides for knowledge of results and feedback. This practice is consistent with research on motivation, instruction, and assessment. Frequent assessment increases student effort, and puts them in an active role.	Chapter 7 Chapter 8 Chapter 10 Chapter 14
Use a criterion-referenced assessment system and emphasize learning rather than performance. You might even put the students' scores on the back page of their tests and quizzes and tell them that you don't want them to share their scores.	Criterion referencing and emphasizing learning helps promote a learning-focused rather than a performance-focused classroom. Telling them them not to share scores won't prevent them from doing so, of course, but it will allow you to refer to it as a rationale when you discuss motivation.	Chapter 11 Chapter 14

SUGGESTED PROJECTS

The following are projects you might consider having your students complete as part of the course.

1. **Case Study**: You might have students complete a case study in which applications of the content of the chapters are utilized. Case studies from chapter opening pages could be used as models. The following are four possible classroom scenarios for which students could prepare case studies:
    *   teacher-student and student-student dialog illustrating a learner-centered approach (see Chapter 8)
    *   a teacher implementing constructivist approaches to problem solving (see Chapter 8)
    *   a teacher implementing several of the variables to promote student motivation (see Chapter 11)
    *   a teacher implementing cognitive views of learning (see Chapter 7)

    An advantage in having the students combine the applications in a single case study is that it will help them see and integrate content from different areas of study such as learning, motivation, and instruction.

2. **Class Presentations:** Since the way topics are represented is a critical factor in what and how much students learn, and research indicates that teachers with strong content backgrounds don't always possess adequate pedagogical content knowledge (discussed in Chapter 1), you might require that students select one or more topics and prepare representations for those topics. Have them present their representations and discuss rationales for their selections. This can be effectively done in groups, i.e., each group selects and presents a topic, or by individual students. To help students understand the requirement, provide some examples of the ways teachers represent their topics. You might refer them to Jenny Newhall's lesson at the end of Chapter 2, to David Shelton's lesson at the beginning of Chapter 7, to Laura Hunter's and Sue Brush's lessons at the beginning and end of Chapter 9, or to Scott Sowell's and Judy Holmquist's lessons at the beginning and end of Chapter 13.

3. **Peer Taught Lessons**: Ask students to select a topic and teach that topic in a peer setting. You might require that the lesson focus on a particular aspect of the content you're emphasizing in your class, such as applications of constructivist approaches to instruction, teaching for transfer, promoting learner motivation, or learner-centered instruction. Students could critique one another's lessons using some kind of observation guide. Samples of observation guides can be found in this manual in *Observing in Classrooms: Exercises and Activities.*

4. **Commercial Movies**: Consider requiring students to watch one or more commercial movies and then discuss the relationships between the movies and their lead characters and the content of your class. Some possibilities might include: *Mr. Holland's Opus, Stand and Deliver, Dead Poet's Society,* or *Dangerous Minds.* They could be encouraged to select others with your approval.

5. **Research Articles**: You might require students search journals, such as the *Journal of Educational Psychology, Journal of Educational Research, Review of Educational Research,* etc. to summarize a selected number of articles and their implications for learning and teaching. You might require that the reference dates for articles be older than a particular year, 1993 or even 1995, for example. Suggest students share the results of their efforts with the whole class.

6. **Debates:** Debates provide opportunities for students to think about important issues about educational psychology. Topics for debates could be discussed as you begin a new chapter. Then, require students, working in teams, to research topics using references from the chapter and searches they can do via the Internet. Possible topics for debate might include:
   - Eliminating the use of grade cards
   - Ungraded classes
   - Gender segregated classrooms and schools
   - Values/character education in the curriculum
   - Minimum competency testing for graduation from high school

7. **Concept Mapping:** Concept maps provide opportunities for students to make connections among concepts. Request students to try constructing concept maps using only the key concepts listed at the end of individual chapters) or, ask students to link concepts from several chapters (e.g., 7 and 13, 7, 10 and 13, or 4, 12 and 13). Students should be able to verbally describe their concept maps in student groups or to the whole class by putting them on the board or a transparency. Any discussion that follows should enable students to see how concepts may be understood differently because of cultural perspectives or educational experiences.

8. **Item Writing:** To encourage a greater depth in the processing of information ask students to write several assessment items over the content they study. We've had good luck with asking students to write multiple-choice items, because writing good stems and distracters seems to encourage a deeper processing of content knowledge. The items students write can then be used in several ways: 1) as review items to be discussed in a whole class activity, 2) as homework review, or 3) as an opportunity to talk about the item writing process.

9. **Journals:** Encouraging students to keep journals and enter personal reflections and reactions to chapter content can be an effective learning tool. Students should make entries on a weekly basis. Use questions, such as the following, to encourage critical thinking for these reflections. Note that we have found students freer to express their opinions when these assignments are pass or fail.
   - What ideas in the chapter will be most useful or valuable to you in a future teaching situation?
   - How has the content of this chapter changed your view of teaching and learning?
   - How might you design your classroom using the ideas in this chapter?

10. **Field Work:** If you have a field component attached to your course, or you can arrange field experiences for your students, consider having students complete field assignments outlined at the end of this Instructor's Manual under the heading, *Observing in Classrooms: Exercises and Activities.*

OBSERVING IN CLASSROOMS: EXERCISES AND ACTIVITIES

This section provides your students with exercises designed to help them in field service experiences. These exercises include suggestions for observing teachers as they work with their students, observing students in learning activities, and conducting interviews with teachers and primary, elementary, or secondary students.

It is wise to remind students before they begin any classroom visitations that professional courtesy should be extended to teachers and classrooms in which your students are guests. At the end of this section are guidelines you can hand out to students or use as a transparency to inform your students of appropriate, professional behavior and procedures when visiting classrooms and writing cases based on classroom experiences.

The following are specific suggestions for students to use for their classroom observations.

Chapter 1: Teaching in the Real World

Learning to Teach
Teacher Interview: This exercise is intended to gather information with respect to teachers' beliefs about learning to teach. The following are some suggested questions:
1. How important is knowledge of content in being an effective teacher? Is knowledge of content all that is necessary? Why do you think the way you do?
2. How important is experience in schools in learning to teach? Is experience all that is necessary? Explain.
3. If a person has a good command of their subject matter and they are able to acquire experience in schools, is that sufficient in learning to teach? Please explain.

Reflection
Teacher Interview: This exercise focuses on teachers as reflective practitioners. To begin the interview you may want to provide a brief overview of the topic of reflection (See text pages 16-17). The following are some suggested questions:
1. Is reflection relatively important or relatively unimportant in a teacher's development? Why do you feel the way you do?
2. When do you find opportunities to reflect about your teaching?
3. Can you give me a specific example where you were involved in reflection in the last day or two?
4. Can you give me an example of how the process of reflection changed your teaching?
5. How do the following stimulate your thinking about teaching?
    *   Interactions with students
    *   Evaluations of student work
    *   Interactions with parents or guardians
    *   Conversations with other professionals
    *   Research?
6. What changes in your professional life would give you greater opportunities to reflect?

Diversity
Student Observation: The purpose of this exercise is to gather basic information about the diversity found in the classroom. Seat yourself at the side of a room so that you can observe students during a lesson and as they enter and leave the room. Gather the following information:
1. Describe the students' physical development. How much do they differ in size? Who is the largest? Smallest?
2. How many males and females are there? How do they interact with each other?
3. Notice the students' clothes. Do they dress alike or is there considerable variation? Are the clothes new or do they appear well worn? Are they clean and in good repair? What do their shoes tell you?

4. How many different cultures appear to be represented? How can you tell? To what extent do students from different cultures interact?

Teacher interview: Explain to the teacher that the purpose of the interview is to gather information about diversity in classrooms. The following are some suggested questions.
1. How much do your students differ in ability?
2. What is the socioeconomic status of most students in your class? What is the range? How does this influence your teaching?
3. How many different cultures are represented in your classroom? For what percentage is English their first language? Is English spoken in the home? How does culture and language influence your teaching?
4. Do the boys and girls in your class do equally well in all subjects? Do they participate equally? Does student gender influence your teaching? If so, how?

Chapter 2: Development of Cognition and Language

Cognitive Development

Student Interview: The purpose of this exercise is to provide you with some experiences in conducting Piagetian tasks with students. If possible, conduct the interviews with a 5-6 year old, a 9-10 year old, and a 13-14 year old and compare their responses. If this isn't possible, interview several students at one grade level and compare their responses.
1. *Conservation of Mass*: Give the student two equal balls of clay. After the student confirms that they are equal, flatten one of the balls into a pancake shape. Ask:
    . Are the amounts of clay in the two pieces the same or different? How do you know?
2. *Conservation of Volume*: Show the student two identical clear containers partially filled with water. Ask if the amounts are the same. Then pour the water from one of the containers into a larger clear container. Ask:
    . Are the amounts of liquids in the two containers same or different? How do you know?
3. *Conservation of Number*: Arrange ten coins in two rows as they appear on page 40 of the text. Ask if the number of coins in the two rows is the same. Then rearrange them so the lower row is spread out. Ask:
    . Are the number of coins in the two rows the same or different? How do you know?
4. *Control of Variables*. Present the following problem to the student: I have ten puppies and I want to find out which of two kinds of dog food will make the puppies grow faster.
    . What kind of experiment could I do to answer the question?
    . Is there anything else I need to do?

Accommodating Developmental Diversity

Teacher Interview: Interview a teacher to determine how developmental diversity influences teaching. The following are some suggested questions:
1. How do the age and developmental level of your students influence your teaching? Can you give me specific examples?
2. How has your view of students changed as a result of working with them over time?
3. To what extent do you use the following strategies to accommodate diversity:
    . Design classroom experiences to specifically address background differences
    . Use concrete examples to illustrate abstract ideas
    . Use classroom interaction to encourage students to share their diverse experiences?

Students' Language Differences

Teacher Interview: The purpose of this exercise is to examine language development and its effect on classroom performance. Interview a teacher. The following are some suggested questions:
1. Do all students speak English fluently?
2. Describe the differences in your students' language development.

3. What do you do to accommodate those differences?
4. Are there any English dialects spoken in your classroom? Do these dialects have any effect on classroom performance, such as in oral reports? Do they have any effect on the way the students interact with each other? Can you describe the effects?
5. Do you do anything to work with the dialects? If so, what?

Student Interview: Ask the teacher to help you identify several students who differ in their verbal skills. The following are some suggested questions:
1. Do you like school? What's the best part? The worst part?
2. Do you have many friends at school? Who are they? What do you do with them? Do your friends like school?
3. What is your favorite subject? Why do you like it? What is the hardest subject? What makes it hard?
4. If you could change one thing about school, what would it be? Why?

English as a Second Language

Teacher Interview: The following are some suggested questions for gathering information about students who are not native English speakers.
1. How many students are there with English as a second language? What countries do they come from?
2. How are the students performing? Can you give some specific examples?
3. What programs exist for these students? How successful are they?
4. What do you do in the classroom to accommodate these language differences?

Student Observation: (Select several of these students and observe them during classroom instruction.) Try and answer the following questions:
1. How much do they participate in class? Do they volunteer?
2. Who do they talk to in class? Out of class? Who are their friends?
3. What special help are they given in the classroom? From the teacher? Other students? Special material? Pullout programs?

Chapter 3: Personal, Social and Emotional Development

Moral Development

Student Interview: As with the previous developmental exercises try to select several students at different age levels to interview. If this is not possible, interview several students at the same level and pose these hypothetical dilemmas:
1. Cheating. You may want to simplify it if you use it with younger students.

Steve, a high school junior, is working at a night job to help support his mother, a single parent of three. Steve is a conscientious student who works hard in his classes, but he doesn't have enough time to study. History isn't Steve's favorite course, and with his night work, he has a marginal D average. If he fails the final exam, he will fail the course, won't receive credit, and will have to alter plans for working during his senior year. He arranged to be off work the night before the exam so he could study extra hard, but early in the evening his boss called, desperate to have Steve come in and replace another employee who called in ill at the last moment. His boss pressured him heavily, so reluctantly Steve went to work at 8:00 p.m. and came home exhausted at 2:00 a.m. He tried to study, but fell asleep on the couch with his book in his lap. His mother woke him for school at 6:30.
    Steve went to his history class, looked at the test, and went blank. Everything seemed like a jumble. However, Jill, one of the best students in the class, happened to have her answer sheet positioned so he could clearly see every answer by barely moving his eyes.

. Is it OK for Steve to cheat? Why do you think so?
. What information in the story influenced your decision?
. Is it ever alright to cheat? If yes, when and why? If not, why not?

2. Honesty: Share the following situation with the students.

Kenny is walking to the store. It's his mother's birthday on Saturday. He's feeling bad because he hasn't been able to save up enough money to get her the present he'd like to give her. Then, on the sidewalk he finds a wallet with $10 in it--just what he needs to buy the present; but there's an identification card in the wallet telling the name and address of the owner.
. What should Kenny do? Why?
. What information in the story influenced your decision?
. Is it ever alright to keep something that doesn't belong to you? If yes, when and why? If not, why not?

Chapter 4: Learner Differences

Students: Individual Differences
Student Observation: The purpose of this exercise is to begin exploring the individual differences found in students. Ideally, it should be done in at least two different classes or at two different grade levels. Observe students and describe the following:

Physical Differences:
1. Describe the physical differences in the students.
2. Do these differences seem to have any effect on the way the students interact with each other or the way they behave in class? If they do, explain, including specific examples.

Energy and Attention Span:
1. How capable are students of monitoring their own attention spans?
2. How much do they fidget, play, and doodle during class?
3. How often does the teacher have to remind students to attend? Is it the group as a whole or certain students?

Gender Differences:
1. Do boys and girls participate equally? If not, who participates more? Is this in all classes or just certain ones?
2. Who do students sit next to? Talk to? Play with?
3. Are there differences in terms of behavioral problems?

Ability Differences
Teacher Interview: Interview a teacher to gather information about the differences in student ability. The following are some suggested questions:
1. How much does the ability of your students vary?
2. What kind of information do you gather to help you deal with ability differences?
3. How do you group your students to deal with ability differences? How does it work?
4. What other strategies do you use to deal with ability differences?

Student Observation: Ask the teacher to identify two high and two low-ability students to observe. As you observe them describe the following:
1. How do the two pairs of students differ in their ability to pay attention and stay on task?
2. Compare the participation of the two pairs. Specifically count the number of times students:
. raise their hands to participate.
. are called on.
. answer questions correctly.
. are given positive feedback about their answers.
3. How do the two pairs of students differ in terms of behavior problems?

Student Interview: If possible, interview the students and ask the following questions:
- How much do you like school?
- What is your favorite part of school?
- What is your best subject?
- What is your hardest subject?

Socioeconomic Status

Teacher Interview: . This exercise involves interviewing a teacher to examine how SES influences learning. The following are some suggested questions:
1. Describe the socioeconomic status of your students. How much do they vary?
2. How many of your students qualify for free or reduced-cost meals?
3. How many of your students come from single-parent families?
4. Do the parents support their children's efforts? Are they supportive of the school?
5. What do you do to accommodate the differences in SES among your students?

Culture

Teacher Interview: Interview a teacher and observe a classroom to examine how culture affects learning. The following are some suggested questions:
1. How many cultures are represented in your classroom?
2. How does culture affect learning in your classroom? Can you give me specific examples?
3. What modifications have you made in your teaching to accommodate cultural differences? How successful have they been? Can you give some specific examples?
4. What suggestions do you have for a beginning teacher working with students from different cultures?

Student Observation. Ask the teacher to provide you with a seating chart and identify students from different cultures. Observe the students and ask yourself the following:
1. Where do these students sit? (Is it by choice or assigned?)
2. Who do these students interact with?
3. How does the participation of these students compare to the participation of non-minorities?
4. How does their behavior (in terms of classroom management) compare to other students?

Chapter 5: Learners with Exceptionalities

Individuals with Disabilities Education Act (IDEA)
Teacher Interview: Interview a teacher to discover how different components of IDEA are implemented in the classroom. The following are some suggested questions:

Due Process through Parental Involvement:
1. How are parents involved in the process?
2. What obstacles exist for greater parent involvement?
3. How are language barriers dealt with?

Protection against Discrimination in Testing:
1. What provisions are made for ESL students?
2. How are classroom performance and general adaptive behavior assessed?

Least Restrictive Environment:
1. How does the concept of least restrictive environment work in your school?
2. Besides mainstreaming, what other options exist?

Individualized Education Program (IEP):
1. What does an IEP look like?
2. From your perspective what are the most important parts of the program? How well do they work? How could they be improved?

Students with Learning Problems

Teacher Interview: This exercise is intended to give you some information about a student having an exceptionality. Talk with a teacher to gather background experience about the student. The following are some suggested questions:
1. What kind of learning problem does the student have?
2. How did you discover this problem?
3. What help did you have in diagnosing the problem?
4. How do you use the IEP (Ask to see it.) to adapt instruction to the needs of the student?
5. What kinds of approaches (e.g., strategy instruction, social skills training) are being used to help the student?
6. Is supplementary instruction integrated or pull out?
7. How well is the student integrated into the regular flow of the classroom?
8. How well is the student accepted by other students?

Students with Physical Impairments

Teacher Interview: Work with the regular classroom teacher to identify a student with a physical impairment. Interview the teacher. The following are some suggested questions:
1. What kind of physical impairment is it?
2. How does it affect the student's classroom performance?
3. How is instruction being adapted for the student?
4. How well is the student integrated into the regular flow of the classroom?
5. How well is the student accepted by other students?

Students Who are Gifted and Talented

Teacher Interview: Interview a teacher and observe a program for students who are gifted and talented. The following are some suggested questions:
1. How are students who are gifted and talented defined?
2. How are these students identified?
3. What percentage of the student population is identified as gifted and talented?
4. Does the program emphasize enrichment or acceleration?
5. How well are students who are gifted and talented accepted and integrated into the regular classroom?

Chapter 6: Behaviorism and Social Cognitive Theory

Classical Conditioning: Classroom Climate

Classroom Observation: Observe in a classroom to investigate how the physical and social environment interact to create the classroom climate. Ask yourself the following questions:

Physical Environment:
1. What kinds of things are on the wall (e.g., pictures, charts, diagrams)? Are there any plants? Does the room look like an inviting place in which to be?
2. What student work is displayed? (e.g., art work, projects, etc.)?
3. How are the desks arranged? What does this tell you about instruction?
4. Are there areas where students can go when their work is finished?
5. Are rules and procedures posted on the walls? Are these stated in a positive way?

Social Climate:
1. How do students enter the room? Do they seem glad to be there?
2. Do classes start in a positive, inviting way?
3. How does the teacher relate to students?
4. Is interaction in the classroom relaxed and easy?

Operant Conditioning
Classroom Observation: Observe a classroom and describe how the following are used:

Reinforcers:
1. Verbal reinforcers (e.g., praise, positive comments)
2. Tangible reinforcers (e.g., candy, pencils, etc.)
3. Token reinforcers (smiling faces, tickets, etc.)
4. Activity reinforcers (e.g., extra recess, time to work on the computer)

Punishment:
1. Verbal Reprimands (e.g., "Mary, be quiet." "Jared, turn around.")
2. Non-verbal Reprimands (e.g., stern look, hand to lips)
3. Time out (e.g., isolation in corner of room or hall)
4. Lost privileges (e.g., Decreased recess, lunch time).
5. Call to parents
6. Visit to principal's office

Reinforcement Schedules
Classroom Observation: Observe a classroom and describe how different reinforcement schedules are implemented in the following areas:

Verbal Interaction:
1. Are correct responses reinforced every time? If not, how often are they reinforced?
2. How are incorrect, incomplete, or no responses reacted to?

Homework:
1. How often is homework given and collected?
2. Is homework graded every time, periodically, or sporadically? Do students know when it will be collected and graded?

Tests and Quizzes:
1. Are tests and quizzes announced beforehand?
2. Are tests and quizzes given on a regular basis? Is it determined by time or work (units) completed?

Modeling
Classroom Observation: Talk to a teacher and find out when they'll be using modeling to teach some concept or skill. Observe the lesson in terms of the following processes:

Attention:
1. What did the teacher do to attract the class's attention?
2. How did the teacher introduce the new content? Was it linked to a previously learned concept?

Retention:
3. As the new skill was modeled did the teacher point out key characteristics or steps?
4. Did the teacher think out loud, modeling the cognitive process as he or she proceeded?

Reproduction:
1. Were students given opportunities to try the new skill?
2. Did the teacher provide feedback?

Motivation:
1. How was the skill introduced? Did the teacher explain how it would be useful later on?
2. Were students provided with reinforcement as they practiced the skill?

Types of Modeling:
1. What types of modeling do you see displayed in the classroom (e.g., direct, symbolic, synthesized,)? Provide specific examples.

Modeling Outcomes:
1. Describe the modeling outcomes you see (e.g., learning new behaviors, facilitating existing ones).

Chapter 7: Cognitive Views of Learning

Attention/Perception
Classroom Observation: Observe a classroom lesson and interview the teacher afterwards to clarify your observations. During the observation ask yourself the following questions:
1. How did the lesson begin? Were all students drawn into the lesson? Did the lesson maintain student attention?
2. How successful were these strategies?
3. What other strategies does the teacher use to gain and maintain student attention?
4. Was there a problem with student inattention? If so, describe the problem. What appears to be the reason for the problem?
5. What did the teacher do to check the students' perceptions? Did any of the students appear to be misperceiving the teacher's materials?

Working Memory
Classroom Observation: Observe a lesson to determine how the teacher accommodates limitations of working memory. As you observe, ask yourself the following questions:
1. How long does the teacher talk before pausing and asking questions to connect material? How does this relate to developmental characteristics of students?
2. What visual aids (e.g., chalkboard, overhead, charts) does the teacher use to supplement the oral presentation? How effective are these?
3. How does the teacher identify important points in the presentation?

Long-Term Memory and Encoding
Classroom Observation: Observe a lesson and interview the teacher to determine how the teacher insures that information is stored in long term memory. Ask yourself the following questions as you observe:
1. Did the teacher involve the students in rehearsal? Describe specifically what the teacher did.
2. How active were the students during the lesson? What did the teacher do to promote activity?
3. How did the teacher organize the information for the students? What did the teacher do that encouraged the students to organize their own information?
4. What kinds of questions did the teacher ask that encouraged the students to elaborate on what they already knew?

Metacognition
Student Interview: Interview four students (two high and two low achievers) to assess the development of their metacognitive abilities.

Meta-attention:
To determine how aware the students are of the role that attention plays in the learning process ask:
1.   Where do you go when you study or have school work to do?
2.   Does noise bother you when you're studying? What do you do if it does?
3.   Do you ever drift off when your teacher is talking? What do you do when this happens?

Metamemory:
To determine how aware the students are of the process of memory and the role it plays in learning ask:
1.   If you had a telephone number to remember to call five minutes later, what would you do? What if you had to remember it for tomorrow?
2.   If I gave you a list of ten objects (like shoe, ball, tree, etc.) to study for a minute and then remember, how many do you think you could remember? How would you try to do this?
3.   If you had a list of spelling (or foreign language vocabulary) words to remember for a quiz on Friday, what would you do? Why?

Diversity and Information Processing
Teacher Interview: Interview a teacher to determine the impact of student diversity on information processing in the classroom. The following are some suggested questions:
1.   Can you describe the differences in background experiences that your students bring to school? Can you give me some specific examples? How does this influence their learning?
2.   How often do you do the following to accommodate students' background diversity? Please offer a specific example of where you did each of the following:
    .   Assessed their background knowledge prior to a lesson
    .   Assessed student perceptions of new material through questioning
    .   Provided background experiences when they are lacking
    .   Used the background experiences of peers to augment the backgrounds of others

Chapter 8: Constructing Understanding

Characteristics of Constructivism
Teacher Interview: Interview the teacher to determine the extent to which he or she understands constructivism and implements lessons based on constructivist views of learning. The following are some suggested questions:
1.   What is your typical approach to instruction, i.e., when you teach a topic, how do you typically teach it? Explain.
2.   How often do you do lessons that are discovery or guided-discovery in their orientation? Please explain how you decide to do the number that you do.

Constructivism in Classrooms
Classroom Observation: Observe a lesson to determine the extent to which the teacher bases the instruction on constructivist views of learning. As you observer ask yourself the following questions:
1.   What examples and other representations did the teacher use to provide background knowledge for the students?
2.   Did the teacher guide the students' developing understanding with questioning, or did the teacher rely on explanations?
3.   To what extent did the teacher connect the content to the real world?

Cooperative Learning
Teacher Interview: This exercise focuses on cooperative learning activities. Interview the teacher to see how she organized her groups. The following are some suggested questions:
1.   How did you form the teams?

2. What did you do to be sure that the groups were about equal in ability, gender and cultural background?
3. What did you do to train the students to effectively interact with each other?

Classroom Observation: Now observe the class and answer the following questions:
1. Does everyone have meaningful tasks to perform during the activity?
2. Do tasks use a variety of skills and call on a variety of knowledge?
3. Do tasks provide opportunities for all students to make contributions?
4. How does the teacher monitor the groups as they work?

Chapter 9: Complex Cognitive Processes

Concepts and Relationships Among Concepts
Classroom Observation: Observe a lesson in which a concept is being taught, or examine a textbook and identify a section where a concept is presented. Ask yourself the following questions:
1. How complete was the definition? Was a superordinate concept identified in the definition? Were characteristics clearly specified?
2. Were positive and negative examples provided? Did they contain characteristics that enabled students to differentiate between the two? Were positive examples familiar to students? Did the negative examples help differentiate the target concept from coordinate concepts?
3. Was the concept linked to other, related concepts?
4. Was the concept presented in context, or was it presented in isolation?
5. What did the teacher do to accommodate differences in the students' background knowledge?

Classroom Observation: Observe a class in which a principle, generalization, or academic rule is being taught. Ask yourself the following questions:
1. Was the relationship among the concepts in the principle, generalization, or rule clearly presented?
2. Was the principle, generalization, or rule applied in a real-world setting?
3. What did the teacher do to accommodate differences in the background knowledge of students?

Study Skills
Student Interview: Interview several students to determine their knowledge and use of different study strategies. If possible, select two high and two low-achieving students and compare their responses. Ask the following questions:
1. When you're studying a chapter (e.g., social studies, science) for the first time what do you usually do to help you learn the material? Why?
2. Have you ever used any of the following strategies? When do you use them and why? Do they help?
   . Underlining
   . Note taking
   . Summarizing
   . Spatial representations (e.g., concept maps, diagramming, hierarchies)
3. Have you ever been taught any study strategies? Do you ever use them? When and why?

Problem Solving
Classroom Observation: Observe a lesson in which problem solving is being taught. Ask yourself the following questions:
1. How was the lesson introduced? Had students been introduced to problem solving before? Were the problems well or ill-defined?
2. What did the teacher do to assist students' learning during the following stages?
   . Identify the problem
   . Represent the problem
   . Select a strategy

. Implement the strategy

. Evaluate·the results

3. What types of practice and feedback were provided?

Transfer of Learning

Teacher Interview: Interview a teacher to determine how the teacher teaches for transfer. The following are some suggested questions:

1. What specific things do you do to promote transfer? Can you give me some specific examples?
2. What are the biggest problems you have getting the students to transfer?

Chapter 10: Theories of Motivation

Perceptions of Motivation

Teacher Interview: Interview a teacher to gather information about their views of motivation. Based on the views, try to determine what aspects of their views are humanistic, behavioral, or cognitive in their orientation. The following are some suggested questions:

Motivation to Learn:

1. What do you believe is most important for the motivation of the students you teach? What do you do to capitalize on these motivators?
2. How much of the responsibility for student motivation is yours? How much is theirs?

Behavioral Approaches:

1. How important do you think it is to praise students? How much praise do you use? Why?
2. Do you use any other kinds of rewards to motivate your students to study? Can you give me some specific examples?

Humanistic Views:

1. How important do you think it is for you to try and help students develop their self-concepts? What do you do to help students develop their self-concepts? Can you give me a specific example?
2. How important do you think it is for students to believe that teachers care about them as people? Is this part of your job? Why or why not?

Cognitive Views:

1. What do you do to capitalize on students' curiosity? Can you give me some specific examples?
2. What can teachers do to make students feel responsible for their learning? What do you do? How well does it work?
3. What do you do to make the students feel that what their learning is important or worthwhile? Can you give me some specific examples?
4. How important do you think it is to challenge your students? Do they feel better about what they've learned when it has been challenging? Can you give a specific example to illustrate your point?

Maslow's Hierarchy of Needs

Teacher Interview: Make a copy of Maslow's Hierarchy of Needs, and interview a teacher. The following are some suggested questions:

1. Where on the hierarchy are most of your students? How can you tell (i.e., what specific behaviors do you observe that suggest this)?
2. How do you adapt your teaching to accommodate the needs of your students?

Attributions

Student Interview: Interview two high and two low-achieving students to investigate their views about success and failure. Ask the following questions:

1. How well do you usually do in school? Why do you think you are doing well (or not so well)?
2. Think about the last test that you took. What kind of grade did you get? Why do you think you got that grade?
3. Do you think your grades depend most on you, such as how hard you study, or do you think they depend on something else? If something else, what?

Chapter 11: Motivation in the Classroom

The Model for Promoting Student Motivation

Teacher Observation: The purpose of this observation is to see if teacher expectations influence interaction patterns in the classroom. Ask the teacher to identify four high and four low achieving students. Write these students' names on two sheets of paper and observe them during an interactive instructional segment. Then, answer the following questions for each student:

Teacher Expectations:
1. Where is the student seated with respect to the teacher?
2. How often does the teacher talk to or make eye contact with the student?
3. How often is the student called on during the lesson? How much time is the student given to answer?
4. What does the teacher do when the student is unable (or unwilling) to answer?
5. What kind of praise is given for correct responses?

Classroom Climate: Observation: Observe a classroom to determine how the following variables influence classroom climate. Ask yourself the following questions:
1. Are the students orderly when they enter and leave the classroom? Are the rights of all student guaranteed by the teacher?
2. During lessons are students free to respond without fear of being laughed at, ridiculed, or harassed?
3. Are students able to successfully answer most questions during learning activities? How successful are the students on their seatwork and homework?
4. Does the teacher tell the students *why* they are studying a particular topic?
5. Is the material challenging but learnable? How do you know? Cite a specific example to illustrate your point.

Classroom Instruction: Observation: Observe a classroom to determine how the following variables influence learner motivation. Ask yourself the following questions:
1. What did the teacher do to introduce the lesson? To what extent did it attract the students' attention?
2. How involved were the students in the lesson? What did the teacher do to promote involvement?
3. What did the teacher do to help students personally relate the information they were learning?
4. Describe the kind of feedback students are getting about their progress.

Chapter 12: Creating Productive Learning Environments: Classroom Management

Classroom Procedures and Rules

Teacher Interview: Interview a classroom teacher to find out about the classroom procedures and rules that the teacher is using. The following are some suggested questions:
1. How did you choose the rules and procedures you're using?
2. How did you teach the rules and procedures?
3. What procedures do you feel are most important in your class (e.g., the way papers are turned in, the way students enter and leave the room)?
4. What do you do when a student doesn't follow a procedure?
5. What do you do when a student breaks a rule?

Student Interview: Interview four students. Try to select students from different segments of the class (e.g., high and low achieving, students from different ethnic or cultural backgrounds). Ask the following questions:

1. How do you feel about the rules in this class? Are they fair? What does the teacher do if you break a rule?
2. Do you think rules are important to make learning easier for you? Why do you think so?

Classroom Observation: Observe the class and answer the following questions:

1. Can all the students see the chalkboard, overhead, and other displays?
2. Can all students hear the teacher and each other? If not, what is distracting the students?
3. What does the teacher do if the students are inattentive or if they break a rule?
4. How effective is the lesson in maintaining student attention? Cite specific evidence to support your assessment.

Communication with Parents

Teacher Interview: Interview a teacher to find out how the teacher and the school communicate with parents or guardians. The following are some suggested questions:

1. What does the school do to communicate with parents (e.g., back-to-school night, open house, school newsletters, packets of papers sent home)? How well do they work?
2. What do you personally do to communicate with parents? How well does it work?

Advice for New Teachers

Teacher Interview: Since classroom management is one of the most challenging problems new teachers face, what advice would you give them? Be as specific as possible.

Chapter 13: Creating Productive Learning Environments: Principles of Instruction

Planning for Instruction

Teacher Interview: Interview an experienced teacher to find out how he or she plans for lessons, unit studies, etc. The following are some suggested questions:

1. When you're planning, how do you begin? What do you do second? Third? How does this vary with different topics?
2. Do you use state or district curriculum guides? Do they help you in your planning?
3. Do you use the teacher's edition of your text? If so, how?
4. Do you do any cooperative planning with other teachers? Why or why not?
5. When you plan, what and how much do you write down?
6. Describe your long-term plans. How are they different from daily plans?
7. Do you take affective factors, such as student motivation, into account when you plan?

Teacher Observation: Ask a teacher if you can look at some of his or her plans and then observe a lesson. As you study the plans and observe the lesson, ask yourself the following questions:

1. How detailed are the plans? What does the teacher write down?
2. How closely does the teacher follow the plan? If he or she deviates from it, why do they do so?

Time

Teacher Interview: Interview a teacher to determine how he or she thinks about time. The following are some suggested questions:

1. How do you decide how much time to devote to a particular topic?
2. What do you do about the "dead time" periods in your classes?
3. What do you do when you see that students aren't paying attention?
4. How can you tell if students are "getting it" when you teach?

Teacher Observation: Now, observe the teacher. Ask yourself the following questions as you observe:
1. How much time does the teacher allocate to the topic?
2. How much of the allocated time is actually devoted to instruction?
3. How did the teacher begin the lesson? Did he or she purposely do something to attract the students' attention? If so, what? How well did it work?
4. Did the teacher review during the lesson? If so, when?
5. What does the teacher do when a student "drifts off?"

Student Observation: Observe four students during the course of a lesson (Ask the teacher to select two that are high achieving and two that are low achieving). Seat yourself so that you can observe their faces during the lesson. Focus on each student at fifteen-second intervals and decide whether the student was attending to the lesson. A "Y" indicates yes, an "N" indicates no, and a question mark indicates that you cannot tell. At the end of the twenty-minute observation period, compute averages for each student and the group as a whole. (Engagement Rate = # of times engaged/Total # of observations.)

	Student A	Student B	Student C	Student D
Minute 1				
Minute 2				
Minute 3				
Minute 20				

Ask yourself the following questions:
1. Did the engagement rates vary during the course of the presentation? If so, why?
2. What did the teacher do differently when the students were paying attention compared to when they were inattentive?
3. How did the attentiveness of the high and low achievers compare?

Questioning
Teacher Observation: Observe a second lesson, and devote your observation specifically to the teacher's questioning patterns. Make out a seating chart for the students. Sit in the room so you can easily see who is being called on. Every time the teacher asks a question, put a check mark by the student being called on. If the student is called on because of attempting to volunteer (such as raising a hand), put an X by the student's name. Observe the lesson and tally the teacher's questions. Then ask yourself the following questions:
1. Does the teacher call on students by name, or are students called on only when they volunteer?
2. Are all the students in the class called on?
3. Are students allowed to call out answers?
4. What does the teacher do when students are unable or unwilling to answer?
5. When the teacher asks a question, how long does he or she wait for the student to answer?
6. Does the teacher direct a similar number of questions to boys and girls? To cultural minorities and non-minorities?

Chapter 14: Assessing Classroom Learning

Teachers' Assessment Patterns
Teacher Interview: Interview a teacher about his or her attitudes toward testing and assessment patterns. The following are some suggested questions:
1. How important do you feel testing is in the assessment of your students? Can you explain?
2. Do you usually make out your own tests, or do you use tests that come with your textbook?
3. What kinds of performance assessments do you use? Can you give me some specific examples of some that you use in your class?

Test Construction

Observation: Obtain a teacher-made test, examine its contents, and ask yourself the following questions:
1. What format was used (e.g., multiple-choice)? Most of the questions were written at what level (e.g., knowledge, comprehension)?
2. To what extent were the items consistent with the guidelines provided in your text?

Teacher Interview: Interview the teacher to gather information about the way he or she prepared the test you examined. The following are some suggested questions:
1. What were your goals in constructing the test? How were the items designed to measure different types of knowledge?
2. What did you do to be sure that the content you wanted covered was covered?
3. Did you use any kind of chart or matrix in designing the test?
4. Did you utilize a computer in any way as you designed your test?
5. How will you grade the test? Will any part of it be machine scored?

Test Administration

Teacher Interview: Interview a teacher who has recently administered a test to gather some information about the ways students are prepared for tests. The following are some suggested questions:
1. Do you do anything to help your students deal with test anxiety? If so, what?
2. Do you, or have you, taught your students specific test-taking strategies? Can you describe specifically how you did this?
3. Did you have your students practice on some items similar to those that will be on the test?
4. How carefully do you supervise the students while they are taking tests?
5. Is cheating ever a problem? If so, what do you do about it?
6. When you hand tests back to the students, do you go over them? Why or why not?

Grading

Teacher Interview: Interview a teacher and get a copy of the course expectations (if available) and a copy of a sample report card. The following are some suggested questions:
1. How do tests and quizzes contribute to the final grade in your class?
2. How do you use homework and seatwork in your grading system?
3. Do you use a point or a percentage system for your grading? Why?
4. Do you use computers to help you in your grading? If so, how?

Diversity and Assessment

Teacher Interview: Interview a teacher to determine how student diversity influences the assessment process. The following are some suggested questions:
1. How does the diversity of student backgrounds in your class affect the assessment process?
2. Do you make any special provisions in preparing students for tests? If so, what are they?
3. Is language ever a problem for students as they take tests? If so, what do you do to accommodate the problem?

Chapter 15: Assessment Through Standardized Testing

Teacher Interview: Interview a teacher about his or her experiences with standardized testing. The following are some suggested questions:
1. Is the emphasis placed on standardized tests appropriate? Too much emphasis? Too little emphasis? Why do you think so?
2. What roles do you play in selecting and administering standardized tests?
3. Is high-stakes testing increasing, decreasing, or having no effect on learning? Why do you think so?

GUIDELINES FOR WORKING IN SCHOOLS

1. ## Try to be unobtrusive.

    To the extent that you can, avoid interrupting classroom routines. It is a simple courtesy, and the information you gather will be more accurate if you aren't noticed.

2. ## Maintain the confidentiality of the teachers and students you observe.

    In any reports you make, avoid using last names and don't identify specific persons. You want to prevent even the most remote possibility of embarrassing someone.

3. ## Keep the information you gather as factual as possible and avoid making premature judgements.

    The purpose of your classroom visits is to observe how the concepts you learn about in your text is applied in classrooms; it is not to assess a teacher's performance. While you will certainly have some reactions to what a teacher does, try to report your observations as objectively as possible.

CHAPTER 1: TEACHING IN THE REAL WORLD

CHAPTER OVERVIEW

Chapter 1 serves as the student's entry into the book and introduces them to the role of research and theory in professional decision making. The student is introduced to the different kinds of knowledge–knowledge of content, pedagogical content knowledge, general pedagogical knowledge, and knowledge of learners and learning–in learning to teach. They then see the different kinds of research that lead to a professional knowledge base, how that research is evaluated, and the link between research and theory. Students are reminded that using research and theory effectively requires critical, practical, and artistic decision making. The chapter closes with a description of the use of case studies in educational psychology.

CHAPTER OBJECTIVES

- Identify the different kinds of knowledge required in learning to teach.

- Explain how research leads to knowledge that can be applied to classroom practice.

- Describe the relationships between research and theory.

- Explain how professional decision making affects teaching.

- Explain how reflective teaching uses educational psychology to improve professional decision making.

TRANSPARENCIES

The transparencies exist in both acetate form and as PowerPoint slides.

T 1.1   Learning and Teaching Inventory
T 1.2   Learning and Teaching Inventory: The Research Base
T 1.3   Knowledge Needed for Expert Teaching
T 1.4   Different Types of Research
T 1.5   Evaluating Research Studies

TRANSPARENCY MASTERS

The transparency masters are included in this manual beginning on page 230.

TM 1.1   The INTASC Principles
TM 1.2   Questions for reflective teaching

VIDEO

Looking Through Classroom Windows Tape 1-Segment 1: "Demonstrating Knowledge in Classrooms"

This video episode illustrates the different forms of knowledge required of teachers. It exists in four segments. The first involves a kindergarten teacher discussing planting a garden with her children; the second is a seventh-grade teacher illustrating the concept of symmetry; the third is a chemistry teacher discussing Charles' law; and the fourth is a history teacher presenting information about the Vietnam War.

It is also the closing case study for this chapter.

CHAPTER OUTLINE

I. Educational psychology: Teaching in the real world
II. Knowledge and learning to teach
    A. Knowledge of content
    B. Pedagogical content knowledge
    C. General pedagogical knowledge
        1. Instructional strategies
        2. Classroom management
    D. Knowledge of learners and learning
        1. Knowledge of learners
        2. Knowledge of learning
    E. The INTASC standards: States respond to the need for professional knowledge
III. The role of research in acquiring knowledge
    A. Descriptive research
        1. Evaluating descriptive studies
    B. Correlational research
        1. Evaluating correlational research
    C. Experimental research
        1. Evaluating experimental research
    D. Action research
    E. Conducting research in classrooms: Action research strategies
    F. Research and the development of theory
IV. Research and teacher decision making
    A. Critical decision making: The role of classroom context
    B. Practical decision making: The need for efficiency
    C. Artistic decision making: Creativity in teaching
    D. Assessment and learning: Gathering information for decision making
    E. Reflection and decision making
V. The use of case studies in educational psychology
    A. Video cases
    B. The Praxis exam
        1. Scoring the Praxis
        2. Keys to success on the Praxis

PRESENTATION OUTLINE

Teaching suggestions in the outline will be marked with the symbol ■. In most cases, the suggested activities can be done individually and discussed as a whole group, or they can be done in small groups, and the small-group results can be discussed with the whole class. To be consistent with our understanding of knowledge construction, we recommend that you promote as much discussion–both in small groups and with the whole class–as possible.

Enrichment Information, which includes elaborations of text topics as well as topics not included in the text, will be boxed as you see here.

I. Educational psychology: Teaching in the real world
II. Knowledge and learning to teach
    A. Knowledge of content
    B. Pedagogical content knowledge
    C. General pedagogical knowledge

1. Instructional strategies
2. Classroom management
   D. Knowledge of learners and learning
      1. Knowledge of learners
      2. Knowledge of learning

■ *The purpose of this activity is to help students understand the different kinds of knowledge required in learning to teach.*

1. Display T 1.1 *"Learning and Teaching Inventory"* and ask students to identify the statements as true or false. Some of the results will be intuitively sensible, while others will not.

2. For each item, ask students (or groups) to write a brief explanation as to why they think the statement is true or false.

3. To provide a brief explanation for each of the items together with a research citation that documents the results display T 1.2 *"Learning and Teaching Inventory: The Research Base."* Display T 1.3 *"Knowledge Needed for Expert Teaching."* As you discuss each of the results, have the students identify the type of knowledge–knowledge of content, pedagogical content knowledge, general pedagogical knowledge, or knowledge of learners and learning–required to respond correctly to the item. (Point out that each of the items is discussed in detail in the chapter.)

4. To help students understand the different forms of knowledge that professional organizations expect of them–even as first year teachers, display TM 1.1 *"The INTASC Principles."* Have them identify the type of knowledge addressed in each of the principles. For example, Principle 1: Knowledge of Content addresses both knowledge of content and pedagogical content knowledge, because it says, "Teachers understand the knowledge they teach and can make the content meaningful for students."

Video: You might want to show the video episode "Demonstrating Knowledge in Classrooms" at this point in your discussion of the chapter.

The Constructed Response questions at the end of the chapter ask the students to identify the type of knowledge each teacher demonstrates in the video.

III The role of research in acquiring knowledge
   A. Descriptive research
      1. Evaluating descriptive studied
   B. Correlational research
      1. Evaluating correlational studies
   C. Experimental research
      1. Evaluating experimental research
   D. Action research
   E. Conducting research in classrooms: Action research strategies
   F. Research and the development of theory

■ *The purpose of this activity is to help the students understand the differences between descriptive, correlational, and experimental research and how to evaluate each type of study.*

1. **Display T 1.4 *"Different Types of Research,"* and T 1.5 *"Evaluating Research Studies."* Give them some examples, such as the following:**

   - **Descriptive Research: Researchers found that teachers, after asking a question, often give students very little time to think about their answers before turning the question to someone else or providing a prompt to help the student.**
   - **Correlational Research: Researchers have found that a caring teachers are more successful with students placed at risk than teachers who are less warm.**
   - **Experimental Research: Researchers systematically manipulated the amount of time teachers waited for students to answer, and they found that the longer wait times caused an improvement in the quality of students' answers.**

2. ***To further increase the students' understanding of the relationship between theory and research:***
   have the students decide whether or not the statement:

   "Success is *the* primary factor that increases student motivation and self-esteem,"

   is true or false. After you've polled the students, point out that research indicates that the statement is false (Baron, 1998; Ryan & Deci, 1998). Then note that we can *explain* why the answer is false by using *Expectancy x Value Theory* (discussed in Chapter 10). This theory suggests that learners will be motivated to the extent that they *expect* to succeed on a task times the amount of *value* they place on the task, and learners value challenging tasks much more than they value trivial tasks. This allows us to *predict* that learners must be challenged if their motivation is to be increased. (You might want to point out that Expectancy *times* Value is important. This means if either is zero the product is zero. So, if learners don't value success, no amount of success will increase motivation to learn.)

Criticisms of Educational Research. Educational research is often criticized by those both in and outside the profession. Some critics even suggest that there is no body of knowledge in education. This is wrong, as evidenced by the expanding body of research described in this and many other books and research articles. In fact, we know a great deal about the connection between teaching and learning, and this body of knowledge continues to grow.

Other critics discount the results of educational research because gaps exist in our body of knowledge, and research results are sometimes conflicting. They would have us ignore what we know, because we don't know everything. Others assessing the gaps in the knowledge base observe, "It is better to have some information about what is more likely to happen than to have no information at all" (Floden & Klinzing, 1990, p. 16).

Ignoring knowledge is antithetical to the very process of education. Every profession–medicine, law, architecture, engineering, and education–operates with partial knowledge, and fills in with sound judgment where research results are unclear or lacking. Further, education is certainly not unique in depending on uncertain research results. For instance, in the late 1980s, over 10,000 male physicians took an aspirin every other day, while a comparable control group took a placebo. After 5 years, less than 1% of the experimental group and less than 2% of the control group had had heart attacks. In spite of the very small percentage of heart attacks in either group, as well as the select population (male physicians) the results made national headlines, and people rushed to take aspirin in an effort to prevent heart attacks. By the standards typically held for studies in education, the research results were certainly weak, yet they had a significant impact on behavior.

Conflicting research results are also not unique to education. For example, for years people with high blood pressure were told to restrict their sodium intake. Then, another study indicated that sodium intake wasn't harmful after all. In another case, several studies indicated that elevated cholesterol levels are dangerous and that oat bran helped decrease cholesterol levels, so people consumed enormous quantities of bran muffins and oatmeal. Then, another study found that oat bran didn't decrease cholesterol levels after all. The same kinds of uncertainties exist in areas such as the dangers of "Type A" personalities, how much exercise is necessary to be beneficial, and the dangers or benefits of consuming alcohol. (One study indicated that three to five glasses of red wine a day was optimal for reducing the likelihood of heart disease!)

Similar discrepancies exist in economics (e.g., the controversy over supply-side economic policy) history (e.g., the reasons Japan attacked the United States in 1941), and many others.

The point is that education is not the only profession in which the developing body of knowledge is far from perfect. In all cases, we continue to gather as much information as possible, search for patterns, and then use the patterns as we make decisions about our actions whether it is teaching students or maintaining a healthy life-style.

IV   Research and teacher decision making
    A.   Critical decision making : The role of classroom context
    B.   Practical decision making: The need for efficiency
    C.   Artistic decision making: Creativity in teaching
    D.   Assessment and learning: Gathering information for decision making
    E.   Reflection and decision making

■ *The purpose of this activity is to help students understand that decision making is part of being a professional.*
Have the students identify examples in the case study where Keith Jackson and/or Jan Davis demonstrated critical, practical, and artistic decision making in their teaching.

■ *To model the processes you intend to use as you teach the course:*
Display TM 1.2 *"Questions for Reflective Teaching"* and share your thinking with the students as you display the information. For example:
*   identify your goals for teaching this chapter.
*   explain why you think they're important.
*   explain why you chose to begin the chapter by having them respond to the items on T 1.1 *"Learning and Teaching Inventory."*
Sharing this information will demonstrate how you reflect on your teaching.

V.   The use of case studies in educational psychology
    A.   Video cases
    B.   The Praxis exam
        1.   Scoring the Praxis
        2.   Keys to success on the Praxis

■ *To help students understand the use of case studies in educational psychology:*
1.   Refer them to the case study at the beginning of the chapter and point out that every chapter begins and ends with a case study.

2.   Point out that the "Constructed Response" questions and the "Document-Based Analysis" items parallel the kinds of items they will experience on the Praxis exam. Also, tell them that feedback for all the items is available on the Companion Website at www.prenhall.com/eggen.

To enrich your students' backgrounds related to the science and art of teaching, you might want to discuss some of the following information.

Teaching: Art or Science? The issue of artistry in teaching is a controversial one. Some argue that teaching is primarily art (Rubin, 1985) while others emphasize the scientific side (Gage, 1978, 1985). Excellent teaching has elements of both.

Gage (1985) describes art as "any process or procedure whose tremendous complexity . . . makes the process in principle one that cannot be reduced to systematic formulas" (p. 4). Based on this definition, teaching is surely an art. No formula tells you how to intervene when your students become inattentive, how to know when students are ready to move to the next activity, or how to maintain control of your class without sacrificing a climate of support and encouragement. Making these decisions quickly and efficiently so the process proceeds smoothly day after day requires a high level of artistry. Michael Jordan was praised as peerless in making his complex moves look so easy–he was an artist on the basketball floor. In an analogous sense, an artist in the classroom makes managing the complexity appear effortless to the casual observer (Doyle, 1986).

Artistry in teaching involves three components: (a) pursuing educational aims of high worth, (b) using creative ways to achieve these aims, and (c) pursuing these aims with skill and dexterity (Rubin, 1985). The music teacher in the episode presented in the chapter displayed artistry in at least three ways. First, she had ambitious goals for her class; she was not willing to let "good enough" do (remember, this was the fourth time she taught the topic). Second, she pursued these goals in energetic and creative ways, linking difficult and abstract ideas to students' lives and ways of knowing. Finally, she put the lesson together with skill, motivating students and actively involving them in the lesson. This was a clear example of artistic decision making.

This artistry doesn't happen by chance, however. Effective teachers don't "shoot from the hip." They base their decisions on a thorough understanding of students, the way they learn, what motivates them, and the most efficient ways of managing and delivering instruction. This could be called the scientific basis for their art. This is where educational psychology can be invaluable.

DISCUSSION STARTERS

1. Of the different roles that teachers perform--manager, motivator, instructor, and evaluator--which is most important to your grade level or content area? Least? How does the context of your teaching situation influence your answer?

2. In the future which side of teaching–artistic or scientific–is likely to become more important? Why?

3. What is the role of research in teacher decision making? How does knowledge of classrooms help in this process?

4. How can research make teachers more reflective? Besides a thorough knowledge of the research base, what else can teachers do to make themselves more reflective?

5. What are some personal characteristics that make teachers effective? Can these be taught or developed?

6. What are some of the reasons for the increased diversity in our schools? What kinds of things can teachers do to make themselves more effective teachers of students whose backgrounds are diverse?

BACKGROUND READINGS

Berliner, D. (1994). Expertise: The wonder of exemplary performances. In J. Mangieri & C. Collins (Eds.), *Creating powerful thinking in teachers and students* (pp. 161-186). Fort Worth, TX: Harcourt Brace. This chapter describes the continuum from novice to expert that has become popular in descriptions of professional development.

Borko, H., & Putnam, R. (1996). Learning to teach. In D. Berliner & R. Calfee (Eds.), *Handbook of educational psychology* (pp. 673-708). New York: Simon & Schuster Macmillan. This chapter provides an excellent overview of the processes involved in learning to teach.

Bullough, R. (1989). *First-year teacher: A case study.* New York: Teachers College Press. A readable account of the growth of a teacher in her first year in the classroom.

Carter, K. (1990). Teachers' knowledge and learning to teach. In W. R. Houston (Ed.), *Handbook of research on teacher education* (pp. 291-310). New York: Macmillan. This chapter describes research and the various kinds of knowledge required of beginning teachers.

Gage N. (1991). The obviousness of social and educational research results. *Educational Researcher 20*(1) 10–16. Gage makes a convincing case that educational research is not just reinventing the wheel.

Murray, F. (1996). *The teacher educator's handbook.* San Francisco: Jossey Bass. This edited work contains a number of valuable chapters on teacher education and learning to teach.

FEEDBACK FOR CONSTRUCTED RESPONSE AND DOCUMENT-BASED ANALYSIS QUESTIONS

Constructed Response Items_____

1. What type or types of knowledge did Rebecca Atkins primarily demonstrate?

Rebecca demonstrated several types of knowledge in her lesson, but the one that was most salient was her knowledge of learners and learning. She understood basic information about plants and gardening–content knowledge, and she had a well managed classroom and used an effective teaching strategy–general pedagogical knowledge. Her knowledge of learners and learning was demonstrated in at least two ways. First, she understood that young children need to be actively involved in learning, and she also used active questioning to activate her students' background knowledge.

2. What type or types of knowledge did Richard Nelms demonstrate in his lesson? Identify at least two decisions that Richard made in an attempt to help his lesson progress smoothly.

Richard Nelms primarily demonstrated Pedagogical content knowledge in his middle school lesson. Pedagogical content knowledge focuses on a teacher's ability to illustrate abstract and difficult to learn ideas. Richard did this by using concrete examples such as a starfish and a student to illustrate different types of symmetry. In doing this he also demonstrated the other forms of teacher knowledge.

Some instructional decisions Richard made in the lesson were the choice of examples (concrete and effective), the decision to have Jason come to the front of the room (motivating), and his example of cutting Jason in half which was clear and vivid. All of these contributed to the effectiveness of his lesson.

3. What type or types of knowledge did Didi Johnson primarily demonstrate? Identify at least two decisions that Didi made in an attempt to help her lesson progress smoothly.

Didi Johnson primarily demonstrated general pedagogical knowledge in his lesson. General pedagogical knowledge involves understanding general principles of instruction and management. Her understanding of instruction was demonstrated in several ways. First, she made the decision to use concrete physical objects as a demonstration to illustrate Charles' Law. Then she strategically used questioning to focus students' attention on important aspects (temperature and volume) of her demonstration. Didi's demonstration also reflected her pedagogical content knowledge.

4. What type or types of knowledge did Bob Duchaine primarily demonstrate?

Bob Duchaine obviously knew his subject matter, an essential element of content knowledge. However, the fact that he primarily lectured suggested that he might not be as knowledgeable about other dimensions of teacher knowledge.

Document-Based Analysis_____

Three days after the presentation in his lesson, Bob Duchaine gave the following items on a brief quiz.
1. In what decade was Vietnam established as a colony?
2. What country was defeated in the battle of Dien Bien Phu?
3. What year was the battle of Dien Bien Phu fought?
4. Describe the "Domino Theory," including at least two countries, other than Vietnam, that were identified.
5. Who was the leader of South Viet Nam that refused to hold the free elections provided for in the peace talks after Dien Bien Phu?
Analyze the effectiveness of Bob's quiz based on the descriptions of effective assessment in the chapter.

Effective assessment gathers information about students' thinking, which allows teachers to make strategic decisions about instruction. The quiz was effective if the goal of Bob's lesson was primarily factual information; four of the five questions focused on dates and names. It wasn't effective if his goal was having students understand the causes and effects of the Viet Nam War.

CLASSROOM EXERCISES

1. Misha Pauley stood at the front of his classroom and smiled broadly as his students filed in for their first meeting. He was excited about his first day. He had his notes, motivation plan, and management system ready. He was confident that his double-major in history and English would make him a stellar teacher. He was especially lucky in that he'd obtained an emergency certificate and hadn't been forced to waste all that time in teacher education classes. If Misha's experience is consistent with patterns identified by research, is Misha likely to be relatively successful or relatively unsuccessful in his first year of teaching? Explain.

2. A sixth grade teacher presents an introductory math lesson on multiplying fractions. During the lesson, she notices that several of the students ask for clarification of the terms "numerator," "denominator," and "reduce." She reflects that evening after school, and plans to go back and review the basics of fractions by using concrete materials (manipulatives) that will allow her students to understand these abstract concepts. What concept from the chapter is the teacher best illustrating by using the manipulatives to illustrate multiplication of fractions.

3. In general, biology teachers carefully and accurately explain the process of photosynthesis in green plants. Yet many learners mistakenly believe that we "feed" green plants, much as we feed animals, instead of understanding that green plants manufacture their own food. Explain how each of the types of knowledge described in the chapter is required to deal with this problem.

4. We see a person struggle to solve a brain teaser, simply for the experience of solving it. We conclude, "People have an innate desire to understand how the world works. When they don't, they struggle until they do." Of the *Important Concepts* that are listed at the end of the chapter, which two are best illustrated by our conclusion? Explain.

5. The process of making decisions is essential in teaching. Assuming teachers are reflective, which two of the *Important Concepts* at the end of the chapter are most important in the process of making decisions? Explain.

FEEDBACK FOR CLASSROOM EXERCISES

1. If Misha's experience fits patterns identified by research, he is likely to be somewhat unsuccessful. His double major doesn't ensure that he has the pedagogical content knowledge to be an effective history or English teacher, and his lack of knowledge of learners and learning is likely to detract from his effectiveness. His thinking illustrates the misconception that majoring in a subject provides all the knowledge needed to teach the subject.

2. Knowing that concrete examples are necessary to understand abstract ideas and being able to prepare the concrete examples illustrates pedagogical content knowledge.

3. Knowledge of content is required to understand the process of photosynthesis. Pedagogical content knowledge is required to enable teachers to represent the process of photosynthesis in such as way that students don't confuse it with the intake of food–as occurs with animals. General pedagogical knowledge is needed to have the questioning skills, for example, to guide learners' understanding, and knowledge of learners and learning is required to understand why learners are likely to have the misconception in the first place and what can be done to help eliminate it.

4. The two concepts best illustrated by the comment are *principle* and *theory*. A theory is a set of related principles that is used to explain observations. We explain the person's efforts based on the theory that people have a need for order, predictability, and understanding. This is the basic premise on which cognitive theories of motivation are based. The principles are; "People have an innate desire to understand how the world works," and "When people don't understand how the world works, they struggle until they do."

5. The two concepts are *research* and *theory*. Research and theory make up the knowledge base teachers use for making decisions. (Since theories are based on principles, they are also important.)

CHAPTER 2: DEVELOPMENT OF COGNITION AND LANGUAGE

CHAPTER OVERVIEW

In this chapter students examine the development of cognition and language. The chapter begins with a definition and description of principles that apply to all forms of development. Within this framework, Piaget's theory of intellectual development is then discussed, followed by an examination of Vygotsky's description of development. Piaget's and Vygotsky's views are then compared in the context of constructivism. The chapter closes with a discussion of language development, language diversity, and English as a second language.

CHAPTER OBJECTIVES

- Explain how cognitive development is influenced by learning, experience, and maturation.

- Describe basic concepts in Piaget's theory of cognitive development.

- Explain the role of social interaction, language, and culture in Vygotsky's theory of cognitive development.

- Explain how language development contributes to other aspects of development.

TRANSPARENCIES

The transparencies exist in both acetate form and as PowerPoint slides.

T 2.1   Factors influencing human intellectual development (Figure 2.1, p. 34)
T 2.2   Principles of development and examples
T 2.3   Maintaining equilibrium through the process of adaptation (Figure 2.3, p. 38)
T 2.4   Piaget's stages and characteristics
T 2.5   An example of centering (the cartoon on page 19 of Chapter 1)
T 2.6   An example of egocentrism (the cartoon on page 14 of Chapter 1)
T 2.7   Learning and development in a cultural context (Figure 2.7, p. 56)
T 2.8   The zone of proximal development
T 2.9   Scaffolding tasks in three zones of proximal development (Figure 2.8, p. 61)

TRANSPARENCY MASTERS

The transparency masters are included in this manual beginning on page 230.

TM 2.1   The drive for equilibrium
TM 2.2   An example of development in the real world
TM 2.3   Measuring thinking
TM 2.4   Preoperational characteristics in adults' thinking
TM 2.5   Principles of instruction for applying Piaget's theory in classrooms
TM 2.6   A comparison of Piaget's and Vygotsky's views of knowledge construction
TM 2.7   Principles of instruction for applying Vygotsky's theory in classrooms
TM 2.8   Types of bilingual programs

VIDEOS

Looking Through Classroom Windows: "Properties of Air."

This video episode illustrates the thinking of first graders as they try to explain why water doesn't go into a glass that is inverted and immersed in a fishbowl of water. It is described in detail in the Media Guide of this manual. It is also the closing case study for this chapter.

Concepts in Classrooms: "Examining Development: Analyzing Learner Differences." The video illustrates learner developmental differences in three ways:
■ Two Piagetian conservation tasks that illustrate differences in the thinking of young children and older students.
■ A segment from the first-grade lesson in the on the properties of air that illustrates differences in the thinking of the students based on background experiences.
■ A segment from a fourth-grade lesson illustrating differences in students' thinking about a problem.. The segment demonstrates that the thinking of some of the fourth graders remains preoperational.

CHAPTER OUTLINE

I.   Development: A definition
   A.   Principles of development
   B.   The human brain and cognitive development
      1.   Research on brain development
         a.   Early brain development
         b.   Critical periods
         c.   Optimal environments
      2.   Putting brain research into perspective
II Piaget's theory of intellectual development
   A.   The drive for equilibrium
   B.   Organization and adaptation: The development of schemes
      1.   Achieving equilibrium: The process of organization
      2.   Maintaining equilibrium: The process of adaptation
   C.   Factors influencing development
      1.   Experience with the physical world
      2.   Social experience
   D.   Stages of development
      1.   Sensorimotor stage (0 to 2 years)
      2.   Preoperational stage (2 to 7 years)
         a.   Conservation
      3.   Concrete operational stage (7 to 11 years)
         a.   Seriation and classification
      4.   Formal operational stage (11 to adult)
         a.   Characteristics of formal thought
      5.   Stages of development: Research on student thinking
   E.   Assessment and learning: Assessing students' cognitive development
      1.   Assessing aspects of formal thinking
      2.   Assessing aspects of concrete operational thinking
   F.   Technology and Learning: Using technology to develop formal thinking
      1.   Laboratory simulations
   G.   Applying Piaget's work in classrooms: Instructional strategies
   H.   Putting Piaget's theory into perspective

III   A sociocultural view of development: The work of Lev Vygotsky
    A.   Social interaction and development
    B.   Language and·development
    C.   Culture and development
    D.   The relationship between learning and development
    E.   Vygotsky's work: Instructional strategies
        1.   Zone of proximal development
        2.   Scaffolding: Interactive instructional support
    F.   Piaget's and Vygotsky's views of knowledge construction
IV. Language development
    A.   Theories of language acquisition
        1.   Behaviorism and language development
        2.   Social cognitive theory
        3.   Nativist theory
        4.   A sociocultural view of language development
    B.   Stages of language acquisition
        1.   Early language: Building the foundation
        2.   Fine-tuning language
        3.   Increasing language complexity
    C.   Language diversity
        1.   English dialects: Research findings
        2.   Dialects in the classroom: Implications for teachers
    D.   English as a second language
        1.   Types of bilingual programs
            a.   Maintenance bilingual programs
            b.   Transitional bilingual programs
            c.   English as a second language (ESL) programs
        2.   Evaluating bilingual programs
        3.   Teaching ELL students: Instructional strategies

PRESENTATION OUTLINE

Teaching suggestions in the outline will be marked with the symbol ■. In most cases, the suggested activities can be done individually and discussed as a whole group, or they can be done in small groups, and the small-group results can be discussed with the whole class. To be consistent with our understanding of knowledge construction, we recommend that you promote as much discussion–both in small groups and with the whole class–as possible.

> *Enrichment Information,* which includes elaborations of text topics as well as topics not included in the text, will be boxed as you see here.

I.   Development: A definition
    A.   Principles of development
    B.   The human brain and cognitive development
        1.   Research on brain development
            a.   Early brain development
            b.   Critical periods
            c.   Optimal environments
        2.   Putting brain research into perspective

■ *The purpose of these activities is to help students understand the concept "development" and principles that influence all forms of development.*

1. Ask the students to describe what the term "cognitive development" means to them. Guide them to conclude that it describes changes in thinking that result from learning, experience, and maturation. Ask them if they, as adults, also develop. They will likely conclude that they do, and you can then emphasize the role of learning and experience in their development.

2. Describe ways that the term *development* is commonly used, such as *developmental approaches to curriculum and instruction*, and topics, problems, or issues that are *developmental*. Point out that when someone says they use a developmental approach it usually means that they begin with concrete experiences and gradually move to more abstract experiences.

   Even university students approach topics "developmentally," meaning they first look at the topics concretely before they're able to deal with the topics in the abstract.

3. Display T 2.1 "*Factors Influencing Human Intellectual Development*." Ask students for some examples from their personal lives that illustrate each of the three factors.

4. Display T 2.2 "*Principles of Development and Examples*," which includes the principles and an example of each. Have the students identify other examples from their own experiences.

5. Have the students suggest implications that brain development has for education. Some possibilities include:
   • Teaching foreign languages to young children, rather than waiting until they're in middle school, as is present practice.
   • Creating stimulating environments for infants and young children.
   • Placing even more emphasis on language and reading with young children than presently exists.
   Remind students that brain research is still in its infancy, and applying the research in classrooms should be approached with caution.

II   Piaget's theory of intellectual development
   A.   The drive for equilibrium

■ *The following activities are intended to help students understand the concept of equilibrium and why it is the cornerstone of Piaget's theory*:

1. Ask the following question: "How many of you in this class are married or living with someone?" You will have a sprinkling of hands. Then ask, "For those of you who are, do you have your side of the bed that you sleep on every night, and does your husband/wife have his/her side?" Since people almost always have their own side of the bed, this usually results in some laughter. Tell them to keep the question in mind, and that the point in it will be clear in a moment.

2. Display TM 2.1 "*The Drive for Equilibrium*" (keeping the title of the transparency covered) and have the students identify what the examples have in common. After a series of responses, use both the examples on TM 2.1 and the question about their side of the bed to introduce the idea of equilibrium. Point out that this concept is the cornerstone of Piaget's Theory of Intellectual Development.

3. Ask students to cite additional examples of people's need for equilibrium. (During the discussion, point out that most of them tend to sit in the same seat each time they come to class, which is a personal, real-world example.)

To enrich your students' understanding of Piaget you might want to share some personal information about him.

Piaget's Background. He died in 1980; he was originally a biologist and his experience with studying mollusks helped form his ideas about adaptation. He observed that mollusks living in swiftly flowing water developed different body structures than did mollusks living in still water. From these observations he developed his concept of adaptation. Much of his initial theory was based on his observations of his own children. America was slow to accept his work, because it was clinical–based on intensive observation of only a few subjects–rather than the laboratory-based behaviorist orientation that predominated at the time. You might also point out that Piaget's work is a prominent example of descriptive research, which was discussed in Chapter 1.

B. Organization and adaption: The creation of schemes
   1. Adapting schemes

   ■ *The purpose in the following suggestions is to help the students understand the relationships among the concepts* equilibrium, organization, scheme, adaptation, assimilation, accommodation, experience, *and* development.
   1. Display T 2.3 *"Maintaining Equilibrium Through the Process of Adaptation."* Students commonly have difficulty with the concepts *assimilation* and *accommodation*, often confusing the two. Emphasize that accommodation involves modifying the original scheme and creating a new scheme.

   2. To help students understand how forming schemes helps us function in the world, display TM 2.2 *"An Example of Development in the Real World."* Have them complete the activity as suggested in the directions. Discuss their products, and display the feedback at the bottom of the exercise.

   3. Have students identify other examples of development using the same concepts.

C. Factors influencing development
   1. Experience with the physical world
   2. Social experience
D. Stages of development
   1. Sensorimotor stage (0 to 2 years)
   2. Preoperational stage (2 to 7 years)
      1. Conservation

      ■ *The suggestions in this section are designed to help the students understand the characteristics of preoperational thinking.*
      1. Display T 2.4 *"Piaget's Stages and Characteristics."* Review the information briefly.

      2. Display T 2.5 *"An Example of Centering"* and T 2.6 *"An Example of Egocentrism"* to illustrate the concepts *centering (centration)* and *egocentrism* in the thinking of young children.

3. Concrete operational stage (7 to 11 years)
   1. Seriation and classification
4. Formal operational stage (11 to adult)
   1. Characteristics of formal thought
E. Assessment and learning: Assessing students' cognitive development
   A. Assessing aspects of formal thinking
   B. Assessing aspects of concrete operational thinking

■ *The suggestions in this section are designed to help the students understand differences in the thinking of preoperational, concrete operational, and formal operational learners.*
1. **Display TM 2.3 *"Measuring Thinking."* Emphasize that the objects are solids and cubes. Point out that solids are treated as non-compressible, and remind them that this information is relevant for their responses. Have them decide what stage of development would be required to answer correctly, and discuss the results.**

   The answers are as follows:
   1. *True.* We can see that A is bigger than B. A *preoperational* thinker would be able to respond correctly to this item, since it is perceptual.
   2. *False.* The balance is balanced, so they have the same weight. This requires *concrete operational* thinking. Young children *center* on the size and conclude that A is heavier. (Technically the balance measures mass, but using weight is acceptable for this discussion.)
   3. *False.* Since their weights (masses) are the same and A is larger, it is less dense than B. Again many students center on the size and conclude that A is more dense. Your students are likely to conclude that this is a formal operational task. However, they can *see* that block A is larger than block B, and they can readily conclude (based on the concrete materials) that the blocks are the same weight, so it is a *concrete operational* task. (Point out that curriculum writers often present the concept of density in 5th grade science books, which is evidence that the curriculum writers view concrete thinkers as *capable* of understanding the concept.)

40

4. *True.* If the two objects have the same weight, they cannot be made of the same substance. This is an abstract idea, and requires hypothetical thinking. This is a *formal operational* task.

5. *True.* In order to make the balloons the sizes of the blocks, more air would have to be put into balloon 1, so it would be heavier. This is also abstract and hypothetical–a *formal operational* task.

6. Emphasize that research indicates that few people are formal operational outside their own areas of expertise. Point out that you use as many concrete examples in your instruction as possible, because they are likely to be concrete operational with respect the many of the topics you cover in this class. Note that you are also concrete operational in areas where you lack experience.

Video: You might want to show the video segment "Examining Development: Analyzing Learner Differences" from the *Concepts in Classrooms* Video, Tape One. Have the students share their reactions. The following include some of the reactions that should result from the discussion:

- The 6-year-old in the segment doesn't conserve. He centers on the most perceptually obvious aspect of the events, leading him to conclude that the amounts are different in each case. The older students do conserve, noting that the ball was simply flattened in the first example, and the liquid was simply poured into a wider jar in the second. This illustrates differences in thinking of students at different ages.

- Samantha, because of her experience in the swimming pool with her dad, was able to explain that the air kept the water out until the glass was tipped. Her comments illustrate the influence of experience on development.

- Danielle, in spite of the explanations that she had heard, continued to center on the number of blocks on the balance and ignored the distance from the fulcrum. Mavrin, in contrast, offered a valid explanation. This illustrates developmental differences in the thinking of two students at the same age.

---

7. To demonstrate that adults sometimes demonstrate preoperational thought display TM 2.4 *"Preoperational Characteristics in Adults' Thinking."* Have the students identify the two concepts best illustrated in the examples (the same two concepts in each example). (These are real-world examples, so you can point out that fact to the students.)

F. Technology and learning: Using technology to develop formal thinking
   1. Laboratory simulations

Using CD-ROM Technology. To enrich their understanding of formal operational thinking and give them some experience with CD-ROM technology, you might have the students complete the "Using Technology in Your Study of Educational Psychology: Examining Cognitive Development" experience with the CD-ROM that is part of the media package for the book.

Feedback for the questions in the chapter is as follows:

1. Formal operational thinking is characterized by isolating one variable, such as the length, keeping the values of the weight and angle constant, and seeing what effect changing the length has on the frequency. Failing to control all the variables but one indicates that students haven't yet reached formal operations.

2. Lack of experience is the most likely reason the students haven't reached formal operations.

3. The students in the video (7th graders) were concrete operational in their thinking. They simultaneously changed the weight, length and angle. It wasn't until the teacher intervened that they began to control variables.

    G.   Applying Piaget's work in classrooms: Instructional strategies
    H.   Putting Piaget's work into perspective

    ■ *To help the students understand how Piaget's work can be applied in classrooms:*
    1.   Display TM 2.5 *"Principles of Instruction for Applying Piaget's Work in Classrooms."* Have the students offer examples of each principle.

    2.   Have the students identify examples of how Piaget's work has influenced instruction and curriculum development. Some examples include:
        •   **Hands-on science**
        •   **The use of manipulatives in math**
        •   **Language experience and whole language in reading and writing**
        •   **Project methods in social studies**

        The focus in each of these is beginning instruction with direct experiences and moving from the concrete to the abstract.

III. A sociocultural view of development: The work of Lev Vygotsky
    A.   Social interaction and development
    B.   Language and development
    C.   Culture and development
    D.   The relationship between learning and development
    E.   Vygotsky's work:: Instructional strategies
        1.   Zone of proximal development
        2.   Scaffolding: Interactive instructional support

    ■ *The purpose in the following suggestions is to help the students understand the concepts involved in Vygotsky's theory and how they can be applied in classrooms.*
    1.   Display T 2.7 "Learning and Development in a Cultural Context." Then, refer to your own teaching in this chapter. Have the students state specifically what you ask them to do with the examples, such as those in TM 2.1 *"The Drive For Equilibrium,"* and TM 2.2

"An Example of Development in the Real World." Guide them to notice that they:
- were involved in a great deal of social interaction through the discussions (and perhaps worked in groups).
- worked collaboratively on the solution to problems--to identify the common characteristics in the examples.
- used language, as you encouraged them to put their understanding into words.

2. Ask them what your role was in the activities. (You provided enough, *but not too much*, guidance to help them make *their own* progress–this is the essence of *scaffolding*, and students often miss the distinction. You arranged the learning activity to be in their *zones of proximal development*, and you provided the scaffolding.) Display T 2.8 *"The Zone of Proximal Development"* and T 2.9 *"Scaffolding in Three Zones of Proximal Development"* to further emphasize your points.

F. Piaget's and Vygotsky's views of knowledge construction

■ *To help students begin to understand constructivism and how Piaget's and Vygotsky's views differ:*
3. Display TM 2.6 *"A Comparison of Piaget's and Vygotsky's Views of Knowledge Construction,"* and discuss the information included on it.

4. Remind students that constructivism will be discussed in depth in Chapter 8, and applications of constructivism are presented in Chapter 9.

5. To summarize and relate Piaget's and Vygotsky's theories to constructivism, display TM 2.7 *"Principles of Instruction for Applying Vygotsky's Theory in the Classroom"* and have the students compare the principles to those in TM 2.5 *"Principles of Instruction for Applying Piaget's Work in Classrooms."* Note that Piaget and Vygotsky are both constructivists, but they differ somewhat in their views.

V. Language development
   A. Theories of language acquisition
      1. Behaviorist theory
      2. Social cognitive theory
      3. Psycholinguistic theory
      4. A constructivist view of language development

■ *To help the students understand the importance of language development*
1. Point out that research indicates that early language experience is one of the strongest determiners of success in school.

2. Have them decide which of the theories of language acquisition tends to offer strong support for these results, and which of the theories tends to offer limited support for these results. Share the groups' results in a whole-class discussion.

   B. Stages of language acquisition
      1. Early language: Building the foundation
      2. Fine-tuning language
      3. Increasing language complexity
   C. Language diversity
      1. English dialects: Research findings

2.　Dialects in the classroom: Implications for teachers
　D.　English as a second language
　　　1.　Types of bilingual programs
　　　　　a.　Maintenance bilingual programs
　　　　　b.　Transitional bilingual programs
　　　　　c.　English as a second language (ESL) programs
　　　2.　Evaluating bilingual programs
　　　3.　Teaching ELL students: Instructional strategies

■ *To help students understand the different types of bilingual programs*:
1. **Display TM 2.8 "Types of Bilingual Programs."**

2. **Have the students explain the research results on bilingual programs using Piaget's and Vygotsky's work as a basis for their explanation. Discuss their explanations.**

Dialects in the Classroom. In reference to dialects, you might want to remind the students that since the dialect is functional for the child outside the classroom, using it as a base for the gradual evolution of Standard English is a sensible approach. (Interestingly, this is the same approach recommended for parents wanting to develop young children's language; adults use events to elicit language and then build on them by modeling correct language [Snow, Perlmann, & Nathan, 1987]).

Most important, students who use different dialects need to feel accepted and valued. Knowing that nonstandard dialects are not inferior forms of language and that students who speak them are as capable as other students can help teachers maintain appropriate expectations. Further, understanding nonstandard English dialects can increase teachers' sensitivity to the diversity in their students and can help them use students' language backgrounds as the foundation for growth in reading and writing (Washington & Miller-Jones, 1989). In working with these students, teachers need to separate grammatical and pronunciation differences from the message itself. Overemphasis on correct pronunciation during oral reading lessons can divert important energy from the central task--understanding the reading passage (Anderson et al., 1985). This is admittedly difficult for teachers schooled in the importance of correct grammar, but sensitivity and awareness can help teachers focus on the essential meaning of students' messages rather than the surface features of different dialects.

DISCUSSION STARTERS

1. Should age-driven grade levels be abolished and replaced by developmentally-driven groupings? What implications would this have for the curriculum? For instruction? What does "developmentally-driven groupings" mean?

2. Can maturation take place without experience? Offer a concrete example to support your point.

3. Can experience contribute to development without maturation? Offer a concrete example to support your point.

4. Should teachers and schools attempt to accelerate cognitive development? If so, how? If not, why not?

5. Which of the following concepts from Piaget's theory are most useful to teachers? Why are they useful? Which of the concepts are least useful? Why aren't they?
   * Equilibrium
   * Organization

- Adaptation
- Centration
- Conservation
- Developmental Stages

6. Do Piaget's descriptions of development have more or fewer implications for curriculum and instruction than do Vygotsky's descriptions? Explain.

7. Is the link between language development and Piaget's work stronger or weaker than the link between language development and Vygotsky's work? Explain.

8. If a teacher uses lecture as a primary method, do students still construct their own understanding of the topics they study? Explain.

BACKGROUND READINGS

Abbeduto, L. (2000). *Taking sides: Clashing views on controversial issues in educational psychology.* Guilford, CT: Dushkin/McGraw-Hill. This edited work presents contrasting views on some of the prominent issues in learning and teaching, such as whether or not brain research has implications for classroom instruction, and whether or not English immersion should replace bilingual education.

Ackerman, E. (1998). New trends in cognitive development: Theoretical and empirical contributions. *Learning and Instruction, 8*(4), 375-385. This article provides a succinct overview of current thinking in cognitive development.

Bredo, E. (1997). The social construction of learning. In G. Phye (Ed.), *Handbook of academic learning: Construction of knowledge* (pp. 3-45). San Diego: Academic Press. This chapter provides a succinct view of Vygotsky's theory of development including a clear description of the relationship between development and learning.

Bruer, J. (1999). In search of brain-based education. *Phi Delta Kappan, 89*(9), 649-657. This article raises questions about the efficacy of trying to apply brain-based research in classrooms.

Byrnes, J. P. (2001). *Minds, brains, and learning: Understanding the psychological and educational relevance of neuroscientific research.* New York: Guilford Press. Takes a critical and analytical look at neuroscientific research.

DeVries, R. (1997). Piaget's social theory. *Educational Researcher, 26,* 4-18. This article provides a good overview of Piaget's theory, and helps eliminate some misconceptions about Piaget's position on the role of social interaction in development.

Fowler, R. (1994, April). *Piagetian versus Vygotskian perspectives on development and education.* Paper presented at the Annual Meeting of the American Educational Research Association, New Orleans. This paper provides an in-depth comparison of Piaget's and Vygotsky's views of development. It is a very good resource for students who have some background in Piaget's and Vygotsky's work.

Gauvain, M. (2001). *The social context of cognitive development.* New York: Guilford Press. Places Vygotsky's work into the larger context of social constructivism and sociocultural views of learning.

Paris, S., & Cunningham, A. (1996). Children becoming students. In D. Berliner, & R. Calfee (Eds.), *Handbook of educational psychology* (pp. 117-147). New York: Macmillan. This chapter focuses on development during the preschool and primary years.

Wadsworth, B. (1996). *Piaget's theory of cognitive and affective development* (5th ed.). New York: Longman. The author presents a comprehensive and conceptual account of Piaget's work in an understandable way. A good beginning point for anyone interested in further study of Piaget's theory.

Wigfield, A., Eccles, J., & Pintrich, P. (1996). Development between the ages of 11 and 25. In D. Berliner, & R. Calfee (Eds.), *Handbook of educational psychology* (pp. 148-185). New York: Macmillan. This chapter examines development during early adolescence, adolescence and young adulthood.

FEEDBACK FOR CONSTRUCTED RESPONSE AND DOCUMENT-BASED ANALYSIS QUESTIONS

Constructed Response Items_____

1. At what level of cognitive development were Jenny's students likely to be? Was her instruction effective for that level? Explain.

Jenny's students demonstrated characteristics of preoperational learners. For instance, Jessica's reason for the towel staying dry was, "Cause it's inside and the rest is outside," and Anthony concluded that "A water seal," had kept the towel dry. This is perceptually based reasoning, which is characteristic of preoperational learners.

Jenny's instruction was quite effective for this level, because she provided direct and concrete experiences for the students. For example, to demonstrate that air was in the glass, she tipped it sideways to allow a bubble to escape. Later in the lesson, when she was trying to guide the students to the idea that the air kept the card on the glass, she first held the card on with her hand to demonstrate that her hand held the card on the glass, and when she removed her hand, and the card stayed on the cup, she led the students to conclude that air was the only thing that could be holding the card on the cup. She also allowed the students to experiment with the materials in a followup hands-on activity, which provided even more direct experience.

2. Why was the medium of water important for Jenny's lesson? How does this relate to Piaget's levels of development?

The water was concrete and perceptual. Without the water, for example, the students wouldn't have been able to see air bubbles escape from the glass, so they wouldn't have had any direct experience with air being in the glass. Preoperational students need direct experiences to provide the foundation for logical thought, which marks the next step in development.

3. When Samantha and Terry disagreed about the condition of the inside of the glass, how did Jenny respond? What other alternatives might she have pursued? What are the advantages and disadvantages of these alternatives?

Jenny described the disagreement as a problem to be solved. This is a desirable approach from a constructivist perspective.

She could simply have told the students that the inside of the glass was dry. She could also have asked other students to come up and check on the glass. The disadvantage of telling the students is that it wouldn't be convincing for those who believed that it was wet. The disadvantage of having other students come up is simply time and management. The advantage in having others check the glass is that more students would have directly experienced feeling the inside of the glass.

5. Were Jenny's students in the zone of proximal development for the lesson she was teaching? What forms of scaffolding did Jenny provide? How effective was the scaffolding?

While we don't have enough evidence to determine if all the students are in the zone of proximal development, the comments of several indicated that they were in the zone.

Jenny provided very effective scaffolding in the form of questions, prompts, and altering materials (e.g., tipping the glass to allow the air bubbles to escape, and having the students try the activities themselves).

Document-Based Analysis

A student is given a series of conservation tasks. When two equal pieces of clay are shown to the child he agrees they are equal, but when one is flattened, he replies, "It's not the same because that one is flattened out like a pancake."

Two equal beakers of liquid are show to the child, and he concludes that the amounts are equal. When one is poured into a larger beaker, he is asked again whether they are equal. He replies that the one has more because, "It's taller."

When two rows of coins are shown to the same child, he agrees that the rows contain the same number of coins. When one row is spread out, he is asked again whether they still contain the same number of coins. He replies that one is "bigger."

The boy's responses indicate thinking at which of Piaget's stages of development. Explain, based on the characteristics of thinking at that stage.

These responses suggest that the student was at the pre-operational stage of development because his thinking was influenced by obvious or salient aspects of the problems. Rather than focusing on the logical fact that size, height, and number didn't change during the physical operation, and that these operations were reversible, the child instead centered on perceptually salient aspects of the environment. The size of the pancake, the height of the beaker, and the spacing of the rows of coins all took precedence over the logical arguments that neither mass, volume, or number actually changed, and that the operations could be reversed, resulting in the initial state.

CLASSROOM EXERCISES

1. In our everyday life, we commonly see prices written as 1.29^9 for gas, for example, and an article of clothing for $39.95, as another example. What concept from Piaget's theory best explains why retailers present prices in this way? Why wouldn't they simply price the gasoline at $1.30 and the clothing at $40, for instance?

2. We periodically get frustrated when we want to change a procedure or something else in a business, and the people in charge want to continue doing business the way it's been done in the past, offering the rationale, "This is the way we've always done it." Using Piaget's work as a basis, explain why they would offer such a rationale.

3. One of the most basic principles in science is: "All objects in the universe want to be at their lowest energy level." Explain how this principle relates to Piaget's concept of equilibrium.

4. Consider the aphorisms, "Still water runs deep," and "Make hay while the sun shines." Describe the meaning that a concrete operational thinking would give to each. Then, describe the meaning a formal operational thinker would give to each.

5. Look again at the cartoon on page 17 of your text. Using Piaget's theory as a basis, explain specifically why the child responds as he does. What stage of development is best illustrated in the cartoon?

6. Trudge (1990) found that when pairing a student who was a conserver in the *"conservation of volume"* task with a nonconserver, and asking the pairs to try and explain the differences in the water level, 80% of the nonconservers in the pairs reached conservation, whereas only 50% reached conservation in regular classroom instruction. Does Piaget's or Vygotsky's theory better explain these experimental results? Defend your conclusion based on your understanding of the two theories.

7. Andrew, a fourth grader in private school, visits a classmate at his home for the first time. Andrew is struck by the obvious opulence of his friends home compared to his own. He is particularly impressed that his friend has such a big bedroom, and he is quick to notice the computer and television in it.

   Andrew's mom picks him up after his afternoon of playing and on the way home Andrew asks his mom why his friend doesn't attend private school since his family is so rich. What concept from Piaget's theory best accounts for Andrew thinking that his classmate should attend private school? Explain.

8. Sandy and Shirley host a trip to Las Vegas each fall including their various friends, neighbors, and relatives. It's a women-only trip that they have arranged for several years. Sandy loves to play blackjack and usually budgets $300 to play. Shirley prefers slot machines and she budgets $200. On their return Sandy's husband, Lou, picks both of the women up at the airport and quizzes them about their success. Shirley says with a grin that she won $100; Sandy reports that she shot her wad and lost it all. When Lou asks Sandy if that was a good use of money, Sandy shakes her head at Lou and tells him,"You can't look at it that way." What concept from Piaget's theory of cognitive development best explains Sandy's view of winning? Provide the explanation.

9. Sydney, age 5, responds that she still only has two feet when her grandmother tells her that she's grown another foot since the last time she visited Sydney.

   Bart, age 8, asks his mom, "What's for dinner?" Affectionately and laughing, she suggests having his baby back ribs and his sister's ham hocks–referring to a running family joke about the size of his baby sister's legs. The next morning Bart quizzes his mom, "Mom, I was thinking, if you love us why would you want to eat us?"

   Joan, an adult, listens as her friend, Shasta, tells a first-person joke. After the punch line she asks–with concern–if Shasta's story is really true.

What major topic from the chapter best explains Sydney's, Bart's, and Joan's thinking in these cases?

FEEDBACK FOR CLASSROOM EXERCISES

1. We tend to center on the $1.29 and the 39, making it look like the price is less than it actually is. The perception of $1.30 and $40 is quite different from the perception of $1.29^9 and $39.95.

2. Doing it the way we've always done it allows us to remain at equilibrium. Any change disrupts our equilibrium, at least to a certain extent.

3. Being at equilibrium is a lower energy state than being at disequilibrium. Research indicates that when we're at disequilibrium, we're motivated to re-establish equilibrium. Our motivation can be explained by suggesting that we want to return to our lower energy state.

4. Concrete operational thinkers tend to describe the aphorisms literally, such as, "When the water isn't moving fast it is deep." Formal operational thinkers describe it metaphorically, such as "Reflective thinkers are likely to remain quiet about their thoughts until they've carefully considered the ideas."

5. The child is demonstrating preoperational thought. All he can see is the water and the faucet, he responds perceptually, and he concludes that all the water is in the faucet.

6. Vygotsky's work better explains the results. When the learners work in pairs, the level of social interaction is higher than in regular class instruction. Vygotsky places greater emphasis on social interaction than does Piaget. The citation for the study is:

> Trudge, J. (1990). Vygotsky, the zone of proximal development. In L. Moll (Ed.), *Vygotsky and education* (pp. 155-174). Cambridge: Cambridge University Press.

7. Centration is the concept best illustrated. Andrew is centering on the perceived wealth of his friend's family and assumes that private school is a logical choice for people with money.

8. Egocentrism is the concept best illustrated. Sandy's comment, "You can't look at it that way," indicates that she is not inclined to consider the incident from someone else's point of view. Adults are susceptible to barriers of logical thought. In this case Sandy is focusing on her enjoyment and views this as an appropriate expense.

9. Their thinking can best be explained on the basis of constructivism. Sydney, Bart and Joan are constructing their own understanding of the incidents based on their background experiences and the interaction involved.

CHAPTER 3: PERSONAL, SOCIAL, AND EMOTIONAL DEVELOPMENT

CHAPTER OVERVIEW

In this chapter we continue the discussion of learner development by examining their personal, social, and moral development. The chapter begins with an examination of the general characteristics of personal and social growth, followed by a description of Erikson's theory of psychosocial development. Self-concept and factors that influence it are then discussed. The chapter continues with a discussion of moral development, reviewing first Piaget's views on moral development and then Kohlberg's descriptions of moral reasoning. The chapter closes by considering the relationship between moral development and classroom structure, as well as the moral education versus character education debate.

CHAPTER OBJECTIVES

- Identify factors that influence personal development.

- Describe factors influencing social development.

- Explain the implications of Erikson's theory for teaching.

- Explain the relationship between self-concept and academic achievement and what teachers can do to influence each.

- Identify different stages of moral reasoning and how they apply to classroom practice.

TRANSPARENCIES

The transparencies exist in both acetate form and as PowerPoint slides

T 3.1   Influences on personal development (Figure 3.1, p. 80)
T 3.2   Parenting styles and patterns of personal development
T 3.3   Erikson's stages of psychosocial development
T 3.4   States in identity development
T 3.5   The relationships among the dimensions of self-concept and achievement (Figure 3.2, p. 96)
T 3.6   Kohlberg's stages of moral reasoning

TRANSPARENCY MASTERS

The transparency masters are included in this manual beginning on page 230.

TM 3.1   Parenting styles: An application
TM 3.2   Principles of instruction for promoting social development
TM 3.3   Assumptions and corollaries involved in Erikson's theory
TM 3.4   Positive and negative resolutions of crises
TM 3.5   Principles of instruction for promoting psychosocial and self-concept development
TM 3.6   Erikson's theory in the classroom
TM 3.7   Self-esteem in our popular culture
TM 3.8   Moral reasoning on the interstate
TM 3.9   An application of Piaget's description of moral development
TM 3.10   A classroom dilemma
TM 3.11   Stages of moral reasoning: An application
TM 3.12   Emotional factors in moral development: An application

TM 3.13   A comparison of character education and moral education
TM 3.14   Principles of instruction for promoting moral development

CHAPTER OUTLINE

I.   Personal development
      A.   Heredity
      B.   Parents and other adults
      C.   Peers
II.   Social development
      A.   Perspective taking
      B.   Social problem solving
           1.   Violence and aggression in schools
      C.   Assessment and learning: Assessing students' social development
      D.   Promoting social development: Instructional strategies
      E.   Technology and learning: Using the Internet to promote social development
III. Integrating personal, emotional, and social development: Erikson's theory
      A.   Erikson's stages of psychosocial development
      B.   Putting Erikson's work into perspective
      C.   Supporting psychosocial development
           1.   Early childhood
           2.   The elementary years
           3.   Adolescence
IV.   The development of identity and self-concept
      A.   The development of identity
           1.   Patterns in identity development
      B.   The development of self-concept
           1.   Self-concept and self-esteem
      C.   Self-concept and achievement
           1.   Academic self-concept
      D.   Promoting psychosocial and self-concept development: Instructional strategies
      E.   Ethnic pride: Promoting positive self-esteem and ethnic identity
           1.   Self-esteem and ethnicity
           2.   Ethnic pride and identity formation
V.   Development of morality, social responsibility, and self-control
      A.   Increased interest in moral education and development
      B.   Piaget's description of moral development
      C.   Kohlberg's theory of moral development
           1.   Level I: Preconventional ethics
                a.   Stage 1: Punishment-obedience
                b.   Stage 2: Market exchange
           2.   Level II: Conventional ethics
                a.   Stage 3: Interpersonal harmony
                b.   Stage 4: Law and order
           3.   Level III: Postconventional ethics
                a.   Stage 5: Social contract
                b.   Stage 6: Universal principles
           4.   Putting Kohlberg's theory into perspective
                a.   Research on Kohlberg's theory
                b.   Criticisms of Kohlberg's theory
                c.   Gender differences: The morality of caring

D. Emotional factors in moral development
E. The moral education versus character education debate
F. Promoting moral development: Instructional strategies

PRESENTATION OUTLINE

Teaching suggestions in the outline will be marked with the symbol ■. In virtually all cases, the suggested activities can be done individually and discussed as a whole group, or they can be done in small groups, and the small-group results can be discussed with the whole class. To be consistent with our understanding of knowledge construction, we recommend that you promote as much discussion–both in small groups and with the whole class–as possible.

Enrichment information, which includes elaborations of text topics as well as topics not included in the text, will be boxed as you see here.

I. Personal development
   A. Heredity
   B. Parents and other adults
   C. Peers

■ *The purpose in the following suggestions is to help students understand factors that influence personal development.*
   1. **To introduce the factors that influence personal development display T 3.1 "***Influences on Personal Development.***"**

   2. **Display TM 3.1 "***Parenting Styles: An Application***" and have the students discuss which of the three they believe is most effective. Ask them to provide specific evidence from the examples to support their conclusions.**

   3. **Display T 3.2 "***Parenting Styles and Patterns of Personal Development.***" Lead the students to conclude that the first example in TM 3.1 (Ellen) illustrates an authoritarian parenting style, the second (Tanya) an autoritative style, and the third (Jan) a permissive style.**

   4. **Have the students offer specific examples of teacher actions or behaviors that would parallel each of the styles.**

II Social Development
   A. Perspective taking
   B. Social problem solving
      1. Violence and aggression in the schools
   C. Assessment and learning: Assessing students' social development
   D. Promoting social development: Instructional strategies
   E. Technology and learning: Using the Internet to promote social development
      1. How the Internet influences communication
      2. Using the Internet to promote social development

■ *The purpose in the following suggestions is to help students understand what teachers can do to promote social development.*
   1. **Have the students explain why young children typically are not good at perspective**

taking. Remind them that Piaget's theory helps us understand that young children tend to be egocentric.

2. **Display TM 3.2** *"Principles of Instruction for Promoting Social Development."* **Have them identify where Teresa Manteras (on page 86) applied each of the principles in her work with her students. (Encourage the students to first look for the principles before reading the paragraphs that follow the case.)**

III. Integrating personal, emotional, and social development: Erikson's theory
   A. Erikson's stages of psychosocial development
   B. Putting Erikson's work into perspective
   C. Supporting psychosocial development
      1. Early childhood
      2. The elementary years
      3. Adolescence

■ *The purpose in the following suggestions is to help the students begin to understand Erikson's theory.*

1. **Ask the students if they know people who seem to be somewhat "paranoid," or always feel that someone is out to take advantage of them. Also ask them if they know others who are inclined to take people at face value unless they get evidence to the contrary. (Erikson's theory helps us understand these people by suggesting that those in the first category didn't effectively resolve the trust-mistrust crisis.)**

2. **To provide some background and to put Erikson's work into context, display T 3.3 *"Erikson's Stages of Psychosocial Development"* and TM 3.3 *"Assumptions and Corollaries Involved in Erikson's Theory."* They identify Erikson's stages and summarize the assumptions on which his work is based.**

3. **Ask the students to describe what they believe positive and negative resolutions of the psychosocial challenges (crises) at each stage would be. Then, provide feedback for the discussion by displaying TM 3.4 *"Positive and Negative Resolutions of Crises."* TM 3.2 describes the characteristics of a positive and negative resolution of each stage in adults.**

4. **Display TM 3.6 *"Erikson's Theory in the Classroom,"* have the students respond to the questions, and discuss their results.**

5. **As a way of helping your students visualize Erikson's work, tell them to imagine a circle, and think of the circle as representing the perfectly formed personality. This means that all the crises have been and remain resolved to this point in an individual's life. Now tell them to visualize an imperfect circle–one with indentations at various points. It remains approximately circular, but it is less than perfect. We all have personality imperfections, and the indentations in the circle help us visualize those imperfections. The imperfections don't mean that we can't cope with life, or that we remain stuck at a particular stage. Depending on the situation we're in, they might prevent us from functioning as effectively as we would if the imperfections didn't exist, but this is typical of most people. This is another way of thinking about Erikson's descriptions of the personality and their implications for the way we operate in the world.**

IV The development of identity and self-concept
   A.   The development of identity
        1.   Patterns in identity development
   B.   The development of self-concept
        1.   Self-concept and self-esteem
   C.   Self-concept and achievement
        1.   Academic self-concept
   D.   Promoting psychosocial and self-concept development: Instructional strategies
   E.   Ethnic pride: Promoting positive self-esteem and ethnic identity
        1.   Self-esteem and ethnicity
        2.   Ethnic pride and identity formation

■ *The purpose in following suggestions is to help students understand identity development and relationships between self-concept, self-esteem and school achievement.*

1.   **Ask students for a definition of identity development. Then, display T 3.4 *"States in identity development."* Ask them to offer some perceptions about their own identity development.**

2.   **Remind students of the differences between self-concept and self-esteem, and then, to promote some discussion related to issues involved in the development of self-concept and self-esteem, pose the following question:**

   "Is the improvement of self-esteem an appropriate and worthwhile goal for schools?"

   Most students will say it is, and you can then ask, "How do we go about improving self-esteem?"

2.   **Point out that distinctions between self-concept and self-esteem are sometimes missed and what implications missing these distinctions has for schools and schooling. TM 3.7 *"Self-Esteem in Our Popular Culture,"* includes a quote from Pintrich & Schunk (1996) that directly addresses this issue.**

3.   **Display T 3.5 *"The Relationships Among the Dimensions of Self-Concept and Achievement."* Then, summarize the information in this section by displaying TM 3.5 *"Principles of Instruction for Promoting Psychosocial and Self-Concept Development."* Have them identify where John Adler (on page 97) applied the principles with his students. (Encourage them to look for the principles in the case study before they read the paragraphs that follow it.)**

■ *To illustrate a recurring theme that appears throughout the book:*

1.   **Read or display the following statement:**

   "Minority students need to know that their cultures are valued and that the languages they bring to school are assets rather than obstacles or liabilities. Teachers play a crucial role in making every student feel wanted and loved by the overt and implicit messages they send through their teaching."

2.   **Refer students to this statement and then ask them to identify ways that they can communicate these messages to their students. Require that they give specific and concrete responses.**

V.   Development of morality, social responsibility, and self-control
  A.   Increased interest in moral education and self-control
  B.   Piaget's description of moral development

  ■ *The purpose in the following suggestions is to introduce the students to moral reasoning.*
  1.   **Display TM 3.8 "*Moral Reasoning on the Interstate.*" It is an example that some of the students may have experienced and all can relate to. Ask students why they think you are or are not justified in feeling you are being treated unfairly and why the highway patrol's position is more or less justified than yours.**

  2.   **Have students identify some examples of moral issues that exist today, at both the national and local levels. Among those they identify some might include:**
       •   **abortion.**
       •   **sex education.**
       •   **affirmative action.**
       •   **controversial judicial decisions (such as disallowing evidence because of not following procedures).**
       •   **gun control.**
       •   **the influence of political action committees.**
       •   **censorship.**
       •   **product liability.**

  3.   **Display TM 3.9 "*An Application of Piaget's Description of Moral Development.*" Have the students describe the reasoning of each of the three students in the example. Lead them to conclude that Talitha and Dwain each displayed external morality, whereas Krystal demonstrated thinking that reflected internal morality. Also point out that authoritarian parenting and teaching styles (as opposed to authoritative styles) tend to retard the development of autonomous morality.**

  C.   Kohlberg's theory of moral development

  ■ *The following suggestions are designed to help the students understand what is meant by a "moral dilemma" and to introduce Kohlberg's work.*
  1.   **Display TM 3.10 "*A Classroom Dilemma,*" have students decide whether they would or would not pass Dave, and give their rationales.**

  2.   **Have students first respond as individuals and have them write their reasons down. (You can then collect the papers and use them later when you discuss "Gender differences: The morality of caring.")**

  3.   **After the students have responded individually in writing, have them discuss the issue in their groups, or you may choose to discuss the issue as a whole group from this point on.**

  4.   **Display T 3.6 "*Kohlberg's Stages of Moral Development*" and have students classify some of the reasons they've offered into one of the stages. (At this point you might again display TM 3.8 "*Moral Reasoning on the Interstate*" and have them decide which stage is best represented by your reasoning and which stage is represented by the highway patrol's reasoning.)**

1. Level I: Preconventional ethics
   a. Stage 1: Punishment-obedience
   b. Stage 2: Market exchange
2. Level II: Conventional ethics
   a. Stage 3: Interpersonal harmony
   b. Stage 4: Law and order
3. Level III: Postconventional ethics
   a. Stage 5: Social contract
   b. Stage 6: Universal principles

■ *The following suggestion is designed to deepen your students' understanding of Kohlberg's stages of moral reasoning.*
    1. Display TM 3.11 "*Stages of Moral Reasoning: An Application*" and have the students classify each of the reasons into one of Kohlberg's stages.

4. Putting Kohlberg's theory into perspective
   a. Research on Kohlberg's work
   b. Criticisms of Kohlberg's work
   c. Gender differences: The morality of caring

■ *The following suggestion is designed to illustrate Gilligan's work.*
    1. From the papers the students turned in that included their rationales for passing or failing Dave, do an informal study to see if the women in your class were more inclined than the men to offer rationales for passing or failing Dave that would be classified into Kohlberg's stage 3, and also see if the men were more inclined than the women to offer reasons that would be classified into stage 4. (Most of the reasons students offer for passing or failing will fall into stage 3 or stage 4.) Discuss the results with the class.

Using CD-ROM Technology. To enrich their understanding of moral reasoning and give them some experience with CD-ROM technology, you might have the students complete the "Using Technology in Your Study of Educational Psychology: Assessing Moral Reasoning" experience with the CD-ROM that is part of the media package for the book.

Feedback for the questions in the chapter is as follows:

1. Assessing moral development is problematic, and critics, such as Gilligan (1982), argue that Kohlberg's work has a bias favoring males in it. Other researchers, e.g. Eisenberg, Martin, & Fabes, 1996, state, "The research has not supported Gilligan's assertion that males score higher on Kohlberg's rights- and justice-oriented scheme of moral judgment" (p. 374).

2. Research indicates that people often respond at different stages, and the fact that this occurs is cited as a criticism of Kohlberg's work.

3. Some researchers, e.g., Rest, Narvaes, Bebeau, & Thoma (1999), question the validity of using interview data in the assessment of moral thinking, arguing that people are often unable to articulate their thinking. They favor a multiple choice version of assessing moral thinking called the *Defining Issues Test (DIT)*. An interview would probably be effective in assessing an individual's thinking, whereas the DIT would be much more effective with a group.

D. Emotional factors in moral education
C. The moral education versus character education debate
F. Promoting moral development: Instructional strategies

■ *To apply the information in this section:*
1. **Display TM 3.12 *"Emotional Factors in Moral Development: An Application"* and have them respond to the items at the bottom. Note that experiencing the emotions Melissa felt represent an advance in moral development.**

2. **Display TM 3.13 "A Comparison of Moral Education and Character Education." Have the students offer examples of each approach.**

3. **Display TM 3.14 "Principles of Instruction for Promoting Moral Development." Have the students identify where in the case study illustrating Rod Leist's work with his students (p. 110) Rod applied each of the principles.**

DISCUSSION STARTERS

1. How would Erikson respond to the following educational practices?
   - Retention in grade
   - Ability grouping
   - Competitive grading systems
   - Failing grades
   - Competitive sports
   - Vocational education

   (When we have introduced these to our students we have found the issues are much more complex than they appear at first glance.)

2. Ask students if they agree or disagree with the following statement: "Differences between religions as well as differences between people who are and are not religious are so great that there would be little agreement on the application of Kohlberg's theory in the classroom."

3. How much of instruction should be targeted toward the development of self-concept? What specific things can teachers do to help develop positive self concepts?

4. What should be the school's role in helping students in the process of identity development? How would Erikson respond to this question? How would Kohlberg respond? How would Gilligan respond? What specific things can teachers do to aid in this process?

5. This text takes the position that moral issues cannot be avoided, and the most appropriate approach is for schools and teachers to deal with the issues openly and honestly. Do you agree or disagree with that position? Why do you feel the way you do?

6. Erikson studied under the famous Sigmund Freud's daughter Anna. How were his views of personality development influenced by these experiences? Explain.

7. Some prominent thinkers believe that schools' concerns for children's self-concepts and their self-esteem are misplaced, and the business of the school is to teach knowledge and cognitive skills. What is your position regarding this issue? Explain.

BACKGROUND READINGS

Forgas, J. P. (Ed.) (2001). *Handbook of affect and social cognition*. Mahwah, NJ: Erlbaum. This edited work provides current perspectives on personal, social, and emotional development.

Gilligan, C. (1982). *In a different voice: Psychological theory and women's development*. Cambridge, MA: Harvard University Press. Gilligan critiques Kohlberg's theory from a feminist perspective.

Grolnick, W., Kurowski, C., & Gurland, S. (1999). Family processes and the development of children's self-regulation. *Educational Psychologist, 34*(1), 3-14. This article examines the influence of families on children's personal and social development.

Harter, S. (1999). *The construction of the self: A developmental perspective*. New York: Guilford Press. An insightful look at how students construct their own views of self.

Kohn, A. (1997). How not to teach values. *Phi Delta Kappan, 78*(6), 429-439. This article and the one that accompanies it examines character education from different perspectives.

Skaalvik, E., & Valas, H. (1999). Relations among achievement, self-concept, and motivation in mathematics and language arts: A longitudinal study. *Journal of Experimental Education, 67*(2), 135-149. This article discusses the relationships between achievement and self-concept and examines the implications of these relationships for learner motivation.

Turiel, E. (1998). The development of morality. In W. Damon (Editor-in-chief) & N. Eisenberg (Vol. Ed.), *Handbook of child psychology: Vol. 3. Social, emotional, and personality development* (pp. 863-932). New York: Wiley. An excellent review of the research on the development of morality.

Wigfield, A., Eccles, J., & Pintrich, P. (1996). Development between the ages of 11 and 25. In D. Berliner & R. Calfee (Eds.), *Handbook of Educational Psychology* (pp. 148-185). New York: Macmillan. This chapter examines several dimensions of learner development, including the development of self-concept.

FEEDBACK FOR CONSTRUCTED RESPONSE AND DOCUMENT-BASED ANALYSIS QUESTIONS

Constructed Response Items_____

1. How might Erikson explain Kim's behavior in Helen's class?

   Based on Erikson's work we might conclude that Kim hasn't positively resolved the industry/inferiority crisis with respect to English. He says, "I'm no good at English," for example. On the other hand, he presumably feels a sense of accomplishment with respect to basketball, since Helen described him as "poetry in motion."

2. Using research findings from the research on self-concept, explain Kim's behavior.

   Research indicates that the strongest correlations exist between specific academic self-concepts and achievement. This is corroborated in Kim's case. His self-concept in English is low, but in math and science it appears to be better. Also, his physical self-concept for basketball, and perhaps athletics in general is probably quite high, since, according to Helen, he's very good at basketball.

3. Using concepts from Kohlberg's theory, analyze Helen's cheating problem. From Kohlberg's perspective, how well did she handle this problem?

Helen's handling of the cheating problem was ineffective. First, her classroom structure promoted a form of external morality; for example, her comment to Nathan was, "Nathan, remember my first rule?" and ". . . if you speak without permission again, it's a half hour after school."

Second, her comment to the students with respect to the cheating was again consistent with external morality–"If I catch anyone cheating on Thursday, I'll tear up your quiz and give you a failing grade. Now, go to work." A more effective approach would have been to try to promote internal autonomous morality by discussing the issue of cheating, and by describing teaching and learning as social contracts. When students take tests they are in a contract that requires them to do the work on their own. While this orientation certainly won't stop all cheating, it creates a more mature and effective climate than the one in which Helen was operating.

4. If you think Helen's teaching could have been improved on the basis of the information in Chapter 3, what suggestions would you make? Again, be specific.

Several things in Helen's approach to her classroom and her instruction could have been improved. In addition to the emotional climate, as indicated by her response to Nathan and her threat to tear up papers if others were caught cheating, her expectations for students were negative. For example, she commented to them, "You did so poorly on the quiz, and I explained everything so carefully. You must not have studied very hard." While we can't be completely sure, it appears that her instruction is very teacher centered, and built around abstract rules rather than dealing with the rules in the context of written work and developing an understanding of the rules based on interaction between the teacher and the students and the students with each other.

Document-Based Analysis

Two students are presented with the moral dilemma involving Steve, the high school senior who cheated (see page 102). When asked if Steve's cheating was justified, Student A replies, "No, because he'll get caught and kicked out." Student B replies, "No, because there are classroom and school rules against cheating."

At which Kohlberg stage is Student A? Provide evidence to document your answer.

At which Kohlberg stage of development is Student B? Provide evidence to document your answer.

Student A's response suggests that he is at the Punishment-Obedience Stage of Kohlberg's theory. This stage suggests that issues of right and wrong are determined by immediate consequences in terms of rewards and punishment. "Getting caught and kicked out" clearly focuses on immediate consequences rather than more abstract issues of right and wrong.

Student B's response, by comparison, suggests that he is at Kohlberg's Law and Order Stage of moral development. Emphasizing "classroom and school rules against cheating" suggests adherence to law and rules for their own sake, a key characteristics of this stage of development.

CLASSROOM EXERCISES

Four generations were gathered together at a recent family reunion. During an after-dinner discussion the subject of continuing education came up among Bridget, the 40-year-old mother of two; Barbara, her mother; Mary, her grandmother; Severn, Bridget's son; and little Terese, Bridget's four-year-old daughter.

Mary shared her criticism of art she saw at an antique gallery, commenting, "The prices of the watercolors I saw were obscene, and the quality wasn't as exacting as the art we produced during the course I took two years ago."

"Well, Gram, why haven't we seen some of your work?" Bridget queried.

"Your grandmother never stays in one spot long enough to do any serious painting, she's always traveling," Barbara commented. "I always wished I had chosen a career like interior design, something that I really could have grown with over the years."

"You know mom," Bridget advised,"It's never too late to go back to school."

"That's right", Severn chimes in. "Mom is going to school to be a teacher and she's old."

"Thanks a lot, sport;" Bridget says as she ruffles Severn's hair.

"He's right, Mom; your study skills might be a little rusty, but you'd be at the top of your class--you're a bright lady."

"Now that I'm in one spot for awhile I think I'll buy some paint and get started again with some projects," Mary interjects. "I think the kids are right, Barb; why don't you go and take a design course at the Community College to see if you like it? All that is at stake is the cost of the course."

"Hey Mom, remember that pottery class we took at the community school last year?" Severn asks. "I'd like to do that again. Remember the big deal the teacher made about the bowl I threw on the pottery wheel?"

"Yeah, Sev, you really showed some talent. I think you must get it from your grandmother and great grandmother. The pottery teacher had all the right stuff. In fact, his commitment to his students really influenced my decision to teach. I really think I can make a difference in people's lives," Bridget said enthusiastically.

"Bridget, you've always had a positive, can-do attitude. For me I think it's a good dream, just a little too late. I was never the student you were. I struggled just to get out of high school. All I had the skills for was secretarial school. My teachers all said that college just wasn't the place for me," Barbara sighed.

"Terese, since you've climbed up on the stepstool, will you help Mommy wash the dishes in the sink?" Bridget said smiling as she glanced behind her. Terese grinned and nodded "Yes." She stepped off the stool and pushed it over to the sink so she could reach.

1. According to Erikson's stages of psychosocial development what outcome did Bridget encourage by handling the step stool incident in the manner in which she did with Terese? Explain.

2. Using the information from the dialogue, which of Erikson's stages is Severn most likely illustrating?

3. Identify the stage of development that embodies Bridget's view of continuing education for herself.

4. What stage of psychosocial development has Barbara most likely not resolved? What evidence do you have for this?

5. What stage of development has Mary successfully resolved?

An article in a prominent newspaper contained an article entitled "What's a Secretary to Do When the Boss Asks Her to Lie?" The article described some secretaries as being extremely loyal to their bosses, and committing acts, such as shredding important documents that may have destroyed evidence. In one case the secretary explained in court that in her commitment to her boss, her policy was, ". . . not to ask questions and just follow orders."

7. Based on Kohlberg's stages of moral development, in what stage does the secretary's policy fall?

8. The newspaper article further describes a secretary in California who, with the promise of protection from being fired, blew the whistle and corroborated meat-contamination cover-ups, allowing investigators to gather crucial evidence. Based on Kohlberg's work, which stage of moral reasoning does this represent?

9. Another example of what secretaries do when bosses asks them to lie, according to the article, is a woman in the midwest whose boss was falsifying home addresses on payroll records so friends could pay lower taxes in a neighboring state. She confronted him, but was ignored. She decided not to contact the police for fear of losing her job. What stage of moral reasoning, according to Kohlberg, does she best illustrate?

10. What if the same midwestern secretary, described in Item 8, decided–after she confronted her boss's wrong-doing–not to contact the police for fear she might lose her job because she is a single mom charged with raising two small school-aged children. What if instead, she looked for another job and eventually left the company? What stage of Kohlberg's moral development would this illustrate?

11. The relationship and the confidences shared between a minister, priest, or rabbi and a member of his or her congregation is privileged and would prevent that religious leader from revealing to another the nature of any confidence, no matter how dire the incident being described, if the member sharing it did not wish it to be revealed. Often a boss and secretary operate under the same set of ethics. Which stage of moral development is operating here?

FEEDBACK FOR CLASSROOM EXERCISES

1. Bridget encouraged a positive resolution of Autonomy vs. Shame and Doubt. While Terese's age suggests the Initiative vs.Guilt (and this would have been the case if Terese had intended to wash the dishes when she climbed the step stool), in this instance she was climbing the step stool to simply climb. Bridget provided structure and support by suggesting that her climb have a purpose--washing the dishes.

2. Severn's interest and enthusiasm in taking the pottery class, and his enjoyment and the recognition he received from the teacher and his mother suggest that he is successfully resolving the Industry vs. Inferiority stage.

3. Bridget's commitment, as indicated by her comment, "I really think I can make a difference in people's lives," suggests that she is successfully resolving the Generativity vs. Stagnation crisis.

4. Barbara appears to have failed to successfully resolve the Industry vs. Inferiority crisis. In Barbara's eyes her teachers and her academic accomplishments suggested a path other than college or some other career besides secretarial school. It seems from the dialogue that her interests seem to lie in the direction of art/design area, one that was not encouraged or recognized as a strength by significant others.

6. Though being the grandmother of a 40-year-old might suggest Integrity vs Despair, Mary remains in the mainstream of life, and has continued interest in living productively with her travel and painting. This suggests Generativity vs. Stagnation.

7. The secretary is demonstrating Stage 3: Interpersonal Harmony, ethics. Loyalty to someone else illustrates this stage. Since the focus is on loyalty as opposed to fear of repercussion, or some personal favor, we see no evidence of Stage 1 or Stage 2 thinking.

8. This case illustrates Stage 2: Market Exchange. The key is the promise of protection in exchange for providing corroborating evidence. ·

9. Her reasoning is at Stage 1: Punishment and Obedience. The consequence of being fired if her boss's deed is discovered or reported caused the secretary to keep silent and continue to work for him as she always has.

10. In this case, the secretary's behavior indicates Stage 3: Interpersonal Harmony. Her decision not to contact the police was out of concern for the welfare of her children if she were fired from her job.

11. This reasoning suggests Stage 5: Social Contract. Agreements about keeping confidences is made among the people involved, the sanctity of which is kept until mutually agreed upon changes are made.

CHAPTER 4: LEARNER DIFFERENCES

CHAPTER OVERVIEW

Learner differences are the focus of this chapter. The chapter begins by outlining different conceptions of intelligence. This discussion is followed by an examination of socioeconomic status, culture–including ethnicity, voluntary and involuntary minorities and culturally responsive teaching–and gender differences. In the last section of the chapter, students placed at risk, the development of resiliency, and effective schools and teachers for students placed at risk are discussed in detail.

CHAPTER OBJECTIVES

- Explain how different views of intelligence influence your teaching.

- Define socioeconomic status and explain how it may affect school performance.

- Explain the role that culture plays in school success.

- Describe the influence of gender on different aspects of school success.

- Describe ways that schools and classrooms can be adapted to meet the needs of students placed at risk.

TRANSPARENCIES

The transparencies exist in both acetate form and as PowerPoint slides.

T 4.1 Sources of learner individuality (Figure 4.1, p 118)
T 4.2 Gardner's theory of multiple intelligences
T 4.3 Sternberg's triarchic model of intelligence (Figure 4.2, p. 121)
T 4.4 Types of ability grouping in elementary schools
T 4.5 Suggestions for reducing the negative effects of grouping
T 4.6 U.S. census ethnicity comparisons
T 4.7 Characteristics of students placed at risk

TRANSPARENCY MASTERS

The transparency masters are included in this manual beginning on page 230.

TM 4.1   Instructional applications of Gardner's multiple intelligences
TM 4.2   Applying analytic, creative, and practical thinking in different content areas
TM 4.3   Ability grouping, behavior, and achievement
TM 4.4   Criticisms of ability grouping
TM 4.5   The influence of SES on learning
TM 4.6   Principles of instruction for culturally responsive teaching
TM 4.7   Making students feel welcome in school
TM 4.8   Gender differences in the classroom
TM 4.9   Principles of instruction for reducing gender bias and stereotyping
TM 4.10 Schools that promote resilience
TM 4.11 Principles of instruction for teaching students placed at risk
TM 4.12 Ethnicity and computer use
TM 4.13 Household income and computer use

CHAPTER OUTLINE

I. Intelligence
    A.   Intelligence: What does it mean?
    B.   Intelligence: One trait or many?
        2.   Gardner's theory of multiple intelligence
           a.   Gardner's theory: Applications and criticisms
        3.   Sternberg's triarchic theory of intelligence
           a.   Processing components
           b.   Contextual components: Intelligence and the environment
           c.   Experiential components: Adapting to unique experiences
           d.   Improving intelligence
    C.   Intelligence: Nature versus nurture
    D.   Assessment and learning: Cultural controversies in measuring intelligence
    E.   Ability grouping
        1.   Ability grouping: Research results
        2.   Ability grouping: Implications for teachers
    F.   Learning styles
        1.   Learning preferences: Research results
        2.   Learning styles: Implications for teachers
II. Socioeconomic status (SES)
    A.   Influence of SES on learning
        1.   Basic needs and experience
        2.   Parental involvement
        3.   Attitudes and values
    B.   SES: Some cautions and implications for teachers
III. Culture
    A.   Ethnicity
    B.   Culture and schooling
        1.   The cultural basis for attitudes and values
        2.   Cultural differences in adult-child interactions
        3.   Classroom organization: Working with and against students' cultures
        4.   School-culture matches and mismatches
        5.   Culture and learning: Deficit or difference?
    C.   Culturally responsive teaching: Instructional strategies
IV. Gender
    A.   Differences in the behavior of boys and girls
    B.   Gender stereotypes and perceptions
        1.   Perceptions of male and female domains
        2.   Single-gender classrooms and schools
    C.   Responding to gender differences: Instructional strategies
V. Students placed at risk
    A.   Resilience
        1.   Schools that promote resilience
        2.   Teachers that promote resilience
    B.   Teaching students placed at risk: Instructional strategies
    C.   Technology and learning: Equity issues
        1.   The digital divides
        2.   Implications for teachers

PRESENTATION OUTLINE

Teaching suggestions in the outline will be marked with the symbol ■. In most cases, the suggested activities can be done individually and discussed as a whole group, or they can be done in small groups, and the small-group results can be discussed with the whole class. To be consistent with our understanding of knowledge construction, we recommend that you promote as much discussion–both in small groups and with the whole class–as possible.

Enrichment Information, which includes elaborations of text topics as well as topics not included in the text, will be boxed as you see here.

I. Intelligence
   A. Intelligence: What does it mean?

   ■ *The purpose in the following suggestion is to help students understand theoretical views of intelligence:*
   1. Have students take out a sheet of paper and number it from 1 to 10. This activity is effective if you give them no directions other than to number their paper. They will wonder what is "going on," and they usually react to the nature of the questions as you ask them. Give them no background or information until you're finished.

   2. Ask the following questions orally and have them respond in writing to them. (Asking the questions orally is consistent with the way the WISC-III is administered, but the students' responses are also oral, rather than in writing as you're doing here.) (If you have access to the WISC-III, an even better activity would be to select some actual items from it and administer them to the students.)
      1. In what continent is Colombia? (South America)
      2. What is the capital of Syria? (Damascus)
      3. How far is it from Seattle to Atlanta? (2618 miles; Accept 2300-3000)
      4. What is the most abundant gas in our atmosphere? (Nitrogen)
      5. Who was Albert Einstein? (Creator of theory of relativity)
      6. If four pieces of candy cost 10 cents, what will be the cost of 28 pieces? (70 cents)
      7. Ed bought a sweater from his friend for $18. He paid 3/4 of what the sweater cost new. What did the sweater cost new? ($24)
      8. A pair of walking shorts for $27 was on sale for 1/3 less. When no one bought the shorts, the store owner reduced the sale price by 1/2. How much did the shorts cost after the second reduction? ($9)
      9. How are a *river* and a *plateau* alike? ("Topographical features" would be a 2-point response; "things we find in nature" would be a 1-point response, and "made of water and rocks" would be a 0-point response)
      10. How are *freedom* and *justice* alike? ("Social ideals" would be a 2-point response, "civil rights" would be a 1-point response, and "both mean peace" would be a 0-point response.)

   3. After the students have responded, ask them what they just did. Someone will know that they responded to items similar to those on intelligence tests. Also, ask them what the 2-point answers have in common that make them different from the 1-point answers, and the 0-point answers. Someone will note that the 2-point answers are the most abstract and the 0-point answers are the most concrete.

4.   Have students discuss what the differences in the 2-point, 1-point, and 0-point answers as well as the items themselves indicate about experts' conceptions of intelligence. Ask them why they think experts believe that an item, such as "What is the capital of Syria?" is an indicator of intelligence. You might also ask them how they feel about the experts' conceptions of intelligence.

5.   Emphasize that intelligence tests measure experience to a considerable extent. This has important implications for teaching--we want to provide as much meaningful experience for our learners as possible.

6.   Display T 4.1 "Sources of Learner Individuality" and remind students that you have begun your study of learner differences with the study of intelligence.

B.   Intelligence: One trait or many?
   1.   Gardner's theory of multiple intelligence
      a.   Gardner's theory: Applications and criticisms

   ■ *The following suggestions are intended to help students understand Gardner's work:*
   1.   Display T 4.2 *"Gardner's Theory of Multiple Intelligences."* Point out that one of the most important contributions of Gardner's work is that he helps us reconceptualize and expand our view of what it means to be intelligent. (*This is an emotionally satisfying conception for people who haven't excelled in linguistic or logical-mathematical intelligence, which are the two most strongly emphasized in traditional school curricula.*)

   2.   To examine classroom implications of Gardner's work display TM 4.1 *"Instructional Applications of Gardner's Multiple Intelligences."*

   3.   To further emphasize Gardner's work, have students identify other topics and describe how they would try to capitalize on the different intelligences in learning activities.

   4.   Point out that Gardner's work has been strongly criticized because of some of his assumptions.

Understanding Gardner's Work. To enrich the students' understanding of Gardner's work, you might point out that people often misinterpret Gardner's conceptions of intelligence, interpreting them as preferences instead. For example, *interpersonal intelligence* means that an individual has insight into the way other people think and operate. They have a good sense of people's inclinations and needs and what it takes to work effectively with them. It does not necessarily mean that they are socially oriented or prefer being with people to being alone.

The same applies to the other areas. People with high *intrapersonal intelligence*, for example, are not necessarily loners nor do they necessarily prefer to be alone. Rather it means that they have a good sense of who they are and how they, as individuals, work most effectively.

---

   2.   Sternberg's triarchic theory of intelligence
      a.   Processing components
      b.   Contextual components: Intelligence and the environment

c. Experiential components: Adapting to unique experiences
d. Improving intelligence

■ *The purpose in the following suggestions is to help students understand Sternberg's conception of intelligence:*

1. **Display T 4.3 "Sternberg's Triarchic Model of Intelligence."**

2. **Encourage application by having the students describe, based on Sternberg's work, what would represent intelligent behavior versus unintelligent behavior on a school-related task, such as solving a word problem in math.**

3. **To illustrate Sternberg's recent views, display TM 4.2 *"Applying Analytic, Creative, and Practical Thinking in Different Content Areas."* Have the students offer some additional applications in their own specialty areas.**

4. **To further emphasize Sternberg's work, have them examine the implications of his views for classroom practice and suggest learning activities that will require students to relate new experiences to old. With some awareness and practice, designing activities of this sort isn't as difficult as it might initially appear.**

■ *To summarize this section*:

1. **Have the students compare early conceptions of intelligence, such as Spearman's notion of "g" to today's conceptions. You might also have them compare the implications of Sternberg's and Gardner's theories for their work with their own students.**

C. Intelligence: Nature versus nurture

■ *To help your students understand the nature/nurture debate*:

1. **Have them think about where they personally fall. Have them give their reasons, and require that they document the reasons with evidence instead of a mere opinion. Ask them where they believe Gardner and Sternberg would fall.**

Enriching concepts of intelligence. To prompt some additional discussion, you might share the following correlations, and ask the students what the information suggests to them about the nature versus nurture question.

I. Q. Correlations*

Foster parent-child	.20
Parent-child	.50
Siblings reared together	.49
Fraternal twins	.53
Identical twins reared apart	.75
Identical twins reared together	.87

*Erlenmeyer-Kimling and Jarvik, 1963

D. Ability grouping
   1. Ability grouping: Research results
   2. Ability grouping: Implications for teachers

■ *The purpose in the suggestions in this section is to help students understand the controversies surrounding ability grouping.*

1. To check students' perceptions and beliefs with respect to ability grouping begin this section by displaying TM 4.3 *"Ability Grouping, Behavior, and Achievement,"*

2. Have the students respond to the four items. Discuss the explanations.

3. Display T 4.4 *"Types of Ability Grouping in Elementary Schools,"* and TM 4.4 *"Criticisms of Ability Grouping."* Ask students why they think placements are sometimes incorrectly made and why the placements tend to become permanent. Have them relate the process of placing students to intelligence testing and what intelligence tests measure. In the discussion, point out that schools are busy, complex places, and school officials and teachers, like people in general want to simplify their work. Maintaining a placement is simpler than moving students from one ability group to another.

4. Ask the students to use Erikson's theory to explain the lowered self-esteem and motivation of students in elementary schools placed in low ability groups. Have them also explain for junior high and high school students placed in low-ability tracks.

■ *To Summarize this section:*

1. Display T 4.5 "Suggestions for Reducing the Negative Effects of Grouping." Discuss the suggestions.

Differences between high- and low-ability students. You might also want to point out that students in high- and low-ability classes, in addition to the *amount* of time they tend to be off-task, differ in *when* they're off task. High-ability students tend to complete assignments, such as seatwork, and then go off task, whereas low-ability tend to go off task during the time they're involved in the assignment. As a result, they often fail to complete the assignment in class, it's left to be completed at home, it may not be completed, or may be completed incorrectly, and achievement declines.

E. Learning styles
  1. Learning preferences: Research results
  2. Learning styles: Implications for teachers

■ *To help students understand some of the controversies involved in the concept of learning styles:*

1. Point out that "learning style" means different things to different people, and much of what people refer to as learning *style* is really learning *preference.*

2. Also note that little research supports the contention that a relationship exists between learning preferences and academic achievement.

II. Socioeconomic status (SES)
  A. Influence of SES on learning
    1. Basic needs and experiences
    2. Parental involvement
    3. Attitudes and values
  B. SES: Some cautions and implications for teachers

■ *The suggestions in this section are intended to help your students understand the impact of SES on achievement.*

1. Introduce students to this section of the chapter by again displaying T 4.1 *"Sources of Learner Individuality,"* and identifying socioeconomic status as the source of individuality that you are focusing on in this section.

1. Display TM 4.5 *"The Influence of SES on Learning,"* which summarizes the research on the differences between students from high and low SES backgrounds.

3. Strongly emphasize that the information in TM 4.5 is in the form of generalizations, and many exceptions exist. Also emphasize that the results can lead to stereotyping students from low SES backgrounds and inappropriately lowering their expectations as a result. Ask them what they would do to accommodate students who come to their classes without some of the school related experiences that other students might have.

III. Culture
   A. Ethnicity
   B. Culture and schooling
      1. The cultural basis of attitudes and values
      2. Cultural differences in adult-child interactions
      3. Classroom organization: Working with and against students' cultures
      4. School-culture matches and mismatches
      5. Culture and learning: Deficit or difference?
   C. Culturally responsive teaching: Instructional strategies

■ *The purpose of the suggestions in this section is to attract attention and increase your students' awareness of the impact that cultural differences can have on learning.*

1. If you teach in a college or university where Caucasian students are in the majority, begin this section by asking those students to predict how they might feel if they were in a school situation where they were a minority.

2. Ask the ethnic minorities in your class, if they were in schools that were largely populated by white students, how they felt during their K-12 experiences. Ask the minority students if they ever felt unwelcome, and if so, why. Discuss their responses.

3. Ask minority students who went to schools largely populated by minorities, such as African-American students who went to schools largely populated by African- Americans, how they felt during their K-12 experiences. Discuss any similarities or differences.

4. Refer the students back to your study of Chapter 3 and the issues of ethnic pride and self-esteem.

5. Display T 4.6 *"U.S. Census Ethnicity Comparisons"* to see how the ethnic makeup of our country is changing.

6. Display TM 4.6 *"Principles of Instruction for Culturally Responsive Teaching."* Have the students identify where in the case study Gary Nolan (on page 138) applied the principles in his work with his students.

7. **Display TM 4.7 *"Making Students Feel Welcome in School,"* which includes some additional ideas for making members of cultural minorities feel welcome in teachers' classrooms.**

IV. Gender
    A. Differences in the behavior of boys and girls
    B. Gender stereotypes and perceptions
        1. Perceptions of male and female domains
        2. Single-gender classrooms and schools
    C. Responding to gender differences: Instructional strategies

    ■ *The purpose in the following suggestions is increase your students' awareness of differences in the ways boys and girls are treated in schools.*
        1. **Pose the question, "How do girls' behaviors compare to boys' behaviors in classrooms?" After students have offered their perceptions, display TM 4.8 *"Gender Differences in the Classroom"* and discuss the patterns and their implications.**

        2. **Display TM 4.9 *"Principles of Instruction for Reducing Gender Bias and Stereotyping."* Have the students identify where in the case study on page 143 Marti Barnes attempted to apply the principles in her work with her students.**

Title IX: Title IX of the Education Amendment Act (a federal law passed in 1972) specifically forbids racial or sexual discrimination in any program receiving federal funds. The preamble to this statute reads in part:

No person in the United States shall, on the basis of sex, be excluded from participation in, be denied the benefits of, or be subjected to discrimination under any education program or activity receiving federal financial assistance.

Title IX provides for gender-free access to:
.   Course offerings
.   Vocational education
.   Athletics
.   Facilities.

One area in which Title IX has had a significant impact is in women's sports. In the 10-year span from 1970 to 1980, women's participation in school sports rose 570% (Sadker & Sadker, 1982). In the period from 1972 to 1987 female participation in high school sports increased from 4% to 26% (American Association of University Women, 1992). Major differences still exist, however. In most schools, girls' teams do not receive comparable funding, facilities, equipment, publicity, travel budgets, or practice opportunities compared to boys.' For example, while women comprise 51% of college undergraduates,they comprised only 34% of the athletes and received only 36% of the scholarships (Knight, 1995). This is one area where individual teachers in a school can point out inequities and perhaps make a difference.

V. Students placed at risk
    A. Resilience
        1. Schools that promote resilience
        2. Teachers who promote resilience
    B. Teaching students placed at risk:: Instructional strategies

    ■ *The following suggestions are designed to help your students understand the characteristics of students placed at risk and the implications these characteristics*

have for learning and teaching.
1. Begin the discussion by asking the students to predict characteristics of students placed at risk.

2. Display T 4.7 *"Characteristics of Students Placed at Risk,"* and compare the information to the students' predictions. Discuss the similarities and differences.

3. Emphasize that these characteristics are generalizations, and because a student comes from a low SES, inner-city background and is male, for example, doesn't mean that he or she will automatically experience the educational problems displayed in T 4.7.

4. Display TM 4.10 *"Schools That Promote Resilience."* Point out that these characteristics are important for *all* schools, not just those with large populations of students placed at risk.

5. Display TM 4.11*"Principles of Instruction for Teaching Students Placed At Risk."* Ask the students to identify where in the case study on page 148 Diane Smith applied each of the principles. After displaying TM 4.11, ask students how instruction for students placed at risk compares to effective instruction in general. They will note that they are essentially the same.

C. Technology and learning: Equity issues
    A. The digital divides
    B. Implications for teachers

    ■ *To help students understand what is commonly called the "digital divide":*
    A. Display TM 4.12 *"Ethnicity and Computer Use"* and TM 4.13 *"Household Income and Computer Use."* Discuss the implications these statistics have for us as teachers.

DISCUSSION STARTERS

1. To what extent should schools attempt to make students more homogeneous, i.e., encourage minority students to adopt the behaviors and values of the majority or white culture? What benefits are there to the student? To society? What drawbacks are there to the student? To society? What does educational psychology tell us about the possibility or desirability of this approach?

2. Parents at an elementary school back-to-school night wanted to know why their child wasn't ability grouped in every content area. They felt their child was being held back by the lack of ability grouping. How would you answer their question?

3. A parent comes to see you, says that she has had her daughter tested and that her intelligence is quite high. Still, the daughter only does slightly above average in school. How would you explain these results to the parent?

4. Based on the information in the text on the effects of SES on learning, describe an ideal family learning environment and explain how it promotes intellectual development.

5. There has been an abrupt change of fortune for two families with children. One, an upper class family has suddenly lost most of its wealth. The other, a lower SES family, has recently become unexpectedly wealthy. How might these economic changes influence the educational experiences of the children in these families?

6. Research on the composition of the public school population shows that while 29% of the students are minority, only 3 of the teachers are (National Center for Statistics, 1993). What problems does this cause for culturally responsive teaching? What long and short term solutions to this problem can you suggest?

7. Why is the teaching force primarily female? How does this influence teaching and learning in our schools?

BACKGROUND READINGS

American Association of University Women (1992). *How schools shortchange girls.* Annapolis Junction, MD: AAUW. This book provides an overview of the issues involved in achieving gender equity in our schools.

Eisenberg, N, Martin, C., & Rabes, R. (1996). Gender development and gender effects. In D. Berliner, & R. Calfee (Eds.), *Handbook of educational psychology* (pp. 358-397). New York: Macmillan. This chapter provides a comprehensive review of the influences of gender on learning.

Gardner, H. (1999). *Intelligence reframed: Multiple intelligences for the 21st century.* New York: Basic Books. This book provides an excellent overview of Gardner's theory.

Gardner, H. (1999). *The disciplined mind: What all students should understand.* New York: Simon & Schuster. In this book, Gardner provides detailed descriptions of multiple intelligences theory in classrooms.

Grant, C. A., & Gomez, M. L. (2001). *Campus and classroom: Making schooling multicultural* (2nd ed.). Upper Saddle River, NJ: Merrill/Prentice Hall. An excellent guide to integrating multicultural concepts into the classroom.

Jew, C., Green, K., Millard, J., & Posillico, M. (1999, April). *Resiliency: An examination of related factors in a sample of students from a urban high school and a residential child care facility.* Paper presented at the Annual Meeting of the American Educational Research Association, Montreal. This paper identifies the characteristics that lead to resiliency in youth placed at risk.

Neisser, U. (Ed.) (1998). *The rising curve: Long-term gains in IQ and related measures.* Washington, DC: American Psychological Association. This book examines the research on the nature versus nurture question.

Ogbu, J. (1999, April). *The significance of minority status.* Paper presented at the Annual Meeting of the American Educational Research Association: Montreal. In this paper Ogbu outlines factors related to academic achievement in cultural minority groups.

Sternberg, R. (1998). Applying the Triarchic Theory of Human Intelligence in the classroom. In R. Sternberg, & W. Williams (Eds.), *Intelligence, instruction, and assessment* (pp. 1-16). Mahwah, NJ: Erlbaum. This chapter describes classroom applications of Sternberg's theory and attempts to dispel myths about intelligence.

FEEDBACK FOR CONSTRUCTED RESPONSE AND DOCUMENT-BASED ANALYSIS QUESTIONS

Constructed Response Items_____

1. What strategies did Teri use to eliminate gender bias in her classroom? What else might she have done?
   The most prominent strategy Teri used to eliminate gender bias was to call on all students–both male and female–equally. Other strategies she might have employed include: strategically assigning girls to key roles in small groups, openly talking about the problem in class, and bringing female role models into her class.

2. One of the principles of effective teaching for students paced at risk recommends the use of high quality examples that supplement students' background knowledge. How well did Teri apply this principle?

The overheads that Teri used to illustrate mercantilism minimized the role of previous background knowledge by containing all of the essential characteristics.

3. Success and challenge are essential for effective instruction for students placed at risk. Evaluate Teri's attempts to provide these components.

Teri provided challenge by asking her students to find commonalities between the two examples of mercantilism. She encouraged success by structuring her questioning strategies so that students were able to construct the concept from the examples.

4. What strategies did Teri use to actively involve her students?

She actively involved her students in two ways. First she had them work in groups, and then she used interactive questioning to involve them in the lesson.

Document-Based Analysis_____

A first-grade teacher prepares the following lesson plan for the concept "mammal."

Unit: Warm-Blooded Animals

Objective: First graders will understand mammals, so when given a series of pictures of different animals, they will identify all the mammals.

Rationale: Mammals are the most advanced members of the animal kingdom, and humans are mammals. Understanding mammals will contribute to children's understanding of themselves as well as different ways that animals adapt to ensure their survival.

Content: Mammals are warm-blooded animals that have hair, and nurse their young. Most mammals are born live, but some, such as the duckbilled platypus are egg-layers. Mammals also have four-chambered hearts and seven neck vertebrae. Some examples are cows, horses, people, wolves, seals, whales, kangaroos, and tigers. (The teacher decides, based on the developmental level of the children, to include only common mammals. Not all mammals give live birth, for example.)

Procedures:
1.   Ask students to give some examples of different kinds of animals. Explain that they are going to learn about a special kind of animal. Emphasize that all can learn this content. Stress the need to pay attention.
2.   Show students a guinea pig, and have them touch and feel it.
3.   Have them describe what they saw and felt. Accept all answers. Write responses on board. Prompt for feels warm and has hair.
4.   Show them a picture of a cow with a calf. Ask how the calf eats. Prompt them to conclude that the calf nurses from its mother.
5.   Add "nurses" to "warm-blooded" and "has hair" as characteristics of mammals on the board.
6.   Show a picture of a dog. Ask how many of them have a dog. Ask them to describe the picture. Link to essential characteristics of mammals. Prompt if necessary and positively reinforce correct characteristics.
7.   Show them a picture of an eagle sitting on a nest of eggs.
8.   Ask students to identify the similarities and differences between the eagle and the guinea pig, cow, calf, and dog.
9.   Show them a picture of a mother whale and baby whale. Prompt them to conclude that some mammals live in water.
10.   Call for a definition of mammals based on the characteristics they've described. Write it on the board.
11.   Ask for additional examples and help students determine if they are mammals.

Materials: A student's pet guinea pig.
            Pictures of a cow with calf, dog, eagle and whale with calf

Assessment: Show students a series of pictures of animals. Have them circle those that are mammals.

Assuming that the teacher follows the plan when she teaches, assess the effectiveness of the lesson plan for students placed at risk. Identify both strengths and weaknesses. Offer at least two suggestions that would make the lesson more effective for students placed at risk.

Several strengths of the lesson were the use of high-quality examples and actively involving students through questioning. In addition, this lesson began by emphasizing that all could learn and that students needed to pay attention.

Some potential weaknesses of the lesson were that the beginning of the lesson failed to link the concept "mammal" to students' own lives. Instead it was presented as an abstract lesson to learn. A second potential weakness was the lack of involvement of all students. A simple groupwork activity like Think-Pair-Share would provide more opportunities for all students to actively participate.

CLASSROOM EXERCISES

Gavin, a seventh grader, has more trouble in school than many of his peers, particularly with word problems in math and other areas that aren't tangible. In spite of high motivation, he still struggles, and new situations and problems "throw him" more than they do his classmates. In order to succeed, he needs a lot of practice, and his approach is somewhat more "mechanical" than that of his peers. He comments, "I need to be able to 'see it' to understand it. Some of these ideas are just too abstract for me. Who cares what caused Columbus to want to go to the Far East. I can get it though, if I get enough practice." When he gets frustrated, he retreats to his room where he plays his guitar; he has even done some of his own arrangements. Gavin is very skilled at working with people, and some of his peers turn to him as an arbitrator when clashes occur in club and other organizational meetings.

1. Using traditional conceptions of intelligence, assess Gavin's intelligence compared to his peers. Explain.

2. Consider Gavin's intelligence based on Gardner's Theory of Multiple Intelligences. Assess Gavin's intelligence on this basis. Explain.

3. Consider Gavin's intelligence according to Sternberg's Triarchic Theory of Intelligence. Based on the case study and Sternberg's work, assess Gavin's intelligence. Explain your thoughts.

Carrie is a fifth grader at Gorrie Elementary school--a school near an affluent neighborhood in a suburb of a major city. Carrie, who lives with her divorced mother--a high school dropout with a steady job as a minimum wage housekeeper--seems to have limited background experiences. In a discussion of the "Old West," for example, she asked what a saddle horn was, when Mrs. Williams talked about the saddles cowboys used. Also, she had never heard of a wild turkey, thinking only of the turkeys people eat on Thanksgiving. However, Carrie "picks up" new ideas in class more quickly than most of her classmates, and she periodically asks questions atypical of fifth graders, such as, "Wouldn't our country be better off if some of the money the Congress spends fighting with each other went to educating poor people instead?"

4. Based on the information in the case study, how will Carrie's score on a traditional intelligence test compare to the scores of her typical peers? Explain.

5. Based on researchers' conceptions of intelligence, would Carrie be considered more, less, or similar in intelligence to that of her typical peers? Explain.

6. How does Carrie's socioeconomic status compare to that of her typical peers? Explain.

7. If Carrie fits typical patterns for students with her background and socioeconomic status, is the likelihood of her dropping out of school at some point before graduation greater, less, or similar to the likelihood of her typical peers dropping out? Explain.

8. If Mrs. Williams questioning patterns are similar to those identified by research, is Carrie more, less, or similarly likely to be called on, compared to typical boys in her class. Is she likely to be asked high- or low-level questions? Explain.

9. Of the following groups--Cambodian refugee, Chinese Americans, Native Americans, or Filipino Americans-- which is most likely to be *involuntary minorities?* Explain.

FEEDBACK FOR CLASSROOM EXERCISES

1. He is probably less intelligent than his typical peers. Traditional conceptions of intelligence include the ability to learn, the ability to solve problems, and the ability to think in the abstract. Gavin appears to be a bit behind his classmates in all three areas.

2. Gavin would be described as less intelligent in areas such as logical-mathematical intelligence, more intelligent in others, such as musical and interpersonal. We don't have information about Gavin's behavior or about other intelligences he might possess such as spatial or bodily kinesthetic.

3. Sternberg views the ability to effectively deal with new or novel situations as an indicator of intelligent behavior. Gavin has difficulty with these situations, so according to Sternberg's view, he would be considered less intelligent than his typical peers.

4. Carrie is likely to score lower on traditional intelligence tests, since they measure experience, and Carrie's experience is limited compared to her affluent peers.

5. Traditional conceptions of intelligence include the ability to learn, the ability to solve problems, and the ability to think in the abstract. Carrie picks up ideas rapidly and tends to think more in the abstract than do her peers. According to traditional conceptions of intelligence, Carrie would be considered more intelligent than her typical peers.

6. Her mother is a high school dropout with a low status, low paying job, so Carrie's socioeconomic status would be lower than that of her peers.

7. Students from low SES backgrounds are about twice as likely to drop out as students from the general population, so Carrie would be more likely to drop out than would her typical peer.

8. Teachers typically call on boys more often than girls, so it is likely that Carrie will be called on less than the boys in her class. Also, teachers tend to ask boys more high-level questions than they ask girls.

9. Involuntary minorities are those that have been brought to this country against their will, such as African Americans, or have been conquered, such as Native Americans. Of the choices given, Native Americans are most likely to be involuntary minorities.

CHAPTER 5: LEARNERS WITH EXCEPTIONALITIES

CHAPTER OVERVIEW

This chapter continues the focus on learner differences, looking at students who may need special help to reach their full potential. A theme for this chapter is the classroom teacher's role in identifying and working with students with exceptionalities. The chapter begins by describing The Individuals with Disabilities Education Act, the changing views of special education, the evolution towards inclusion and the legal framework for working with students with exceptionalities. The discussion continues by examining learning problems including mental retardation, learning disabilities, behavioral disorders and communication, visual and hearing impairments.

The chapter also includes a discussion of students who are gifted and talented and concludes with a section examining effective practices for working with students with exceptionalities in the regular classroom, including identifying, teaching, and helping these students grow emotionally and socially. Emphasis is placed on strategy instruction, positive expectations, and integration of students with exceptionalities into all phases of school life.

CHAPTER OBJECTIVES

- Describe the laws and regulations that influence teachers' work with students with exceptionalities

- Explain how specific exceptionalities–mental retardation, learning disabilities, communication disorders, visual and hearing impairments–affect student learning.

- Describe different methods of identifying and teaching students who are gifted and talented.

- Explain the role of classroom teachers in working with students with exceptionalities

- Explain how instructional strategies can be adapted to meet the needs of students with exceptionalities.

TRANSPARENCIES

The transparencies exist in both acetate form and as PowerPoint slides.

T 5.1 The Individuals with Disabilities Education Act (IDEA)
T 5.2 Educational service options for implementing the LRE (Figure 5.1, p. 161)
T 5.3 The population of students with disabilities (Figure 5.3, p. 166)
T 5.4 Characteristics of students with learning disabilities
T 5.5 Characteristics of students with behavior disorders
T 5.6 Instructional adaptations for students with exceptionalities

TRANSPARENCY MASTERS

The transparency masters are included in this manual beginning on page 230.

TM 5.1 Mental retardation, learning disabilities, and behavioral disorders
TM 5.2 Attention deficit/hyperactivity disorder (ADHD)
TM 5.3 Teaching students with behavior disorders
TM 5.4 Kinds of speech disorders
TM 5.5 Symptoms of potential visual problems
TM 5.6 Indicators of hearing impairment
TM 5.7 Working with students who have hearing disabilities
TM 5.8 Characteristics of the gifted and talented

CHAPTER OUTLINE

I.   Changes in the way teachers help students with exceptionalities
    A.   Individuals with Disabilities Education Act (IDEA)
        1.   A free and appropriate public education (FAPE)
        2.   Least restrictive environment: The evolution towards inclusion
            a.   Collaborative consultation: Help for the classroom teacher
            b.   Putting inclusion into perspective
        3.   Protection against discrimination in testing
        4.   Due process through parental involvement
        5.   Individualized education program
    B.   Amendments to the Individuals with Disabilities Education Act
II.   Students with learning problems
    A.   The labeling controversy
    B.   Mental retardation
        1.   Levels of mental retardation
        2.   Programs for students with mental retardation
    C.   Learning disabilities
        1.   Characteristics of students with learning disabilities
        2.   Identifying and working with students who have learning disabilities
            a.   The use of classroom-based information for identification
            b.   Adaptive instruction
    D.   Attention deficit/hyperactivity disorder
    E.   Behavior disorders
        1.   Kinds of behavior disorders
        2.   Teaching students with behavior disorders
            a.   Teacher flexibility and sensitivity
    F.   Communication disorders
        1.   Helping students with communication disorders
    G.   Visual disabilities
        1.   Working with students who have visual disabilities
    H.   Hearing disabilities
        1.   Working with students who have hearing disabilities
    I.   Assessment and Learning: Assessment trends in special education
        1.   Curriculum-based assessment
        2.   Adaptive behavior
III.   Students who are gifted and talented
    A.   Creativity: What is it?
    B.   Identifying students who are gifted and talented
    C.   Teaching gifted and talented students: Instructional strategies
IV.   The teacher's role in inclusive classrooms
    A.   Identifying students with exceptionalities
    B.   Teaching students with exceptionalities: Instructional strategies
        1.   Instructional support
        2.   Seatwork and homework
        3.   Reading materials
        4.   Learning strategies

5. Social integration and growth
    a. Developing classmates' understanding and acceptance
    b. Helping students learn acceptable behaviors
    c. Strategies for promoting interaction and cooperation
C. Technology and learning: Assistive technology

PRESENTATION OUTLINE

Teaching suggestions in the outline will be marked with the symbol ■. In most cases, the suggested activities can be done individually and discussed as a whole group, or they can be done in small groups, and the small-group results can be discussed with the whole class. To be consistent with our understanding of knowledge construction, we recommend that you promote as much discussion–both in small groups and with the whole class–as possible.

> Enrichment Information, which includes elaborations of text topics as well as topics not included in the text, will be boxed as you see here.

I. Changes in the way teachers help students with exceptionalities
  A. Individuals with Disabilities Education Act (IDEA)
    1. A free and appropriate public education (FAPE)
    2. Least restrictive environment: The evolution towards inclusion
      a. Collaborative consultation: Help for the classroom teacher
      b. Putting inclusion into perspective
    3. Protection against discrimination in testing
    4. Due process through parental involvement
    5. Individualized education program
  B. Amendments to the Individuals with Disabilities Education Act

■ *The suggestions in this section are designed to help your students understand the law and their roles as teachers in working with students having exceptionalities.*

1. Ask them what Public Law 94-142 (PL 94-142), the *Individuals with Disabilities Education Act* (IDEA), means to them. This will give you some insight into their backgrounds and perceptions. You might then want to highlight some information about it, such as:
    . it was passed in 1975; updated in 1997.
    . it is commonly associated with the term "mainstreaming and inclusion."
    . it ensures a free and appropriate public education for all students with exceptionalities.
    . it means that regular classroom teachers are highly likely to have students with exceptionalities in their classrooms.
    T 5.1 *"The Individuals With Disabilities Education Act"* summarizes this information.

2. Ask the students to what other topics that they've already studied PL 94-142 relates. They should identify it as an anti-discrimination law, which makes it a moral issue, so it relates to Chapter 3. Having exceptionalities also represents learner differences, so the topic also relates to the study of Chapter 4.

3. To help the students summarize the information in this section, display T 5.2 *"Educational Service Options for Implementing the LRE."*

4. Remind the students that a sample IEP is shown in Figure 5.2 on page 164 of their text.

Options for Implementing the LRE. To help students understand the options for implementing the LRE, and how they relate to mainstreaming and inclusion offer an example of two students which could be described as follows:

The first student has a learning disability, and in the judgment of the student's individualized implementation plan team, this student is able to cope with the regular classroom environment when given some extra support from the regular classroom teacher. As a result, the student is at or near the top of the options for implementing the LRE (on T 5.4 "Educational Service Options for Implementing the LRE")

The second student is mainstreamed for most of the day, and is pulled out for part of the day to receive specialized help with reading. The second student would be at the third or fourth position down of the options for implementing the LRE (on T 5.4); the exact location would be determined by the IEP team.

The least restrictive environment for the first student is full mainstreaming; the least restrictive environment for the second student is partial mainstreaming.

If an inclusion model were implemented, a special resource teacher would be in the regular classroom to work with the second student, and the regular classroom teacher and the specialist would collaborate in working with the student. The student would not be pulled out of the regular classroom.

Inclusion is a philosophy and is not legally mandated. As a result many inclusion models exist, and the way inclusion is implemented in one school may not be the same as the way it is implemented in another school.

II.   Students with learning problems
    A.   The labeling controversy
    B.   Mental retardation
        1.   Levels of mental retardation
        2.   Programs for students with mental retardation
    C.   Learning disabilities
        1.   Characteristics of students with learning disabilities
        2.   Identifying and working with students who have learning disabilities
            1.   The use of classroom-based information for identification
            2.   Adaptive instruction
    D.   Attention deficit/hyperactivity disorder
    E.   Behavior disorders
        1.   Kinds of behavior disorders
        2.   Teaching students with behavior disorders
            a.   Teacher flexibility and sensitivity

■ *The purpose in the following suggestion is to introduce students to the exceptional student population and their relative frequencies.*

1.   **Display T 5.3 *"The Population of Students With Disabilities."* They will see that students with learning problems–mental retardation, learning disabilities, and behavior disorders–make up the majority of the population (nearly three-fourths of the population [actually 71%]).**

2.   **T 5.4 *"Characteristics of Students with Learning Disabilities"* summarizes the characteristics of students with learning disabilities.**

3.   **TM 5.2 *"Attention Deficit/Hyperactivity Disorder (AD/HD)"* summarizes the legal**

issues and characteristics of AD/HD.

The Relationship Between AD/HD and Learning Disabilities. In clarifying the relationship between AD/HD and learning disabilities you might emphasize that AD/HD is not a type of learning disability nor is it a subset of learning disabilities. It does not qualify for special funding and support under IDEA *as its own category.* It is, however, commonly associated with learning disabilities, and this is the reason it is presented in this section of the chapter. If a learner who has AD/HD is also classified as learning disabled, the learner then qualifies for special education support. Since the laws and policies governing special education are often somewhat murky, these descriptions may quickly change.

---

4.   **T 5.5** *"Characteristics of Students With Behavior Disorders"* **summarizes the general characteristics of behavior disorders and both externalizing and internalizing behavior disorders.**

5.   **To summarize and relate the information in this section, have the students identify the similarities and differences between mental retardation, learning disabilities, and behavioral disorders (emotional disabilities or emotional handicaps). TM 5.1** *"Mental Retardation, Learning Disabilities, and Behavioral Disorders,"* **summarizes these characteristics.**

4.   **To help the students apply the content of this section to a classroom situation, have them examine the case study at the end of the chapter, and have them determine how Mike Sheppard, the teacher in the case study, worked with his students having learning disabilities and behavior disorders. Have them identify the specific strategies Mike used, and have them also assess the extent to which Mike applied the strategies for working with students having learning disabilities and the strategies for working with students having behavior disorders.**

F.   Communication disorders
  1.   Helping students with communication disorders
G   Visual disabilities
  1.   Working with students who have visual disabilities
H.   Hearing disabilities
  1.   Working with students who have hearing disabilities
I.   Assessment and learning: Assessment trends in special education
  1.   Curriculum-based assessment
  2.   Adaptive behavior

■ *The purpose in the following suggestions is to increase your students' awareness of communication, visual, and hearing problems in learners.*
1.   **In the lower elementary grades identifying communication, visual, or hearing problems is important. A communication disorder in a first grader, for example, may be undetected, whereas an undetected communication disorder in an 8th grader is unlikely.**

2.   **Emphasize that a primary role of teachers in the middle elementary grades and beyond**

in working with students having communication disorders is to ensure that they feel like they belong and that they are welcome in the classroom.

3. TM 5.4 *"Kinds of Speech Disorders"* describes and illustrates common speech disorders.

4. TM 5.5 *"Symptoms of Potential Visual Problems,"* summarizes some of the signs and symptoms of possible visual problems.

5. Point out that even though most children are visually screened, a young child with a visual impairment may remain undetected, so sensitivity to the symptoms is important.

6. Emphasize that lowered self-concept and the possibility of learned helplessness are possibilities for visually impaired learners.

7. TM 5.6 *"Indicators of Hearing Impairment,"* summarizes some of the symptoms of hearing problems.

8. TM 5.7 *"Working With Students Who Have Hearing Disabilities"* offers suggestions for regular classroom teachers in working with hearing impaired students who are mainstreamed into their classrooms.

III. Students who are gifted and talented
    A. Creativity: What is it?
        1. Measuring creativity
    B. Identifying students who are gifted and talented
    C. Teaching gifted and talented students: Instructional strategies

■ *The suggestions in this section are intended to help your students understand the characteristics of gifted and talented students, together with options for maximizing their learning.*

1. Display TM 5.8 *"Characteristics of the Gifted and Talented,"* which summarizes the characteristics of gifted and talented students.

> **Myths associated with giftedness.** As you discuss the information on TM 5.8, emphasize some of the myths associated with giftedness such as: people who are gifted being poorly adjusted, having emotional problems, or other difficulties with life. While some people who are gifted and talented certainly do have problems, the percentage in the gifted population is lower than the percentage in the population as a whole.
>
> Also point out that learners who are gifted and talented tend to somewhat naturally do the things that we encourage in all learners, such as searching for relationships, identifying applications, solving problems, and thinking in the abstract. In fact, students who are gifted and talented will sometime identify relationships in ideas that technically don't exist.

2. To introduce the students to the concept of creativity, have students identify as many uses as possible for a brick, a discarded car tire, or some other object of your choice. If you do the activity in groups, you might want to have the groups compete to see which group can come

up with the most uses. (If you want to focus the groups somewhat, you might also require that the uses be practical.) Discuss the groups' results with the whole class.

3. After the groups have reported, you might examine the list in terms of *flexibility*, *originality*, and *fluency*.

4. Have students think back to the conceptions of intelligence discussed in Chapter 4, such as traditional IQ tests (e.g., the WISC-III [the WISC-III is discussed in the text's Appendix]), Guilford's conception of intelligence, Gardner's Multiple Intelligences, and Sternberg's view of intelligence. Have the students consider how effective or difficult identifying students who are gifted and talented would be based on these conceptions.

5. TM 5.9 *"Options in Enrichment and Acceleration Programs,"* outlines some options for working with students who are gifted and talented.

> **The Needs of All Students.** Point out that while some students are gifted and talented, they still have the same needs and concerns that are typical of students in general. Also note that some irony exists in programs and courses for the gifted. Teachers tend to assume that because the students are gifted that they don't need instructional support, and students in these programs are often given long, detailed projects without adequate instruction. These criticisms are somewhat controversial, of course.

VI. The teacher's role in inclusive classrooms
    A. Identifying students with exceptionalities
    B. Teaching students with exceptionalities: Instructional Strategies
        1. Instructional support
        4. Seatwork and homework
        5. Reading materials
        6. Learning strategies
        7. Social integration and growth
            a. Developing classmates' understanding and acceptance
            b. Helping students learn acceptable behaviors
            c. Strategies for promoting interaction and cooperation
    C. Technology and learning: Assistive technology

■ *The suggestions in this section are designed to help your students understand their roles in working with students in their classrooms who have exceptionalities.*
1. Display TM 5.10 *"The Teacher's Role in Inclusive Classrooms"* which summarizes teachers' roles and responsibilities.

2. TM 5.11"*Principles of Instruction for Teaching Students With Exceptionalities*" provides a framework for regular classroom teachers who have students with exceptionalities in their classrooms.

3. T 5.6 *"Instructional Adaptations for Students With Exceptionalities"* offers some suggestions for helping students with exceptionalities in the regular classroom.

4. TM 5.12 *"Working With Students With Exceptionalities: An Application,"* and have them work in their groups to respond to the questions. Discuss their response with the whole class.

They should have identified the following in their responses:

Question 1: Based on the evidence in the case study Joan implemented prereferral strategies by calling Lon's parents and checking on the school procedures. No evidence exists, however, to indicate that she tried alternative strategies with Lon, that she documented any strategies, or that she checked Lon's records.

Question 2: The school officials violated the provisions of IDEA by giving him the test in English. A second possible violation depends on interpretation and judgment. The placement appears to have depended largely on the WISC-III, and if this is the case it is a violation, since IDEA calls for more than one measure. On the other hand, Joan's observations of Lon's performance and behavior are other measures, and if they were considered in the placement, it could be argued that the placement decision was not a violation.

Question 3: Lon appears to have a learning disability. This is based both on his classroom performance and his uneven performance on the WISC-III.

Question 4: Since a disproportionate number of cultural minorities exist in the special education population, school officials should ask themselves if the performance is in fact an exceptionality, or is it a developmental lag, a language-based problem, or a lack of school-related experience.

DISCUSSION STARTERS

1. Given the past trends in these areas of special education what do you predict for the future? In particular, what would you predict about the future of inclusion?

2. Will the future role of the classroom teacher expand or contract in terms of dealing with students with exceptionalities? Why do you think so?

3. Research shows that a disproportionate number of minorities are placed in special education classes. How might we explain this finding? What can be done to address this problem?

4. Should all teachers be required to take a course in teaching students with exceptionalities? If so, what should it contain? If not, why is such a course unnecessary?

5. How are effective strategies and programs for children with exceptionalities similar to those for at-risk students? How are they different?

6. How well do the following practices in the general area of special education meet the special needs of students who are gifted and talented?
   - mainstreaming
   - IEP
   - mainstream assistance teams
   - collaborative consultation

BACKGROUND READINGS

Clark, B. (2002). *Growing up gifted* (6th ed.). Upper Saddle River, NJ: Merrill/Prentice Hall. An excellent overview of issues and practices in gifted education.

Davies, S., Luftig, R., & Witte, R. (1999). *Self-management and peer-monitoring within a group contingency to decrease uncontrolled verbalizations of children with attention-deficit/hyperactivity disorder.* Paper presented at the annual meeting of the American Educational Research Association, Montreal. This paper outlines strategies for developing self-regulation in students diagnosed as AD/HD.

Hallahan, D., & Kauffman, J. (2003). *Exceptional children* (9th ed.). Englewood Cliffs, NJ: Prentice-Hall. This is an excellent introduction to the field of special education. It clearly describes the different kinds of mental and physical handicaps and what the classroom teacher can do to accommodate the special needs of these students in the regular classroom.

Hardman, M., Drew, C. & Egan, W. (2002). *Human exceptionality* (7th ed.). Needham Heights, MA: Allyn & Bacon. This book does an excellent job of exploring the social issues involved with exceptionalities.

Heward, W. (2003). *Exceptional children: An introduction to special education* (7th ed.). Columbus, OH: Merrill. The author provides an overview of the field that is both comprehensive and practical. This book is especially useful for the classroom teacher.

Keogh, B., & MacMillan, D. (1996). Exceptionality. In D. Berliner, & R. Calfee (Eds.), *Handbook of educational psychology* (pp. 311-330). New York: Macmillan. This chapter focuses on three groups of students with exceptionalities: mildly mentally retarded, learning disabled, and gifted and talented.

Piirto, J. (1999). *Talented children and adults: Their development and education* (2nd ed.). Upper Saddle River, NJ: Merrill/Prentice Hall. An interesting look at developmental aspects of giftedness.

Turnbull, A., Shank, M., Turnbull, R., Leal, D., & Smith, S. (2002). *Exceptional lives: Special education in today's schools* (3nd ed.). Columbus, OH: Merrill. This introductory special education text has an update of the 1997 IDEA principles, takes a humanistic, philosophical approach in its description of inclusion and collaboration. It is an innovative and definitive text that describes all categories of disabilities including AD/HD as covered by Section 504.

In addition to the above references, you may also wish to contact the National Information Center for Children and Youth with Disabilities (NICHCY) for video information and other resource materials:

NICHCY
P.O. Box 1492
Washington, DC 20013-1492
http://www.nichcy.org

FEEDBACK FOR CONSTRUCTED RESPONSE AND DOCUMENT-BASED ANALYSIS QUESTIONS

Constructed Response Items_____

1. How did Mike create a warm academic climate for his students? Cite specific evidence from the case study.
    The climate he developed was positive and supportive. He smiled at his students, willingly repeated part of the problem for Gwenn, and offered encouragement by telling them in a positive tone that he was going to call on them first in the lesson. He also provided support to other students, such as whispering, "That's terrific," to Todd and 'thumping' him on the back, encouraging Herchel when he said, "I . . . I . . . don't

know," and moving toward Horace and prompting him when Horace didn't respond. While each of these behaviors alone is relatively minor, when combined they result in a climate of support and positive expectations.

2. How did Mike attempt to ensure success in his teaching?

First, Mike was consistently positive with the students, and he stated positive expectations throughout the lesson. Second, he taught the lesson in small steps and prompted students whenever they were unable to answer (e.g., Herchel and Horace).

3. What did Mike do to alter instruction for his students with learning disabilities? How effective were these modifications?

First, he had the three students with learning disabilities come to class a few minutes early, so he could carefully read his warm-up problem to them and be sure they understood what was asked for in the problem before the rest of the students began. Then he worked with them in a small group while the rest of the students were doing seatwork to give them the extra scaffolding they needed to help get them to the point where they could work on their own.

4. What did Mike do to meet the needs of his students with behavior disorders? How effective were these interventions?

He helped Todd develop a system in which Todd would chart his own behavior, with the goal being the development of self management. He also provided Todd with the emotional support and reinforcement needed to help make the system work. He provided support for Horace by including him in the question and answer activity and being sure that he was able to answer successfully before turning to another student. He also lowered his tone of voice and didn't overemphasize Horace's response to the point where it would call inappropriate attention to him. In this way, he was able to unobtrusively engage Horace, and hopefully, in time, make significant progress with him.

Document-Based Analysis

In developing the Individualized Education Program in Figure 5.2 in this chapter, the following procedures were used.

Mrs. Snow, the regular teacher, initiated the process when she noticed that Joe responded infrequently in class and didn't seem to understand her directions. Mr. Thomas, the resource teacher referred Joe to Mr. Ryan, the school psychologist, for testing after a meeting with Joe. In her note to Mr. Ryan, she suggested that English may not be Joe's first language. After administering an intelligence test to Joe, the school psychologist concluded that he was marginally intelligent enough to stay in the regular class but would need special help. After several unsuccessful attempts to contact Joe's single-parent mother who worked three jobs, the group decided to meet anyway.

Analyze the extent to which the processes used in initiating and completing the I.E. P. were consistent with accepted procedures.

The purpose of constructing an Individualized Education Program is to ensure that instructional modifications meet the learning needs of a student. There were several questionable or problematic aspects of the process in this case. First, teachers need to gather as much information as possible before initiating the process. Unfortunately in this case, there was little information about active attempts by the teacher to gather information from other teachers or the student's cumulative file. In addition, the law stipulates that any testing must be in the student's native language; the case doesn't provide any evidence of this. Finally the law stipulates that parents should be involved in the process. In terms of this case, this is a difficult one to judge; several attempts were made to involve the mother.

CLASSROOM EXERCISES

Teress, age 3, loves to observe her friends as they play at a mothers' "morning out" program she attends three times a week. Her teachers describe her as very well behaved little girl who is somewhat shy, but usually all smiles. Teress is happy to draw and color and seldom talks unless she says "please" and "tank-you". One day Teress's mother, Anita, overhears one of her daughter's classmates tell her mother that she thinks Teress doesn't like her because she doesn't answer her questions.

At home she is quite imaginative as she sets up tea parties and school for her stuffed animals. Teress is also quite adept at using the family computer and has several preschool programs that she uses at will. Outside, she enjoys kicking the soccer ball with Roberto, her brother, or playing a game of two-square. Her chalk drawings on the driveway rival the stick figures that her brother makes.

When Teress talks however, she asks her mother and her brother to help her communicate her needs. Teress's father looks to Anita and Roberto to help him understand Teress's answers to his questions about her day. Anita and Roberto frequently have to help neighbors, friends and grandparents decipher Teress's answers to their questions.

Anita takes Teress and Roberto to have physicals each year which include hearing and vision tests. Both children come away with a clean bill of health each time. Neither child has ever experienced ear infections. One day Anita expressed her concern to her sister-in-law, Louisa, about having to continually decipher Teress's responses to her husband's questions, who Anita thought by now should be as adept at understanding Teress as she and Roberto are.

Louisa, a pediatric nurse, told Anita about a screening program that was available through the public school system free of charge and suggested taking Teress there for evaluation.

A preliminary screening and a more comprehensive screening administered separately within a three month period revealed that Teress didn't need therapy. Anita, however, pressed the point that Teress's father continues to have difficulty understanding his daughter and Teress continues to be shy among teachers, school mates, friends and relatives. In some cases the shyness overcomes her completely and Teress will ignore someone's question or ask her mother or brother to respond for her. Anita further explained that Teress would be attending private school (affiliated with their religion) and that the kindergarten class was 25 strong and that this large number of children might promote Teress becoming lost in the numbers due to her hesitancy to talk other than in a comfortable setting.

The elementary school's speech therapist agreed to include Teress in her program two days a week for a three-month period at which time Teress's progress would be reviewed. Anita was asked to attend a meeting three days later with the speech therapist, her supervisor and the school district's director. During the meeting a simple plan was drawn up for Teress's therapy. With some discussion and agreement on all points three documents were signed by Anita.

1. Based on the anecdotal evidence present in the paragraphs above describe the (pattern) type of disability illustrated in Teress's behavior.

2. List the behavioral symptoms that may indicate a disorder, and make a case for or against Teress being referred to a school specialist.

3. If Teress were a cultural minority, what impact might this factor have on the identification of any disorder Teress might have? Explain.

4. Based on the available evidence, does Teress have a specific learning disability? Explain.

5. Based on the available evidence, is Teress mentally retarded? Explain.

6. Suppose you are a classroom teacher responsible for someone like Teress. Identify some actions you can take to ensure a safe learning environment.

7. Using your knowledge of the IEP and the information provided describe the legal components and ascertain if all the components were present in the episode.

8. Is LRE (least restrictive environment) being met by having Teress attend speech class at a public elementary school before her mom takes her to her preschool?

In a class of 28 students is Hector Sanchez, a Brazilian-American boy, whose parents make a combined income of $61,000 per year; Sonja Jackson, an African American student, whose mother is an administrative assistant and whose father is an electronics technician; Leroy Jordan, an African American student whose parents are divorced and whose mother is a janitor, and Christopher Montcinous, a Mexican-American boy whose parents make a combined income of $45,000 as language specialists.

9. If the students fit patterns identified by research, which of the four is least likely to be diagnosed as behaviorally disordered? Explain.

10. Which student is most likely to be diagnosed as behaviorally disordered? Explain.

FEEDBACK FOR CLASSROOM EXERCISES

1. Teress's symptoms suggest an expressive communication disorder. Expressive (articulation) disorders involve forming and sequencing sounds. While there is no evidence that Teress is stuttering, she is mispronouncing sounds as in the case of "tank-you." Receptive disorders involve using language to express ideas, and there is no direct evidence of this type of problem.

2. Teress indicates the following symptoms: 1) Seldom speaking even during play, 2) using few words or very short sentences, and 3) over-relying on gestures to communicate. There is anecdotal evidence that Teress seldom speaks to people other than her brother and mother. While there is no evidence about the use of gestures, Teress's strong dependence on the interpretive skills of her brother and mother and her one or two word answers, coupled with the evidence that her father doesn't understand some of her language, would suggest that testing is in order. A school specialist should be contacted.

3. Language disorders are more difficult to detect in non-native English speakers, because they are initially learning English, and their problems may indicate difficulty with the language instead of truly being a disorder.

4. No evidence of a specific learning disability exists. Specific learning disabilities are most commonly problems with learning to read, write, or do math when students are involved in formal schooling. We have no evidence of this in Teress's case.

5. No evidence of mental retardation exists. In fact, Teress's imagination as well as her work with the computer indicates above average intelligence.

6. Some of your actions would include: 1) Identifying the disorder and referring Teress to a specialist, 2) modeling acceptance of Teress for her classmates, 3) following through to be sure that actions are taken, and 4) providing opportunities for small-group interaction.

7. The components include the following: 1) Assessment of a student's current level of performance, 2) long and short term objectives, 3) description of services or strategies, 4) schedule for implementing the plan, 5) criteria to be used in evaluating the plan's success. Although a re-evaluation date was made, there is no evidence that the specifics of how Teress's progress would be evaluated was discussed. Long term objectives seem to hinge on the evaluation at the end of the three-month therapy. All other components were present.

8. The LRE is being met. Teress receives therapy in a small group, but she attends regular preschool.

9. Sonja is least likely to be diagnosed as behaviorally disordered. Girls are less likely than boys to be diagnosed as behaviorally disordered. Since all the students are minorities, no indicators can be identified on that basis.

10. Leroy is most likely to be diagnosed as behaviorally disordered. Leroy comes from a low socioeconomic background and is a cultural minority. Research indicates minority students from low SES backgrounds tend to be labeled behaviorally disordered more often than other students.

CHAPTER 6: BEHAVIORISM AND SOCIAL COGNITIVE THEORY

CHAPTER OVERVIEW

This chapter begins with a discussion of contiguity and then moves to classical and operant conditioning and their applications. The chapter then turns to social cognitive theory, and the differences between behaviorism and social cognitive theory are outlined. The discussion of social cognitive theory continues by examining different types of modeling and vicarious learning, the effects of modeling on learner behavior, and the processes involved in modeling. The chapter concludes by examining behaviorism and social cognitive theory in the context of working with learners having diverse backgrounds.

CHAPTER OBJECTIVES

- Explain examples of learning through classical conditioning.

- Explain student behavior using concepts such as *reinforcement, punishment, generalization, discrimination, satiation*, and *extinction*.

- Identify examples of modeling and vicarious learning in classroom situations.

- Explain modeling outcomes, processes, and effectiveness in examples of student learning.

- Describe how self-regulation influences student learning.

TRANSPARENCIES

The transparencies exist in both acetate form and as PowerPoint slides.

T 6.1	Types of learning in behaviorism (Figure 6.1, p. 196)
T 6.2	Classical conditioning examples
T 6.3	A comparison of classical and operant conditioning
T 6.4	Consequences of behavior (Figure 6.2, p. 201)
T 6.5	Schedules of reinforcement (Figure 6.3, p. 203)
T 6.6	Reinforcement schedules and examples
T 6.7	Different forms of modeling
T 6.8	Effects of modeling on behavior
T 6.9	Processes involved in learning from models (Figure 6.5, p. 220)
T 6.10	Effectiveness of models

TRANSPARENCY MASTERS

The transparency masters are included in this manual beginning on page 230.

TM 6.1	An introduction to classical conditioning
TM 6.2	Learning to like school
TM 6.3	Operant conditioning in the classroom
TM 6.4	Shaping learner behavior
TM 6.5	Reinforcement schedules in the classroom
TM 6.6	Reinforcement, satiation, and extinction
TM 6.7	Principles of instruction for applying behaviorism in classrooms

CHAPTER OUTLINE

I.   Behaviorist views of learning
    A.   Contiguity
    B.   Classical conditioning
        1.   Classical conditioning in the classroom
        2.   Generalization and discrimination
        3.   Extinction
    C.   Operant conditioning
        1.   Reinforcement
            a.   Positive reinforcement
            b.   Negative reinforcement
            c.   Shaping
            d.   Reinforcement schedules
            e.   Extinction
            f.   Satiation
        2.   Punishment
            a.   Using punishers: Research results
        3.   The influence of antecedents on behavior
            a.   Environmental conditions
            b.   Prompts and cues
            c.   Generalization and discrimination
    D.   Behaviorism in the Classroom: Instructional strategies
        1.   Creating productive learning environments
        2.   Applied behavioral analysis
            a.   Identify target behaviors
            b.   Establish a baseline
            c.   Choose reinforcers and punishers
            d.   Measure changes in behavior
            e.   Reduce frequency of reinforcers
    E.   Putting behaviorism into perspective
II.   Social cognitive theory
    A.   Comparing behaviorism and social cognitive theory
        1.   Views of learning
        2.   Interactions among behavior, the environment and personal factors
        3.   Interpretations of reinforcement and punishment
        4.   Nonoccurrence of expected consequences
    B.   Modeling
        1.   Cognitive modeling
    C.   Vicarious learning
    D.   Effects of modeling on behavior
        1.   Learning new behaviors
        2.   Facilitating existing behaviors
        3.   Changing inhibitions

       4.   Arousing emotions

E.   Technology and learning: The impact of symbolic modeling on behavior
    1.   Symbolic modeling and television viewing
    2.   Television and symbolic modeling: Guidelines for teachers and parents

F.   Processes Involved in Learning From Models

G.   Effectiveness of models

H.   Self regulation
    1.   Cognitive behavior modification
        a.   Goal setting
        b.   Self-observation
        c.   Self-assessment
        d.   Self-reinforcement

I.   Social cognitive theory in the classroom: Instructional Strategies

J.   Assessment and learning: Self-modeling as an assessment tool
    1.   Self-modeling in assessment

K.   Putting social cognitive theory into perspective

III. Addressing diversity: Behaviorism and social cognitive theory

    A.   Classical conditioning: Learning to like and dislike school

    B.   Motivating hesitant learners

    C.   Capitalizing on minority role models

PRESENTATION OUTLINE

Teaching suggestions in the outline will be marked with the symbol ■. In most cases, the suggested activities can be done individually and discussed as a whole group, or they can be done in small groups, and the small-group results can be discussed with the whole class. To be consistent with our understanding of knowledge construction, we recommend that you promote as much discussion–both in small groups and with the whole class–as possible.

Enrichment information, which includes elaborations of text topics as well as topics not included in the text, will be boxed as you see here.

I.   Behaviorist views of learning
    A.   Contiguity
        ■ *The following suggestions are designed to help students understand contiguity.*
        1.   Display T 6.1, "*Types of Learning in Behaviorism,*" to provide an overview of the contents of this portion of the chapter.

        2.   Ask the students a simple factual question, such as, "What's 7 times 8?" They will answer quickly.

        3.   Offer the principle of contiguity which says, "If two sensations occur together often enough, they become associated," noting that 7 times 8 and 56 have occurred together for them over and over, so they have become associated.

        4.   Ask a more obscure fact, such as, "What is the capital of South Dakota?" (Pierre) "When was the Magna Carta signed?" (1215) or "When was the Battle of Hastings fought?" (1066). Many of them will be unable to answer. Have them explain why they weren't able to answer based on the principle of contiguity. (The two stimuli haven't occurred together often enough to become associated.)

based on the principle of contiguity. (The two stimuli haven't occurred together often enough to become associated.)

B. Classical conditioning
    1. Classical conditioning in the classroom
    2. Generalization and discrimination
    3. Extinction

■ *The following suggestions are designed to help students understand classical conditioning.*

1. Display TM 6.1 "An Introduction to Classical Conditioning?" Ask the students what Rod "learned." Lead them to conclude that he learned to feel excited when he heard Latin Music.

2. Ask them how he learned to feel excited when he heard Latin music, and lead them to conclude that he associated the music with his encounter with Kim.

3. Display T 6.2 *"Classical Conditioning Examples"* and have the students identify the common features in the examples. Have them relate the examples to the example with Rod learning to feel excited at the sound of Latin music.

4. Display TM 62 *"Learning to Like School,"* and have the students identify the conditioned and unconditioned stimuli, and the unconditioned and conditioned responses in each case.

    The following are the answers.

	Problem 1	Problem 2
UCS	Jennifer's father	Mrs. Rodriguez's reassuring manner
UCR	Security (with her father)	Feeling better
CS	Mrs. Abbott	Mrs. Rodriguez's classroom
CR	Comfortable	Relaxed

5. Ask the students to compare the examples, so they will see that in one case there is an association between Mrs. Abbott and Jennifer's father ("She puts her arm around Jennifer and chats with her dad as the three of them stand together near the door."), whereas in the second example there is no association between Mrs. Rodriguez and Natasha's mother. There is an association, however, between Mrs. Rodriguez's manner and her classroom ("Each day, Ms. Rodriguez greets Natasha with the same smile and reassuring manner. Now Natasha jumps out of the car and feels quite relaxed as she enters Mrs. Rodriguez's classroom.").

6. Again display TM 6.1 *"An Introduction to Classical Conditioning"* and have the students explain why Rod reacts to Reggae the same way he does to Latin music, and why doesn't he react the same way to Rock and Jazz. Typically *generalization* and *discrimination* are quite easy for students to understand, and they will identify them quickly in the examples.

7. Ask the students what would happen if Rod continued to listen to Latin music, but he never had another encounter with Kim, or if Pavlov's lab assistants kept coming in the

room but stopped bringing meat, or Tim kept taking tests but didn't fail. In each case the conditioned response gradually disappears.

8.   To summarize classical conditioning, have the students explain the following examples using classical conditioning
   •   test anxiety
   •   a medical patient breaking into a sweat when he sees a needle.
   •   A kindergartner developing a pain in the stomach when she and her parents drive into the school parking lot.
   •   a junior high student becoming nervous before gym after a class in which his gym shorts split and other students laughed.

C.   Operant conditioning
   1.   Reinforcement
      a.   Positive reinforcement
      b.   Negative reinforcement
      c.   Shaping
      d.   Reinforcement schedules
      e.   Extinction
      f.   Satiation
   2.   Punishment
      a.   Using punishers: Research results
   3.   The influence of antecedents on behavior
      a.   Environmental conditions
      b.   Prompts and cues
      c.   Generalization and discrimination

■ *The following suggestions are intended to help the students understand operant conditioning and the difference between reinforcers and punishers.*
1.   To introduce this section display T 6.3 *"A Comparison of Classical and Operant Conditioning"* to help the students make the transition to operant conditioning. Then display T 6.4 *"Consequences of Behavior,"* discuss the consequences and TM 6.3 *"Operant Conditioning in the Classroom,"* and have students explain the teachers' and the students' behaviors in each case. (TM 6.3 illustrates both reinforcement and punishment.)

2.   Ask the students for additional examples of reinforcers and punishers
   Positive reinforcers: Praise, high test scores, good grades
   Negative reinforcer: Allowing them to avoid a homework assignment because of their conscientious work
   Presentation punishers: Reprimands, being told "Shh."
   Removal punishers: Loss of privileges, removal of free time.

3.   To illustrate shaping display TM 6.4 *"Shaping Learner Behavior."* Ask the students for additional examples of shaping.

4.   The different types of reinforcement schedules are outlined in T 6.5 *"Schedules of Reinforcement"* and they're illustrated in T 6.6 *"Reinforcement Schedules and Examples."* To increase their understanding of the different schedules, have them identify the reinforcement schedules illustrated on TM 6.5 *"Reinforcement Schedules in the Classroom."* In item 1 on TM 6.5 tell them to focus on the students

doing seatwork. Discuss their conclusions. They should conclude the following:

1. For the students doing seatwork, a variable-interval schedule is being used. It is based on time and is unpredictable.

2. This is a variable-ratio schedule. It is based on a student's response and is unpredictable.

3. Mr. Lombardo's homework system is a fixed-interval schedule, whereas Mrs. Aschliman's is a variable interval schedule. Their quizzes are both fixed interval.

4. Mr. Lombardo's policy with finishing homework illustrates a fixed-ratio schedule. The students can predict when they will be rewarded with free time, and it is based on their behaviors--not on time.

5. Display TM 6.6 *"Punishment, Satiation, and Extinction"* which illustrates the difference in the three concepts. Students often have difficulty in distinguishing among the three. Point out that a difference between removal punishment and extinction depend on the situation. For instance, you might ask students what would make the situation with the student who isn't being called on an example of removal punishment. (If the teacher had been calling on her, and then stops, it would be punishment--being called on is removed. If the student wasn't being called on in the first place, it is extinction--there is nothing removed.)

3. The influence of antecedents on behavior
   a. Environmental conditions
   b. Prompts and cues
   c. Generalization and discrimination

■ *To help the students understand the influence of antecedents on behavior:*

1. Ask the students to identify examples of environmental conditions that serve as cues.

2. Ppoint out that prompting questions are one of the most common forms of cues that teachers use in classrooms. Ask students for some additional examples.

3. Have students explain the difference between generalization and discrimination in a classical conditioning situation and generalization and discrimination in an operant conditioning situation.

4. Present the following examples and ask the students to explain whether generalization or discrimination is being illustrated.
   . Junior high students go from classroom to classroom to meet with different teachers. In some classes they're well behaved; in others they're rowdy.
   . Kevin's English teacher taught outlining skills in his class. Kevin now uses the study strategy in biology and social studies.
   . Students are wild and loud on the playground but quiet down when they enter the classroom.
   . Joe's seventh grade language arts teacher is working on his handwriting. Other teachers have noticed an improvement, too.

D. Behaviorism in the Classroom: Instructional strategies
   1. Creating productive learning environments

2. Applied behavioral analysis
   a. Identify target behaviors
   b. Establish a baseline
   c. Choose reinforcers and punishers
   d. Measure changes in behavior
   e. Reduce frequency of reinforcers

   ■ *The suggestions in this section are designed to help students understand classroom applications of behaviorism.*
   1. Display TM 6.7 *"Principles of Instruction for Applying Behaviorism in Classrooms."* Have the students identify where Erika Williams (in the case study on page 208) applied the principles in her teaching.

   2. Display TM 6.8 *"Applied Behavioral Analysis,"* which outlines the steps in performing applied behavioral analyses.

   3. Have the students turn to the case study at the end of Chapter 5, and identify where in the case study Mike Sheppard completed each of the steps involved in an applied behavioral analysis.

   4. Have them identify the step for which we have the *least* evidence.

   5. The students should find the following:
      . He identified *talking out, swearing, hitting and touching, out of seat* and *being friendly* as his target behaviors.
      . He established a baseline during the week of 2/9 to 2/13.
      . He chose praise as his primary reinforcer.
      . He measured changes in the target behaviors during the weeks of 2/16 to 2/20 and 2/23-2/27.
      . We have the least evidence for gradually reducing the reinforcers as the behavior improves.

E. Putting behaviorism into perspective

   ■ *The following suggestions are intended to help students put behaviorism into perspective by understand its implications for instruction.*
   1. Point out that since behaviorism focuses on observable learning is organized into isolated, specific, and decontextualized pieces that allow instructors to determine if learners display the desired behaviors. If they do, they're reinforced. If not, they're given feedback until they do display the desired behaviors. Gradually, these isolated pieces accumulate, with higher order processes being the final outcome of the cumulative process.

   2. Also point out that the criticisms of behaviorism as a basis for guiding instruction continue to increase. For example, the gap between having students complete decontextualized exercises, such as, "Please come with Karen and (I, me) to the mall," and being effective writers is indeed large.

   2. On the other hand, behaviorism continues to be a very powerful influence as a basis for managing learners and the learning environment. Whether or not this should be the case is open to debate, and you may want to have your students discuss this issue.

II. Social cognitive theory
   A. Comparing behaviorism and social cognitive theory
      1. Views of learning
      2. Interactions among behavior, the environment, and personal factors
      3. Interpretations of reinforcement and punishment
      4. Nonoccurrence of expected consequences

   ■ *The following suggestions are intended to help the students understand the differences between behaviorism and social cognitive theory.*
      1. **To introduce social cognitive theory display TM 6.10 "*Vicarious Learning on the Interstate.*" Have the students try to explain why we slow down when we see the other car pulled over. Lead them to conclude that behaviorism is unable to explain our behavior, which leads us to social cognitive theory.**

      2. **Display TM 6.9 "*Differences Between Behaviorism and Social Cognitive Theory.*"**

      3. **Also emphasize the importance of feedback based on social cognitive theory. (Since reinforcers only work when learners are *aware* of the behaviors that are being reinforced, feedback helps them become aware, by specifying the behaviors they've displayed that are being reinforced, e.g., learners getting feedback on a writing assignment are then better equipped to display the desired behaviors on the next assignment.)**

   B. Modeling
      1. Cognitive modeling

   ■ *The following suggestions are intended to help students understand the concept of "modeling."*
      1. **In its simplest form, the concept of modeling is intuitively sensible. It often goes beyond simple imitation, however. You might want to share some of Bandura's original work with your students, which will help them see the basis for the effects of modeling on behavior that are presented later.**

Bandura's Original Research. Bandura's (1963) original research involved nursery school children assigned to one of five treatments. In the first, the children watched a human adult model verbally and physically attack a life-sized inflated doll. In the second treatment, children saw a film of the same behavior. In the third, they saw cartoon characters carry out the same aggressive actions. Treatment four, which was the control group, saw no behaviors displayed. In the final treatment, the children saw a live model who displayed subdued and inhibited behavior. The children were then placed in situations similar to those they observed. The researchers watched the children through one-way mirrors and counted the children's aggressive acts. The children who observed aggressive behavior–live, on film, and in cartoons–all displayed significantly more aggressive behaviors than did the control group, and the children who observed the subdued model displayed significantly fewer aggressive behaviors than did the control group. (Source: Bandura, A. (1963). The role of imitation in personality development. *Journal of Nursery Education, 18,* 207-215.)

---

      4. **To help students understand how theories contribute to our understanding of the world,**

ask them how behaviorism would explain Bandura's research results. Point out that this is a "trick" question, leading them to conclude that behaviorism can't explain the results.

5. Ask them why it cannot, and lead them to conclude that it can't because nothing happened to the nursery school children. They weren't reinforced or punished, and a neutral stimulus didn't become associated with any unconditioned stimulus. The explanation for their behavior must involve cognition. The children recorded the models' behaviors in their memories, and later reproduced them.

6. Point out that this is the reason we study different theories. Behavior is able to explain the production of emotional and physiological responses based on associations, and it is also able to explain changes in overt behaviors as a result of consequences applied directly to the behaviors, but it cannot explain changes in behavior as the result of observing others.

7. Display T 6.7 *"Different Forms of Modeling,"* which describes and illustrates the different forms of modeling.

8. Have the students describe how Bandura's research led to the concept of *direct* and *symbolic* modeling.

C. Vicarious learning
D. Effects of modeling on behavior
   1. Learning new behaviors
   2. Facilitating existing behaviors
   3. Changing inhibitions
   4. Arousing emotions

■ *The suggestions in this section are intended to help students understand the different effects of modeling.*
   1. Display T 6.8 *"Effects of Modeling on Behavior,"* which describes and illustrates the effects.

   2. Display TM 6.11 *"Modeling Effects in the Classroom"* and have students respond to the questions. Have them share their responses.

   Mention that Kounin (1970), in his study of classroom management, termed the effect of observing another student being reprimanded the "ripple effect." Ask them how social cognitive theorists would explain the "ripple effect." Ask them how social cognitive theorists would explain the effects of a misbehaving student not being reprimanded. Would social cognitive theorist suggest public or private reprimands? Lead them to the following conclusions.
   . Students seeing another student reprimanded would likely experience strengthened inhibitions.
   . Students' misbehaviors would likely increase if a misbehaving student isn't reprimanded, as a result of the nonoccurrence of an expected punisher acting as a reinforcer.
   . Social cognitive theory would recommend public reprimands; otherwise, the observing students wouldn't be able to observe the reprimand and adapt their behavior accordingly.

E. Technology and learning: Technology and social cognitive theory
    1. Symbolic modeling and television viewing
    2. Television and symbolic modeling: Guidelines for teachers and parents

■ *The suggestions in this section are intended to help students understand the relationship between television viewing and symbolic modeling.*

1. **Point out that Bandura's original research was done in response to concerns about the harmful effects of television viewing.**

2. **Have the students explain the harmful effects of television viewing–the wrong kind of television viewing–using social cognitive theory as a basis for their explanations.**

F. Processes involved in learning from models

■ *To understand the mechanism in modeling*:

1. **Display T 6.9 *"Processes Involved in Learning From Models."***

2. **Have students identify one or more topics and describe how the processes would be involved with the topic of their choice.**

G. Effectiveness of models

■ *To illustrate the factors that influence a models' effectiveness:*

1. **Display T 6.10 *"Effectiveness of Models,"* which outlines and illustrates factors influencing a model's effectiveness.**

2. **TM 6.13 *"Effectiveness of Models in the Classroom"* offers an application of the factors, and TM 6.12 *"Under-muscled and Embarrassed"* which is taken from a newspaper clipping is a real-world example of the importance of perceived similarity in modeling effectiveness, and**

■ *The following information summarizes some research on the impact of peer models and mastery compared to coping models in their effects on learner behavior.*

Peer Models. When students are uncertain about the appropriateness of a behavior or have doubts about their capabilities, they are more likely to imitate a peer than an older child or adult (Schunk, 1987). Peer models can have a powerful influence on the development of academic skills. For example, in one study researchers found that elementary students who observed peer models successfully solve subtraction problems, successfully solved significantly more problems themselves than did children who observed a teacher solve the same problems, and both groups solved significantly more problems than children who observed no models (Schunk & Hanson, 1985).

Mastery and Coping Models. An additional factor was involved in Tim's case in the case study at the beginning of the chapter. Though both Susan and Karen were successful, he chose to imitate Susan's rather than Karen's behavior. When learners are fearful about a situation, as Tim was, they are more likely to imitate a *coping* model, or one who struggles to achieve competence, than a *mastery* model, or one whose competence is an accomplished fact (Schunk, 1991). This is where competence and similarity interact. Tim perceived both Karen and Susan to be competent, but he perceived himself to be more similar to Susan, because she too had to struggle with the class, so he imitated her behavior.

H.   Self-regulation
1.   Cognitive behavior modification
   a.   Goal setting
   b.   Self-observation
   c.   Self-assessment
   d.   Self-reinforcement

■ *To illustrate the characteristics of self-regulation and cognitive behavior modification:*

1.   **Pose the question, "Why is self-regulation an important part of social cognitive theory?" The students' responses will give you some insight into both their perception of social cognitive theory compared to behaviorism and what self-regulation means to them.**

2.   **Point out that many reinforcers are delayed significantly, such as studying to get a good grade in a course. Without self-regulation, they wouldn't maintain the behavior until they received the reinforcer.**

3.   **Also point out that behaviorism has a difficult time explaining why people will maintain a behavior when reinforcers are significantly delayed. (As a discussion topic, you might ask them to explain the difference between delayed reinforcement, as social cognitive theorists describe it, and intermittent reinforcement, as behaviorists describe it.)**

■ *To enrich students' understanding of this section:*

4.   **Have them identify goals related to the class, such as setting a goal of writing a response to each of the margin questions, responding to all the applications in the student study guide, or writing a summary statement for each of the sections of the chapters. They will then see how goals, self-observation, self-assessment, and self-reinforcement promote learning.**

I.   Social cognitive theory in the classroom: Instructional strategies

   ■ *To help students understand how social cognitive theory can be applied in classrooms:*
   1.   **Display TM 6.14 *"Principles of Instruction for Applying Social Cognitive Theory in Classrooms."* Have the students identify where Sally Campese (in the case study beginning on page 223) applied each of these principles in her teaching.**

J.   Assessment and learning: Self-modeling as an assessment tool
   1.   Self-modeling in assessment

   ■ *To help students understand how self modeling can be used as an assessment tool:*
   1.   **Note how videotaping can be used as a mechanism for assessing our own behavior. As we watch ourselves on videotape, we serve as self models. Videotaping is particularly powerful as a tool for promoting professional development in teaching.**

K.   Putting social cognitive theory into perspective

   ■ *To help students understand the limitations of social cognitive theory:*
   1.   **Remind the students of the limitations that appear on page 226. Also note that these limitations are one of the reasons we study the learning theories that appear in later chapters.**

III.   Dealing with diversity: Behaviorism and social cognitive theory
   A.   Classical conditioning: Learning to like and dislike school
   B.   Motivating hesitant learners
   C.   Capitalizing on minority role models

   ■ *To apply their understanding of behaviorism to issues of learner diversity:*
   1.   **Have students use classical conditioning to explain why Carlos felt welcome in school, whereas Roberto felt unwelcome.**

DISCUSSION STARTERS

1.   Should corporal punishment be used in the schools today? If so, under what circumstances? If not, why not?

2.   Should students or their parents be informed if teachers are trying to change or shape students' behavior through behavioral principles?

3.   What does research on social cognitive theory suggest about the ethical and moral behavior of teachers?

4.   On what point or points would Piaget and Skinner agree about the nature of learning? On what points would they disagree?

5.   How would Skinner explain the development of moral behavior? How would his explanation differ from Kohlberg's?

6.   Do all learners respond to basically the same reinforcers? Do all cultures? What implications do your answers have for teaching?

7. A great deal of controversy exists about the potentially harmful influences of television and movies on young people. Do you believe that the criticisms of the television and film industry are valid? What would social cognitive theorists say about these criticisms?

8. Cultural minorities and women sometimes complain about the lack of opportunity for them in upper management levels in the business world. How important is it that minorities and women be in these positions? How would social cognitive theorists explain the need for minorities and women in these positions?

BACKGROUND READINGS

Alberto, P., & Troutman, A. (2003). *Applied behavior analysis for teachers* (6th ed.). Upper Saddle River, NJ: Prentice Hall. The authors do an excellent job of explaining how behaviorist principles can increase learning in the classroom.

Baldwin, J., & Baldwin, J. (2001). *Behavior principles in everyday life* (4th ed.). Upper Saddle River, NJ: Prentice Hall. This book provides a number of concrete examples of classical and operant conditioning in the everyday world.

Bandura, A. (1997). *Self-efficacy: The exercise of control.* New York: Freeman. Describes the role of self-efficacy in self regulation.

Gentile, J. (1996). Setbacks in the "Advancement of learning?" *Educational Researcher, 25,* 37-39. In this article, Gentile provides an additional perspective on classical conditioning.

Gredler, M. (2001). *Learning and instruction: Theory into practice* (4th ed.). Upper Saddle River, NJ: Prentice Hall. Behaviorism and social cognitive theory are covered in detail in this text.

Hergenhahn, B. R., & Olson, M. H. (2001). *Introduction to theories of learning* (6th ed.). Upper Saddle River, NJ: Prentice Hall. Places behaviorism and social cognitive theory into a larger perspective.

Kohn, A. (1996). By all available means: Cameron and Pierce's defense of extrinsic motivators. *Review of Educational Research, 66,* 1-4. In this article Kohn argues against the use of behaviorally based motivational systems.

Kratochwill, T., & Bijou, S. (1987). The impact of behaviorism on educational psychology. In J. Glover & R. Ronning (Eds.), *Historical foundations of educational psychology* (pp. 131–158). New York: Plenum. This excellent historical overview of behaviorism, includes the contributions of the most important figures in the field presented in an historical context.

Mazur, J. E. (2002). *Learning and behavior* (5th ed.). Upper Saddle River, NJ: Prentice Hall. A comprehensive look at different theories of learning, including behaviorism and social cognitive theory.

Skinner, B. F. (1968). *The technology of teaching.* New York: Appleton-Century-Crofts. This is a classic in the field written by one of the giants. It is quite readable, and Skinner is persuasive in describing learning and teaching from a behaviorist perspective.

Zirpoli, T., & Melloy, K.. (2001). *Behavior management: Applications for teachers* (3rd ed.). Upper Saddle River, NJ: Merrill/Prentice Hall. An excellent resource for teachers.

FEEDBACK FOR CONSTRUCTED RESPONSE AND DOCUMENT-BASED ANALYSIS QUESTIONS

Constructed Response Items

1. Describe where classical conditioning occurred in the case study. Identify the classical conditioning concepts in your description.

   While we don't have a great deal of evidence from the case study that relates to classical conditioning, Helen's comments to Jenny indicate an emotional reaction to working at the chalkboard. Initially the chalkboard was a neutral stimulus. When it became associated with anxiety, it became a conditioned stimulus, resulting in anxiety, the conditioned response. Warren could try and move the reaction toward extinction by ensuring Helen's success when she worked at the board--assuming he is aware of her reaction.

2. Warren inadvertently allowed himself to be punished in two different places the case study. Explain where they occurred, and describe their likely impact on learning.

   Punishment occurs when consequences weaken behaviors or decrease the frequency of behavior. Punishment occurred twice in the case. The first time was when students protested about doing all of the problems and Warren agreed to students only doing the odd ones. The second time also involved homework, when Warren agreed to have students only do four problems.

3. Warren's modeling had both positive and negative features. Identify and explain one positive and one negative feature.

   He modeled distaste for percents and decimals with his comment, ". . . I'm not wild about them either, but we have no choice, so we might as well buckle down and learn them." Through his comments Warren modeled disliking these math problems

   He positively demonstrated cognitive modeling when he said, "Now, . . . the first thing I think about when I see a problem like this one is, 'What does the jacket cost now?' So, I have to figure out . . . ." He demonstrated the solution and he verbalized his thoughts for the students.

4. Warren capitalized on the positive aspects of perceived similarity in the case study. Explain where and how this occurred.

   Perceived similarity refers to a model being more effective because people think the model is like them. Warren capitalized on perceived similarity when he said to Chris, "Good. That's what we're trying to do. We are all going to make mistakes, but if we catch ourselves, we're making progress. Keep it up. You can do these problems." These positive comments would be powerful because other students would see themselves as similar to Chris.

Document-Based Analysis

A 7th grade teacher has the following list of rules and consequences displayed on the bulletin board at the front of her room.
1. Raise your hand before speaking.
2. Leave your seat only when given permission.
3. Bring all needed materials to class each day.
4. Keep hands and feet to yourself.
5. Do all grooming in the restroom.

First infraction for the day:	Warning
Second infraction for the day:	Half hour of detention
Third infraction for the day:	Referral and call to parents
Each day begins anew.	

Assess these rules and consequences with respect to using behaviorism as a mechanism for creating a productive learning environment. Identify both their strengths and weaknesses based on the content of the chapter.

In terms of strengths, the rules and consequences were clearly stated so that students could understand them. Because of their clarity they established clear standards for acceptable behavior. In addition, they were stated positively, creating a positive emotional tone in the classroom. They also cleared the slate each day ("Each day beings anew."), which helps students refocus their efforts positively. In terms of weaknesses they emphasized negative consequences and did not provide opportunities for positive reinforcement.

CLASSROOM EXERICSES

1. Teachers are discouraged from giving students writing assignments as a form of punishment for misbehavior. Using classical conditioning as a basis, explain why using writing assignments as punishment is unwise practice. Be specific in your explanation.

2. For many people a song, a picture, or even an odor sometimes conjures up feelings or moods that they can't otherwise capture. You've probably had this experience yourself. a) What concept from classical conditioning is illustrated by the song, picture, or odor, and b) what concept from classical conditioning is illustrated by the mood or feeling? Explain in both cases.

3. Suppose you repeatedly hear a song that elicits a warm feeling, but you don't have another positive experience similar to the original one that caused the warm feeling. a) What will eventually happen to the feeling, and b) what concept from classical conditioning does this illustrate? Explain.

4. A teacher says, "Okay, everyone. You've done such a good job of turning in your homework this week that you don't have to do your assignment for the weekend. We'll do it Monday instead." a) What concept from behaviorism is the teacher attempting to apply in this case, b) What is the teacher's goal in making this statement, and c) what is the situation the students must be in, in order for the teacher's strategy to work? Explain.

5. A teacher says, "If everyone is *sitting quietly* in his or her seat when the bell rings, we'll go to lunch. If not, we'll miss some of our lunch period." Suppose that the students are then sitting quietly when the bell rings, and they go to lunch as scheduled. What concept from behaviorism is the teacher applying in this case? Explain.

6. In Chapter 1 we asked, "Have you ever done one job to get it out of the way and saved a more enjoyable one for later?" Assuming the answer is yes, what idea from behaviorism is being illustrated? Explain.

7. Suppose that, in an effort to increase car pooling, a city allowed cars with three or more people to pass through toll booths without paying. Using the information in this section, explain the city's efforts.

8. What reinforcement schedule is best illustrated by people playing slot machines? Explain.

9. You're working with your students in a question and answer session and you ask:

"How does the direction of the ocean current off the coast of Chile affect the rainfall in the Chilean Desert?"

Tanya responds, "The current comes from the south, so the water is cold. The air over the water is more dense than the air over the land, so the air that goes over the land is warmed up, and it doesn't rain."

You want to praise Tanya for her answer. Write down what you would say.

Suppose instead that Tanya responded, "I . . . I'm not sure. The current goes from the south, . . . I think, . . . so . . . the water should be . . . cold. So, . . . the air above is . . . less . . . let's see . . . no, . . . more dense, so the air . . . over the land . . . gets cold, . . . no, warm . . . and, it rains, no . . . doesn't rain."

Again, you want to praise Tanya for her answer. Write down what you would say this time.

10. A person studies hard for a test, takes the test, and receives a high score several days later. Before receiving the score, however, the person continues to study other material related to the course. Behaviorists maintain that the high score is a reinforcer that directly causes the studying behavior. How do social cognitive theorists view the high score? Why do they believe the behaviorist account is inadequate?

11. Suppose a teacher has a classroom rule requiring students to raise their hands before speaking, and further suppose that a student speaks without permission and isn't reprimanded. a) Using social cognitive theory as a basis, what is the likely effect on the rest of the class of not reprimanding the student, and b) what modeling effect does this best illustrate? Explain this effect using the concept of *expectations* as a basis for your explanation.

12. Look again at the case study that introduces the chapter. Susan and Karen, Tim's classmates, were both successful, but Tim chose to imitate Susan's rather than Karen's behavior. Explain why this might have been the case?

FEEDBACK FOR CLASSROOM EXERCISES

1. Punishers can produce negative emotional reactions. The writing assignment might become associated with the punisher--becoming a conditioned stimulus--which produces a negative emotional reaction--as a conditioned response. We don't want students to have negative emotional reactions to classroom assignments.

2. The song, picture, or odor are conditioned stimuli that have become associated with some unconditioned stimulus that produced the original mood or feeling. The mood or feeling is a conditioned response that is similar to the original mood or feeling produced by the unconditioned stimulus.

3. The feeling will eventually disappear. The concept is extinction. If a conditioned stimulus occurs repeatedly in the absence of the unconditioned stimulus, the conditioned response will eventually disappear (become extinct).

4. The teacher is attempting to use negative reinforcement by allowing the students to avoid doing homework. Her goal is to increase the students' "doing homework" behaviors. The students must be in a situation of normally doing homework, or there would be nothing for them to avoid.

5. The teacher is applying negative reinforcement. The teacher is focusing on a desired outcome (sitting quietly) versus an undesired outcome (stopping talking). Also, the students are in control of the outcome. If they're quiet, they get to go to lunch. Negative reinforcement is being illustrated because the students can *avoid* missing some of their lunch period. Under typical conditions, they would get to go to lunch. The teacher is threatening the students with punishment, but she isn't actually punishing them.

6. The idea is the Premack Principle, which says that a more desirable activity can serve as a positive reinforcer for a less desirable activity.

7. The city is attempting to apply negative reinforcement by allowing people to avoid the tolls.

8. Slot machines illustrate variable-ratio schedules. The reinforcers depend on behaviors, not time, and they're unpredictable.

9. In the first case, specific praise in the first case wasn't necessary because the student gave a clear, confident answer. If Tanya's answer were tentative, however, specific praise would emphasize important information and help eliminate uncertainty.

An example in the second case could be: "Very good, Tanya. You recognized that the air would be warmed as it moved over the land. This was because the air above the water was cold, caused by the cold water itself flowing from the south. Good analysis."

10. Social cognitive theorists view the high score as causing *expectations*. According to social cognitive theorists, students study because they "expect" to be reinforced for doing so. They believe the behaviorist account is inadequate because in many cases too much elapses between the behavior and receiving the reinforcer.

11. If students break a rule they expect to be punished. If the punisher isn't given, its nonoccurrence can serve as a reinforcer, and the undesirable behavior is likely to increase. Decreasing inhibitions is the modeling effect that is illustrated.

12. When learners are fearful about a situation, as Tim was, they are more likely to imitate a *coping* model, or one who struggles to achieve competence, than a *mastery* model, or one whose competence is an accomplished fact (Schunk, 1991). This is where competence and similarity interact. Tim perceived both Karen and Susan to be competent, but he perceived himself to be more similar to Susan, because she too had to struggle, so he imitated her.

CHAPTER 7: COGNITIVE VIEWS OF LEARNING

CHAPTER OVERVIEW

This chapter is the first of three that expands the discussion of internal cognitive processes, such as attention, perception, rehearsal, encoding, and retrieval. The chapter begins with a description of information processing, one of the most thoroughly studied cognitive learning theories. Our information processing systems consist of information stores–*sensory memory, working memory* and *long-term memory*, cognitive processes–*attention, perception, rehearsal, encoding,* and *retrieval*–that move information from one store to another, and metacognition, which regulates processing.

CHAPTER OBJECTIVES

• Identify the principles on which cognitive learning theories are based

• Describe the components of our information processing system, including memory stores and cognitive processes.

• Describe the influence of metacognition on learning.

• Implement ways to promote schema development in your classroom.

• Explain the role of assessment in classroom applications of cognitive learning theory.

TRANSPARENCIES

The transparencies exist in both acetate form and as PowerPoint slides.

T 7.1   Tall in the saddle
T 7.2   An information processing model (Figure 7.2, p. 239)
T 7.3   The limitations of working memory
T 7.4   Schema representing Juan's understanding
T 7.5   Schema representing Randy's understanding
T 7.6   Strategies for attracting attention
T 7.7   An exercise in perception
T 7.8   Making information meaningful (Figure 7.7, p. 251)

TRANSPARENCY MASTERS

The transparency masters are included in this manual beginning on page 230.

TM 7.1   Different types of models (TM 7.1 from 5e)
TM 7.2   Research results and working memory
TM 7.3.   Characteristics of the memory stores
TM 7.4   Questions that promote deep processing of information (TM 7.3 from 5e)
TM 7.5   Background knowledge and encoding (TM 7.4 from 5e)
TM 7.6   Elaborating on past experiences (TM 7.6 from 5e)
TM 7.7   Active and passive study strategies (TM 7.7 from 5e)
TM 7.8   Types and examples of mnemonic devices (TM 7.8 from 5e) (fix)
TM 7.9   Children and metacognition (TM 7.9 from 5e)
TM 7.10   Review exercises (Attention and sensory memory)
TM 7.11   Review exercises (Perception, schemas, and metacognition)

TM 7.12   Review exercise (The role of background knowledge)
TM 7.13   Review exercise (Metacognition)
TM 7.14   Principles of instruction for applying information processing in classrooms

VIDEOS

Looking Through Classroom Windows Tape 1-Segment 3: "The Scarlet Letter in a High School English Class"
This video lesson illustrates a teacher's attempts to help her students understand the characters in the novel *The Scarlet Letter*. (This is the chapter's closing case study.)

Concepts in Classrooms Tape 1-Segment 3: "Promoting Encoding: Putting Students in Active Roles."
This video segment includes four episodes that illustrates teachers' attempts to put learners in active roles. It includes:
- A hands-activity with first graders on properties of air
- A whole-group and hands-on activity on graphing in second grade
- A hands-on activity on problem-solving in fifth grade
- A whole-group activity on geography and economy in ninth grade

Concepts in Classrooms Tape 1-Segment 4: "Organizing Information: Applying Dual-Coding Theory."
This video segment illustrates teachers attempts to organize information in different ways to make it meaningful and capitalize on the dual-coding benefits of simultaneously presenting information in visual and verbal forms. It includes the following four episodes:
- A history teacher introducing the Vietnam War with an outline
- A geography teacher examining the relationships between geography and economy using a matrix
- A life-science teacher examining different types of worms with drawings
- A fifth grade teacher introducing problem solving with a schematic

CHAPTER OUTLINE

I.   Cognitive perspectives on learning
    A.   Principles of cognitive learning theory
        1.   Learners are active
        2.   Understanding depends on what learners know
        3.   Learners construct rather then record understanding
        4.   A definition of learning
II. Information processing
    A.   Models: Aids to understanding
    B.   Sensory memory
    C.   Working memory
        1.   Limitations of working memory
        2.   Cognitive load theory: Overcoming the limitations of working memory
            a.   Chunking
            b.   Automaticity
            c.   Dual processing
    D.   Long-term memory
        1.   Representing declarative knowledge in memory: Schemas
            a.   Schemas as scripts
            b.   Organizing knowledge in memory: implications for teaching and learning
        2.   Representing procedural knowledge in memory: Conditions and actions
            a.   Developing procedural knowledge
            b.   Developing procedural knowledge: Implications for learning and teaching
    E.   Cognitive processes

1. Attention: The beginning of information processing
   a. Attracting and maintaining student attention
2. Perception: Finding meaning in stimuli
   a. The influence of background knowledge on perception
3. Rehearsal: Retaining information through repetition
4. Meaningful encoding: Making connections in long-term memory
   a. Organization
   b. Dual-coding theory: Imagery in long-term memory
   c. Elaboration
   d. Activity
5. Levels of processing: An alternate view of meaningful encoding
6. Forgetting
   a. Forgetting as interference
   b. Forgetting as retrieval failure

F. Metacognition: Knowledge and control of cognitive processes
   1. The development of metacognition
      a. Meta-attention: Development of attention strategies
      b. Metamemory: Development of memory strategies

G. Impact of diversity on information processing
   1. Diversity and perception
   2. Diversity, encoding, and retrieval
   3. Instructional adaptations for background diversity

IV. Information processing in the classroom: Instructional Strategies
   A. Schema production: Acquiring integrated declarative knowledge
   B. Promoting schema production in classrooms: An instructional strategy
      1. Meaningful verbal learning: The work of David Ausubel
   C. Understanding and automaticity: Acquiring procedural knowledge
   D. Promoting understanding and automaticity: An instructional strategy
      a. Introduce and review
      b. Develop understanding
      c. Practice: The associative stage and automatic stages
      d. Homework
   E. Assessment and learning: The role of assessment in cognitive instruction
      1. Assessment and instruction
      2. The importance of alignment
   F. Putting information processing into perspective

PRESENTATION OUTLINE

Teaching suggestions in the outline will be marked with the symbol ▪. In most cases, the suggested activities can be done individually and discussed as a whole group, or they can be done in small groups, and the small-group results can be discussed with the whole class. To be consistent with our understanding of knowledge construction, we recommend that you promote as much discussion--both in small groups and with the whole class--as possible.

Enrichment Information, which includes elaborations of text topics as well as topics not included in the text, will be boxed as you see here.

I. Cognitive perspectives on learning
   A. Principles of cognitive learning theory
      1. Learners are active

2. Understanding depends on what learners know
3. Learners construct rather then record understanding
4. A definition of learning

■ *The following activities are suggestions for introducing the chapter. The purpose in the activities is to help the students understand that behaviorism, with its emphasis on stimuli, responses, and reinforcers as a way of explaining behavior is unable to account for their--the students' own--responses in each case. This will allow you to demonstrate that explanations focusing on internal, mental processes are necessary to account for student responses. The activities also allow you to provide a motivating introduction to cognitive views of learning.*

1. **Tell the students that you're going to do three simple activities, and the point in them will be clear after you've completed and discussed them.**

2. **For the first activity, tell the students that you're going to display a phrase on the overhead for two seconds, and that you want them to write it down. Then display T 7.1 "Tall in the Saddle," keeping the title of the transparency covered. Quickly cover the transparency and have the students write what they "see" on the overhead. (Most of the students will miss the second "the" in the phrase.)**

3. **Remind the students of the activity on page 236. (You may want to try it with them, and see how many answer "Go" to the question about what people do at a green light, in spite of the fact that they read about it. Those that do further illustrate cognition.) Encourage them to try the activity with their friends, and see how many answer "Go."**

4. **For the third activity, display T 7.7 "An Exercise in Perception." Ask the students how many see the young woman in the picture, and then ask how many see an old woman in the picture. Ask the students to see if they can identify one and then the other. Point out that they will almost be able to "feel" their minds click back and forth.**

5. **Now ask the students what these activities have in common. After several student comments, ask what the "stimulus" was in each case (the phrase, the question, "What do we do at a green light?" and the picture respectively). Then ask, since the stimulus was the phrase in the first case, the question in the second, and the picture in the third, why did different students respond differently? Point out that they were not responding only to the stimuli, but were also responding to their past experience and expectations. For example, saying "Pots," established expectations for them, and they responded to their expectations instead of the actual stimulus.**

6. **Point out that behaviorism is unable to explain events such as these; cognitive psychology suggests that the learner isn't responding only to the environment, but is also using internal cognitive processes to interpret and make sense of the environment. Note that examples such as these led to interest in what actually is going on in people's minds. This leads to the idea of cognitive views of learning.**

II. Information Processing
    A. Models: Aids to understanding

   ■ *The purpose of the suggestions in this section is to help the students understand that models, such as the information processing model, are representations that help them visualize what they can't observe directly.*

1. Ask the students to give you some examples or definitions of models. Some possibilities are:
    *   A miniature representation of something, such as a model car or a globe
    *   Someone who poses for an artist
    *   Someone who displays merchandise
    *   Someone who displays behavior that is imitated (as was presented in Chapter 6)

2. Now point out that the definition that is useful when we discuss information processing is: "A representation that allows us to visualize what we can't observe directly." Note that even though we can't directly observe the information this model represents, it is valuable nevertheless, because it helps us visualize and think about the information stores and cognitive processes involved in processing information.

    TM 7.1 lists *"Different Types of Models."*

    This can lead you to the next activity.

■ *The point in this activity is to help students understand that a great deal of information can be derived from models, such as the information processing mode*

1. Display T 7.2 *"An Information Processing Model."* Have the students make two columns on their papers. In the left column make as many observations of the model in T 7.2 as possible. Give them an example or two, such as, "In the model there are fewer lines to the right of 'attention' than there are to the left of attention," or "In the model, working memory is smaller then either sensory memory or long-term memory." This will give them a feel for what you're looking for in the observations.

2. Then, in the right column, have them make possible conclusions (inferences) based on the observations. For example, based on the observation that there are fewer lines to the right than to the left of attention we might infer that attention acts as a screen; stimuli that we don't attend to are lost.

    Use your judgment about the amount of time you allot for the activity, such as 10-15 minutes. Then discuss their findings.

    After you've completed the discussion, remind students again that even though models may not directly correspond to a physical reality, they summarize and describe many of the important features of our information processing systems.

B. Sensory memory

■ *The following simple exercises are designed to help students understand the characteristics of sensory memory.*

1. Have the students wiggle their fingers back and forth in front of them and ask them what they observe (a "shadow" of their fingers as it's moving). Then have them press their forefingers on their opposite arms and note that the feeling of pressure remains briefly after their fingers are removed. Point out that the "shadow" that "trails" after their fingers as they wiggle them, and the slight feeling of pressure that briefly remains are the memory traces retained in sensory memory.

Note also that in reading we must retain the first part of the sentence in sensory memory long enough to extract meaning from the whole sentence. If information was lost immediately, it would be impossible to get any meaning from reading.

1. Ask the students to summarize the characteristics of sensory memory (this can be done either as a small-group or whole-group activity). They should identify the following characteristics:
   - **Virtually unlimited capacity**
   - **Retains exact copy of stimuli (information is "unprocessed")**
   - **Holds information very briefly (a second or two)**

C. Working memory
   1. Limitations of working memory
   2. Cognitive load theory: Overcoming the limitations of working memory
      a. Chunking
      a. Automaticity
      b. Dual processing

■ *The purpose in the following activities is to help students understand the limitations of working memory.*
1. **Display TM 7.2 "Research Results and Working Memory," and ask the students to try and identify what the examples have in common.**

2. **Then display T 7.3 "The Limitations of Working Memory." Tell the students that you're going to show them some letters for about 1 second, and that after you've shown them, they should write them down. Then show the first row only (for about a second). Have the students write the letters. Then repeat the process with the other four rows. (Be careful to avoid displaying the words at the bottom of T 7.3.)**

3. **After you're finished, display the letters and ask them how many got the letters in each case. Nearly all will get the letters in the five-letter row, and fewer will get all the letters in each succeeding row. Point out that the typical adult capacity is from 5 to 9 bits of information, and that these capacities are lower for younger children.**

4. **Ask students to recall some of the observations and inferences (conclusions) they made about working memory. They should note that:**
   - It is limited in capacity.
   - It is the "conscious" part of our processing system.
   - If it becomes overloaded, information from it will be lost.

   Again display TM 7.2 to emphasize the importance of working memory's limited capacity.

■ *The following information is designed to help students understand the importance of understanding relationships in information instead of learning information in isolated pieces.*
1. **To illustrate the process of *chunking* display the words at the bottom half of T 7.3. This displays the same letters in the exercise "chunked" into one or two units. They will see that remembering all the letters in the "chunked" information is easy to remember in each case.**

2. **Point out that remembering patterns and relationships is also a form of chunking**

which frees working memory space. This is the reason that in this class we emphasize relationships rather than isolated pieces of information. When several items of information are related to each other, they essentially become a "chunk." (For example, with continued thought and effort, the information processing model becomes a chunk rather than several pieces of information.)

■ *The following exercises are designed to help students understand that we perform many activities automatically. Performing activities automatically frees working memory space for more complex tasks.*
1. Ask the students to identify some things they do "without thinking about it." These are essentially *automatic*. After you have a list, offer the term "automaticity" if they haven't already used it. Some examples include:
    - driving a car.
    - typing on a computer keyboard.
    - recognizing words.
    - math facts.
    - writing.

2. Ask them to identify several ideas that must be automatic for them to do well in this class. The information processing model and its components are examples. Definitions of concepts are other examples. Have them explain why these ideas must be automatic.

    An example and explanation is as follows:
    If the information processing model and its organization are not automatic, they (the students) will use working memory space to recall elements of the model, and they won't have enough working memory space available to solve the problems in the case studies you ask them to analyze.

■ *The following exercises are designed to help students understand the role of visual representations in learning and how they relate to dual processing theory.*
1. Point out that–in virtually all cases–you supplement your descriptions with visual materials, such as information on the overhead.

2. Point out that these visual representations, combined with you class discussions, are intended to capitalize on the dual-processing capabilities of working memory.

3. Summarize dual processing by having the students explain what dual processing means. Lead them to conclude that dual processing theory suggests that working memory consists of a visual and an auditory store that work independently and additively, i.e., combining visual and verbal representations not only does not overload working memory, but in fact help overcome its limitations.

■ *The purpose in the following suggestions is to have students understand the implications for instruction of working memory's limitations.*
1. Have students identify as many implications of working memory's limitations as possible.

    Some of these implications include:

- practicing basic skills to automaticity, so that they don't have to use working memory space to recall basic information.
- forming schemas of interrelated information, so the schemas become *chunks* of information instead of isolated pieces.
- teaching in short steps and providing practice to allow learners time to process information and transfer it to long-term memory.

The Significance of a Limited Working Memory. You might want to point out that some experts (e.g., Bruer, 1993) believe that a limited working memory is the most significant aspect of our information processing systems. Further, cognitive load theorists (e.g. Sweller, van Merrienboer, & Paas, 1998) point out that while our working memories can hold about 7 bits of information, processing also requires working memory space, so we are probably only able to hold–and process–about 2 bits of information.

On the other hand, Sweller, et al., (1998) point out that while the *number* of bits of information is limited, the *size* is not. This makes the development of inter-related schemas an even more important goal for learning.

D. Long-term memory
  1. Representing knowledge in long-term memory: Schemas
     a. Schemas as scripts
     b. Organizing knowledge in memory: Implications for teaching and learning

■ *The purpose of the suggestions in this section is to help students understand the characteristics of long-term memory.*

1. **Have the students identify similarities and differences in each of the memory stores.**

2. **Display T 7.4 *"Schema Representing Juan's Understanding"* and T 7.5 *"Schema Representing Randy's Understanding."* Have the students describe and compare the information in the transparencies. Remind the students that they are models that help us visualize the way Randy and Juan organized and stored information in their long-term memories. Guide them to the definition that schemas are the way knowledge is organized in memory.**

3. **Have the students describe as much information as they can about the information processing model and what implications this information has for learning and teaching. The information they offer will be in the form of declarative knowledge organized in a schema.**

4. **As you ask them to tell you how they recalled the information, some are likely to say that they "pictured" the model, which you can point out as an example of *imagery*. They might also say that they *saw* sensory memory on the left, working memory in the middle and long-term memory on the right. You can then offer this as a form of linear ordering.**

5. **Point out that virtually infinite numbers of schemas exist. You can also point out that one of your goals in this section is for them to develop a complex and**

115

integrated schema about information processing and what implications it has for learning and teaching.

Using CD-ROM Technology. To enrich their understanding of background knowledge in the form of schemas and give them some experience with CD-ROM technology, you might have the students complete the "Using Technology in Your Study of Educational Psychology: "Bartlett's Ghosts" experience with the CD-ROM that is part of the media package for the book.

Feedback for the questions in the chapter is as follows:

1. The students' omissions, transformations, and additions will be individual and will depend on their background knowledge related to the original story.

2. While all three–omissions, transformations, and additions–are problematic, transformations and additions are probably most significant because they result in the most misconceptions. (Your students will make arguments for all three being problematic, and they all are to some extent.) Misconceptions–once formed–are very difficult to eliminate.

Teachers can do two things to help minimize schema errors. First, they can build their instruction around high quality examples and representations. The examples and representations help provide accurate background knowledge from which learners develop understanding. Second, high levels of interaction are essential. During discussions misconceptions are revealed and hopefully eliminated.

3. Each would result in more accurate recall of the information in the written passage. This fact has two implications for teaching. First, we must try to assess learners' background knowledge, and second, we must try to supply it in the form of effective examples and representations when it is lacking.

---

2. Representing procedural knowledge in memory: Conditions and actions
   a. Developing procedural knowledge
   b. Developing procedural knowledge: Implications for teaching and learning

■ *The goal of the following suggestions is to help students understand the differences between declarative knowledge and procedural knowledge.*

1. Review declarative knowledge and use it as a link to procedural knowledge by pointing out that the focus of your discussion to this point has been on declarative knowledge. Ask them to describe some procedural knowledge related to your discussion. (When they actually teach based on the implications of information processing, they will demonstrate procedural knowledge.)

2. Also ask the students to give you some additional examples of procedural knowledge. Some examples include:
   - finding a book in the library.
   - changing a tire.
   - using a computer.

.   solving a word problem in math.
.   writing an essay.

3.   **Ask the students why we care about the difference between declarative and procedural knowledge--the "so what" question. They should note that the two types of knowledge are learned differently; declarative knowledge involves items of information being linked to each other, whereas procedural knowledge involves** *conditions* **and** *actions*. **Ask the students to offer some examples of conditions and actions, such as in the case of finding a book in the library, writing a persuasive versus a descriptive essay, or different types of word problems**

4.   **Summarize this section by asking the students what kind of knowledge has predominated to this point in the course you're teaching (declarative). Ask them how conditions and actions have been illustrated to help them develop procedural knowledge. (The classroom examples and the written and video cases are the best examples, primarily because they provide context for the topics they're studying.)**

5.   **Display TM 7.3** *"Characteristics of the Memory Stores"* **which summarizes the similarities and differences.**

E.   Cognitive processes
  1.   Attention: Information processing from a learner perspective
     a.   Attracting and maintaining student attention
  2.   Perception: Finding meaning in stimuli
     a.   The influence of background knowledge on perception
  3.   Rehearsal: Retaining information through practice

■ *The purpose of the activities in this section of the chapter is to help students understand how the cognitive processes move information from sensory memory to working memory, and from working memory to long-term memory.*

1.   **Begin this section by asking students to recall what you did to begin your discussion of the chapter. They should remember that you began with the "Say 'pots,'" activity, and the "Tall in the saddle," and old lady/young woman examples. Ask them what these examples illustrated. They should note that first the examples were attention getters. Second, they should recall that "Say 'pots'" set up expectations in them that influenced their perceptions, which in turn resulted in them saying "Stop," when you asked, "What do you do at a green light?" Perception was also involved with the other examples. They tend to miss the second 'the' in "Tall in the the saddle," because we rarely see it (experience), and the fact that some people see a young woman, whereas others see an older woman is a classic perceptual example.**

2.   **Have the students identify other examples of attention getters that you've used throughout your instruction in the course.**

   Then have the students identify other topics, and have them determine how they might begin a lesson on the topic to best attract attention.

   Have the students share and discuss their ideas. In the discussion, point out that beginning lessons to attract attention often requires only some imagination. It doesn't need to require a great deal of extra preparation.

3.   **T 7.6** *"Strategies for Attracting Attention"* **provide some additional examples.**

117

4.   Ask the students how they will determine if their learners are accurately perceiving the information they present. (Asking students is the simplest and most effective way.)

        Ask them what kinds of questions are particularly effective. They should identify open-ended questions as being ideal. You can then remind them that open-ended questions are also very effective in working with cultural minorities, so they are appropriate for an additional reason.

5.   Ask the students how they remember a phone number long enough to dial it. The technique they describe will likely illustrate a form of rehearsal, since they will have repeated the number enough times to retain it in working memory until they could dial it.

6.   Point out that rehearsal is a low-level process, used to retain factual information. Point out that rehearsal and practice are not the same process. Practice can involve high-high level operations, such as problem solving and writing whereas rehearsal is low level, involving memorization.

4. Meaningful encoding: Making connections in long-term memory
   a. Organization
   b. Dual-coding theory: Imagery in long-term memory
   c. Elaboration
   d. Activity

■ *The purpose of the activities in this section of the chapter is to help students understand the concept of "meaningfulness" and that meaningfulness is increased with organization, elaboration, and activity.*

1.   Display T 7.8 *"Making Information Meaningful"* as an organizer for this section. To illustrate the concept of *meaningfulness*, again display T 7.4 and T 7.5 that illustrate the difference between Juan's and Randy's schemas. In them we see the same numbers of ideas, yet more links exist among the ideas in Juan's schema than exist in Randy's. As a result, Juan's understanding is greater. (For example, there are 12 links in Juan's schema, whereas there are only 6 in Randy's. This helps visualize the idea that the information is more meaningful for Juan than it is for Randy.)

2.   To illustrate organization, display transparencies that you have used to teach topics from earlier chapters, such as a matrix, a hierarchy, and another form of organizer (such as the information processing model from this chapter). Ask the students what they have in common. Guide them to conclude that they all helped *organize* the content you were teaching. Then, take one or two specific examples and have the students describe how the organizer makes the information more meaningful. (*Emphasize that each organizer illustrates associations or connections in the content.*)

3.   As you discuss the organizers in each case, point out how they all incorporate imagery, and remind the students that dual-coding theory suggests that information that can be visualized is stored more efficiently in long-term memory than is information that can only be described verbally. This helps us understand why a concept like *tree* is easier to remember than a concept like *honesty*.

> **Video:** At this point you might want to show the video segment "Organizing Information: Applying Dual-Coding Theory" (described at the beginning of this chapter).

■ *To illustrate the process of elaboration:*

1. Display TM 7.6 *"Elaborating on Past Experiences."* As the students to explain the two examples and then display the feedback at the bottom.

2. Point out that producing examples is probably the most effective form of elaboration that exists. Also note that this is the reason you've emphasized the use of examples so strongly in your teaching.

3. Point out that using analogies and mnemonic devices are two strategies that capitalize on elaboration. Display TM 7.8 *"Types and Examples of Mnemonic Devices."*

■ *To illustrate the role of activity:*

1. Display TM 7.7 *"Active and Passive Study Strategies,"* and have the students decide which of the three students are likely to learn the most.

2. Ask the students what other kinds of learning experiences promote activity.

> **Video:** At this point you might want to show the video segment "Promoting Encoding: Putting Students in Active Roles" (described at the beginning of this chapter.

■ *To illustrate the importance of background knowledge in meaningful encoding:*

1. Display TM 7.12 *"Review Exercise (The Role of Background Knowledge)."* It offers an example of the role of background knowledge in making information meaningful. Have the students respond to the exercise and then discuss the results.

2. If you had the students complete the exercises involved in "Bartlett's Ghosts," you might refer them to their experiences with the CD.

5. Levels of processing: An alternative view of meaningful encoding

■ *The suggestions in this section are designed to help students see how levels of processing theory relate to encoding in the information processing model.*

1. To illustrate different levels of processing, ask the students to offer some specific questions that promote deep processing and some others that promote only shallow processing. Some questions and examples that promote deep processing are illustrated in TM 7.4 *"Questions That Promote Deep Processing of Information."*

6. Forgetting
   a. Forgetting as interference

b.   Forgetting as retrieval failure

c.   The role of context in retrieval

■ *The suggestions in this section are intended to help students understand that interference is one explanation for why we forget information.*

1.   To illustrate information in this section, ask students to offer two related ideas that are confusing for them. Ask them to try and explain why they're confusing. Point out that theorists would explain that one interferes with the other.

2.   Identify some concepts, such as *assimilation* and *accommodation* in Chapter 2 or *positive* and *negative reinforcement* in Chapter 6, that you've studied in the class which can potentially involve interference.

■ *To help students understand that some theorists suggest that "forgetting" is really the inability to retrieve information:*

1.   Use the discussion of interference to help students understand that effective encoding is the key to retrieval. Ask the students what would help them clarify the confusing ideas.

2.   Ask one of the students to state the months of the year. He or she will quickly say "January, February, . . . December."

3.   Now ask the student to name the months of the year alphabetically. He or she will struggle and laborously say, "April, August, . . . " Point out that this illustrates the fact that we've encoded the months of the year in a chronological context. When we have to state the months alphabetically, we have to reprocess the information.

F.   Metacognition: Knowledge and control of cognitive processes

■ *The suggestions in this section are designed to help students understand metacognition and how it influences learning.*

1.   To begin this section, ask the students what they might do if they were up late the night before class and know they might have trouble staying awake in class. Some examples might be:

.   Drink some coffee before (or during) class.

.   Move to the front of the room.

.   Take more notes.

.   Fidget/move around in their seats.

2.   Point out that these examples illustrate that they're *aware of*, and are exercising *control over*, their attention.

3.   Also point out that their tendency to take notes and/or highlight parts of the book, work the exercises in the Student Study Guide, take the practice quizzes, and respond to the margin notes in the book illustrate metacognition, because by doing these activities they demonstrate *knowledge of* and *control over* their understanding of the content they're studying.

4.   Also note that exercising metacognition and using study strategies is part of being self-regulated.

120

5. Again display T 7.2 *"An Information Processing Model"* to illustrate metacognition in our information processing systems.

6. TM 7.11 *"Review Exercise (Perception, Schemas, and Metacognition)"* and TM 7.13 *"Review Exercise (Metacognition)"* include exercises that help the students better understand metacognition.

1. Development of metacognition
   a. Meta-attention: Development of attention strategies
   b. Metamemory: Development of memory strategies

   ■ *The purpose in the following suggestions is to illustrate developmental differences in metacognition.*
   1. Display TM 7.9 *"Children and Metacognition."* Have the students offer a brief explanation for the child's behavior in the cartoon. (The students will likely say that the child is egocentric, and from a Piagetian perspective egocentrism is demonstrated. From an information processing perspective, the cartoon illustrates lack of metacognition; the child is unaware that he isn't able to communicate clearly.)

   2. Remind the students that meta-attention and metamemory are types of metacognition, and then ask what type is illustrated by the cartoon and see if they're able to identify "metacommunication," as a type of metacognition.

   3. Also, have the students predict what the two children will do in the example at the bottom of TM 7.9. (The kindergartner will likely do nothing, whereas the 6th grader will say something, such as, "I can't hear," or do something such as try to move closer to the front of the room.)

   4. . Summarize this section by asking how a first grader and a fifth grader might differ in their approach to learning how to spell a list of words.

G. Impact of diversity on information processing
   1. Diversity and perception
   2. Diversity, encoding, and retrieval
   3. Instructional adaptations for background diversity

   ■ *The suggestions in this section are intended to help students see how learner diversity influences the way they perceive information.*
   1. To illustrate this point, share the following teaching anecdote:

      A social studies teacher was curious about the following statement written by a student: "The French wrote insulting letters to the Americans." When questioned, the student showed the teacher the place in the text that said, "The French Revolution corresponded *roughly* to the American Revolution."

   2. Discuss how the anecdote relates to perception. Ask the students what other experiences you've had with perception (the old woman and the young lady). You might want to point out that perception is always an issue when dealing with test items that are above the knowledge/recall level, since they require interpretation. Again, ask the students what we as teachers do about the fact that our students may perceive the information

we present in a way that is different from the way we intended it. (Ask the students how they interpret the information. It is the simplest and most effective way we have.)

3.   You might also point out that you're doing a perception check whenever you ask students to interpret some information, or when you simply ask them what a display or example represents.

■ *To illustrate how diversity in backgrounds influences encoding and retrieval:*
1.   Display TM 7.5 *"Background Knowledge and Encoding."* Have the students decide what each passage is about and offer their interpretations.

   After they've offered their interpretations point out that the first is about Christopher Columbus and his voyage to the New World, and the second is about washing clothes.

2.   Ask students why neither passage was very meaningful for some of them. They will probably point out that they weren't told what the passages were about. In the discussion, note that being told what the passages are about activates background knowledge of Columbus and their experience with washing clothes. Point out that in these examples background knowledge was there, just needing to be activated. Often, background knowledge is absent and needs to be provided. Also, F. Bartlett's classic 1932 study, *Remembering: A study in experimental and social psychology* (Cambridge Press) contains additional amusing examples of garbled encoding.

■ *To help the students understand how instruction can be adapted to accommodate differences in their learners' backgrounds:*
1.   Tell them to think of themselves as teachers with classes having students with widely varying backgrounds. Ask them what kinds of relatively simple and practical things they might do to accommodate those differences in backgrounds.

   Based on the information processing model and their reading, they should identify the following:
   .   Ask students what they know about the topic you're planning to teach.
   .   Provide background for the students in the form of examples and other representations.
   .   Check students' perceptions of your examples by using open-ended questions.
   .   Have students in your classes share experiences to increase each others'
   ·   backgrounds.

III. Information processing in the classroom: Instructional Strategies
   A.   Schema production: Acquiring integrated declarative knowledge
   B.   Promoting schema production in classrooms: An instructional strategy
        1.   Meaningful verbal learning: The work of David Ausubel
   C.   Understanding and automaticity: Acquiring procedural knowledge
   D.   Promoting understanding and automaticity: An instructional strategy
        a.   Introduce and review
        b.   Develop understanding
        c.   Practice: The associative stage and automatic stages
        d.   Homework
   E.   Assessment and learning: The role of assessment in cognitive instruction
        1.   Assessment and instruction
        2.   The importance of alignment

■ *The purpose of this section is to understand instructional applications of information processing.*

    1.   **Display TM 7.14 *"Principles of Instruction for Applying Information Processing in Classrooms."* Have the students identify where Darren Anderson (in the case study beginning on page 264) and Sam Barnett (in the case study beginning on page 267) applied each of the principles in their teaching.**

F.   Putting information processing into perspective

■ *The purpose of this section is to identify some of the strengths and weaknesses of information processing.*

    1.   **Ask the students to identify some factors that influence the amount they study. Some of their responses can include:**
- **how well they like the material.**
- **how well they like the teacher.**
- **how they feel.**
- **what they expect to learn and what they expect from the teacher.**
- **what they believe about the content, the teacher, and the course.**

    2.   **Point out that information processing doesn't take learners' emotions, beliefs, needs, and expectations into account, and its failure to do so is commonly cited as weaknesses and limitations in the information processing view of learning.**

    3.   **Point out that, on the other hand, most researchers and theorists accept the basic architecture of information processing–a sensory memory, working memory, and long-term memory, together with cognitive processes that move information from one store to another. Note that areas of study, such as cognitive-load theory and dual-processing theory focus on the limitations of working memory and what can be done to help overcome them.**

DISCUSSION STARTERS

1.   What similarities and differences exist between behaviorist, social cognitive, and information processing views of learning? Are either more valuable to teaching at different grade levels? In different subject matter areas? For different topics? Which and why?

2.   Is information processing more closely related to Piaget's or to Vygotsky's theory? What specific concepts from each are related? Describe the relationship.

3.   Which aspect or aspects of an information processing view of memory and learning have the most important implications for instruction? What are these implications?

4.   Using information from this chapter explain how long-term memory might differ for the following groups of people:
    a.   A three-year-old vs. senior citizen
    b.   A first year biology student and a doctoral student in the same area
    c.   A first year and experienced teacher
    4.   A student who has memorized information for a fill-in-the-blanks test and one who studies for an essay exam

5. How useful are mnemonic devices in the classroom? Should teachers place more emphasis on these strategies? Are they more useful at some levels and in certain content areas than others? Which and why?

6. Which theory of forgetting--interference or retrieval failure--seems most useful to teachers? Why? What are the implications of each for instruction?

7. Does diversity primarily influence the information stores or the processes in the information-processing model? Explain, using information from the chapter.

BACKGROUND READINGS

Bransford, J., Brown, A., & Cocking, R. (Eds.). (2000). *How people learn: Brain, mind, experience, and school.* Washington, DC: National Academy Press. This comprehensive book cognitive learning in detail and the implications these views of learning have for planning, instruction, and assessment.

Bruning, R., Schraw, G., & Ronning, R. (1999). *Cognitive psychology and instruction* (3rd ed.). Englewood Cliffs, NJ: Prentice Hall. This book provides in-depth coverage of information processing and constructivism. Separate chapters discuss memory, encoding, and retrieval, as well as cognitive frameworks for reading, writing, math, and science.

Byrnes, J. P. (2001). *Minds, brains, and learning: Understanding the psychological and educational relevance of neuroscientific research.* New York: Guilford Press. This book describes neuroscientific research and relates it to cognitive theories of learning.

Greeno, J., Collins, A., & Resnick, L. (1996). Cognition and learning. In D. Berliner & R. Calfee (Eds.), *Handbook of Educational Psychology* (pp. 15-46). New York: Macmillan. This chapter examines learning, motivation and transfer from behaviorist, cognitive, and situative/sociohistoric views. It includes discussions of assessment and creating classroom environments that facilitate learning.

Mayer, R. (1998). Cognitive theory for education: What teachers need to know. In N. Lambert & B. McCombs (Eds.). *How students learn: Reforming schools through learner-centered education* (pp. 353-377). Washington, DC: American Psychological Association. This chapter examines learning from behaviorist, information processing, and constructivist perspectives and describes the implications of constructivist views of learning for learner-centered instruction.

Mayer, R. (2002). The promise of educational psychology, Volume II: Teaching for meaningful learning. Upper Saddle River, NJ: Prentice Hall. This book by a well-known author discusses a variety of topics related to cognitive learning.

Reisberg, D. (1997). *Cognition: Exploring the science of the mind.* New York: W. W. Norton. An excellent overview of theory and research on cognition.

Schacter, D. L. (1999). The seven sins of memeory: Insights from psychology and neuroscience. *American Psychologist, 54,* 182-203/

Schunk, D. (2000). *Learning theories: An educational perspective* (3rd ed.). Upper Saddle River, NJ: Prentice Hall. This text provides a detailed description of information processing, among other views of learning.

FEEDBACK FOR CONSTRUCTED RESPONSE AND DOCUMENT-BASED ANALYSIS QUESTIONS

Constructed Response Items_____

1. Assess the extent to which Sue applied the principles of cognitive learning theory in her lesson. Include both strengths and weaknesses in your assessment.

   There are four basic principles of cognitive learning theory:
   1. *Learners are active in their attempts to understand their experiences. Sue capitalized upon this principle by having them write in their journals and through her interactive questioning.*
   2. *The understanding that learners develop depends on what they already know. Sue built upon students' background knowledge by referring to Hester Prynne and events in previous lessons.*
   3. *Learners construct, rather than record, understanding. Sue facilitated the knowledge construction process by having students pretend in their journals that they were either Hester Prynne or Dimmesdale. Since one of her goals was for students to understand Dimmesdale's character, she might have been more analytical in her questioning, helping students to form a more complete picture of his character. One suggestion might have been to make the lesson more concrete, such as with pictures. For example, she might have brought in several possible pictures of Dimmesdale and asked the class to select one and defend it, using information from the text.*
   4. *Learning is a change in a person's mental structure. Since learning is a change in structures, teachers need to ensure that the structures students create are organized, coherent, and accurate. To do this, Sue could have used the end of her lesson to summarize the class's findings and conclusions about Dimmesdale.*

2. Assess the extent to which Sue applied information processing theory in her lesson. Include both strengths and weaknesses in your assessment.

   Attention is an essential process in the Information Processing Model. Sue focused the class's attention in several ways. First, she challenged them to find evidence in the book that Dimmesdale was the illicit lover. She also used the passage from the book describing Dimmesdale's speech in a similar way, as an attention getter. In each instance she used student responses to check their perceptions.

   Sue demonstrated that she understood the limitations of working memory by allowing the students enough time to process the information at each step in the discussion. She typically asked one question at a time and gave them time to consider their answers.

   Sue facilitated encoding into long-term memory in several ways. First, she encouraged the students to use imagery to imagine what Dimmesdale looked like. Then, they wrote in their journals, which put them in an active role which helps make the information meaningful. Finally, she again placed students in an active role when they role played each of the characters during Dimmesdale's speech.

3. Which cognitive process from information processing theory was most prominent in Sue's lesson? Explain.

   Encoding was most prominent in her lesson. Sue facilitated encoding into long-term memory in several ways. First, she encouraged students to use imagery to imagine what Dimmesdale looked like. Then, they wrote in their journals, which put them in an active role, which helps make the information meaningful. Finally, she again placed students in an active role when they role played each of the characters during Dimmesdale's speech.

   Sue encouraged meaningfulness in the encoding in several ways. She used elaboration when she encouraged students to interconnect information in the text to defend their conclusion that Dimmesdale was the father. She used organization when she had students compare and contrast the feelings of Hester and Dimmesdale during his speech. She used activity when she asked them to cast Dimmesdale's part in a movie and when she asked them to role play Hester and Dimmesdale.

4. Identify at least one instance in Sue's lesson that was focused on declarative knowledge. Identify another that was focused on procedural knowledge. Was the primary focus of Sue's lesson the acquisition of declarative knowledge or procedural knowledge?

Declarative knowledge is knowledge of facts, definitions, procedures and rules; procedural knowledge involves knowing how to perform tasks. Sue focused on declarative knowledge when she reviewed the novel's plot at the beginning of the lesson. The primary focus of the lesson was on procedural knowledge - knowing how to analyze a text, and using information from the text to bolster arguments. Sue did this when she asked students how they knew the baby was Dimmesdale's, requiring them to defend their answers with information from the text. She also did this when she asked them to describe Dimmesdale in their journals.

Document-Based Analysis_____

After her lesson, Sue prepared the following assessment.

Even though The Scarlet Letter was set in a Puritan community centuries ago, the moral dilemmas of personal responsibility, and consuming emotions of guilt, anger, loyalty and revenge are timeless. Describe how these dilemmas and emotions were illustrated in the novel, and support your conclusions with details from the novel.

Analyze Sue's assessment based on the case study and the content of the chapter. Include both strengths and weaknesses of her assessment.

Sue's essay question emphasized the importance of understanding the novel at multiple levels, which promoted meaningful encoding. Another aspect of the question, asking students to support their answers with details from the novel, also encouraged deeper processing and more meaningful encoding. In addition, asking students to respond to the novel from multiple perspectives helps ensure well developed and integrated schemas. While the primary function of assessment is to gather data for instructional decision making, it can also be an effective instructional device, encouraging meaningful studying and comprehensive, coherent learning.

CLASSROOM EXERCISES

1. Look at the following telephone numbers:
    731-9586
    249-7132
    852-1657
    965-3841

What do they have in common?
Why do you suppose this commonality exists?

2. Lecture has always been and still remains the most common teaching method in junior highs, high schools, and universities. Using the characteristics of working memory as the basis, explain why lecture is so popular. (Respond to this item from the perspective of the teacher. In other words, how does the use of lecture relate to teachers' working memories?)

3. Teachers are encouraged to used sophisticated forms of instruction, such as guided discovery in their teaching. (A discussion and example of guided discovery begins on page 293 of your text.). Again, using the characteristics of working memory as the basis, explain what the teachers must do in order to successfully use a strategy such as guided discovery.

4. When teachers become expert at using a strategy, such as guided discovery, are they primarily demonstrating declarative knowledge or procedural knowledge? Explain.

5. You have an electric garage door opener, and one morning as you're in a bit of a rush to get to school or work, you realize that you can't remember if you've put the garage door down or not, so you drive back several blocks to check, and you see that you have indeed put the garage door down. What concept from information processing best explains why you originally couldn't remember if you put the garage door down?

6. Research indicates that experts in a field, as widely ranging as teaching, physics, or even chess, think differently than novices in those same fields. Some of the differences include the following:
- Experts are more metacognitive in their approaches to problems.
- Experts have more of their knowledge stored in interconnected schemas, whereas novices have more of their knowledge stored in isolated bits.
- More of experts' knowledge is automatic than is the knowledge of novices.

Which of the following concepts–*sensory memory, attention, perception, working memory,* or *rehearsal*–is most closely related to these expert-novice differences? Explain the relationship between the concept and these differences in the thinking of experts and novices.

7. Missy Somers, a business consultant and mother, was asked to attend a meeting of an auxiliary which raises money for an organization that helps abused children. Before Missy agreed to attend she asked her friend to send her information about the charity and the auxiliary's financial budget. After poring over the information her friend sent her, which Missy found impressive, she agreed to attend the next meeting with the knowledge that some of her energies would be devoted to participating in one of the group's fundraisers.
    While attending the meeting the following month, Missy met other first-time members who were unaware of the auxiliary's track record and were simply there at the invitation of friends to meet other women. During the meeting, the charity's director shared some statistics on the number abused children taken in by the agency on a monthly basis. She continued her talk by including details of the direct impact of the money raised by the auxiliary on the children's lives. Murmurs among the prospective members after the meeting revealed that some of them

were unaware of the group's three fund raising efforts and the requirement to work on at least one. Others talked of their shock on the number of children abused each year. Missy was not surprised by either of these concerns, but she did detect a sort of factionalization of the group in terms of interest in belonging.

Using the information from the chapter, explain why Missy's reaction differs with other first-time members.

8. Would Missy's schema for the organization apt to be more or less detailed than another business consultant whose mother had died from a long-term battle with breast cancer and who attended a similar membership drive for the American Cancer Society?

9. You are working on these exercises. What concept from "making information meaningful" in the chapter is best illustrated by your work on these exercises?

FEEDBACK FOR CLASSROOM EXERCISES

1. Each of the numbers is composed of seven digits. Working memory is capable of holding approximately seven bits of information.

2. Lecture is the simplest form of instruction, so it is less likely to overload teachers' working memories than are more sophisticated forms of instruction. The instructor only has to think about organizing and presenting the content, and the students are typically not disruptive. In addition to organizing and presenting the content, more sophisticated forms of instruction, such as guided discovery, require the teacher to ask questions, monitor students' answers and ask questions based on those answers, and look for inattention or disruptive behavior. These requirements can overload teachers' working memories.

3. Skills, such as questioning, must be automatic, so working memory space is available to monitor the students and the flow of the lesson.

4. They are demonstrating procedural knowledge. They are identifying conditions and taking actions based on the appropriateness of the conditions.

5. The concept is automaticity. You put the garage door down "without thinking about it."

6. These differences most closely relate to working memory. Interconnected schemas become large chunks of information that actually take up less working memory space than do isolated pieces, and automaticity also frees working memory space. Since experts are more effective at saving working memory space, they have working memory available for metacognition.

7. Because of her background knowledge, Missy's perception of the meeting's details was different from the perceptions of the other women.

8. Missy's schema would be more detailed about the abused children's charity than the other consultant. Her schema was based on her study. The other consultant's experiences weren't relevant to the organization.

9. These exercises are intended to put you in an active role in applying the information in the chapter to new situations.

CHAPTER 8: CONSTRUCTING UNDERSTANDING

CHAPTER OVERVIEW

This chapter includes a discussion of constructivism, including different interpretations of constructivism, characteristics common to most views of constructivism, and the suggestions for classroom practice that can be derived from constructivism. The chapter continues with an examination of the role of assessment in constructivist classrooms and a discussion of applications of constructivist views of learning, including guided discovery, inquiry, discussions, and cooperative learning. implications of constructivism for learning and teaching, complete the chapter completes the chapter.

CHAPTER OBJECTIVES

- Identify the essential elements of constructivist views of learning.

- Describe differences between social constructivist and cognitive constructivist perspectives.

- Explain how knowledge construction and learners' cognitive architectures are related.

- Describe classroom applications grounded in knowledge construction frameworks.

TRANSPARENCIES

The transparencies exist in both acetate form and as PowerPoint slides.

T 8.2   The persistence of Suzanne's thinking about balance beams
T 8.3   Characteristics of constructivism (Figure 8.1, p. 283)
T 8.4   Suggestions for classroom practice (Figure 8.2, p. 285)
T 8.5   Using technology to represent content (Figure 8.3, p. 286)
T 8.6   Assessing understanding of balance beams

TRANSPARENCY MASTERS

The transparency masters are included in this manual beginning on page 230.

TM 8.1   Some conclusions from kids
TM 8.2   Constructing understanding about movie ratings
TM 8.3   Constructing understanding of balance beams
TM 8.4   Principles of instruction for applying constructivism in classrooms
TM 8.5   Steps in inquiry instruction
TM 8.6   Characteristics of cooperative learning
TM 8.7   Capitalizing on diversity with cooperative learning

VIDEO EPISODES

Looking Through Classroom Windows Tape 1-Segment 4: "Constructing Understanding: Instructional Applications"
This video lesson illustrates the thinking of fourth graders as they attempt to construct understanding of the principle that makes a beam balance. (This is the chapter's opening case study.)

Looking Through Classroom Windows Tape 1-Segment 5: "Designing Experiments in Seventh Grade"
This video lesson illustrates the thinking of students as they attempt to design and conduct an experiment to measure the influence of length, weight, and angle on the frequency of a simple pendulum. (This is the chapter's closing case study.)

CHAPTER OUTLINE

I.   What is constructivism?
II   Different views of constructivism
III. Characteristics of constructivism
    A.   Learners construct understanding that makes sense to them
    B.   New learning depends on current understanding
    C.   Social interaction facilitates learning
    D.   Meaningful learning occurs in real-world tasks
IV.   Implications of constructivism for teaching
    A.   The teacher's role in knowledge construction
    B.   Suggestions for classroom practice
        1.   Provide a variety of examples and representations of content
            a.   Technology and learning: Using technology to represent content
        2.   Connect content to the real world
        3.   Be skeptical about explanations
        4.   Promote high levels of interaction
            a.   Learning benefits for students
            b.   Instructional benefits for teachers
    C.   Assessment and learning: The role of assessment in constructivist classrooms
V.   Constructivism in classrooms: Instructional Strategies
    A.   Guided discovery
    B.   Inquiry
    C.   Discussion
    D.   Cooperative learning
        1.   Introducing cooperative learning
        2.   Cooperative learning strategies
            a.   Reciprocal questioning
            b.   Scripted cooperation
            c.   Jigsaw II
            d.   Student Teams Achievement Divisions
        3.   Cooperative Learning: A Tool for Capitalizing on Diversity
VI.   Putting constructivism into perspective

PRESENTATION OUTLINE

Teaching suggestions in the outline will be marked with the symbol ■. In most cases, the suggested activities can be done individually and discussed as a whole group, or they can be done in small groups, and the small-group results can be discussed with the whole class. To be consistent with our understanding of knowledge construction, we recommend that you promote as much discussion–both in small groups and with the whole class–as possible.

I.   What is constructivism?
II.   Different views of constructivism
III. Characteristics of constructivism
    A.   Learners construct understanding that makes sense to them
    B.   New learning depends on current understanding
    C.   Social interaction facilitates learning

D. Meaningful learning occurs in real-world tasks

■ *The goal of the suggestions in this section is to help students understand constructivist views of learning.*

1. **Begin your discussion of constructivism by displaying TM 8.1 *"Some Conclusions From Kids."* Beginning with TM 8.1 allows you to accomplish at least three goals:**
    a. **To remind the students that you're beginning your presentation with an attention getter.**
    b. **To show the students some examples that are attractive and funny.**
    c. **To illustrate the process of knowledge construction.**

2. **Then, display TM 8.2 *"Constructing Understanding About Movie Ratings."* Point out that, obviously, the students who made these conclusions developed or "constructed" them on their own; they weren't presented by a teacher. (The examples in TM 8.1 come from 6th graders, and Andrew, in TM 8.2, is a seventh grader).**

3. **Display T 8.3 *"Characteristics of Constructivism"* and ask students which of the characteristics they believe are best illustrated in TM 8.1 and TM 8.2.**

IV. Implications of constructivism for teaching
  A. The teacher's role in knowledge construction
  B. Suggestions for classroom practice
     1. Provide a variety of examples and representations of content
        a. Technology and learning: Using technology to represent content
     2. Connect content to the real world
     3. Be skeptical about explanations
     4. Promote high levels of interaction
        a. Learning benefits for students
        b. Instructional benefits for teachers
  C. Assessment and learning: The role of assessment in constructivist classrooms

■ *The goal of the suggestions in this section is to help students understand the implications of constructivist views of learning for teaching.*

1. **Show the video episode *"Constructing Understanding: Instructional Applications"* from *Looking Through Classroom Windows* Tape 1-Segment 4. This segment is directly integrated with the chapter content.**

2. **After the students have seen the video segment, display TM 8.3 *"Constructing Understanding of Balance Beams,"* and have the students respond to the questions. Discuss their responses (but do not display the feedback).**

3. **As you discuss their responses, display T 8.1 *"Suzanne's Thinking About Balance Beams,"* and T 8.2 *"The Persistence of Suzanne's Thinking About Balance Beams."* They concretely illustrate Suzanne's thinking during the lesson and interview. Also display T 8.4 *"Suggestions for Classroom Practice,"* and have the students use this information in their discussion.**

4. **Display the feedback in TM 8.3 *"Constructing Understanding of Balance Beams."* (Some of the students' views might be different from those presented on the feedback. If so, you can use this as an example of people constructing understanding that makes sense to them.)**

5. Display T 8.6 *"Assessing Understanding of Balance Beams."* It illustrates how understand of the balance beam principle could be systematically assessed.

V. Constructivism in classrooms: Instructional Strategies
   A. Guided discovery
   B. Inquiry
   C. Discussion
   D. Cooperative learning
      1. Introducing cooperative learning
      2. Cooperative learning strategies
         a. Reciprocal questioning
         b. Scripted cooperation
         c. Jigsaw II
         d. Student Teams Achievement Divisions
      3. Cooperative Learning: A Tool for Capitalizing on Diversity

■ *The goal of the suggestions in this section is to help students understand the principles that guide teachers as they plan and conduct learning activities based on constructivist views of learning.*
1. Display TM 8.4 *"Principles of Instruction for Applying Constructivism in Classrooms."* Remind them that these principles apply to each of the instructional strategies in this section.

2. Have the students identify the principles in the case studies that illustrate guided discovery (page 293 of the text), inquiry (page 295), and discussions (page 297). (You may want to display TM 8.5 *"Steps in Inquiry Instruction"* as a review for the students."

3. Display TM 8.6 *"Characteristics of Cooperative Learning."* Have the students describe how these characteristics are embedded in each of the cooperative learning strategies discussed in the chapter.

4. Display TM 8.7 *"Capitalizing on Diversity With Cooperative Learning,"* to demonstrate how cooperative learning can be a tool for accommodating diversity. Have the students describe how Maria Sanchez (in the case study beginning on page 302) capitalized on the suggestions in TM 8.7.

VI. Putting constructivism into perspective

■ *To help students understand the limitations of constructivism:*
1. Point out that while evidence overwhelmingly indicates that learners do indeed construct understanding, not all forms of understanding are equally good, and a reality independent of individual understanding exists. If this weren't true, teachers would have little role in education.

2. Also point out that the fact that learners construct their own understanding makes the teacher's job more difficult, not easier. As they saw with the *Constructing Understanding* segment of the "Concepts in Classrooms" video, simply explaining often doesn't work very well, which makes guiding learners' understanding more demanding and sophisticated.

■ *To summarize the chapter:*
1. Point out the applications of constructivism that are being employed in your class. Some examples of applications could be:

- You do a considerable amount of groupwork followed by discussion of the groups' findings. This is an application of social interaction as a factor that facilitates learning.
- As the students discuss the topics, complete the exercises, take quizzes, and receive feedback, they are in the process of constructing understanding.
- You are making an effort to link each topic to topics that you have already studied. This capitalizes on the role of background knowledge in learning.
- You link the topics you study to classrooms through the case studies, video episodes, applications, and examples. Since classroom application is a major theme of the class, these are authentic learning tasks.

2. Point out that you are attempting to use your class as a model of instruction based on constructivist views of learning.

Video: You might also want to show the video segment "Designing Experiments in Seventh Grade," which further illustrates how problematic students' knowledge constructions can be.

DISCUSSION STARTERS

1. What are some important similarities and differences between information processing and constructivism?

2. If teachers lecture, do learners still construct their own understanding? Why or why not?

3. If teachers are basing their instruction on constructivist views of learning, will they have their students practice basic skills to automaticity? Why or why not?

4. Some educational psychologists suggest that constructivism is more a principle than a theory. Explain why you either agree or disagree with that assertion.

5. Do teachers have a more important or a less important role when conducting learner-centered instruction than when conducting teacher-centered instruction?

6. Is assessment a more or less important for learner-centered instruction compared to teacher-centered instruction?

7. Teachers often have goals for which real-world applications are not immediately apparent. If they are basing their instruction on constructivist views of learning, should they avoid teaching those topics? Why or why not?

8. To what extent to learners' beliefs influence their constructions of understanding? Explain.

BACKGROUND READINGS

Bransford, J., Brown, A., & Cocking, R. (Eds.). (2000). *How people learn: Brain, mind, experience, and school.* Washington, DC: National Academy Press. This comprehensive book discusses the implications that constructivist views of learning have for planning, instruction, and assessment.

Bruning, R., Schraw, G., & Ronning, R. (1999). *Cognitive psychology and instruction* (3rd ed.). Englewood Cliffs, NJ: Prentice Hall. This book provides in-depth coverage of constructivism, including different views of constructivism and their implications for instruction.

Cassady, J. (1999, April). *The effects of examples as elaboration in text on memory and learning.* Paper presented at the annual meeting of the American Educational Research Association, Montreal. This paper describes the role of examples in the process of knowledge construction.

Fosnot, C. T. (Ed.) (1996). *Constructivism: Theory, perspectives, and practice.* New York: Teachers College Press. This edited book provides excellent perspectives on different facets of constructivism.

Greeno, J., Collins, A., & Resnick, L. (1996). Cognition and learning. In D. Berliner & R. Calfee (Eds.), *Handbook of Educational Psychology* (pp. 15-46). New York: Macmillan. This chapter examines learning, motivation and transfer from behaviorist, cognitive, and situative/sociohistoric views. It includes discussions of assessment and creating classroom environments that facilitate learning.

Mayer, R. (2002). The promise of educational psychology, Volume II: Teaching for meaningful learning. Upper Saddle River, NJ: Prentice Hall. This book by a well-known author discusses a variety of topics including applications of constructivist views of learning, such as guided discovery.

Nuthall, G. (2001, April). *Student experience and the learning process: Developing an evidence based theory of classroom learning.* Paper presented at the annual meeting of the American Educational Research Association, Seattle. This paper describes the contribution of constructivism to a comprehensive view of cognitive learning theory.

Spivey, N. N. (1997). *The constructivist metaphor: Reading, writing, and the making of meaning.* San Diego: Academic Press. Relates constructivism to the language arts.

FEEDBACK FOR CONSTRUCTED RESPONSE AND DOCUMENT-BASED ANALYSIS QUESTIONS

Constructed Response Items

1. Describe the extent to which the characteristics of constructivism were demonstrated in Scott's lesson.
   The characteristics of constructivism are:
   a. *Learners construct understanding that makes sense to them. Unfortunately, this characteristic also results in misconceptions, as we saw when the students thought they were solving the problem by changing a number variables at one a time.*
   b. *New learning depends on current understanding. Again, the students in the focal group had background knowledge, but it wasn't always accurate. For example, they knew that they had to manipulate variables, but didn't understand that these had to be changed systematically, varying only one at a time.*
   c. *Social interaction facilitates learning. Social interaction occurred in the lesson in two forms. Scott's questions helped them reconsider their procedures, and talking to each other provided different perspectives on ways to identify and isolate key variables.*
   d. *Meaningful learning occurs within real-world tasks. This was probably one of the strongest aspects of Scott's lesson from a constructivist perspective. By actually handling the equipment, students could see how the abstract variables they were considering related to the real world.*

2. Assess how effectively Scott implemented the "Suggestions for Classroom Practice" described in the section that discussed the implications of constructivism for teaching.
   Let's consider these suggestions one at a time, starting with the strengths of the lesson. One of the suggestions was to "Promote high levels of interaction." Scott did this effectively through his groupwork, which allowed students to dialogue about the process. A second suggestion is to "Be skeptical about the effectiveness of explanations." Scott's lesson was also strong here. He didn't lecture about controlling variables; instead, he provided experiences and asked questions, guiding students in their knowledge

135

construction. Additional suggestions are: "Connect content to the real world: and "Provide learners with a variety of examples and representations of content." While Scott presented students with a concrete, hands-on task, it is likely that they will need additional practice controlling variables with other experiments to really understand the process.

3. Which of the instructional strategies did Scott most nearly employ in his lesson. Identify each of the parts of the strategy.

   Inquiry is a strategy in which learners gather facts and observations, and use them to investigate real-world problems. Inquiry involves five steps:
   a. *Identify a question or problem. This occurred at the beginning of the lesson when Scott asked what factors influenced the period of a pendulum.*
   b. *Form hypotheses. Students did this in their small groups when they identified length, weight, and angle and release as possible variables.*
   c. *Gather data to test hypotheses. This occurred when students used the string and paper clips to investigate the different variables.*
   d. *Draw conclusions from data. Scott assisted with this both through his questions to the small group and to the whole class.*
   e. *Generalize on the basis of conclusions. Time ran out so Scott wasn't able to encourage the class to consider generalizations to follow when students encountered a similar problem. This was his real goal for the lesson.*

4. Assess the effectiveness of Scott's lesson for learners with diverse backgrounds.

   Groupwork provides several positives for students with diverse backgrounds. It provides opportunities for students from different backgrounds to learn to work together. While not evident from the written description, the focal group consisted of an Asian American, African American, a Caucasian, and a recent immigrant from Russia. Scott's task provided an opportunity for these students to positively work together on a common problem and to learn about each other while working together on a productive task. In addition , his learning task provided concrete experiences for students to use in trying to figure out how to control variables.

Document-Based Analysis

In the Chapter 4 closing case study you saw that Teri Hall wanted her 8th graders students to understand the concept mercantilism, which she defined as: A strategy countries used to make money in colonial times, which included using colonies to produce raw materials that they sent back to the mother country, selling finished products back to the colonies, and using the mother countries' ships to transport both the raw materials and finished products. She then used the following vignettes as examples.

In the mid 1600's the American colonists were encouraged to grow tobacco, since it wasn't grown in England. The colonists wanted to sell it to France and other countries but were told no. In return the colonists were allowed to import textiles from England, but were forbidden from making their own. All the materials were carried on British ships.

Early French colonists in the New World were avid fur trappers and traders. They got in trouble with the French monarchy, however, when they attempted to make fur garments and sell them to Spain, England and others. They were told that the produced garments would be sent to them from Paris instead. The monarchy also told them that traps and weapons would be made in France and sent to them as well. Jean Forjea complied with the monarchy's wishes but was fined when he hired a Dutch ship to carry some of the furs back to Nice.

Using the suggestions in the chapter, assess the effectiveness of Teri's vignettes for providing background knowledge for her 8th graders. Describe both strengths and weaknesses of the vignettes she used.

From a constructivist perspective, the value of vignettes such as these lies in their ability to provide students with raw materials for knowledge construction. The strengths of Teri's vignettes were that they clearly illustrated the concept of mercantilism, providing two different examples of mercantilism in action. In addition to having the essential characteristics of the concept embedded in them, the vignettes also tended to be authentic, because of the use of stories of actual people.

CLASSROOM EXERCISES

1. Teachers commonly believe that children must memorize basic math facts, such as 7 x 8 = 56, and 9 x 6 = 54. Assume that the teachers' beliefs are valid. Which theory–information processing or constructivism–better explains this assertion? Explain.

2. You are in a class where the teacher lectures virtually all the time. Does this imply that you *do not* construct understanding of the ideas being presented? Explain why it does or does not.

3. What is meant by the term *cognitive architecture*? Where in our cognitive architectures is understanding constructed? Explain.

4. Tim, a fourth-grader, concludes that we're closer to the sun in the summer than we are in the winter. When asked to explain why he thinks so, he says, "When I stand close to the fireplace, I feel warm, and when I stand far away, I feel cooler." Which two characteristics of constructivism are illustrated by Tim's reasoning? Explain.

5. Offer one important reason why guided discovery is considered to be more nearly grounded in constructivist views of learning than is lecture.

6. Which of the following *least* illustrates a learning activity based on constructivist views of learning? Describe what could be done to more nearly apply principles of instruction that guide teachers as they plan and conduct instruction based on constructivist views of learning.
   a.   Geography students use longitude and latitude to describe how to tell a friend to find a remote camping location in the mountains.
   b.   Math students look at manufacturing costs and the prices marked on a series of soap products to determine the percentage of profit.
   c.   Science students explain why a can of pork and beans explodes--if a hole isn't poked in the can--when placed in a campfire.
   d.   Language arts students rewrite a series of sentences, each of which contains grammatical errors.

Explain your thinking.

Use the following vignette for exercises 7 and 8.

Four teachers want their students to understand the rule saying that non-essential clauses in sentences are set off by commas.

   Janet Reeve displays six sentences on the overhead, three of which contain essential clauses and three others that contain non-essential clauses. She points out the clauses, correctly punctuates them, and explains why they are punctuated in this way. She then gives the students several sentences for practice, directing them to correctly punctuate the clauses in the sentences.
   Javier Sanchez presents a paragraph which contains three underlined essential clauses and three other underlined non-essential clauses, each punctuated correctly. The class discusses the common features of the underlined and italicized clauses, and, with Javier's guidance they arrive at a rule for punctuating essential and non-essential clauses. Javier then directs the students to write a paragraph containing at least three examples of essential clauses and three other examples of non-essential clauses, all punctuated correctly.
   Steve Smith presents several sentences which contain essential clauses and other sentences that contain non-essential clauses. He directs the students to look for clauses in the sentences that have commas around them, and he guides them to conclude that the clauses set off by commas are not essential, whereas those that don't have commas around them are essential. He then gives the students some additional sentences to punctuate correctly.

Susan Welna presents a passage in which several examples of essential and non-essential clauses are embedded. She asks the students to describe the passages, and after they have made several observations, she punctuates the sentences properly, explaining the rule in the process.

7. Which teacher in the vignette *most* nearly based his or her learning activity on the principles of instruction that guide teachers as they plan and conduct instruction based on constructivist views of learning? Explain.

8. Which teacher in the vignette *least* nearly based his or her learning activity on the principles of instruction that guide teachers as they plan and conduct instruction based on constructivist views of learning? Explain.

FEEDBACK FOR CLASSROOM EXERCISES

1. Information processing better explains this assertion. The memorized facts are automatic, so they don't use working memory space. Constructivism doesn't address this issue.

2. It does not imply that you are not constructing understanding. However, constructing understanding on the basis of a lecture is more difficult than constructing understanding based on effective representations of content and social interaction.

3. *Cognitive architecture* refers to our information processing system–sensory memory, working memory, long-term memory, and the cognitive processes that move information from one memory store to another. The process of constructing understanding occurs in working memory, and it depends on our attention, perception, and existing background knowledge.

4. The characteristics "Learners construct understanding that makes sense to them" and "New learning depends on current understanding" are both illustrated in Tim's thinking. To him, it made sense that we're closer to the sun in summer, since he got warmer when he got closer to the fireplace. And, his experience with fireplaces was the background knowledge he used to construct his conclusion.

5. The primary reason guided discovery is views as more nearly grounded in constructivist views of learning is the emphasis on social interaction. The importance of social interaction is a characteristic of constructivism, and "Promote high levels of interaction" is one of the instructional principles that guide teachers in their attempts to base instruction on constructivism. In addition, as students describe their thinking during guided discovery lessons, teachers can informally assess their current levels of understanding, and assessment is an essential part of instruction based on constructivism.

6. Choice d least illustrates a learning activity based on constructivist views of learning. It is the least "real world" of the tasks. It could be more nearly based on constructivism if the grammatical errors were first embedded in the real-world context of a written passage instead of isolated sentences. Then, students could discuss the parts of the passage that were punctuated correctly and other parts that were not, so social interaction would be incorporated, and finally students should again write passages rather than isolated sentences.

7. Javier Sanchez most nearly based his learning activity on the principles of instruction that guide teachers as they plan and conduct instruction based on constructivist views of learning. First, Javier presented the rules in the context of a paragraph, which is more nearly connected to the real world than presenting the rules in isolated sentences. Second, he capitalized on social interaction by having the class discuss the common features of the underlined and italicized clauses, and, he further capitalized on social interaction by guiding the students to the rule for punctuating essential and non-essential clauses. Finally, he further connected his content to the real world by having the students write a paragraph containing at least three examples of essential clauses and three other examples of non-essential clauses, all punctuated correctly.

8. Janet Reeve least nearly based her learning activity on the principles of instruction that guide teachers as they plan and conduct instruction based on constructivist views of learning. First, Janet illustrated the rule in the form of sentences which is less connected to the real world than embedding the rule in the context of a passage would have been. Then, she did not capitalize on social interaction when she pointed out the clauses, correctly punctuated them, and explained why they were punctuated in this way. Finally, she again failed to connect her content to the real world by giving the students sentences for practice.

CHAPTER 9: COMPLEX COGNITIVE PROCESSES

CHAPTER OVERVIEW

Our analysis of cognitive learning continues in this chapter with a focus on complex cognitive processes. The chapter includes a discussion of concept learning, focusing on the role that examples, nonexamples, prototypes and play in learning concepts. Problem solving follows in the second section of the chapter, with the discussion examining a general problem solving strategy, expert-novice differences in problem solving ability, and what teachers can do to help students become better problem solvers.

The third section of the chapter examines the strategic learner with emphasis on basic and complex study strategies, together with critical thinking. The chapter closes with a discussion of transfer, including positive and negative transfer, general and specific transfer, and factors that influence transfer of learning.

CHAPTER OBJECTIVES

- Explain the application of concept learning to classroom activities.

- Apply problem-solving strategies to well-defined and ill-defined problems.

- Explain how critical thinking can be used in classroom learning activities.

- Describe how study strategies can be used to increase student learning.

- Discuss ways of increasing transfer of learning.

TRANSPARENCIES

The transparencies exist in both acetate form and as PowerPoint slides.

T 9.1	Theories of concept learning
T 9.2	First learner's network for the concept *novel* (Figure 9.3, p. 316)
T 9.3	Second learner's network for the concept *novel* (Figure 9.4, p. 317)
T 9.4	A general problem solving model (Figure 9.5, p. 321)
T 9.5	Expert-novice differences in problem solving ability
T 9.6	Helping learners become better problem solvers
T 9.7	Characteristics of effective strategy users
T 9.8	Elements of critical thinking (Figure 9.6, p. 335)
T 9.9	Factors affecting the transfer of learning

TRANSPARENCY MASTERS

The transparency masters are included in this manual beginning on page 230.

TM 9.1	Concepts from educational psychology
TM 9.2	Commonly held misconceptions
TM 9.3	Principles of instruction for promoting concept learning
TM 9.4	Cases that are and are not problems
TM 9.5	The druggist's problem
TM 9.6	Principles of instruction for developing problem solving ability
TM 9.5	Utilizing PQ4R with this text
TM 9.6	Principles of instruction for developing strategic learning

VIDEOS

Looking Through Classroom Windows Tape 1-Segment 6: "Finding Area in Elementary Math."
This video lesson illustrates the thinking of fifth graders as they deal with the problem of how much carpeting they need to cover an irregularly shaped portion of their classroom. In the episode we see problem-solving processes illustrated concretely. (It is the opening case study of the chapter.)

Looking Through Classroom Windows Tape 2-Segment 1: "Graphing in Second Grade Math."
This video lesson illustrates a teacher attempting to use real-world experiences to help her second graders understand bar graphs. The lesson includes several applications at learning centers around the classroom.. (It is the closing case study of the chapter.)

Concepts in Classrooms Tape 1–Segment 5: "Improving Transfer: Applications in Classrooms."
This video segment takes excerpts from the fifth grade lesson on finding area and a seventh grade lesson on designing experiments. The segment concretely demonstrates that transfer is often problematic, and students have difficulty transferring problem solving skills, even when the target problem is very similar to the initial problem.

CHAPTER OUTLINE

I. Concept learning
    A. Concepts: Categories that simplify the world
    B. Theories of concept learning
    C. Examples: The key to learning and teaching concepts
    D. Concept mapping: Embedding concepts in complex schemas
    E. Concept learning: Misconceptions and conceptual change
    F. Learning and teaching concepts: Instructional strategies
II. Problem solving
    A. Well-defined and ill-defined problems
    B. A problem-solving model
        1. Identifying the problem
        2. Representing the problem
        3. Selecting a strategy
            a. Algorithms
            b. Hueristics
        4. Implementing the strategy
        5. Evaluating the results
    C. Expert-novice differences in problem solving ability
        1. Developing expertise: The role of deliberate practice
    D. Helping learners become better problem solvers
        1. Present problems in real-world contexts
        2. Capitalize on social interaction
        3. Provide scaffolding for novice problem solvers
            a. Cognitive apprenticeship
            b. Analyzing worked examples
        5. Teach general problem-solving strategies
    E. Using technology to improve problem-solving ability
    F. Problem-based learning
III. The strategic learner
    A. Metacognition: The foundation of strategic learning
        1. Broad background knowledge
        2. A repertoire of strategies
    B. Study strategies

       1.   Basic study skills
       2.   Comprehension monitoring
          a.   Summarizing
          b.   Elaborative-questioning
          c.   PQ4R

  C. Developing strategic learning in students: Instructional strategies
  D. Critical thinking
       1.   Component skills
       3.   Domain-specific knowledge
       4.   Metacognition
       5.   Motivational

IV. Transfer of learning
  A. General and specific transfer
  B. Factors affecting the transfer of learning
       1.   Similarity between the two learning situations
       2.   Depth of original understanding
       3.   Quality of learning experiences
       4.   Context for learning experiences
          a.   Situated learning
       5.   Variety of learning contexts and experiences
       6.   Emphasis on metacognition
  C. Assessment and learning: The role of assessment in transfer

PRESENTATION OUTLINE

Teaching suggestions in the outline will be marked with the symbol ■. In most cases, the suggested activities can be done individually and discussed as a whole group, or they can be done in small groups, and the small-group results can be discussed with the whole class. To be consistent with our understanding of knowledge construction, we recommend that you promote as much discussion–both in small groups and with the whole class–as possible.

I. Concept learning
  A. Concepts: Categories that simplify the world
  B. Theories of concept learning
  C. Examples: The key to learning and teaching concepts
  D. Concept mapping: Embedding concepts in complex schemas

■ *The goal in the following suggestion is to introduce your students to concepts and concept learning.*

  1.   **Tell the students that what you're about to do may seem a little silly but to simply pay attention to what you're doing.**

  2.   **Walk over to the wall and push on it. Ask the students what you're doing. Prompt them to simply say that you're *pushing* on the wall. Then pull on the chalkboard tray, or a cabinet or some other object. Again prompt them to say that you're *pulling*. Ask them if they know what a push or a pull is called. Someone is likely to say "force." (If they don't, simply tell them that any push or pull is called a force.)**

  3.   **Now, have a student come and sit on a chair in front of the room, and pull the student and the chair across the front of the room.**

  4.   **Ask the class what you're doing and prompt them to say that you're exerting a force**

(pulling). Ask them what is different about the force you're exerting now and the force you exerted when you pulled on the chalkboard tray (or whatever you pulled on). Prompt them to say that movement was involved.

5. Ask them if they know what the combination of force and movement is called. (If they don't know, simply tell them)

6. Ask them what they learned, and prompt them to say "concepts". Display TM 9.1 *"Concept From Educational Psychology"* for additional examples of concepts from educational psychology that they've studied to this point.

7. Point out that pushing on the wall and pulling the student across the room were attention getters, which relate to information processing in Chapter 7.

8. Ask the students to identify the characteristics of *force* and *work*.

9. Display T 9.1 *"Theories of Concept Learning"* and ask the students which theory of concept learning: rule-driven, prototype, or exemplar best explains how they learned the concepts *force* and *work*. Point out that the concepts have very well-defined characteristics, so rule-driven theories provide an effective explanation.

10. Have the students offer cases of concepts best explained by rule-driven, prototype, and exemplar theories. Have them explain why they chose the cases they did. Lead them to conclude that prototype and exemplar theories best explain concepts that don't have specific and well-defined characteristics.

11. Continue the discussion by asking the students how they learned the concepts *force* and *work* (or would have learned the concepts if the concepts weren't already familiar to them). Prompt them to recognize that you pushing on the wall and pulling on the tray were *examples* of the concept *force* and you pulling the student across the room was an example of the concept *work*.

12. Have them demonstrate *force* at their desks (such as pushing down on the desk). Have them demonstrate *work* (such as sliding a book across their desks).

13. Ask them how "easy" it was for them to learn the concepts *force* and *work* compared to concepts such as *square* and *socialism*. They will see that *force, work,* and *square* are all much easier to learn than is *socialism*. Ask them why. They should note that *force, work,* and *square* are easy to learn because they have only a few characteristics, and the characteristics are tangible or observable, whereas the concept *socialism* has abstract characteristics and there isn't universal agreement on what the characteristics are. Point out that prototype theories probably better explain how we learn *socialism* than do rule-driven theories.

14. Ask the students how the ease of learning concepts relates to the developmental level of the students. They will see that kindergartners, for example, understand concepts, such as *square*, whereas concepts like *socialism* are rarely taught before the middle or junior high school years, and even then students' understandings of them are often uncertain.

■ *To help the students understand concept mapping:*

1. Display T 9.2 *"First learner's network for the concept* novel*"* and T 9.3 *"Second learner's network for the concept* novel*."* Then, have them construct a concept map of content in their subject matter area or at their level.

E. Concept learning: Misconceptions and conceptual change
F. Learning and teaching concepts: Instructional strategies

■ *The suggestions in this section are intended to help your students understand that learners acquire many misconceptions in their learning, and to reinforce the fact that learner background knowledge influences the understandings they construct.*

1. Push again on the wall. Ask the students if you're doing any work. In spite of the activity you've just completed, a number of them are likely to say "yes." Ask them why they responded as they did.

2. Point out that this experience illustrates that many learners have misconceptions about the concepts they study.

3. Display TM 9.2 *"Commonly Held Misconceptions"* which contains examples of misconceptions.

4. Ask the students to identify the key concept in each of the statements. Remind them that the concept or concepts may not be stated explicitly. The key concepts in each case are:
   1. The sun
   2. Living things
   3. Green plants
   4. Northern hemisphere
   5. Europe
   6. Living things
   7. Movement
   8. The Great Lakes
   9. Negative reinforcement
   10. Frogs
   11. Whales
   12. Spiders
   They are likely to be somewhat uncertain about the concepts and argue that #5 is as much about the United States as it is about Europe. Point out that in each case the statement provides information about characteristics learners attribute to the concept (mistakenly). As another example, in concluding that any movement requires a force, they're mistakenly attaching force as a characteristic of movement.

5. Ask which theory of learning–behaviorism, social cognitive theory, information processing, or constructivism–best explains why misconceptions exist. Lead them to conclude that the fact that learners construct understanding, rather than record it, help us understand why misconceptions about the world exist. Learners construct understanding in an effort to make the world make sense, and their constructions are sensible to them.

6. Ask them how they would try to eliminate the misconceptions in each case. During the discussion remind them that research indicates that misconceptions must be directly confronted to be eliminated. Ask them how they might directly confront some of the misconceptions. (In a case of misconceptions about the differences between insects and

145

spiders, a simple example might be to bring in an insect and a spider to class and point out that the spider has eight legs, but the insect has only six.)

7.   Have the students identify some additional topics and describe specifically how they would represent the topics to accommodate differences in students' background experiences.

8.   Display TM 9.3 *"Principles of Instruction for Promoting Concept Learning."* Have the students identify Have the students identify where Carol Lopez (in the case study beginning on page 318) applied each of the principles in her teaching.

II.   Problem solving
    A.   Well-defined and ill-defined problems

> **Video:** You might want to introduce this section of the chapter by showing the video lesson "Finding Area in Elementary Math" at this point in your discussion of the chapter.

■ *The goal of the suggestions in this section is to help your students understand the characteristics of problem solving and what teachers can do to help learners become better problem solvers.*

1.   Introduce this section by displaying TM 9.4 *"Cases That Are and Are Not Problems,"* which shows 6 brief incidents. Have the students identify the similarities and differences in the incidents.

2.   Lead the students to conclude that examples 2, 3, 4, and 5 are problems, but that 1 and 6 are not problems. There is virtually no uncertainty about what to do about the flour, for example. You simply run to the store. The same is true for the situation in number 6. You simply write a check or go to an automated banking machine.

Examples 2 and 5 are well defined problems. The goal stated is clear (getting to your friends' house at the desired time, and getting Jerome to bring his book to class).

Examples 3 and 4 illustrate ill-defined problems. The goal state isn't clear in either one, and no generally agreed upon strategy exists for moving toward a goal state.

3.   In discussing the problems point out that the line between well-defined and ill-defined problems can sometimes be blurred. (For example, wanting to know *why* Jerome consistently fails to bring his book to class is not well defined.) Also note that the existence of problems isn't cut and dried; they depend on the person and the situation. For instance, running out of flour might be a problem if it is late at night and the stores are closed, or the person is a guest from out of town and doesn't know there is a store nearby.

    B.   A problem-solving model
        1.   Identifying the problem

■ *The purpose of the suggestions in this section is to help your students understand a general problem solving strategy.*

1.   Introduce this section by displaying T 9.4 *"A General Problem-Solving Model."* Tell the students to keep the general strategy in mind as you move through the steps in the process.

2. To illustrate this part of the problem solving process, again display TM 9.4 *"Cases That Are and Are Not Problems"* and focus on Example 3. Have the students identify the problem and report to the whole class. The "problems" they identify will vary, which will help them understand that identifying problems is often difficult.

3. To further illustrate the process of identifying problems as well as the role that domain-specific knowledge plays, display TM 9.5 *"The Druggists' Problem,"* and have the students identify the problem and suggest a solution. Even in this situation some of the students may have difficulty in identifying the problem, and many will lack the domain-specific knowledge in algebra needed to solve the problem.

    Since some or your students might voice frustration, point out that their lack of experience in problem finding is the reason they have difficulty. Ask them how much experience they've had in identifying problems. Most will say very little, and acknowledging this factor should alleviate their frustration.

    The bottom of TM 9.5 *"The Druggist's Problem"* defines the problem and provides an equation that can be used to solve the problem.

2. Representing the problem
3. Selecting a strategy
    1. Algorithms
    2. Heuristics

    ■ *The suggestions in this section are designed to help your students understand how problems can be represented and how algorithms and heuristics are used.*
    1. Represent the druggist's problem with a drawing of a beaker or graduated cylinder that illustrates the original 15% solution and another representing the 6% solution. Seeing the visual representation often helps learners work toward a solution.

    2. The equation that appears at the bottom of TM 9.5 *"The Druggist's Problem"* is an algorithm. It is a standard way of solving percent mixture problems.

    3. Ask the students to identify other examples of algorithms. Many exist, such as the algorithms for adding, subtracting, multiplying, and dividing numbers, simplifying algebraic expressions and many others.

    4. Ask the students to what other form of content algorithms relate. (They are actually rules. The fact that they're arbitrary is illustrated by the fact that some children spontaneously create their own algorithms for addition and subtraction, for example.)

4. Implementing the strategy
5. Evaluating the results

    ■ *The suggestions in this section are designed to help your students see how strategies are implemented and results are examined.*
    1. To illustrate the process of evaluating results, have the students estimate the number of grams of the 6% solution that should be added to create the 10% solution. Ask them

how many grams would seem to make sense. Do the same thing with Example 2 in TM 9.4 *"Cases That Are and Are Not Problems."* Point out that estimating and then checking answers against the estimate is a powerful strategy for evaluating results in math.

    2.   Ask the students how they might evaluate the results in the case of an ill-defined problem, such as the curriculum evaluation problem in TM 9.4 or the problem with your old car (Example 4 in TM 9.4).

C.   Expert-novice differences in problem solving ability
    1.   Developing expertise: The role of deliberate practice
    2.   Acquiring expertise: The importance of motivation

    ■ *The suggestions in this section are intended to help your students understand differences between experts and novices in their problem-solving abilities.*
    1.   To begin this section display T 9.5 *"Expert-Novice Differences in Problem Solving Ability."* Ask the students what theme they see illustrated in the descriptions of expert-novice differences.

    2.   The two most important factors are domain-specific knowledge and experience. You can point out that experts solve problems quickly, for example, because they've seen similar problems in the past, which allows them to use "Drawing Analogies" as a strategy. With experience they also acquire the disposition to evaluate their results, i.e., their metacognitive abilities improve. This discussion can then lead to the next section.

    3.   Pose the question, "How do learners acquire the domain-specific knowledge and experience needed to acquire expertise?" Deliberate practice is the primary way.

    4.   Point out that your approach to teaching the class is designed to provide them with the practice they need to acquire expertise. Offer examples of where you provide feedback, where you attempt to link what you're studying to topics you've already covered (to take existing knowledge into account), why you quiz frequently and discuss the results (to provide knowledge of results and feedback), and why you have them involved in the group problem-solving activities that you present.

D.   Helping learners become better problem solvers: Instructional strategies
    1.   Present problems in meaningful contexts
    2.   Capitalize on social interaction
    3.   Provide scaffolding for novice problem solvers
        a.   Cognitive apprenticeship
        b.   Analyzing worked examples
    4.   Teach general problem solving strategies
E.   Technology and learning: Using technology to improve problem-solving ability
F.   Problem-based learning

    ■ *The suggestions in this section are designed to help your students understand how they can help learners become better problem solvers.*
    1.   Display TM 9.6. *"Principles of Instruction for Promoting Problem Solving Ability."* Have them identify where Laura Hunter (in case study on page 324) applied each of the principles in her work with her students.

2. **Point out that the *"The Druggist's Problem"* (TM 9.5) also illustrates the use of worked examples.**

3. **Point out that Laura Hunter's lessons are examples of problem-based learning.**

> **Video:** You might want to summarize this section of the chapter by showing the video lesson "Graphing in Second Grade Math." Constructed response questions at the end of the chapter encourage further analysis of the lesson.

III. The Strategic Learner
    A. Metacognition: The foundation of strategic learning
        1. Broad background knowledge
        2. A repertoire of strategies

> ■ *The suggestions in this section are designed to help your students understand the characteristics of effective strategy users.*
1. **Give your students the following task:**
    1. **Have them identify as many strategies as they can think of that they use in their own study. Emphasize that the strategies they offer must be ones they actually use.**
    2. **Have them identify how many different strategies are discussed.**
    3. **Have them describe differences in the strategies they use in class compared to the strategies they use when studying for tests and quizzes.**
    4. **Ask them if they ever think about the strategies they use and how effective the strategies are. Ask them to describe specifically how they analyze the effectiveness of their strategies**

2. **Have them report their results, and discuss them with the class.**

3. **Display T 9.7 *"Characteristics of Effective Strategy Users,"* and relate the information on it to what the groups report.**

    B. Study strategies
        1. Basic study skills
        2. Comprehension monitoring
            a. Summarizing
            b. Elaborative Questioning
            c. PQ4R
        3. Developing strategic learning in students: Instructional strategies

> ■ *The suggestions in this section are designed to help your students understand both basic study skills and sophisticated comprehension monitoring abilities.*
1. **Introduce the information in this section by having the students again think about the strategies they use.**

2. **Relate effective and ineffective study skills to the concept of *activity* from Chapter 7. For example, many students highlight "passively," highlighting entire sections of the text and avoiding the decision about what is most important to highlight. Making a**

decision puts them in a more "active" role. Point out that even if they make an incorrect decision, the fact that they've thought about it will allow them to correct it based on class discussions or further reading. If they haven't thought about it however, they won't know. In any case, being active results in more meaningful learning.

3.   Assign the students a section of the chapter (or another chapter), have them prepare some summaries of the sections and "self questions" related to the sections. (You might want the students to prepare the self questions and summaries on transparencies to allow them to be displayed.) Have some of the students display their results and discuss them with the class to identify the characteristics of effective self-questions and summaries.

4.   Have the students work for a few minutes to identify the way this text capitalizes on PQ4R. Then display TM 9.7 *"Utilizing PQ4R With This Text."* The way the strategy can be applied to this text is outlined at the bottom of TM 9.7.

5.   Display TM 9.8 *"Principles of Instruction for Developing Strategic Learning."* Have them identify where Donna Evans (in the case study on page 333) applied each of the principles in her teaching.

D.   Critical thinking
   1.   Component skills
   2.   Domain-specific knowledge
   3.   Metacognition
   4.   Motivation

■ *The suggestions in this section are designed to help your students understand what "critical thinking" means and what teachers can do to promote it in their learners.*
   1.   Display T 9.8 *"Elements of Critical Thinking,"* which identifies *component skills, domain-specific knowledge, metacognition* and *motivation* as the elements of thinking.

   2.   Have the class identify the component skills they used when you conducted the activity with the concepts *force* and *work*, which was used to introduce the chapter.

   3.   Ask the students to identify other ways in which you've emphasized critical thinking in your instruction. Also, ask them what forms of metacognition you've promoted.

   4.   Have the students identify one or more topics and describe how they might teach the topic to maximize the emphasis on critical thinking. Have them present their ideas, and discuss the ideas with the class.

IV.   Transfer of learning
   A.   General and specific transfer
   B.   Factors affecting the transfer of learning
      1.   Similarity between learning situations
      2.   Depth of original understanding
      3.   Quality of learning experiences
      4.   Context for learning experiences
         a.   Situated learning
      5.   Variety of learning contexts and experiences

6. Emphasis on metacognition
C. Assessment and learning: The role of assessment in transfer

■ *The suggestions in this section of the chapter are designed to help your students understand what is meant by "transfer" and what can be done to promote it.*

1. T 9.9, *"Factors Affecting the Transfer of Learning"*, identifies and illustrates the different factors affecting transfer. Begin this section by displaying T 9.9 and then follow with the activities described in the sections below.

2. Have the students assess the extent to which the activity you did with *force* and *work* promoted transfer. Have them specifically consider *variety* of examples, *quality* of examples, and *context* for examples in their assessment of the activity.

3. After discussing the activity with *force* and *work*, have the students identify topics and decide how they will represent the topics to make the likelihood of transfer the greatest. Have the students present their ideas, and discuss them as a whole class.

> **Video:** You might want to summarize this section of the chapter by showing the video segment "Improving Transfer: Applications in Classrooms," which illustrates how problematic transfer can be.

DISCUSSION STARTERS

1. Which of the different kinds of cognitive learning–concept learning, problem solving, or cognitive strategies–is most important for your content area or level? Least? Why?

2. There has been a long-time and on-going debate about the relative value of teaching students content, such as concepts, versus processes (e.g., study skills and critical thinking). Which should the schools emphasize more? Why? What do you predict will happen to this emphasis in the future?

3. How does the developmental level of the student (e.g., first grade versus high school) influence the answers to Question 2?

4. How will the increasing use of computers and technology in the future influence the answers to Question 2?

5. You are going to make a presentation to parents about your emphasis on transfer in your classroom. How would you explain and defend it from a research perspective? What strategies will you propose to use?

6. Some people have advocated placing greater emphasis on critical thinking through the introduction of a separate course on critical thinking. What advice do you have for them based upon the research in this chapter?

7. Much of the research and emphasis on problem solving has occurred in areas such as math where many of the problems are well defined. How might schools focus on problem solving using ill-defined problems to a greater extent than now typically occurs?

8.   Research indicates that learners typically receive little formal instruction in the use of study strategies. Why is this the case? Are study strategies best taught within the context of a particular content area, such as history, or are they better taught "context-free?" Why do you think so?

BACKGROUND READINGS

Bruning, R., Schraw, G., & Ronning, R. (1999). *Cognitive psychology and instruction* (3rd ed.). Upper Saddle River, NJ: Prentice Hall. This book devotes a chapter to an in-depth coverage of problem solving and critical thinking.

Gardner, H. (2000). *The disciplined mind: Beyond facts and standardized tests, the K-12 education that every child deserves.* New York: Penguin Books. Gardner describes how to translate current research on thinking into classroom practice.

Halpern, D. F. (1998). Teaching critical thinking for transfer across domains. *American Psychologist, 53*, 449-455. This article examines how critical thinking can transfer across different content areas.

Hofer, B. K., & Pintrich, P. R. (2002). *Personal epistemology: The psychology of beliefs about knowledge and knowing.* Mahwah, NJ: Erlbaum. This book describes the influence of personal epistemological beliefs on knowledge construction.

Mayer, R., & Wittrock, M. (1996). Problem-solving transfer. In D. Berliner, & R. Calfee (Eds.), *Handbook of educational psychology* (pp. 47-62). New York: Macmillan. This chapter provides an excellent overview of the issues involved in transfer of learning. .

Perkins, D. N., Tishman, S., Ritchhart, R., Donis, K., & Andrade, A. (2000). Intelligence in the wild: A dispositional view of intellectual traits. *Educational Psychology Review, 12*, 269-293. An excellent review of affective factors and intelligence.

Schunk, D. (2000). Learning theories: An educational perspective (3rd ed.). Upper Saddle River, NJ: Prentice Hall. This book devotes a chapter each to concept learning, problem solving, and transfer.

FEEDBACK FOR CONSTRUCTED RESPONSE AND DOCUMENT-BASED ANALYSIS QUESTIONS

Constructed Response Items

1. How effectively did Suzanne teach problem solving in her lesson? To what extent did she apply the instructional strategies for helping students become better problem solvers?
> *Suzanne did a generally good job of teaching problem solving with young children. She posed the situation and asked the children how they would solve the problem. In this way she provided some practice in identifying the problem and selecting a strategy for solving it. The learning-center work gave the students experience in applying their understanding of graphing to other problems.*
>
> *Suzanne did a very good job of presenting her problem in a meaningful context, and she provided considerable scaffolding for the children who had difficulty with the process and the applications.*

2. To what extent did Suzanne encourage critical thinking in her lesson? What could she have done to give students more practice in developing critical thinking abilities?
> *Suzanne did quite well at promoting critical thinking in her lesson. For example, she asked the students to make observations of the information in the graphs, and she asked the students to confirm their conclusions with observations (e.g., "How did you get that answer?" "Why is it not 24?").*

She could have increased the emphasis on critical thinking by giving her students the chance to practice more of the basic processes. For instance, she might have posed questions, such as, "Suppose we went around the school and asked people what their favorite flavor of jelly bean is. What do you think they would say?" After the students predicted, she could ask them for the basis for their prediction (such as the information in their graph).

3. How effective would Suzanne's lesson have been for promoting transfer? What could Suzanne have done to increase the likelihood of transfer in her students?

Promoting transfer was one of the strengths of Suzanne's lesson. After she conducted the whole-group activity, she had the students work at a series of centers, each of which focused on gathering information and preparing bar graphs. In this way the students had a variety of high quality experiences, all of which were in realistic contexts.

4. Describe the ways that Suzanne assessed the children's understanding of bar graphs. Describe what she could have done to improve her assessment.

Assessment provides teachers with information about what is occurring in students' heads so they can adjust subsequent instruction accordingly. Suzanne assessed her students' learning progress in several ways. First, she used classroom questions to obtain a snapshot of learning progress. Then she had students work at learning centers. In both of these, her assessment would have been more effective if she had systematically gathered information about learning progress from each student. Both of her assessments provided timely data, but they didn't gather information systematically from each student.

Document-Based Analysis

In Chapter 4 you saw the following lesson plan developed by a first-grade teacher.

Unit: Warm-Blooded Animals
Objective: First graders will understand mammals, so when given a series of pictures of different animals, they will identify all the mammals.
Rationale: Mammals are the most advanced members of the animal kingdom, and humans are mammals. Understanding mammals will contribute to children's understanding of themselves as well as different ways that animals adapt to ensure their survival.
Content: Mammals are warm-blooded animals that have hair, and nurse their young. Most mammals are born live, but some, such as the duckbilled platypus are egg-layers. Mammals also have four-chambered hearts and seven neck vertebrae. Some examples are cows, horses, people, wolves, seals, whales, kangaroos, and tigers. (The teacher decides, based on the developmental level of the children, to include only common mammals. Not all mammals give live birth, for example.)
Procedures:
1. Ask students to give some examples of different kinds of animals. Explain that they are going to learn about a special kind of animal. Emphasize that all can learn this content. Stress the need to pay attention.
2. Show students a guinea pig, and have them touch and feel it.
3. Have them describe what they saw and felt. Accept all answers. Write responses on board. Prompt for feels warm and has hair.
4. Show them a picture of a cow with a calf. Ask how the calf eats. Prompt them to conclude that the calf nurses from its mother.
5. Add "nurses" to "warm-blooded" and "has hair" as characteristics of mammals on the board.
6. Show a picture of a dog. Ask how many of them have a dog. Ask them to describe the picture. Link to essential characteristics of mammals. Prompt if necessary and positively reinforce correct characteristics.
7. Show them a picture of an eagle sitting on a nest of eggs.
8. Ask students to identify the similarities and differences between the eagle and the guinea pig, cow, calf, and dog.

9. Show them a picture of a mother whale and baby whale. Prompt them to conclude that some mammals live in water.
10. Call for a definition of mammals based on the characteristics they've described. Write it on the board.
11. Ask for additional examples and help students determine if they are mammals.

Materials: A student's pet guinea pig.
            Pictures of a cow with calf, dog, eagle and whale with calf

Assessment: Show students a series of pictures of animals. Have them circle those that are mammals.

Suppose this lesson plan were designed for 7th graders. Again, assess the effectiveness of the plan for the older students. Describe developmental differences between 1st graders and 7th graders that would influence teachers' thinking in both cases.

Transfer occurs when students are able to take information learned in one context and apply it in different ones. In terms of this lesson plant, it would involve applying the concept "mammal" to new examples and in different contexts. This lesson was strong in terms of transfer in several ways. First, because of the liberal use of high quality examples, the depth of original understanding should be good. The quality of learning experiences, both in terms of good examples and teachers questions that targeted essential characteristics, was also good. From a transfer perspective the lesson plan could have been improved by more and varied examples, both positive (e.g. bats, humans) and negative (e.g. turtles). In addition, helping students understand that they are learning a concept would not only enhance immediate learning but also concept learning in the long term.

Seventh graders are both more conceptually and developmentally advanced than first graders. Having said that, there still is a critical need for positive and negative examples, but these could be more varied (e.g. bats and marsupials) and students could be asked to take a more active role in analyzing them. In addition, because of the conceptual sophistication of seventh graders, the teacher could delve into some of the more subtle mammalian characteristics such as a four-chambered heart, exploring its evolutionary and physiological significance.

CLASSROOM EXERCISES

Look at the two paragraphs below that are taken from your text.

Think about some of your everyday experiences. Are you bothered when something doesn't make sense? Do you want to world to be predictable? Are you more comfortable in classes when the instructor specifies the requirements, schedules the classes, and outlines the grading practices? Does your life in general follow patterns more than random experiences? Most people's do.

According to Piaget (1952, 1959), people have an innate need to understand how the world works and to find order, structure, and predictability in their existence. He calls this need the drive for equilibrium, or a state of cognitive balance between our understanding of the world and our experiences.

1. What kind of learning is being promoted in this section—concept learning, problem solving, or strategic learning? Explain.

2. Identify the examples used to illustrate the topic in this section.

3. What do you not see in the paragraphs that is often emphasized in teaching this type of topic?

4. Was the approach to presenting the topic more expository than inductive, or more inductive than expository? (As an example of an inductive lesson, look at the case study with Diane Smith and her students at the end of Chapter 4.) Explain.

Use the following information for Items 5-8.

As you're studying these paragraphs, you say to yourself, "I still don't quite get this idea. . . . I'll try to write an answer to margin question 2.2 to help me understand it better. . . . I'll look in the Student Study Guide too, to see if that will help."

5. What concept are you best demonstrating when you say to yourself, "I still don't quite get this idea." Explain.

6. The concept that you're demonstrating when you say, "I still don't quite get this idea," most relates to what theory of learning? Explain.

7. To what major section of the chapter--*concept learning, problem solving, the strategic learner*, or *transfer of learning*–are your comments, "I'll try to write an answer to margin question 2.2 to help me understand it better. . . . I'll look in the Student Study Guide too, to see if that will help," most closely related? Explain.

8. Your friend is also struggling with the idea, and she too wants to use Margin question 2.2 to help her, so she looks up the answer in the Student Study Guide. Explain why your approach is better than hers.

9. Look at the following passage.

Jefferson, one rural **county** among several **counties**, has six **schools**—one high **school**, two elementary **schools**, and one middle **school**. Five of the **schools** are in Brookesville, the largest city in Jefferson **county**. **Schools** in the three **cities** nearest Brookesville are Brookesville's biggest rivals. The **schools** in all the cities hold an annual athletic and scholastic competition.

The two **women** advisors of the debate team and the **woman** who coached the softball team were proud of both the performance of the **students** from Big Tree High School and their appearance. (The school is named after a 600-year-old **tree** that stands prominently in a grove of oak **trees** near the school grounds.) One **student** took all-around honors, and four other **students** won medals. One **girl** and one **boy** were honored for their work in math, and two **boys** and two **girls** wrote exemplary essays. One essay was voted top of the competition. It described a **child** and how she helped several other **children** learn to cope with difficulty.

The **students** all looked the part of **ladies** and **gentlemen**. Each young **gentleman** wore a shirt and tie, and each young **lady** wore a dress or pant suit.

Explain why this passage is effective for promoting transfer of teaching the rules for forming plural nouns. Be very specific and refer directly to the passage in presenting your explanation.

10. On page 322 of the text, after the example with Holt and the boy, we say, "Situations like this are common in classrooms. Once students get an answer, they're satisfied, regardless of whether or not it makes sense." Is the tendency of students to accept any answer, regardless of whether or not it makes sense a well-defined or an ill-defined problem? Explain. Describe some steps that you might take to solve this problem. What heuristic is likely to be the most effective? Provide a rationale for your choice.

FEEDBACK FOR CLASSROOM EXERCISES

1. The topic is equilibrium, which is a concept. The desire for order, stability, and predictability are its characteristics.

2. The examples include the questions:
   . Are you bothered when something doesn't make sense?
   . Do you want to world to be predictable?
   . Are you more comfortable in your classes when the instructor specifies the requirements, schedules the classes, and outlines the grading practices?
   . Does your life in general follow patterns more than random experiences?

   Another example includes students' tendencies to sit in the same seats in their classrooms, and married couples' tendencies to sleep on the same side of the bed.

3. No "non-examples" are presented in the three paragraphs.

4. The approach tended to be inductive. First, the concrete examples were presented, and then the concept was identified.

5. You are demonstrating one characteristic of metacognition--knowing that you don't understand the idea.

6. Metacognition is an important part of information processing; it controls the cognitive processes to move information from one store to another.

7. Your comments most closely relate to *the strategic learner*. Writing an answer to a margin question and looking in the study guide are strategies designed to reach the goal of improved understanding.

8. By writing the answer, you put yourself in a more active role than does your friend.

9. The passage has high quality examples in it. For instance, students don't have to know that "county" is singular, because it says "one rural county." Likewise, they don't have to know that "counties" is plural because it says "several counties." All the information the students need to understand the rules is in the passage.

   The passage also has adequate variety. There are two different examples of each part of the rule in the passage.

   The rules are embedded in the context of the passage.

   The passage has all three--high quality examples, adequate variety of examples, and context for examples.

10. This is an ill-defined problem. The problem is that learners tend to accept answers that make no sense, or they tend to not evaluate their solutions. The problem isn't as specific as, for example, finding the area of a room to determine how much carpet is necessary.

   A means-ends analysis is likely to be the most effective heuristic. A series of subgoals could be identified, and efforts to reach each could be made in succession.

   High levels of interaction will be the most effective teaching strategy.

CHAPTER 10: INCREASING LEARNER MOTIVATION

CHAPTER OVERVIEW

This chapter begins by defining and comparing extrinsic and intrinsic motivation, which is followed by theoretical descriptions of motivation including an examination of behaviorist, cognitive and humanistic perspectives. The discussion then turns to specific theories of cognitive motivation, including expectancy x value theory, self-efficacy, goals, attribution theory and self-determination theory. The chapter closes with a discussion of affective l factors in motivation, including self-worth theory, and arousal and anxiety. As students study this chapter, encourage them to think about their own motivation and factors that influence it.

CHAPTER OBJECTIVES

- Describe differences between extrinsic and intrinsic motivation

- Explain learner motivation on the basis of behavioral, humanistic, and cognitive theories.

- Apply rewards in ways that can increase intrinsic motivation.

- Demonstrate strategies that can increase students' motivation to learn.

- Describe how affective factors in learners influence their motivation.

TRANSPARENCIES

The transparencies exist in both acetate form and as PowerPoint slides.

T 10.1   Extrinsic and intrinsic motivation (Figure 10.1, p. 350)
T 10.2   Theories of motivation (Figure 10.2, p. 351)
T 10.3   Maslow' hierarchy of needs (Figure 10.3, p. 354)
T 10.4   Expectancy x value theory (Figure 10.5, p. 360)
T 10.5   Factors affecting self-efficacy (Figure 10.6, p. 362)
T 10.6   The influence of self-efficacy on behavior and cognition
T 10.7   Goals, motivation, and achievement
T 10.8   Psychological needs according to self-determination theory

TRANSPARENCY MASTERS

The transparency masters are included in this manual beginning on page 230.

TM 10.1   Principles for using rewards to increase intrinsic motivation
TM 10.2   An illustration of deficiency and growth needs
TM 10.3   Principles for applying humanistic motivation theory in classrooms
TM 10.4   An exercise in cognitive motivation
TM 10.5   Effective and ineffective goals
TM 10.6   Analyzing attributions and self-worth
TM 10.7   Principles for promoting goals, self-efficacy and positive attributions in students
TM 10.8   Teacher behavior and self-determination
TM 10.9   Principles for developing students' self-determination
TM 10.10 Motivation, anxiety, and performance
TM 10.11 Principles for increasing self-worth and decreasing learner anxiety

I.   Extrinsic and intrinsic motivation
    A.   Motivation to learn
II. Behavioral views of motivation
    A.   Using rewards in classrooms
    B.   Criticisms of behavioral approaches to motivation
    C.   Using rewards in classrooms: Instructional strategies
III. Humanistic views of motivation
    A.   Development of the whole person
        1.   Development of the whole person: Maslow's hierarchy of needs
            a.   Deficiency and growth needs
            b.   Putting Maslow's work into perspective
        2.   The need for positive regard: The work of Carl Rogers
    B.   Humanistic views of motivation: Instructional strategies
IV. Cognitive theories of motivation
    A.   Expectancy x value theory
        1.   Expectancy for success
        2.   Factors influencing task value
            a.   Intrinsic interest
            b.   Importance
            c.   Utility value
            d.   Cost
    B.   Self-efficacy: Beliefs about capability
        1.   Factors influencing self-efficacy
        2.   The influence of self-efficacy on learner behavior
    C.   Goals and goal orientation
        1.   Learning and performance goals
        2.   Goals and theories about the nature of intelligence
        3.   Social goals
        4.   Work-avoidance goals
        5.   Using goals effectively
            a.   Effective goal setting
            b.   Goal monitoring
            c.   Strategy use
            d.   Metacognition
    D.   Attribution theory
        1.   Impact of attributions on learners
        2.   Learned helplessness
        3.   Attribution training
    E.   Beliefs, goals, and attributions: Instructional strategies
    F.   Self-determination theory
        1.   The need for competence
            a.   Attributional statements
            b.   Praise and criticism
            c.   Emotional displays
            d.   Offers of help
        2.   The need for control
        3.   The need for relatedness
    G.   Assessment and learning: The role of assessment in self-determination
    H.   Developing students' self-determination: Instructional Strategies
V.   Affective factors in motivation

A. Self-worth theory
B. Arousal and anxiety
C. Accommodating affective factors in motivation: Instructional strategies

PRESENTATION OUTLINE

Teaching suggestions in the outline will be marked with the symbol ■. In most cases, the suggested activities can be done individually and discussed as a whole group, or they can be done in small groups, and the small-group results can be discussed with the whole class. To be consistent with our understanding of knowledge construction, we recommend that you promote as much discussion–both in small groups and with the whole class–as possible.

Enrichment Information, which includes elaborations of text topics as well as topics not included in the text, will be boxed as you see here.

I. Extrinsic and intrinsic motivation
   A. Motivation to learn

  ■ *The suggestions in this section are intended to help your students understand the relationships between extrinsic and intrinsic motivation.*

    1. As an attention getter for this section ask students how many of them would study as hard as they now do if there were no tests, and if the class was ungraded. Many will admit that they study primarily for grades. Some will point out that potential employers focus heavily on grades.

    2. Point out that studying for the purpose of getting high grades is extrinsic motivation; the studying is a means to an end–the end being the high grade.

    3. Display T 10.1 *"Extrinsic and Intrinsic Motivation"* and point out that extrinsic and intrinsic motivation are not mutually exclusive, and many learners display characteristics of both. (Some students will probably say that they study to both get high grades and understand the content.)

    4. Emphasize that, as teachers, we attempting to increase motivation to learn, and point out that intrinsic motivation often is not possible.

II. Behavioral views of motivation
   A. Using rewards in classrooms
   B. Criticisms of behavioral approaches to motivation
   C. Using rewards in classrooms: Instructional strategies

  ■ *The suggestions in this section are intended to help your students understand behavioral approaches to motivation, together with some of the criticisms of this approach.*

    1. Display 10.2 *"Theories of Motivation"* and note that you will initially focus on behaviorist views of motivation.

    2. Describe some of the common criticisms of behaviorist approaches to motivation.

    3. Display TM 10.1 *"Principles for Using Rewards to Increase Intrinsic Motivation."* Have the

students identify where Amanda Shah (in the case study on page 353) applied each of the principles in her teaching.

You might want to share some additional information with your students regarding the implementation of reinforcers to increase motivation. Stipek (2002) describes the *scarcity principle* which says, "anything available to all students is usually less desirable than something that only a few students can achieve" (p. 25). The fact that high grades are not available to all students, for example, is what makes them reinforcers for many students. For students who don't have a history of high achievement, grades are ineffective reinforcers, and these are the students that most need to be motivated.

The scarcity principle is the basis for organizing exclusive clubs, sororities, fraternities, and other organizations or experiences which are unavailable to most people.

(The scarcity principle tends to not operate with young children in schools, however. They pay less attention to the tangible or symbolic reinforcement other children receive than do older students. As a result, common reinforcers affect young children's behavior more than they affect the behavior of older students.)
[Source: Stipek, D. (2002). *Motivation to learn (4th ed.).* Needham Heights, MA: Allyn and Bacon.]

III. Humanistic views of motivation
    A.   Development of the whole person
        1.   Development of the whole person: Maslow's hierarchy of needs
           a.   Deficiency and growth needs
           b.   Putting Maslow's work into perspective
        2.   The need for positive regard: The work of Carl Rogers
    B.   Humanistic views of motivation: Instructional strategies

■ *To help students understand humanistic views of motivation:*

1. **Display TM 10.2 "*An Illustration of Deficiency and Growth Needs.*" Have the students answer the question and provide an explanation for their choice. Many students select Choice c, others will select Choice b, and a few will select Choice d. Have them give their reasons. Then share the information at the bottom of TM 10.2.**

2. **Display T 10.3 "*Maslow's Hierarchy of Needs*" as the students work.**

3. **Have the students identify several implications of Maslow's work for teachers. Require that they offer concrete examples in their implications. (You might also remind the students of the link between Maslow's work and humanistic views of motivation. The "whole person" is readily observable in Maslow's hierarchy.)**

4. **Display TM 10.3 "*Principles for Applying Humanistic Motivation Theory in Classrooms.*" Have the students identify where Kathy Brewster (in the case study on page 356) applied each of the principles in her work with her students.**

IV. Cognitive theories of motivation

■ *The purpose of the suggestions in this section is to help students understand the basic assumptions in cognitive motivation theory.*

1. **Present the problems on TM 10.4 "*An Exercise in Cognitive Motivation*" to the students.**

2. **Have the students answer the question. Take a class poll to determine the number of students that think the water level will be higher, the number that think it will be lower, and the number that think it will be the same with the jar on the bottom as with the jar on the board. After several**

have offered their answers and their explanations for the answers, make a comment, such as the following, "Okay, very good everyone. Now, let's move on." Someone in the class is likely to ask, "Wait, what is the answer?" You can then explain that the reason you had them do the problem and not give them the answer was to illustrate that they would be dissatisfied with having done the problem and not know what the answer was. Then can point out that this illustrates people's intrinsic need to understand events and "how the world works." This is the basic premise of cognitive theories of motivation.

(The water level is lower with the jar in the water. While the jar is on the board it displaces 200 ml of water (its weight)(water weighs one gram for each milliliter), but when it is at the bottom of the tub it only displaces 40 ml of water (its volume), so the water level is lower.)

3. Ask the students how they feel when they do a paper and don't get any feedback on it, take a quiz and don't discuss the results, and other examples. In each case the "need to know," is illustrated.

A. Expectancy x value theory
    1. Expectancy for success
    2. Factors influencing task value
        a. Intrinsic interest
        b. Importance
        c. Utility value
        d. Cost
B. Self-efficacy: Beliefs about capability
    1. Factors influencing self-efficacy
    2. The influence of self-efficacy on learner behavior
C. Goals and goal orientation
    1. Learning and performance goals
    2. Goals and theories about the nature of intelligence
    3. Social goals
    4. Work-avoidance goals
    5. Using goals effectively
        a. Effective goal setting
        b. Goal monitoring
        c. Strategy use
        d. Metacognition
D. Attribution theory
    1. Impact of attributions on learners
    2. Learned helplessness
    3. Attribution training
E. Beliefs, goals, and attributions: Instructional strategies

■ *The purpose of the suggestion in this section is to help students understand the characteristics of four cognitive theories of motivation–expectancy x value theory, self-efficacy, goal theory, and attribution theory.*
1. Display T 10.4 "Expectancy x value theory." Have them offer additional examples of each of the factors influencing task value.

2. Display T 10.5 *"Factors Affecting Self-Efficacy."* Then, display T 10.6 *"The Influence of Self-Efficacy on Behavior and Cognition,"* and emphasize that your approach–frequent assessment, detailed feedback, high-quality examples, and modeling–is intended to help them be successful on challenging tasks which will increase their self-efficacy.

162

3. **Display T 10.7 *"Goals, Motivation, and Achievement."* Have the students give some additional examples of learning goals, performance-approach and performance-avoidance goals, and social goals.**

4. **Display TM 10.5 *"Effective and Ineffective Goals"* and have the students explain why each is effective or ineffective.**

5. **Display TM 10.6 *"Analyzing Attributions and Self-Worth."* Have the students answer each of the questions. (Tell them that you will discuss Items 4 and 6 a little later.)**

6. **Display TM 10.7 *"Principles for Promoting Goals, Self-Efficacy and Positive Attributions in Students."* Have them identify where Kathy Brewster (in the case study beginning on page 369) applied each of the principles in her teaching.**

F. Self-determination theory
    1. The need for competence
        a. Attributional statements
        b. Praise and criticism
        c. Emotional displays
        d. Offers of help
    2. The need for control
    3. The need for relatedness
G. Assessment and learning: The role of assessment in self-determination
H. Developing students' self-determination: Instructional Strategies

■ *The purpose in the following suggestions is to help students understand self-determination theory.*

1. **Display T 10.8 *"Psychological Needs According to Self-Determination Theory."* Explain that competence helps organisms survive in the world. Note also how stressed people become when they're out of control. Relate the need for competence and control to Piaget's concept of equilibrium.**

2. **Point out that you're treating self-determination theory apart from the other cognitive theories, because it has aspects of humanistic views of motivation in it. Ask the students to identify these aspects (the need for relatedness, which is similar to Maslow's need for belonging).**

3. **Display TM 10.8 *"Teacher Behavior and Self-Determination."* Have the students explain how the teacher's behavior could detract from students' self-determination.**

4. **Display TM 10.9 *"Principles for Developing Students' Self-Determination."* Have the students identify where Elaine Goodman (in the case study beginning on page 375) applied each of the principles in her teaching.**

V. Affective factors in motivation
    A. Self-worth theory
    B. Arousal and anxiety
    C. Accommodating affective factors in motivation: Instructional strategies

■ *The purpose of these suggestions is to help students understand self-worth theory*

163

and the influence of emotional arousal on motivation.

1. Display TM 10.6 *"Analyzing Attributions and Self-Worth"* again. Focus on Billy's behavior and have the students look again at Items 4 and 6 and explain Billy's behavior based on self-worth theory.

2. Display TM 10.10 *"Motivation, Anxiety, and Performance."* Have them decide if their performance is likely to increase, decrease, or remain unchanged in each of the three examples. (Feedback is provided at the bottom of the page.) Point out that this research has important implications for them as students. Since anxiety can increase performance on well-practiced tasks, the better they understand the content they're studying, the less likely anxiety will detract from their performance.

3. Display 10.11 *"Principles for Increasing Self-Worth and Decreasing Learner Anxiety."* Have the students go back to the case studies in the chapter and identify where the teachers applied each of the principles.

DISCUSSION STARTERS

1. How could motivation in the schools be improved through modifications in the present grading system? In attempting to answer this question use as many concepts from the chapter as possible.

2. Defend and justify one of these two polar positions: "Take care of learning and motivation takes care of itself," and "All learning begins with motivation."

3. Does our current emphasis on extrinsic motivation (e.g., grades, prizes, etc.) damage students' intrinsic motivation? If so, what concrete steps can teachers take to remedy the problem? If not, how could the use of these extrinsic motivators be made more effective?

4. Is competition good or bad for classroom motivation? What information from the chapter supports your conclusion?

5. A teacher is assigned to teach the same class but has high-ability, college-bound students in one and low-ability, poorly motivated students in the other. What specifically should the teacher do differently in the two classes?

6. How does the age and developmental level of students affect motivation in the classroom? Specifically, what would you do differently if you were teaching first graders versus high school students?

7. How do culture and SES influence motivation? What can teachers do to make this influence a positive one?

BACKGROUND READINGS

Brophy, J. (1998). *Motivating students to learn.* Boston: McGraw Hill. This book explains motivation to learn and includes two chapters dealing with issues involved in the motivation of low achievers and students who are alienated from school.

Freese, S. (1999, April). *The relationship between teacher caring and student engagement in academic high school classes.* Paper presented at the Annual Meeting of the American Educational Research Association, Montreal. This paper offers insights into the impact of relatedness on learner motivation.

Good, T., & Brophy, J. (2000). *Looking in classrooms* (8th ed.). New York: Addison-Wesley Longman. Good and Brophy include a chapter on motivation in this popular book that applies theories and concepts to classroom practice.

Graham, S., & Weiner, B. (1996). Theories and principles of motivation. In D. Berliner, & R. Calfee (Eds.), *Handbook of educational psychology* (pp. 63-84). New York: Macmillan. This chapter provides a conceptual and historical perspective on theories of motivation.

Pintrich, P., & Schunk D. (2002). *Motivation in education: Theory, research, and applications* (2nd ed.) Englewood Cliffs, NJ: Prentice Hall. This book provides the most up-to-date, comprehensive, and applicable presentation of motivation presently available.

Ryan, R., & Deci, E. (2000). Intrinsic and extrinsic motivations: Classic definitions and new directions. *Contemporary Educational Psychology, 25,* 54-67. This paper describes the complex relationships between extrinsic and intrinsic motivation and learner autonomy.

Stipek, D. (2002). *Motivation to learn* (4th ed.) Englewood Cliffs, NJ: Prentice-Hall. This is a quite readable and reasonably comprehensive book on motivation.

FEEDBACK FOR CONSTRUCTED RESPONSE AND DOCUMENT-BASED ANALYSIS QUESTIONS

Constructed Response Items_____

1. Assess Damon's use of praise to communicate increasing competence in his students.
   Damon's remarks would encourage negative attributions related to task difficulty for those who did well on the test--he commented, "That wasn't that hard a test." Attributions of low ability could be induced in students who did poorly on the test, since they did poorly on a less-than-difficult task. It was a form of "lose-lose" for the students. (He further promoted an attribution of low ability in Jeremy with his comment, "I know you have a tough time with written assignments.")

2. With respect to humanistic views of motivation, assess the extent to which Damon helped students meet the deficiency needs and contribute to the growth needs in Maslow's hierarchy.
   Damon's instruction probably was less effective than it could have been for meeting the needs described in Maslow's hierarchy. For example, he responded, ". . . so that doesn't make sense . . .," which detracts from the need for classrooms to be safe and orderly, and the conduct of the lesson-lecture describing a list of facts-would not appeal to students' need for intellectual achievement. In addition, his giving D's on the test and then remarking that ,"You better get moving... This wasn't that hard a test.", would not do any thing for students' self esteem.

3. With respect to expectancy times value theory, how effectively did Damon promote intrinsic interest in the topic?
   Expectancy x value theory suggests that students are motivated to engage in an activity to the extent they expect to succeed in it times the value they place on the success. His comment, "I know that learning dates and places isn't the most pleasant stuff, but you might as well get used to it because that's what history is about, and they'll be on the next test," would, in all likelihood, completely demolition the value component.

4. Assess Damon's effectiveness in promoting students' feelings of self-efficacy and competence.
   Self-efficacy involves beliefs about one's capabilities to organize and complete courses of action required to accomplish specific tasks. Self-efficacy is influenced by a number of factors including past performance and teacher comments. Students' poor performance on the previous test as well as the following comments would damage student self-efficacy: "You people better get moving. This wasn't that hard a test" and "I know you have a tough time with written assignments. Let me help you."

5. Assess Damon's effectiveness in accommodating students' needs to preserve feelings of self-worth.

Self-worth is an emotional reaction to, or evaluation of, the self. "This wasn't a hard test" (despite the fact that 7 received D's and F's) would be damaging to the self-worth of these students(Not to mention the other students who received passing grades on an easy test.).

Document-Based Analysis_____

Damon's students were writing a summary of the Crusades, including people and events and why they were important. As Damon walked by Jeremy, he saw that Jeremy had written only a few words on his paper, and they had the following exchange:

Damon: (With sympathy)Are you having trouble getting started?

Jeremy: Yeah. . . I don't quite know how to get started.

Damon: I know you have a tough time with written assignments. Let me help you.

(Damon took a blank piece of paper and started writing as Jeremy watched.)

Damon: See how easy that was? That's the kind of thing I want you to do. Go ahead-that's a start. Keep that so you can see what I'm looking for. Go back to your desk, and give it another try.

Assess Damon's interaction with Jeremy based on the content of the chapter.

This interchange with Jeremy was motivationally damaging in several ways. First, he damaged Jeremy's self-worth by suggesting that he wasn't good at writing. This also promoted an attribution of low ability in Jeremy with two comments. First, he attributed low ability in Jeremy when he said, "I know you have a tough time with written assignments." Then, even if Jeremy does a fine job on the assignment, it will be motivationally discounted because Damon said, "See how easy that was?"

CLASSROOM EXERCISES

1. Humanistic thinkers were critical of the reductionist nature of behaviorism and psychoanalysis. Predict how humanistic thinkers would react to cognitive psychology, and particularly information processing.

2. Humanistic views of motivation emphasize the "whole person." Explain how the "whole person" is illustrated in Maslow's hierarchy.

3. Both White (1959) and Connell and Wellborn (1991) suggest that "competence" is a basic human need. Offer an explanation as to why competence might be a basic need. What concept from Piaget's work is closely related to the need for competence. Explain how the concept is related.

4. Two students are equally successful on a task, but the teacher praises only one of them. Suppose someone observes this happen. Which of the two students does the observer assume has higher ability?

5. Suppose two students fail, and one is criticized. Which of the two will the observer conclude has higher ability?

6. Suppose learners have an entity view of ability. Are they more likely to adopt learning goals or performance goals? Why would they be likely to have this goal orientation?

7. Do affective needs precede or follow intellectual needs? (Give an example of an affective need. Give an example of an intellectual need.) On what basis do you make your conclusion about which precedes the other? On what theoretical view of motivation are you basing your conclusion about which precedes the other?

8. Time is perhaps the most powerful indicator of caring that exists. Explain why giving someone else your time would be such an important indicator.

9. In the chapter we saw that teachers' expectations influence the amount of emotional support they provide, the effort they expend to promote learning and the demands they place on learners, their questioning, and the feedback and evaluations they provide (See Table 10.6 in this chapter). Research also indicates that expectations influence teachers' behaviors in terms of the: 1) attributional statements they make to students about their performance (the explanations teachers offer for success or failure), 2) the way they use praise and criticism, 3) their emotional displays, and 4) their offers of help. Describe the differences in the way a teacher would respond to a high expectation student compared to a low expectation student for each of these four areas.

10. What is the teacher trying to accomplish in the following incident?

I just want to remind you that we agreed to begin our presentations on genetics on Monday, so we need to sign up today. You all know what you have to do in your presentations. For those of you who chose to write a report on genetics instead, remember we discussed that your report must contain at least two common examples of genetic traits, one example of a trait that isn't genetic but is commonly thought to be, and one example in which scientists now think genetics may play a part but aren't sure. Your report is also due on Monday.

11. Consider the relationship between attributions and self-efficacy. Suppose a student is high in self-efficacy and fails at a task. How will her attributions compare to a student who is low in self-efficacy?

Now suppose the student is successful. How will her attributions compare to a low self-efficacy student who is also successful.

FEEDBACK FOR CLASSROOM EXERCISES

1. Advocates of humanistic views would argue that both behaviorists and cognitive theorists tend to dehumanize education in the sense that neither behaviorist techniques, such as programmed learning, nor cognitive approaches, such as discovery learning take into account how students feel about themselves or about learning, teachers, and schooling. The "human" side of learning isn't emphasized enough.

2. The physical person is illustrated in the first two levels, *survival* and *safety*. *Safety* is also often interpreted to mean emotional safety as well, so the emotional person is interpreted by some to be illustrated in the second level. The social person is illustrated through *belonging*, and the personal, emotional person is illustrated through *self-esteem*. The intellectual and aesthetic persons are illustrated in the growth needs, and the entire person is illustrated through *self-actualization*.

3. Increasing competence allows individuals to effectively adapt to the environment. The ability to adapt is a basic need. Effective adaptation keeps an individual at equilibrium. In fact, Piaget suggested that adaptation was the process learners used to arrive at and maintain equilibrium.

Competence motivation is closely related to Piaget's concept of equilibrium; as schemes develop, competence increases and equilibrium is easier to achieve and maintain.

4. The observer is likely to conclude that the one not praised has higher ability. Praise is usually associated with effort, so the one praised is assumed to have exerted the greater effort, and since effort and ability are viewed as inversely related, the observer is likely to conclude that the praised student is lower in ability.

5. It is likely that the one criticized will be assumed to have higher ability. Criticism is associated with lack of effort, so it is assumed that the one criticized didn't try as hard, and therefore must be higher in ability. If he or she wasn't higher in ability, the teacher wouldn't have criticized him or her.

6. They would be more likely to adopt performance goals. Performance goals, such as performing better than peers, allow them to demonstrate high ability. A person with an entity view of ability would be more likely than a person with an incremental view of ability to want to demonstrate high ability.

7. An example of an affective need would be to feel welcome in the class. An intellectual need would be to feel like you understand proofs in geometry, for example. Maslow' hierarchy would suggest that affective needs precede intellectual needs. This is based on humanistic views of motivation.

8. The most significant aspect of time is that we all have the same amount of it. This being the case, it communicates that the person is important enough to allocate time to. If people had different amounts of time, giving time would be less significant.

9. Teachers tend to make statements that attribute success to high ability and failure to lack of effort for high-expectation learners, whereas they tend to attribute failure to lack of ability for low-expectation learners. They tend to praise low-expectation learners more for success than they do high-expectation learners, particularly on easy tasks. They tend to criticize high-expectation learners more for failure. They tend to express sympathy to low expectation learners and anger to high-expectation learners, particularly when they perceive high expectation learners as not exerting effort. They tend to offer low-expectation learners help more readily than high-expectation learners.

10. The teacher is likely attempting to *address learners' needs for autonomy.*

11. High self-efficacy students tend to attribute failure to lack of effort or use of ineffective strategies, whereas students low in self-efficacy tend to attribute failure to lack of ability (Bruning et al., 1999). High self-efficacy students tend to attribute success to effort and ability, whereas low self-efficacy students tend to attribute success to luck, task difficulty, or other external factors.

CHAPTER 11: MOTIVATION IN THE CLASSROOM

CHAPTER OVERVIEW

This chapter presents a model that applies the theories of motivation presented in Chapter 10. The chapter begins with a discussion of learning-focused compared to performance-focused classrooms. It then describes strategies for promoting learner self-regulation. The chapter continues with discussions of teacher characteristics and classroom climate variables that increase learner motivation, and it closes with a discussion of instructional factors that enhance motivation to learn.

CHAPTER OBJECTIVES

- Describe the difference between a learning-focused environment and a performance-focused environment.

- Explain the role of motivation in developing self-regulation.

- Explain how teacher personal characteristics promote student motivation.

- Describe how classroom climate variables promote student motivation.

- Identify instructional factors that promote student motivation.

TRANSPARENCIES

The transparencies exist in both acetate form and as PowerPoint slides.

T 11.1   Comparisons of learning-focused and performance-focused classrooms
T 11.2   A model for promoting student motivation (Figure 11.1, p. 389)
T 11.3   Characteristics of caring teachers

TRANSPARENCY MASTERS

The transparency masters are included in this manual beginning on page 230.

TM 11.1   An example of self-regulation
TM 11.2   Instructional principles for increasing learner self-regulation
TM 11.3   Demonstrating personal qualities that increase learner motivation
TM 11.4   Principles for applying climate and instructional variables in classrooms

VIDEOS

Looking Through Classroom Windows Tape2-Segment 2: "Studying Arthropods in the Fifth Grade."
The video lesson illustrates a teacher, DeVonne Lampkin, attempting to increase her students' interest by using real-world examples to study the concept *arthropods*.

Looking Through Classroom Windows Tape2-Segment 3: "Writing Effective Paragraphs."
The video lesson illustrates the same teacher, DeVonne Lampkin, as she conducts a writing lesson. The class discusses the characteristics of an effective paragraph, they write paragraphs on transparencies, and each paragraph is evaluated by the class.

Concepts in Classrooms Tape 2-Segment 6: "Improving Learner Motivation: Introductory Focus"
This video segment illustrates four episodes in which teachers attempt to attract the attention of students and provide an umbrellas for the lesson which follows: It includes:

- A demonstration with first graders in which the teacher puts baking soda into water and then into vinegar and asks the students to use their senses to try and determine why one "fizzed" and the other didn't.
- A demonstration with seventh graders in which the teacher uses a 20-meter length of tape to introduce the topic of tapeworm parasites.
- A chemistry class in which the teacher demonstrates heat and expansion as an introduction to Charles' Law.

Concepts in Classrooms Tape 2-Segment 7: "Personalizing Content: Increasing Learner Motivation"
This segment illustrates teachers' attempts to personalize content to make it more meaningful to students. It includes:

- An episode with second graders in which the students graph their favorite flavors of jelly beans.
- An episode with seventh graders in which a student from the class is used to illustrate the concept *symmetry*
- A twelfth-grade class in which the teacher asks the students to put themselves in the role of the characters of the novel *The Scarlet Letter*.

CHAPTER OUTLINE

I. Class structure: Creating a learning-focused environment
II. Self-regulated learners: Developing student responsibility
   A. Developing self-regulation: Applying Self-Determination Theory
   B. Helping students develop self-regulation: Instructional strategies
III. Teacher characteristics: Personal qualities that increase student motivation and learning
   A. Personal teaching efficacy: Beliefs about teaching and learning
   B. Modeling and enthusiasm: Communicating genuine interest
   C. Caring: Meeting the need for relatedness
      1. Communicating caring
   D. Teacher expectations: Increasing perceptions of competence
   E. Demonstrating personal qualities that increase motivation: Instructional strategies
IV. Climate variables: Creating a motivating environment
   A. Order and safety: Classrooms as secure places to learn
   B. Success: Developing learner self-efficacy
   C. Challenge: Increasing perceptions of competence and self-determination
   D. Task Comprehension: Increasing perceptions of control and value
V. Instructional variables: Developing interest in learning activities
   A. Introductory focus: Attracting students' attention
   B. Personalization: Links to students' lives
   C. Involvement: Increasing intrinsic motivation
      1. Using open-ended questioning to increase involvement
      2. Using hands-on activities to promote involvement
   D. Feedback: Meeting the need to understand
   E. Applying the climate and instructional variables in your classroom: Instructional strategies
   F. Assessment and learning: Using feedback to increase interest and self-efficacy
VI. Technology and learning: Using technology to increase learner motivation
   A. The motivating effects of technology: Theoretical explanations
   B. Technology and motivation: Cautions and guidelines for teachers
VII. Motivation and diversity
   A. Motivation problems: Student perspectives
   B. Motivation problems: Possible solutions

PRESENTATION OUTLINE

Teaching suggestions in the outline will be marked with the symbol ■. In most cases, the suggested activities can be done individually and discussed as a whole group, or they can be done in small groups, and the small-group results can be discussed with the whole class. To be consistent with our understanding of knowledge construction, we recommend that you promote as much discussion–both in small groups and with the whole class–as possible.

I.   Class structure: Creating a learning-focused environment

■ *The suggestions in this section are designed to help your students understand the differences between a learning-focused and performance-focused classroom, as well as the variables in the Model for Promoting Student Motivation.*

1.   **To introduce the section display T 11.1** *"Comparisons of Learning-Focused and Performance-Focused Classrooms."* **T 11.1 outlines the characteristics that differentiate the two types of classrooms. Have the students identify some things teachers can do to promote a learning-focused versus a performance-focused classroom. Require that students offer** *specific* **and** *concrete* **suggestions.**

2.   **Point out the reasons for some of your practices, such as:**
   •   **Emphasizing that the focus in the course is** *learning.*
   •   **De-emphasizing grades by putting their quiz scores on the last page of their quizzes instead of on the front page.**
   •   **Telling them to not share their scores with each other.**
   •   **Modeling an incremental view of ability**
   •   **Avoiding any comparisons of student performance, such as displaying grades or arrays of scores on quizzes.**

3.   **Display T 11.2 "A Model for Promoting Learner Motivation," which outlines the variables in the Model for Promoting Motivation. Point out that is will be the framework for the study of the chapter.**

> **Video: You might want to show the video segment "Studying Arthropods in Fifth Grade" as an introduction to the chapter. Have the students discuss the lesson and the extent to which it was motivating for learners.**

II.   Self-regulated learners: Developing student responsibility
   A.   Developing self-regulation: Applying Self-Determination Theory
   B.   Helping students develop self-regulation: Instructional strategies

■ *The purpose of these suggestions is to help students understand how self-regulation can be developed in learners.*
   1.   **Display TM 11.1** *"An Example of Self-Regulation."* **Have the students identify the characteristics of self-regulated learners in the vignette.**

   2.   **Discuss the students' responses. The following are some possible conclusions.**
      1.   **She demonstrates metacognition when she says, "But, all the quizzes are application. Just memorizing the definitions won't work."**
      2.   **She sets the goal of doing** *and understanding* **all the items on the practice quiz in the study guide, as well as those on the website.**
      3.   **She monitors progress toward her goal with her chart.**

4. She adapts her strategy; if she doesn't understand some of the items on the practice quizzes, she goes in a sees her instructor.

5. Display TM 11.2 *"Instructional Principles for Increasing Learner Self-Regulation."* Have the students identify where Sam Cook (in the case study beginning on page 390) applied each of the principles in his teaching.

III. Teacher characteristics: Personal qualities that increase student motivation and learning
   A. Personal teaching efficacy: Beliefs about teaching and learning
   B. Modeling and enthusiasm: Communicating genuine interest
   C. Caring: Meeting the need for relatedness
      1. Communicating caring
   D. Teacher expectations: Increasing perceptions of competence
   E. Demonstrating personal qualities that increase motivation: Instructional strategies

■ *These suggestions are intended to help students understand teacher characteristics that promote motivation.*
   1. Display TM 11.3 *"Demonstrating Personal Qualities That Increase Learner Motivation."* Have the students identify where DeVonne Lampkin (in the case study on page 399) demonstrated each of these qualities.

   2. To emphasize the importance of caring, display T 11.3 *"Characteristics of Caring Teachers."* Further emphasize the relationship between caring, respect, and holding students to high standards. Refer the students to the quote on the middle of page 397, for an additional source.

IV. Climate variables: Creating a motivating environment
   A. Order and safety: Classrooms as secure places to learn
   B. Success: Developing learner self-efficacy
   C. Challenge: Increasing perceptions of competence and self-determination
   D. Task Comprehension: Increasing perceptions of control and value
V. Instructional variables: Developing interest in learning activities
   A. Introductory focus: Attracting students' attention

> **Video:** You might want to show the video segment "Improving Learner Motivation: Introductory Focus" to illustrate teachers' attempts to capture and maintain students' attention.

   B. Personalization: Links to students' lives

> **Video:** You might want to show the video segment "Personalizing Content: Increasing Learner Motivation" to illustrate teachers attempts to increase motivation by personalizing the topics they teach.

   C. Involvement: Increasing intrinsic motivation
      1. Using open-ended questioning to increase involvement
      2. Using hands-on activities to promote involvement
   D. Feedback: Meeting the need to understand
   E. Applying the climate and instructional variables in your classroom: Instructional strategies

F. Assessment and learning: Using feedback to increase interest and self-efficacy

■ *The purpose in these suggestions is to help students understand how the climate and instructional variables can be applied in classrooms.*

1. **Display TM 11.4** *"Principles for Applying Climate and Instructional Variables in Classrooms."* **Have the students identify where David Crawford (in the case study beginning on page 410) applied the principles in his work with his students.**

> **Video:** To summarize the chapter you might want to show the video segment "Writing Effective Paragraphs." It is also the closing case study for the chapter, constructed response items, which can guide your analysis, are included.

VI. Technology and learning: Using technology to increase learner motivation
   A. The motivating effects of technology: Theoretical explanations
   B. Technology and motivation: Cautions and guidelines for teachers
VII. Motivation and diversity
   A. Motivation problems: Student perspectives
   B. Motivation problems: Possible solutions

If you haven't already done so, display the quote from Graham (1991) at the bottom of TM 10.7 "Teacher Behavior and Attributions" and discuss the implications of this information for working with cultural minorities.

DISCUSSION STARTERS

1. Respond to the following assertion: "My job as a teacher is to plan to promote learning. Motivation is a student's responsibility."

2. Should teachers be held accountable for increasing the motivation of students who are alienated from school or are disinterested in school?

3. To what extent should motivation be part of teachers' planning?

4. Teachers are encouraged to promote self-regulation in students. Does this include allowing students to set their own learning goals?

5. Which is more important, intrinsic motivation, or motivation to learn? Why do you think so?

6. Is it possible to increase learner motivation in a performance-focused classroom? Why or why not?

7. Describe the characteristics of students for which a learning-focused classroom is most important.

BACKGROUND READINGS

Bruning, R., Schraw, G., & Ronning, R. (1999). Cognitive psychology and instruction (3rd ed.). Upper Saddle River, NJ: Prentice Hall. This text provides additional information on personal teaching efficacy and self-regulation, as well as other topics related to motivation.

Freese, S. (1999, April). *The relationship between teacher caring and student engagement in academic high school classes.* Paper presented at the Annual Meeting of the American Educational Research Association, Montreal. This paper offers some insights into the impact of relatedness on learner motivation.

Good, T., & Brophy, J. (2000). *Looking in classrooms* (8th ed.). New York: Addison-Wesley Longman. Good and Brophy provide a detailed discussion of teacher expectations and their influence on learner motivation and behavior.

Pintrich, P., & Schunk D. (2002). *Motivation in education: Theory, research, and applications* (2nd ed.) Englewood Cliffs, NJ: Prentice Hall. This book provides the most up-to-date, comprehensive, and applicable presentation of motivation presently available.

Ryan, R., & Deci, E. (2000). Intrinsic and extrinsic motivations: Classic definitions and new directions. *Contemporary Educational Psychology, 25,* 54-67. This paper describes the complex relationships between extrinsic and intrinsic motivation and learner autonomy.

Stipek, D. (1996). Motivation and instruction. In D. Berliner, & R. Calfee (Eds.), *Handbook of educational psychology* (pp. 85-113). New York: Macmillan. This chapter provides information about classroom applications of motivation theory.

Stipek, D. (2002). *Motivation to learn* (4th ed.) Englewood Cliffs, NJ: Prentice-Hall. This is a quite readable and reasonably comprehensive book on motivation.

FEEDBACK FOR CONSTRUCTED RESPONSE AND DOCUMENT-BASED ANALYSIS QUESTIONS

Constructed Response Items

1. Feelings of safety are essential for student motivation. Assess the extent to which DeVonne's students felt safe in her classroom.

We can infer that DeVonne's students felt safe based on several facts from the lesson. First, students seemed to volunteer freely. They also were not afraid to have their essays graded by their peers. Third, they volunteered freely to come up to the front of the room to have their essays evaluated by the whole class.

2. Assess DeVonne's application of the instructional variables in her classroom.

DeVonne provided introductory focus by putting the essay about computers on the overhead. She allowed for personalization by allowing student to write their essay on a topic of their choice. She actively involved students through her interactive questioning and provided substantive feedback by displaying the essays and having students discuss and evaluate them.

3. In spite of the fact that they were having their paragraphs publicly evaluated, DeVonne's students were very enthusiastic about displaying their work. Offer an explanation for their enthusiasm.

Their enthusiasm can be explained both by teacher characteristics and climate variables. DeVonne was enthusiastic, caring, and had positive expectations for her students. In terms of climate variables, her class was orderly, she explained the writing task clearly, and the writing assignment provided opportunities for both challenge and success.

175

4. DeVonne's students' backgrounds are very diverse. Assess her classroom environment for learners with diverse backgrounds.

Research suggests that teachers who are successful with diverse learners are enthusiastic, supportive, and have high expectations. They also create lessons that connect to students' lives and have high rates of involvement. DeVonne possessed all of these teacher characteristics, and her lesson connected to students' lives by allowing them to write on a topic of their choice, and they were actively involved throughout the lesson.

Document-Based Analysis

Look again at Justin's paragraph. It was rated a 1.5 by his peers. Based on the information in the chapter, assess how effectively DeVonne handled the class's evaluation of Justin's work.

DeVonne could have done a better job in making the class a safe environment for Justin by moderating the negative feedback Justin received. Though the essay technically didn't meet the criteria for a well-written expository essay, it was quite creative in creating a mood. DeVonne might have taken a few moments to point this out, complimenting Justin on his efforts.

CLASSROOM EXERCISES

A synthesis of Kathy Brewster's lesson on the Crusades is shown below. Read the case study and answer the questions that follow.

1.   "We better get moving," Susan urged Jim as they approached the door of Kathy Brewster's classroom. "The bell is gonna ring, and you know how Brewster is about this class. She thinks it's SO important."

2.   "Did you finish your homework?" Jim asked and then stopped himself. "What am I talking about? You've done your home in every class since I first knew you."

3.   "I don't mind it that much. . . . It bothers me when I don't get something, and sometimes it's even fun. My dad helps me. He says he wants to keep up with the world," Susan responded with a laugh.

4.   "In some classes, I just do enough to get a decent grade, but not in here," Jim responded. "I used to hate history, but Brewster sorta makes you think. It's actually interesting the way she's always telling us about the way we are because of something that happened a zillion years ago. . . . I never thought about this stuff in that way before."

5.   "Gee, Mrs. Brewster, that assignment was impossible," Harvey grumbled as he walked in.

6.   "That's good for you," Kathy smiled back. "I know it was a tough assignment, but you need to be challenged. It's hard for me, too, when I'm studying and trying to put together new ideas, but if I hang in, I feel like I can usually get it."

7.   "Aw, c'mon, Mrs. Brewster. I thought you knew everything."

8.   "I wish. I have to study every night to keep up with you people, and the harder I study, the smarter I get," Kathy continued with a smile. "And, . . . I feel good about myself when I do."

9.   "But you make us work so hard," Harvey continued in feigned complaint.

10.   "Yes, but look how good you're getting at writing," Kathy smiled again, pointing her finger at him. "I think you hit a personal best on your last one. You're becoming a very good writer."

11.   "Yeh, yeh, I know," Harvey smiled on his way to his desk, ". . . and being good writers will help us in everything we do in life," repeating a rationale the students continually hear from Kathy.

12.   Kathy turned to Jennifer as she walked in, and said quietly, "I pulled your desk over here, Jenny," motioning to a spot in the middle of the second row. "You've been a little quiet lately. . . . I almost considered calling your Mom, to see if everything's okay," and she touched Jennifer's arm, motioning her to the spot.

13.   She finished taking roll and then pulled down a map in the front of the room. "Let's look again at the map and review for a moment to see where we are. We began our discussion of the Crusades yesterday. What was significant about them? . . . Greg?"

14.   "You came in with pictures of Crusaders and asked us to imagine what it'd be like to be one of them. . . . Antonio said he didn't think he'd like iron underwear," Greg grinned as the rest of the class giggled.

15.   "All right, that's true." Kathy smiled back. "Now, how did we start the lesson? . . . Kim?"

16.   ". . ."

17.   "Remember, we started by imagining that we all left Lincoln High School and that it was taken over by people who believed that all extracurricular activities should be eliminated. We then asked what we should do about it. What did we decide we should do?"

18.   "We decided we'd talk to them . . . and try and change their minds," Kim responded hesitantly.

19.   "Right. Exactly, Kim. Very good. We said that we would be on a 'crusade' to try to change their minds.

20.   "Now, what were the actual Crusades all about? . . . Selena?"

21.   ". . . The Christians wanted to get the Holy Land back from the Muslims."

22.   "About when was this happening?"

23.   "I . . . I'm not sure."

24.   "Look up at our time line."

25.   ". . . Oh, yeah, about 1100," Selena answered peering at the time line.

26.   "Good, and why did they want them back? . . . Becky?"

27.   "The . . . Holy Lands were important for the Christians. I suppose they just wanted them because of that."

28.   "Yes. Good, Becky," Kathy smiled. "Indeed, that was a factor. What else? . . . Anyone?"

29.   After surveying the class and seeing uncertainty on students' faces, Kathy said, "You might not see what I'm

driving at. . . . Let's look at this," and she then displayed a map that illustrated the extent of Muslim influence in the Middle East, North Africa, and Europe.

30. "What do you see here? . . . Cynthia?"

31. Cynthia scanned the map for several seconds and then said, "It looks like the Muslims are getting more and more territory."

32. "Yes, very good. So, what implication did this have for the Europeans?"

33. "They probably were scared . . . like afraid the Muslims would take over their land," Scott volunteered.

34. "That's a good thought, Scott," Kathy responded. "They certainly were a military threat. In fact, the conflict occurring in Bosnia is a present-day reminder of the clash between Christians and Muslims. How else might they have been threatening?"

35. "Maybe . . . economically," Brad added. "You're always telling us how economics rules the world."

36. "Brilliant, Brad," Kathy laughed. "Indeed, economics was a factor. In fact, this is a little ahead of where we are, but we'll see that the military and economic threats of the Muslims, together with the religious issue, were also factors that led to Columbus's voyage to the New World. . . . Think about that. The Muslims in 1000 A.D. have had an influence on us here today."

37. "Now," Kathy said, "let's get back on track. Why do we study the Crusades? Like, who cares, anyway? . . . Toni?"

38. "They were important in Europe, . . . it affected its development in the Middle Ages, like fashion and war strategies, . . . all the way up to today. The Renaissance wouldn't have been the same without them."

39. "Excellent, Toni! Very good analysis. Now, for today's assignment, you were asked to write a paragraph answering the question, 'Were the Crusades a success or a failure?' You could take either position. We want to learn how to make and defend an argument, so the quality of your paragraph depends on how you defended your position, not on the position itself. Remember, this is a skill that goes way beyond a specific topic like the Crusades. This applies in everything we do.

40. "So, let's see how we made out. Go ahead. . . . Nikki?"

41. "I said they were a failure. They didn't . . ."

42. "Wait a minute!" Joe interrupted. "How about the new fighting techniques they learned?"

43. "Joe," Kathy began firmly, "what is one of the principles we operate on in here?"

44. "We don't have to agree with someone . . . but we have to listen. . . . Sorry."

45. "Go on, Nikki," Kathy continued.

46. "That's okay," Nikki continued nodding to Joe. "It seemed to me that militarily, at least, they failed because the Europeans didn't accomplish what they were after . . . to get the Holy Land back for Christianity," Nikki said. "There were several Crusades, and after only one did they get sort of a foothold, and it only lasted a short time, like about 50 years, I think."

47. "Okay. That's good, Nikki," Kathy responded. "You made your point and then supported it. That's what I wanted you to do in your paragraph."

48. "Now, go ahead, Joe. You were making a point," Kathy said, turning back to him.

49. "I said they were a success because the Europeans learned new military strategies that they used on the Natives . . . here, in the Americas, and they were good at it. If it hadn't been for the Crusades, they probably wouldn't have learned the techniques, . . . at least not for a long time. Then, only the Japanese knew the attacking techniques the Crusaders learned when they went to the Middle East. It even changed our ideas about like guerrilla fighting."

50. "Also good, Joe," Kathy responded, nodding. "This is exactly what we're after. Nikki and Joe took opposite points of view in their paragraphs, but they each provided several details to support their positions. Again, we're more concerned with the support you provide than the actual position you take.

51. "Let's look at one more," she went on. "What was your position, Anita?"

52. "I said they . . . were a success," Anita responded. "Europe, you know, like Western Europe took a lot from their culture, their culture in the Middle East. Like, some of the spices we eat today first came to Europe then."

53. "Now isn't that interesting!" Kathy waved energetically. "See, here's another case where we see ourselves today finding a relationship to people who lived 1,000 or more years ago. That's what history is all about."

54. "Brewster loves this stuff," David whispered to Kelly, smiling slightly.

55. "Yeah," she replied. "History has never been my favorite subject, but some of this stuff is actually kind of

neat."

56. "Okay. One more," Kathy continued, "and we'll move on."

57. The class reviewed another example, and then Kathy told the students to revise their paragraphs in light of what they had discussed that day and to turn in a final product the following day. "Remember, think about what you're doing when you make your revisions," she emphasized. "Read your paragraph after you write it, and ask yourself, 'do I actually have evidence here, or is it simply an opinion?' . . . The more aware you are when you write, the better you work will be."

58. When the period was nearly over, Kathy said, "Excuse me, but the bell is about to ring. Just a reminder, group presentations on the Renaissance are Wednesday and Thursday. You decide what groups will be on each day. For those who chose to write the paper on the Middle Ages, remember we agreed that they should be due next Friday."

Identify the variable in the Model *best illustrated* by each of the following combinations of paragraphs. Remember, it is the *combinations* of the paragraphs. Do not focus on a single paragraph in each case (unless only a single paragraph is identified, as in Item 3 [paragraph 12]).

For example, paragraphs 6-8 best illustrate *Teacher modeling and enthusiasm.*

Now, you identify the variable for the following combinations of paragraphs. Be sure to provide a rationale for your choice in each case.

1.   1-11

2.   5-6

3.   12

4.   7-19

5.   22-25

6.   30-31 (Identify two different variables for these paragraphs.)

7.   37-38

8.   40-43

9.   50

10.   53-54

FEEDBACK FOR CLASSROOM EXERCISES

1. Paragraphs 1-11: Teacher Expectations
Evidence for Kathy's high expectations exists in the students' responses, " ...you know how Brewster is about this class. She thinks it's SO important." (1); ". ..Brewster sorta makes you think," (4); and "But you make us work so hard." (9)

2. Paragraphs 5-6: Challenge
Kathy even uses the word "challenge" in (6).

3. Paragraph 12: Caring
Kathy demonstrates a personal interest in Jennifer by moving her to the middle of the row.

4. Paragraphs 17-19: Personalization
Kathy personalizes the Crusades by using their "crusade" to prevent the elimination of extracurricular activities as a metaphor for their topic.

5. Paragraphs 22-25: Success
Kathy provides a prompt which allows Selena to answer correctly.

6. Paragraphs 30-31: Involvement/Success
Using open-ended questions is a technique for promoting involvement, and they also ensure success. (Either or both answers would be acceptable.)

7. Paragraphs 37-38: Task Comprehension
Kathy wants the students to understand the reasons for studying the Crusades.

8. Paragraphs 40-43: Order and Safety
Kathy creates a safe environment by admonishing Joe for interrupting Nikki.

9. Paragraph 50: Feedback
Kathy provides information about the extent to which goals are being reached.

10. Paragraphs 53-54: Modeling and enthusiasm
Kathy demonstrates her own genuine interest in the topic.

CHAPTER 12: CREATING PRODUCTIVE LEARNING ENVIRONMENTS
CLASSROOM MANAGEMENT

CHAPTER OVERVIEW

This chapter is the first of two focusing on the creation of productive learning learning environments with emphasize on the creation and maintenance orderly classrooms. The chapter begins with a discussion of planning for orderly classrooms, the preparation and teaching of rules and procedures, and communication with parents. It continues with a discussion of management interventions from both cognitive and behaviorist perspectives. The chapter closes with a discussion of serious management problems and school violence.

CHAPTER OBJECTIVES

- Explain how instruction and classroom management contribute to productive learning environments.

- Describe how cognitive approaches to classroom management develop learner responsibility.

- Explain how effective planning can prevent management problems.

- Identify differences between cognitive and behavioral approaches to management.

- Describe how effective intervention techniques can eliminate management problems.

TRANSPARENCIES

The transparencies exist in both acetate form and as PowerPoint slides.

T 12.1 Planning for orderly classrooms (Figure 12.1, p. 429)
T 12.2 Learner characteristics affecting classroom management
T 12.3 Guidelines for preparing rules
T 12.4 Examples of teachers' rules
T 12.5 Guidelines for beginning the school year
T 12.6 Involving caregivers in their children's education
T 12.7 Guidelines for successful interventions
T 12.8 Cognitive interventions
T 12.9 An intervention continuum (Figure 12.4, p. 451)

TRANSPARENCY MASTERS

The transparency masters are included in this manual beginning on page 230.

TM 12.1 Instructional principles for creating and teaching rules
TM 12.2. Sample classroom procedures
TM 12.3 Teaching children procedures
TM 12.4 Beginning the school year
TM 12.5 A behavioral management system

CHAPTER OUTLINE

I.   Classroom management: A definition
  A.   Classroom management and the complexities of the classroom
      a.   Classroom events are multidimensional and simultaneous
      b.   Classroom events are immediate
      c.   Classroom events are unpredictable

I.   Classroom management: A definition
    A.   Classroom management and the complexities of the classroom
        a.   Classroom events are multidimensional and simultaneous
        b.   Classroom events are immediate
        c.   Classroom events are unpredictable
        d.   Classroom events are public
    B.   Cognitive approaches to management: Developing learner responsibility
II. Planning for effective classroom management
    A.   Student characteristics
    B.   The physical environment
    C.   Rules and procedures: Cornerstones of an effective management system
    D.   Creating and teaching rules: Instructional strategies
        1.   Teaching rules
        2.   Beginning the school year
        3.   Monitoring rules
III. Communication with parents
    A.   Benefits of communication
    B.   Involving parents: Instructional strategies
    C.   Communication with parents: Accommodating learner diversity
        1.   Economic, cultural, and language barriers
        2.   Involving minority parents
IV. Dealing with misbehavior: Interventions
    A.   Guidelines for successful interventions
        a.   Demonstrate withitness
        b.   Preserve student dignity
        c.   Be consistent
        d.   Follow-through
        e.   Keep interventions brief
        f.   Avoid arguments
    B.   Cognitive interventions
        1.   Verbal-nonverbal congruence
        2.   I-messages
        3.   Active listening
        4.   Problem ownership
        5.   Logical consequences
    C.   Behavioral interventions
        1.   Assertive Discipline: A structured approach to consequences
        2.   Designing and maintaining a behavioral management system
    D.   An intervention continuum
        1.   Praising desired behavior
        2.   Ignoring inappropriate behavior
        3.   Using indirect cues
        4.   Using desists
        5.   Applying consequences
    E.   Assessment and learning: The role of assessment in classroom management
V.   Serious management problems: Violence and aggression
    A.   Immediate actions
    B.   Long-term solutions

PRESENTATION OUTLINE

Teaching suggestions in the outline will be marked with the symbol ■. In most cases, the suggested activities can be done individually and discussed as a whole group, or they can be done in small groups, and the small-group results can be discussed with the whole class. To be consistent with our understanding of knowledge construction, we recommend that you promote as much discussion–both in small groups and with the whole class–as possible.

Enrichment Information, which includes elaborations of text topics as well as topics not included in the text, will be boxed as you see here.

I.   Classroom management: A definition
    A.   Classroom management and the complexities of the classroom
        a.   Classroom events are multidimensional and simultaneous
        b.   Classroom events are immediate
        c.   Classroom events are unpredictable
        d.   Classroom events are public
    B.   Cognitive approaches to management: Developing learner responsibility
II. Planning for effective classroom management
    A.   Student characteristics
    B.   The physical environment
    C.   Rules and procedures: Cornerstones of an effective management system
    D.   Creating and teaching rules: Instructional strategies
        1.   Teaching rules

■ *The purpose in the following suggestions is to help your students understand the importance of planning for orderly classrooms, together with the differences between a cognitive and a behaviorist approach to classroom management.*

1.   **To check students' perceptions and informally assess their backgrounds with respect to classroom management, have them identify some of the characteristics of effective managers. To help them in their thinking ask them to think about some of their previous teachers. Discuss their results. Record some of their suggestions so that you can refer back to them as you examine the content of the chapter.**

2.   **Ask the students how a management system based on cognitive views of learning would be different from a system based on behaviorist views of learning. Emphasize differences such as:**
    .   **knowing the reasons for rules compared to obeying rules because of fear of negative consequences.**
    .   **focusing on personal responsibility compared to simply complying with rules.**
    .   **emphasizing that rules exist to protect their rights and the rights of their classmates to learn in a safe and orderly environment.**

3.   **T 12.1 *"Planning for an Orderly Classroom"* illustrates the elements that should be considered in planning for rules and procedures, and T 12.2 *"Learner Characteristics Affecting Classroom Management"* identifies some of the learner attributes that should be considered.**

4.   **To illustrate some additional procedures, display TM 12.2 *"Sample Classroom Procedures,"* which outlines some examples of procedures at the elementary as well as**

the middle, junior high, and secondary levels.

5. Using the guidelines listed in T 12.3 *"Guidelines for Preparing Rules"* have the students generate lists of rules that they would use in their classrooms. Discuss their decisions with the whole class.

6. Display T 12.4 *"Examples of Teachers' Rules."* Assess the extent to which they followed the guidelines outlined in T 12.3.

7. Have students describe the way concepts are taught, as was discussed in Chapter 9. Remind them that rules and procedures are no more effectively taught with abstract descriptions than are concepts.

8. To illustrate the way effective teachers teach their procedures and rules, display TM 12.3 *"Teaching Children Procedures."* Have students look at the example, and then have them describe specifically what the teacher did that was effective. They should notice that she modeled the process and provided an example for the children. The children were also actively involved in the learning experience. You might also remind them that Martha was using a form of *direct modeling*, which was designed to teach the children *new behaviors*, which is a link to the content of social cognitive theory in Chapter 6.

9. To help students integrate the content of this chapter with earlier chapters, have them explain--based on some of the topics from earlier chapters (particularly Chapters 2, 6, 7, and 10)--why effective management can increase both achievement and motivation. Some of the connections they make should include:
    .   An orderly classroom helps the students maintain their *equilibrium*--Chapter 2. Disorderly classrooms leave learners with a sense of disequilibrium, which detracts from their ability to think and concentrate on learning.
    .   Orderly classrooms are predictable. According to social cognitive theory--Chapter 6, predictable consequences are important. (They should recall that nonoccurrence of expected reinforcers can become punishers, and nonoccurrence of expected punishers can become reinforcers.)
    .   Orderly classrooms help learners develop schemas for appropriate actions. These schemas then guide their actions as they function in the classroom--Chapter 7. Disorderly classrooms don't allow learners to form effective schemas that help them operate effectively in the classroom.
    .   Orderly classrooms promote a sense of safety, and safety is one of the most basic needs on Maslow's Hierarchy--Chapter 10.

1. Beginning the school year
2. Monitoring rules

■ *The purpose of the suggestions in this section is to help your students understand the importance of beginning the school year effectively and how rules and procedures are monitored.*

1. Display T 12.5 *"Guidelines for Beginning the School Year."* Ask the students to use social cognitive theory to explain why the beginning of the year is so important. Included in their responses should be the fact that the beginning establishes expectations for the kinds of behaviors that will be reinforced

2. Display TM 12.4 *"Beginning the School Year,"* and have them compare the way the two

184

teachers began their year. Discuss the differences as a whole group.

III. Communication with parents
    A. Benefits of communication
    B. Involving parents: Instructional strategies
    C. Communication with parents: Accommodating learner diversity
        1. Economic, cultural, and language barriers
        2. Involving minority parents

> ■ *The suggestions in this section are intended to help your students understand the importance of communication with parents, particularly those coming from diverse backgrounds.*
>
> 1. **Display T 12.6** *"Involving Caregivers in Their Children's Education,"* **which outlines some of the issues related to involving parents, as well as some suggestions for trying to increase parental involvement. Discuss the suggestions and what teachers might do to improve school-home communication.**
>
> 2. **Even though teachers try to communicate with parents and other caregivers, some remain reluctant to get involved in school activities. Have the students brainstorm some additional ways to try and involve parents and other caregivers.**

IV. Dealing with misbehavior: Interventions
    A. Guidelines for successful interventions
        a. Demonstrate withitness
        b. Preserve student dignity
        c. Be consistent
        d. Follow-through
        e. Keep interventions brief
        f. Avoid arguments

> ■ *The purpose of the suggestions in this section is to help your students understand basic approaches to intervention*
>
> 1. **Display T 12.7** *"Guidelines for Successful Interventions"* **which provides examples of each of the interventions.**

    B. Cognitive interventions
        1. Verbal-nonverbal congruence
        2. I-messages
        3. Active listening
        4. Problem ownership
        5. Logical consequences

> ■ *The purpose of the suggestions in this section is to help your students understand cognitive interventions.*
>
> 1. **Ask the students to explain why verbal-nonverbal congruence, I-messages, active listening, and logical consequences are cognitive versus behaviorist.**
>
> 2. **They should conclude that the assumption involved in each is that the learner is an active, thinking being. If verbal and nonverbal behaviors are inconsistent, for example, a learner's equilibrium is disrupted by the inconsistency. They won't react to the verbal**

directive, as behaviorism would predict; rather they react to their perception of the true meaning of the message, which is a cognitive explanation.

3. Display T 12.8 *"Cognitive Interventions,"* which provides examples of each of the cognitive interventions.

C. Behavioral interventions
  1. Assertive Discipline: A structured approach to consequences
  2. Designing and maintaining a behavioral management system

■ *The purpose of the suggestions in this section is to help your students understand behaviorist interventions.*

1. While behavioral management systems are somewhat controversial, many teachers in the field continue to design and use them. TM 12.5 *"A Behavioral Management System"* illustrates one teacher's behavioral management system. You might display TM 12.5 and have the students discuss its strengths and weaknesses.

2. Refer the students back to Erika Williams' management system, described on page 208, as another example of a behaviorist management system.

3. Since many schools and teachers may expect beginning teachers to be able to design a behavioral management system, you may want to have students design a system of their own. In the process, remind them that they can incorporate characteristics that promote responsibility by providing rationales for the rules they design and allowing student input into the rules. (They won't be able to solicit student input in this activity, of course, but they can have this notion in mind as they prepare their rules.)

D. An intervention continuum
  1. Praising desired behavior
  2. Ignoring inappropriate behavior
  3. Using indirect cues
  4. Using desists
  5. Applying consequences
E. Assessment and learning: The role of assessment in classroom management

■ *The purpose of the suggestions in this section is to help your students understand the differences between cognitive and behaviorist approaches to intervention and to be able to apply effective interventions in their own teaching.*
1. Display T 12.9 *"An Intervention Continuum"* and have the students explain each of the points on the continuum from both a cognitive and a behaviorist perspective. As a simple example, from a cognitive perspective, praise is feedback that helps the students understand what is appropriate. From a behaviorist perspective, praise is a positive reinforcer. From a cognitive perspective consequences should be logical and connected to the act, and from a behaviorist perspective, they're punishers than are intended to eliminate the behavior.

2. Have the students describe the differences between a system based on cognitive views of learning compared to behaviorist views of learning. Emphasize differences such as:
  . knowing the reasons for rules compared to obeying rules because of fear of negative consequences.

- focusing on personal responsibility compared to simply complying with rules.
- emphasizing that rules exist to protect their rights and the rights of their classmates to learn in a safe and orderly environment.

3. **As an application exercise have the students compare the effectiveness of Judy Harris' and Janelle Powers's management (the case studies at the beginning and the end of the chapter respectively). Some of the conclusions students should make include:**
   - Janelle could have been better organized by having the students complete a warmup activity while she took roll.
   - Judy demonstrated withitness and overlapping, whereas Janelle did not
   - Judy had well established routines, and Janelle did not.
   - Janelle's communication did not utilize "I-message"s.
   - Judy better maintained lesson momentum in spite of interventions than did Janelle.

4. **As a form of enrichment, you may want to provide some of the following information that emphasizes the role of communication in effective management.**

The Canters (1992) suggest that in communicating with students it is important to have a positive but firm tone. They identify three communication styles, which they label *passive*, *hostile*, and *assertive*. The following are examples.

Kelly waves her hand wildly above her head during seatwork and nearly shouts, "Mr. Hicks, I don't know how to do number 3."
"Please," Mr. Hicks implores, "must you yell? I'll be there in a second. Try to be patient."

Cameron blurts out an answer in a question-and-answer session.
"One more time like that and you're out of here," Mrs. Santo shouts back. "How many times do I have to remind you of the rules in here?"

Zena and Karin are whispering and giggling while Mrs. Kim is explaining a procedure on the board.
"Zena, Karin," she says evenly. "The other students can't hear over your talking. Please be quiet."

The misbehavior in each case was similar, but each teacher's response was different. Mr. Hicks was *passive*, nearly solicitous in his response, which communicated uncertainty about his own ability to manage the class. Mrs. Santo was immediately angry and *hostile*, which was no more effective. In contrast, Mrs. Kim was neither passive nor hostile, but instead communicated clearly in an *assertive*, no-nonsense way that students were interfering with learning and the behavior had to stop. An assertive response style communicates to students that teachers have a right to teach, and students have a right to learn.
While assertiveness is most commonly associated with the Canters' work, several other authorities advocate a similar approach to management. Kounin (1970), Glasser (1985), Jones (1987), and Dreikurs, Grunwald, and Pepper (1982) in their book *Maintaining Sanity in the Classroom* published by Harper and Row, all advocate a clear and firm stance as one effective management skill. (The citations other than Dreikurs, et al., are in the reference list in the text.)
It should be emphasized that firmness or assertiveness is the clear communication of well-defined limits in a climate of respect and openness. It is not harsh or rigid behavior on the part of the teacher. The latter, in fact, is a barrier to effective communication and classroom management.

V. Serious management problems: Violence and aggression
    1. Immediate actions
    2. Long-term solutions

■ *The purpose in the following suggestions is to help your students put serious management problems into perspective.*

   1. **Remind the students that while violence and aggression make dramatic headlines, the incidents are in reality very infrequent. Tell them that in the case of a violent incident that they should break up the incident, if possible, and then get help immediately.**

DISCUSSION STARTERS

1. Have classroom management issues changed over the last 10 years? Fifteen years? Twenty years? Why do you think so?

2. To what extent is effective classroom management a function of teachers' personalities compared to teachers' knowledge? Provide a rationale for your position.

3. We discussed rules and procedures from cognitive and behaviorist views. How would they be designed based on humanistic views of learners?

4. Effective management has been called a "necessary but not sufficient" component of effective teaching. Explain the "necessary" and "not sufficient" parts of this expression.

5. Suppose some high school teachers are moving to elementary schools. What advice would you give them for modifying their existing management plans? What about teachers making the transition the other way?

6. To what extent does classroom management involve moral decisions, both on the part of the teacher and on the part of the students? Use Kohlberg's theory to support your answer.

7. A concerned parent at the beginning of the school year wants to know if you think that Assertive Discipline is an effective way to manage classrooms. How would you answer the parent?

8. How might learners' cultural and SES backgrounds influence the way you manage your classroom? In answering this question choose and describe a specific location where you anticipate you will be teaching.

BACKGROUND READINGS

Charles, C. (2002). *Building classroom discipline: From models to practice* (7th ed.). Upper Saddle River, NJ: Pearson. This short, readable book describes several "models" of classroom management. These models offer a succinct overview of several experts' views on approaches to effective management and discipline.

Doyle, W. (1986). Classroom organization and management. In M. Wittrock (Ed.), *Handbook of research on teaching* (3rd ed.) (pp. 392–431). New York: Macmillan. The chapter, almost a classic, provides a wide-ranging, research-based discussion of effective management issues at both the elementary and secondary school levels.

Emmer, E., Evertson, C., & Worsham, M. (2003). *Classroom management for secondary teachers* (6th ed.). Upper Saddle River, NJ: Prentice-Hall. Based on the practices of effective managers at the secondary level, this book is a source of practical ideas for secondary teachers.

Evertson, C., Emmer, & Worsham, M. (2003). *Classroom management for elementary teachers* (6th ed.). Needham Heights, MA: Allyn & Bacon. This practical and readable text translates the research literature on management in elementary classrooms into concrete suggestions.

Evertson, C., & Randolph, C. (1995) . Classroom management in the learning-centered classroom. In A. Ornstein (Ed.), *Teaching: Theory and practice*. Needham Heights, MA: Allyn and Bacon. This chapter describes the relationship between management and instruction and describes how each contributes to the other.

Good, T., & Brophy, J. (2000). *Looking in classrooms* (8th ed.). New York: Addison-Wesley Longman. This well known text includes two detailed chapters on classroom management.

FEEDBACK FOR CONSTRUCTED RESPONSE AND DOCUMENT-BASED ANALYSIS QUESTIONS

Constructed Response Items _____

1. Analyze Janelle's planning for classroom management.

Teacher planning in terms of management should decrease disruptions and maximize student learning time. Due to ineffective planning Janelle's students were expected to sit quietly while she called the roll, while she went to the file cabinet to get out her transparencies, and while she finished arranging her materials. As a result, her students not only lost valuable instructional time, there were also opportunities for management problems to arise.

2. Evaluate the effectiveness of Janelle's management interventions.

There were several problems with her management interventions. First, Janelle evidenced a lack of withitness; Janelle first admonished Leila when she blurted out, "Stop it Damon," so Janelle initially 'caught' the wrong one, and allowed the incident to disrupt the learning activity to a greater extent than did Judy. Janelle also allowed her encounter with Howard and Manny to disrupt the momentum of her lesson. Janelle's nonverbal behavior also didn't communicate that she was "in charge", or that she meant it when ;she intervened. For example, she glanced up from her papers to admonish Howard and Manfred, and she again "looked up" in response to a hum of voices around the classroom. Also, requiring Manfred to read the rule aloud in front of the class was a form of power play that did nothing to improve the classroom climate, and her comment, "You've been bugging me all week . . ." was inconsistent with recommendations of authorities such as Gordon.

3. The chapter stressed the interdependence of management and instruction. Analyze the relationship between management and instruction in Janelle's class. Include both strengths and weaknesses in the relationship.

Janelle's instruction would have been more effective if it had been more interactive and developed with more supporting materials such as maps and globes. This would have allowed her to involve students more, which usually results in fewer management problems.

Janelle's management was also less effective than it might have been. She wasn't well organized and she didn't communicate as clearly and assertively as she might have to be effective. In Addition she was slightly less "withit" than what would have been desirable and she allowed her interventions with the students to disrupt the momentum and smoothness of her lesson, resulting in more problems with management.

We have several suggestions for improvement. First, Janelle would have been more effective if she had been better organized. A beginning-of-class warmup activity would have helped her better use her time and would also have eliminated "dead" time at the beginning of the lesson during which management problems can occur. Also, her materials should have been ready and waiting, so she didn't have to spend time arranging them while students were supposed to sit quietly. Her verbal and nonverbal channels of communication weren't quite congruent, so her admonishments of students weren't as credible as they might have been, and her interaction with Howard implied a character flaw rather than simple inappropriate behavior. Finally, allowing her intervention with Howard and Manfred to disrupt the flow of her lesson further detracted from the smooth management of her students.

Document-Based Analysis

Brenda Litchfield, a third-grade teacher in an inner-city elementary school, developed the following list of rules for her class.
1. Raise your hand before speaking. Otherwise work quietly.
2. Listen when someone else is talking.
3. Don't leave your seat unless the teacher gives permission.
4. Keep your hands to yourself.
5. When in line, stand quietly and don't bother people in front or back of you.
6. Follow directions the first time they are given.
7. Bring necessary materials to class.

Analyze Brenda's rules based on the guidelines in this chapter. Include suggestions for making the rules more effective.

General guidelines for effective rules include: 1) state rules positively, 2) minimize the number of rules, 3) solicit student input, and 4) emphasize rationales for rules. In addition, rules should be clear enough so students understand them and can follow them.

We don't know if Brenda solicited student input or emphasized the reasons for her rules. However, they were stated positively. One problem might be the number of rules–seven–which might be too many for third graders. In addition, one of the rules, "bring necessary materials to class" is too vague to provide much guidance to students.

CLASSROOM EXERCISES

1. In the chapter we talked about the concept of follow-through, meaning the teacher must follow through to be certain that misbehavior stops when she intervenes. Suppose the teacher asks students to stop misbehaving, but doesn't follow through. Explain what the likely outcomes of failing to follow through would be based on social cognitive theory. Explain for the target students and also explain for other students.

2. In the chapter we said "Assertive discipline is popular because it clearly specifies consequences for breaking and following rules, which eliminates the need for split second decisions by the teacher." Using information processing as a basis, explain why "eliminating split second decisions" is helpful for teachers. Again using information processing theory as a basis, explain why would making "split second" decisions be easier for an expert than for a novice teacher?

3. Duranna Hamilton greets her students with a smile at the classroom door. "How's your new little sister?" she asks Devon, whose mother recently had a baby girl.

   "Be ready today," she smiles and whispers to Cassie as she comes in. "I've been watching you, and you've been a little quiet lately, so I'm going to call on you today. . . . Be ready," she smiles again and ushers Cassie into the room with a touch on her shoulder.

   As she is ushering Cassie to her seat, she says, "Rico and Steve," in response to the students' whispering after the bell stops ringing. "One of the rules we all agreed on was 'Be ready to work as soon as the bell stops ringing.'"

   Duranna watches them carefully, and the boys quickly stop.

   Identify the three guidelines for successful interventions that were best illustrated in the vignette. Explain.

4. Think about the study of psychosocial development in Chapter 3. How would Erikson explain the disruptive behavior of a low-achieving fifth grader? Using Erikson's work as a guide, explain what you might do to help the student.

5. Learners in obedience-oriented classrooms see rules in an absolute "do it or else" frame of reference, whereas learners in responsibility-oriented classrooms learn to obey rules because they understand that we agree upon the rules, and the rules exist to protect their rights and the rights of others. To which of Kohlberg's stages do each of these orientations most closely relate?

6. Read the case study and respond to the question that follows. (This is a real-world example of an encounter between a student and a teacher.) (The paragraphs are numbered for your reference.)

1.   Andrew is a bright but active and talkative sixth grader who periodically blurts out answers in class before his classmates have a chance to respond. He also has a habit of putting pens in his mouth. Mrs. Jones, his teacher uses a classroom management system in which students get "tallies" for misbehavior. She usually gives students one warning if they break a rule, which is then followed by giving a "tally," although students will occasionally get tallies for a first infraction. Receiving three or more tallies in a one-week period results in a half hour of detention.
2.   Andrew is periodically warned about his blurting out answers, and he then stops doing so for several days. He, and other students, periodically receive tallies, but rarely receive three in a week, wanting to avoid the possibility of detention.
3.   As the students are making the transition from the learning activity to seatwork, Mrs. Jones announces quite loudly, "Andrew, Sanchia just told me that you spit on her. . . . We don't behave that way, and we particularly don't spit on each other. You will be receiving a tally."
4.   The students, somewhat startled by Mrs. Jones' announcement look around at Andrew and Sanchia, but they quickly settle down and begin their seatwork, and the rest of the day proceeds without incident.
5.   "Mom!" Andrew nearly screams as he walks into the house after school that day. "Mrs. Jones is so terrible and so mean. She is so unfair," he continues nearly out of control.

6. "Wait, . . . calm down, honey," Suzanne, his mother, says, putting her arm around him and attempting to sooth his feelings. "Tell me what happened."

7. "I'm just working, and out of the blue Mrs. Jones announces in front of the whole class that I spit on Sanchia, and that I have a tally."

8. "Are you sure you were 'just working'?" Suzanne probes. "Did you spit on Sanchia?"

9. "No, no, no, . . . Mom, I really didn't."

10. "You must have don't something," Suzanne continues to probe. "Sanchia wouldn't just make that up out of the clear blue."

11. They talk at length, and during the discussion it comes out that Andrew did indeed have his pen in his mouth and "I maybe pointed it at Sanchia,"

12. "Did it have saliva on it?"

13. "I don't know . . . maybe," Andrew confesses. "But, Mom, it's terrible unfair. I got a tally once for tattling, and now Sanchia says I spit at her, when I didn't really do it, and I get a tally. It just isn't fair. Why didn't she get a tally for tattling?"

14. Suzanne considers the incident, talks to a friend, and decides to write Mrs. Jones a note inquiring about her tally system and how it's administered. In the note Suzanne questions Mrs. Jones giving Andrew a tally when she didn't see the incident–she only used the other student's word, and she also questions the inconsistency in giving tallies.

15. Upon receiving the note, Mrs. Jones calls Andrew out in the hall before class and says, "What's this all about? I got a note from your mom about the tally you received for spitting on Sanchia."

16. "But, Mrs. Jones," Andrew protests. "I didn't spit on her. I swear, . . . I didn't."

17. "Well, that's the way it goes sometimes," Mrs. Jones responds. "Sometimes you need to just shake it off. That's part of life. . . . Now, go back into the classroom. We're about to start."

18. "Do I still have the tally?"

19. "Yes."

Identify at least four things Mrs. Jones did in the encounter with Andrew that were ineffective, specify the paragraphs in which the ineffective behavior is illustrated, and explain why they were ineffective. .

For example:

1. She gave Andrew a tally based on Sanchia's accusation rather than her own observation. (paragraph). As a result, Andrew felt screwed. (In Andrew's perception, he didn't spit on her. She shouldn't have given him a tally unless she observed the infraction. [This also demonstrates a lack of "withitness."])

Now, identify at least three more:

FEEDBACK FOR CLASSROOM EXERCISES

1. Social cognitive theory would suggest that failing to follow through would result in an increase in the undesired behavior. Misbehaving students *expect* to be admonished for their misbehavior. The nonoccurrence of these consequences act as reinforcers, which results in an increase in the misbehaviors.

The nonoccurrence of expected punishers act as vicarious reinforcers for the rest of the students, and they also become more likely to misbehave.

2. Split-second decisions require working memory space. Eliminating the split-second decisions frees working memory space that can be devoted to other aspects of learning and teaching.

Making split-second decisions is easier for experts because more of their knowledge is automatic, so they have more working memory space that can be devoted to making the decision.

3. Duranna first demonstrated *withitness* by quickly recognizing that Rico and Steve were talking inappropriately. second, by watching them carefully until they stopped, she demonstrated *follow through,* and third, she kept the intervention brief. It is likely that she demonstrated the guidelines as well, but we don't have evidence for them in the vignette.

4. Erikson's work would suggest that the fifth grader is disruptive because he or she hasn't achieved a sense of industry that results from success on worthwhile tasks. While difficult, the key is genuine accomplishment on tasks the student perceives as challenging.

5. The first orientation most closely relates to Stage 1. "Do it or else," implies punishment for disobedience. A responsibility orientation is related to Stage 5. When "we agree upon" the rules, they become social contracts. If there wasn't an implied agreement, rules existing to protect everyone's rights implies Stage 3.

6. First, Mrs. Jones is inconsistent in her administering of tallies. (paragraph 1 and paragraph 13)

Second, Mrs. Jones confronts Andrew about Suzanne's note. (paragraph 15). The issue of the note was between Mrs. Jones and Suzanne, not Mrs. Jones and Andrew.

Third, Mrs. Jones teaches Andrew that the world is arbitrary and capricious, rather than orderly and sensible, with the comment, "Well, that's the way it goes sometimes. Sometimes you need to just shake it off. That's part of life." (paragraph 17). Cognitive approaches to management emphasize learner understanding, which can lead to them accepting responsibility for controlling their own behavior. A capricious environment detracts from this understanding.

CHAPTER 13: CREATING PRODUCTIVE LEARNING ENVIRONMENTS
PRINCIPLES OF INSTRUCTION

CHAPTER OVERVIEW

This chapter continues the discussion of the development and maintenance of productive learning environments, with emphasis on the interdependence of effective instruction and orderly classrooms. The chapter begins with an examination of the types of teacher knowledge needed to produce as much learning as possible. It continues with the teacher thinking that is involved in planning instruction, implementing learning activities, and assessing student understanding. The chapter then turns to the abilities, called essential teaching skills, that we expect to see in all teachers regardless of topic or grade level, and closes with a discussion of the relationship of assessment to the planning and implementation of effective learning activities.

CHAPTER OBJECTIVES

- Identify the different types of knowledge expert teachers possess

- Describe the thinking of expert teachers as they plan for instruction

- Identify essential teaching skills that help promote learning for all students at all levels

- Describe the relationships among planning instruction, implementing instruction, and assessing student learning

TRANSPARENCIES

The transparencies exist in both acetate form and as PowerPoint slides.

T 13.1   Teacher knowledge
T 13.2   Processes involved in teacher thinking about planning, implementation, and assessment (Figure 13.1, p. 464)
T 13.3   A taxonomy for learning, teaching, and assessing (Figure 13.2, p. 466)
T 13.4   Essential teaching skills (Figure 13.3, p. 473)
T 13.5   Characteristics of effective praise (Transparency 11.5 from the 5th edition)
T 13.6   Characteristics of effective questioning

TRANSPARENCY MASTER

The transparency master is included in this manual beginning on page 230.

TM 13.1   Instructional alignment

VIDEOS

Looking Through Classroom Windows Tape 2-Segment 4: "Improving Instruction: Essential Teaching Skills" This video lesson illustrates a teacher's attempts to demonstrate each of the essential teaching skills that are presented in the chapter. (This is the chapter's opening case study.)

Looking Through Classroom Windows Tape 2-Segment 5: "Climate, Geography, and Economics in Junior High School Social Studies."
This video lesson illustrates a teacher attempting to help her students understand the relationships between the geography and the economy of four different regions of the United States. (This is the chapter's closing case study.)

CHAPTER OUTLINE

I.   Teacher knowledge and teacher thinking
    A.   Teacher knowledge
    B.   Teacher thinking
II. Planning for instruction
    A.   Deciding what topics are important to study
    B.   Preparing objectives: Deciding what students should know, value, or be able to do?
        1.   Objectives in the cognitive domain
        2.   A taxonomy for cognitive objectives
        3.   Objectives in the affective domain
        4.   Objectives in the psychomotor domain
    C.   Preparing and organizing learning activities
        1.   Task analysis: A planning tool
    D.   Planning for assessment
    E.   Planning in a standards-based environment
III. Implementing instruction: Essential teaching skills
    A.   Attitudes
    B.   Use of time
    C.   Organization
    D.   Communication
        1.   Communication and knowledge of content: Implications for teachers
    E.   Focus: Attracting and maintaining attention
    F.   Feedback
        1.   Praise
        2.   Written feedback
    G.   Questioning
        1.   Questioning Frequency
        2.   Equitable distribution
        3.   Prompting
        4.   Wait-time
        5.   Cognitive levels of questions
    H.   Review and closure
    I.   Classroom interaction: Accommodating learner diversity
        1.   Interacting with diverse learners: Implications for teachers
IV. Assessment and learning: Using assessment as a learning tool

PRESENTATION OUTLINE

Teaching suggestions in the outline will be marked with the symbol ■. In most cases, the suggested activities can be done individually and discussed as a whole group, or they can be done in small groups, and the small-group results can be discussed with the whole class. To be consistent with our understanding of knowledge construction, we recommend that you promote as much discussion–both in small groups and with the whole class–as possible.

I.   Teacher knowledge and teacher thinking
    A.   Teacher knowledge
    B.   Teacher thinking

> ■ *The following suggestions are intended to help your students understand the interdependence of effective teaching and orderly classrooms.*
>
> 1.   **Begin by posing the question, "What is the most effective thing you can do to promote an orderly classroom?"**
>
> 2.   **The students will offer a variety of answers, and many of them will be rather vague.**
>
> 3.   **After listing several of their responses, write on the board, "Teach effectively," and then emphasize that it is virtually impossible to have an orderly classroom in the absence of effective instruction.**
>
> 4.   **Show the video episode "Improving Instruction: Essential Teaching Skills" (described at the beginning of the chapter). (It is also the chapter's opening case study.) Then, display T 13.1 *"Teacher Knowledge."* Have the students identify each of the types of knowledge in Scott's lesson (the teacher in the video).**

II.   Planning for instruction
    A.   Deciding what topics are important to study
    B.   Preparing objectives: Deciding what students should know, value, or be able to do?
        1.   Objectives in the cognitive domain
        2.   A taxonomy for cognitive objectives
        3.   Objectives in the affective domain
        4.   Objectives in the psychomotor domain
    C.   Preparing and organizing learning activities
        1.   Task analysis: A planning tool
    D.   Planning for assessment
    E.   Planning in a standards-based environment

> ■ *The following suggestions are intended to help your students understand the processes involved in planning instruction.*
>
> 1.   **Display T 13.2 *"Processes Involved in Teacher Thinking About Planning, Implementation, and Assessment."* Have the students identify the processes in Scott's lesson.**
>
> 2.   **Display T 13.3 *"A Taxonomy for Learning, Teaching, and Assessing."* Have the students classify Scott's objectives into one of the cells of the taxonomy table. Then, have the students classify some of your objectives for the class into the one of the cells.**
>
> 3.   **Remind the students of the affective and psychomotor domains. Depending on the emphasis you place on these domains in your teaching, you might want to have the students classify some objectives using each of these domains.**

III.   Implementing instruction: Essential teaching skills
    A.   Attitudes
    B.   Use of time
    C.   Organization
    D.   Communication

1. Communication and knowledge of content: Implications for teachers
E. Focus: Attracting and maintaining attention
F. Feedback
 1. Praise
 2. Written feedback
G. Questioning
 1. Questioning Frequency
 2. Equitable distribution
 3. Prompting
 4. Wait-time
 5. Cognitive levels of questions
H. Review and closure

■ *The purpose of the suggestions in this section is to help your students understand the essential teaching skills.*
 1. Display T 13.4 *"Essential Teaching Skills"* and briefly discuss them with students. This will also give you the chance to remind students of your attempts to model the information presented in the text, since your class will be a concrete example of a number of the essential teaching skills.

 2. Have the students identify where Scott demonstrated each of the essential teaching skills in his lesson. List Scott's behavior and the skill he demonstrates on the board for sake of emphasis.

 3. As you discuss Scott's lesson, display T 13.6 *"Characteristics of Effective Questioning"* which summarizes effective questioning techniques. Have the students assess Scott's questioning.

 4. Display T 13.5 *"Characteristics of Effective Praise,"* and have the students assess Scott's use of praise.

 5. To reduce some of the concerns the students will have about getting the "right answer," remind them that your goal is for them to see and understand the essential teaching skills in context and that a great deal of overlap of the skills exists in the real world.

 6. Have the students identify essential teaching skills in your teaching. This will help personalize the topic for them. They will quickly identify examples, such as you starting your class on time, having your materials ready, providing focus when you use the overhead or PowerPoint slides, developing your lessons with questioning and so on.

 7. The classroom exercises at the end of this chapter gives the students additional practice with identifying the essential teaching skills in the context of a lesson.

I. Classroom interaction: Accommodating learner diversity
 1. Interacting with diverse learners: Implications for teachers

 ■ *The purpose of the suggestions in this section is to help your students understand effective classroom interaction with students from diverse backgrounds.*
  1. Ask the students to describe what they believe to be the most important strategy they can use to accommodate learner diversity.

2. Emphasize the concept of *equitable distribution* and ask the students to explain what equitable distribution communicates to students. Point out that it demonstrates that you have similar expectations for all students, and it further communicates that you believe all the students are competent. Remind the students of people's needs for competence as described by self-determination theory in Chapter 10.

IV. Assessment and Learning: Using assessment as a learning tool

■ *The purpose of the suggestions in this section is to help your students understand the role of assessment in promoting learning.*

1. Discuss the students' thinking in Scott's lesson, as presented on page 484 of the text, and emphasize the need for assessment in promoting learning.

2. Again, remind the students that promoting learning is the reason you quiz frequently and provide detailed feedback about their responses. Note that feedback is one of the most important essential teaching skills.

3. Relate frequent assessment and feedback to your study of motivation in Chapters 10 and 11. Assessment and feedback provide information about increasing competence and self-efficacy, both essential for motivation to learn.

4. Summarize the chapter by displaying TM 13.1 *"Instructional Alignment"* and have the students identify which of the examples are aligned and which are not. Have them assess the extent to which Scott's instruction was aligned.

DISCUSSION STARTERS

1. Which of the different types of knowledge expert teachers possess are most important for elementary teachers? Middle and junior high school teachers? Secondary teachers?

2. What would be the advantages of moving to a longer school year (e.g., 240 versus 180 days?) What disadvantages would there be? Weighing these advantages and disadvantages, what would be your recommendation?

3. What are the major barriers to instructional time in the classroom? What concrete steps can teachers take to maximize instructional time?

4. What can teachers do to maximize student engaged time? How do the strategies teachers might use vary in elementary, middle and junior high, and secondary schools.

5. What differences exist in the planning process for teachers in elementary schools, middle and junior high schools, and secondary schools?

6. Are each of the essential teaching skills equally important in elementary, middle and junior high, and high schools? If not, explain the differences.

7. Is assessment equally important for elementary, middle and junior high, and secondary teachers? If not, describe the differences.

BACKGROUND READINGS

Anderson, L., & Krathwohl, D. (Eds.).(2001). *A taxonomy for learning, teaching, and assessing: A revision of Bloom's taxonomy of educational objectives.* New York: Addison Wesley Longman.

Bloom, B., Englehart, M., Furst, E., Hill, W., & Krathwohl, O. (1956). *Taxonomy of educational objectives: The classification of educational goals: Handbook 1. The cognitive domain.* White Plains, NY: Longman. This classic describes the foundation from which later thinking about objectives and assessment has evolved.

Borko, H., & Putnam, R. (1996). Learning to teach. In D. Berliner & R. Calfee (Eds.), *Handbook of educational psychology* (pp. 673–708). New York: Simon & Schuster. This chapter describes in detail the processes involved in learning to teach.

Calderhead, J. (1996). Teachers: Beliefs and knowledge. In D. Berliner & R. Calfee (Eds.), *Handbook of educational psychology* (pp. 709–725). New York: Macmillan. This chapter provides a detailed description of the influence of beliefs on teachers' classroom behavior.

Eggen, P., & Kauchak, D. (2001). *Strategies for teachers* (4th ed.). Englewood Cliffs, NJ: Prentice Hall. This book describes a number of instructional models based upon theories of learning.

Kauchak, D., & Eggen, P. (2003). *Learning and teaching: Research-based methods* (4th ed.). Needham Heights, MA: Allyn and Bacon. These authors describe the planning, implementing, and assessing process in detail.

Marzano, R. (2003). *What works in schools.* Alexandria, VA: ASCD. An excellent overview of current research on effective teaching.

Shuell, T. (1996). Teaching and learning in a classroom context. In D. Berliner & R. Calfee (Eds.), *Handbook of educational psychology* (pp. 726–764). New York: Simon & Schuster. This chapter provides additional research background for the essential teaching skills.

Shulman, L. (1986). Those who understand: Knowledge growth in teaching. *Educational Researcher*, 15(2), 4–14. This article provides the framework for the concept of pedagogical content knowledge.

FEEDBACK FOR CONSTRUCTED RESPONSE AND DOCUMENT-BASED ANALYSIS QUESTIONS

Constructed Response Items_____

1. Describe the types of teacher knowledge Judy displayed in the lesson. Provide evidence from the case study to support your conclusions.

Judy displayed all the different types of teacher knowledge in implementing her lesson. First, her knowledge of content allowed her to structure the lesson so that students could see similarities and differences between the four geographic areas. Pedagogical content knowledge was evidenced by Judy's ability to illustrate abstract relationships about geography and the economy into data that students could analyze to reach those generalizations. General pedagogical knowledge involves an understanding of general principles of instruction and classroom management. Judy's lesson was clearly focused and she effectively used groupwork and was able to move students into and out of their groups with a minimum of distractions. Finally, knowledge of learners and learning was evidenced by her understanding that learners need to be actively involved in lessons. Judy did this through her groupwork and interactive questioning.

199

2. Describe Judy's thinking as she planned the lesson. Identify at least three decisions that she made as she planned.

> *Planning involves a number of decisions. First, Judy had to decide about content–what topics are important to study. Judy did this by selecting the four geographic areas and focusing on their similarities and differences. Second, teachers need to decide on objectives–what students should know and do. Judy wanted her students to understand how geography influenced the economy, the people in a region, and the future for those regions. A third planning decision is organizing learning activities. Judy did this by involving her students in groupwork while they analyzed the matrix. A final planning decision is assessment, which we'll discuss under the Document-based Analysis question.*

3. Analyze Judy's instructional alignment. Offer any suggestions that you might have that would have increased the alignment of the lesson.

> *Alignment refers to the connections between goals, instructional activities, and assessment. Since they weren't explicitly stated, we can only infer that Judy's goals were to have her students understand the relationships between geography and the economy and the people of different regions in the country. If this was her goal, then her instruction was aligned with it, as the primary focus of her lesson was on these factors. We'll discuss evaluation alignment below in the document-based question.*

4. Analyze Judy's application of the essential teaching skills in her lesson. Which did she demonstrate most effectively? Which did she demonstrate least effectively?

> *Judy demonstrated several of the essential teaching skills in her lesson. First, she used her time well and she was well organized. She began the lesson within a minute or two of the time the bell rang, she had her chart already displayed on the wall of her room, and the students moved back and forth from small-group to whole-group activities quickly and smoothly.*
>
> *Judy's communication was also clear. The discourse was well connected, and she used few vague terms in her discussion.*
>
> *The chart that Judy and the students had prepared provided a good form of sensory focus. Introductory focus wasn't evident in the lesson.*
>
> *Judy did a good job of monitoring students, both as they did their groupwork and during the whole-group discussion, and her questioning was quite good. She called on a variety of students, called on girls and boys about equally, called on students by name, and assured success with open-ended questions and prompting.*
>
> *Because of the way the lesson was organized, much of Judy's feedback was a simple acknowledgment of the students' observations, and her review was quite brief, because the period came to a close before the students had a chance to come to complete closure.*

Document-Based Analysis_____

Judy prepared the following items on a short quiz following her lesson.

1. In which of the four states was the citrus industry most prominent?
2. In which state was mining the most important part of the economy?
3. Explain why the lumber industry is important in both California and Alaska but not in Florida and New York.
4. Explain why fishing is an important part of the economy in all four states.

Analyze each of the four items with respect to its alignment with Judy's goal.

Again, assuming that her goal was to understand the relationship between the geography of a region and its economy and people, items 1 and 2 are out of alignment because they focus on isolated facts. By contrast, items 3 and 4 ask students to look for relationships and explain these, so these items are aligned.

CLASSROOM EXERCISES

Read the following case study and answer the questions that follow:

1   Kathy Johnson is a fifth grade teacher with 27 students, about half of whom are classified as placed at risk in
2   her class from mostly low to middle income families in an urban midwestern city. Four of her students have
3   learning disabilities, and two are classified as behaviorally disordered. A veteran of six years, she typically
4   schedules her day as follows:
5

6   8:15- 9:15   Math
7   9:15-10:45   Language Arts
8   10:45-11:00   Break
9   11:00-11:30   Social Studies
10   11:30-12:00   Lunch
11   12:00- 1:25   Reading
12   1:25- 1:35   Break
13   1:35- 2:00   Science
14   2:00- 2:45   Resource (Art, music, P.E., computer)
15

16   In social studies Kathy has begun a unit on the on the Northern and Southern Colonies prior to the Civil War.
17   As the students file into the room from their break, they see a large chart displayed at the front of the room that
18   appears as follows:
19

20

	People	Land and Climate	Economy
Northern Colonies	Small towns Religious Valued education Cooperative	Timber covered Glacial remains Poor soil Short growing season Cold winters	Syrup Rum Lumber Shipbuilding Fishing Small farms
Southern Colonies	Aristocratic Isolated Social class distinction	Fertile soil Hot weather Long growing season	Large farms Tobacco Cotton Unskilled workers Servants and slaves

21 (Northern Colonies row)
22 (Southern Colonies row)

23
24   Kathy is standing at the doorway as her students enter the room. She smiles and jokes with them as they pass
25   by, and reminds them of what they're about to do with comments, such as, "Look carefully at the chart at the front
26   of the room," and "See if you can find anything interesting about it and how the north and south were different?"
27   At 11:02 the students have their social studies books on their desks, Kathy has moved to the front of the room
28   and she begins, "We began talking about the Northern and Southern Colonies yesterday. Let's see what we
29   remember. . . .Where are they compared to where we live?. . . Lorenda?"
30   ". . . They're over here," Lorenda answers, motioning to the right with her hand.
31   "Yes, they're generally east of us," Kathy adds, as she walks quickly and points to the map at the side of the
32   room identifying the general location of the colonies relative to their location with a wave of her hand.
33   "And about how long ago are we talking about, a few years or a long time? . . . Greg?"
34   ". . . A long time. Like when our great, great, great, great grandfathers and grandmothers might have lived."
35   "Yes, very good," Kathy smiles and nods. "We're talking about time during the early and middle 1800s.

36   "We also talked about some important ideas, like 'Economy,'" Kathy continues. "What do we mean by
37 economy?. . . Carol?"
38   ". . . It's . . . like . . . the way they make their money, like when we said that the economy here is based on
39 manufacturing, like making cars and parts for cars and stuff," Carol responds uncertainly.
40   "Very good description, Carol," Kathy nods. "You identified auto manufacturing as an important part of our
41 economy, and that's a good example."
42   "Now, look here," Kathy directs, pointing to the column marked 'Economy.' "We see that the economy for
43 the two groups of colonies is very different. Today we want to see what some of these specific differences are and
44 why the two economies are so different. So, remember as we go through the lesson that we're talking about the
45 way the colonies made their money, and we're trying to figure out why it is so different. . . . Everybody ready?"
46 Kathy surveys the class. "Good. Let's go."
47   She then begins, "What are some of the differences we see in the economies for the two regions? . . . Ann
48 Marie?"
49   ". . ."
50   "What do you notice about the farms in the two colonies?"
51   ". . . The farms were much bigger in the Southern Colonies than they were in the Northern Colonies."
52   "OK, Good observation," Kathy nods energetically. "Now why might that have been the case? . . . Jim?"
53   ". . ."
54   ". . . Would you like me to repeat the question?" Kathy asks, knowing that Jim hasn't heard her.
55   "Yes," Jim responds quickly, with a look of relief.
56
57 [Kathy continues guiding the students' analysis of the information on the chart, in the process finding relationships
58 between the geography, climate, and economy. When students are unable to answer she rephrases her questions
59 and provides cues to help them along. She then has them consider why the economy of their city might be the way
60 it is. We return to her lesson now.]
61
62   You have done very well, everyone," she smiles, pointing her finger in the air for emphasis. "Now, everyone,
63 get with your partner, take two minutes and write two or three summary statements about what we've learned here
64 today. . . . Quickly now, get started.
65
66 [The students start buzzing, pointing at the chart, and one of the two in each pair begin writing. In some cases
67 they stop, crumple their papers and begin again. As they work, Kathy walks among them offering encouragement
68 and periodic suggestions.]
69
70   At the end of two minutes Kathy announces, "One more minute, and we're going to look at what you wrote."
71   After another minute she begins, "OK, let's see what you've got. What did you and Linda say, David?"
72   ". . . We said that the weather and the land had a lot to do with the way the different colonies made their
73 money."
74   "Excellent! That's a good one. How about someone else.. . . Danielle, how about you and Tony?"
75
76 [Kathy has several other pairs offer their summary statements, they further develop the statements as a whole
77 group, and then Kathy collects the papers.]
78
79   At 11:28 she announces, "Almost lunch time. Please put away your papers."
80   The students quickly put their books, papers, and pencils away, glance around their desks for any waste paper,
81 and are sitting quietly at 11:30.

Identify the Essential Teaching Skill *best illustrated* by each of the following sets of lines in the case study. In each case, where appropriate, identify both the skill and the subskill. For example, if you select Organization, also include "Starting on Time" or "Preparing Materials in Advance" or Established Routines. Your answer would then be, for example, "Organization–Established Routines."

Explain your choice in each case.

1. Lines 16-27
2. Lines 28-41
3. Lines 42-46
4. Lines 47-51
5. Lines 62-74
6. Lines 27 and 79
7. Lines 29, 33, 36-37, 47-48, 52
8. Lines 31-32, 40-41, 52
9. In Line 52 Kathy called on Jim, knowing that he wasn't listening (as we see in Line 54). Is this [calling on a student who isn't paying attention] effective teaching strategy? Why do you think so, or why do you think not?
10. Look at the *type* of questions Kathy asked in Lines 47-48 and 50. What kind of questions are these. Give at least three reasons why they're effective.

FEEDBACK FOR CLASSROOM EXERCISES

1. *Organization–Materials prepared in advance*, and *starting on time*.
Kathy had her chart prepared in advance a displayed in front of the room as the students walked in, and she began her instruction two minutes after it was scheduled to begin.

Organization is a better response than "Use of Time" because "Use of Time" doesn't account for the existence of the chart.

2. *Review–Beginning of class review*. Kathy reviewed the time when the events occurred and checked the students' perception of terms such as *economy*.

3. *Focus –Introductory Focus*. Kathy's comment, "So, remember as we go through the lesson that we're talking about the way the colonies made their money, and we're trying to figure out why it is so different. . . . ," provided a conceptual umbrella for the lesson.

4. *Questioning–Prompting*. When Ann Marie wasn't able to answer, Kathy prompted her by saying, "What do you notice about the farms in the two colonies?"

5. *Review and Closure–Closure*. Kathy has the students summarize the information, and they discuss the students' conclusions as a class.

6. *Use of Time–*Of the 30 minutes allocated to social studies, Kathy uses 26 in her lesson.

7. *Questioning–Equitable Distribution*. Kathy calls on individual students by name, and she asks the question first and identifies the person to respond after the question has been asked.

8. *Attitudes–Enthusiasm*. Kathy guides the lesson in an energetic way.

9. Yes, this is an effective technique. It draws the student back into the lesson in a non-punitive way.

10. These are *open-ended* questions. Some reasons they're effective include:
    a. They're safe, and they ensure student success, since a variety of answers are acceptable.
    b. They're easy to ask, so they take some pressure off the teacher.
    c. They're excellent as prompts when students aren't initially able to answer. (This is how Kathy used them in helping Ann Marie to respond.)
    d. They're effective for cultural minorities and non-native English speakers, who sometimes aren't used to the fast-paced drill-type questioning that goes on in classrooms.

CHAPTER 14: ASSESSING CLASSROOM LEARNING

CHAPTER OVERVIEW

This chapter begins by defining and outlining the functions of assessment and describing measurement, evaluation, validity and reliability. These descriptions are followed by a discussion of teachers' assessment patterns together with an examination of reliable and valid traditional assessment items.

The chapter then turns to a discussion of alternative assessment, including the design of performance assessments, evaluation methods with performance assessments, and portfolio assessments.

The discussion of alternative assessment is followed by effective assessment practices, which involve preparing students for assessment, including test-taking strategies and test anxiety, administering assessments, analyzing results, and bias in assessment. The chapter closes with a discussion of grading and reporting.

CHAPTER OBJECTIVES

- Explain basic assessment concepts.

- Describe classroom teachers' assessment patterns.

- Analyze assessment for factors that detract from their validity.

- Construct alternative assessments in your content area or grade level.

- Apply effective assessment procedures in classrooms.

TRANSPARENCIES

The transparencies exist in both acetate form and as PowerPoint slides.

T 14.1   The relationship between validity and reliability
T 14.2   Teachers' assessment patterns
T 14.3   Characteristics of teacher-made tests
T 14.4   Sample rubric for paragraph structure
T 14.5   Designing performance assessments
T 14.6   Effective assessment practices
T 14.7   The total assessment system

TRANSPARENCY MASTERS

The transparency masters are included in this manual beginning on page 230.

TM 14.1   Traditional and alternative measurement formats
TM 14.2. Examples of multiple-choice items
TM 14.3   Guidelines for preparing multiple-choice items
TM 14.4   Interpretive exercise with the multiple-choice format
TM 14.5   Guidelines for preparing and scoring essay items
TM 14.6   Instructional principles for preparing performance assessments
TM 14.7   Rating scale for content representations
TM 14.8   Definitions of values for rating scale

VIDEO

Looking Through Classroom Windows Tape 2-Segment 6: "Using Assessment to Improve Instruction." This video lesson illustrates a fifth grade teachers' use of assessment as a basis for making decisions about instruction. (It is the opening case study of the chapter.)

CHAPTER OUTLINE

I. Classroom assessment
   - A. Functions of classroom assessment
   - B. Measurement and evaluation
     1. Formal and informal measurement
     2. The need for systematic assessment
   - C. Validity: Making appropriate evaluation decisions
   - D. Reliability: Consistency in measurement

II. Traditional assessment strategies
   - A. Teachers' assessment patterns
   - B. Valid test items
   - C. Constructing valid test items: Instructional strategies
     1. Multiple choice items
        - a. The stem
        - b. Distracters
        - c. Assessing higher level learning
     2. Matching items
     3. True-false items
     4. Completion items
     5. Essay items: Measuring complex outcomes
     6. Using rubrics
   - D. Commercially prepared test items

III. Alternative assessment
   - A. Performance assessments
   - B. Designing performance assessments: Instructional strategies
     1. Specifying desired outcomes
     2. Selecting the focus of assessment
     3. Structuring the evaluation setting
     4. Designing evaluation procedures
     5. Performance evaluation strategies
   - C. Portfolios: Involving students in alternative assessment
   - D. Putting traditional and alternative assessment into perspective

IV. Effective assessment practices: Instructional strategies
   - A. Planning for assessment
     1. Tables of specifications: Increasing validity through planning
   - B. Preparing students for assessments
     1. Teaching test-taking strategies
     2. Reducing test anxiety
     3. Specific test-preparation procedures
   - C. Administering assessments
   - D. Analyzing results
   - E. Accommodating diversity in classrooms: Reducing bias in assessment
     1. Carefully wording items
     2. Making provisions for non-native English speakers
     3. Accommodating diversity in scoring

V. Grading and reporting: The total assessment system
   A. Designing a grading system
       1. Formative and summative evaluation
       2. Norm and criterion-referenced evaluation
       3. Tests and quizzes
       4. Alternative assessments
       5. Homework
   B. Assigning grades: Increasing learning and motivation
       1. Raw points or percentages?
   C. Technology and learning: Using technology to improve assessment
       1. Planning and constructing tests
       2. Analyzing test data
       3. Maintaining student records
       4. Technology and portfolios

PRESENTATION OUTLINE

Teaching suggestions in the outline will be marked with the symbol ■. In most cases, the suggested activities can be done individually and discussed as a whole group, or they can be done in small groups, and the small-group results can be discussed with the whole class. To be consistent with our understanding of knowledge construction, we recommend that you promote as much discussion–both in small groups and with the whole class–as possible.

Video: You might want to introduce the chapter by showing the video lesson "Using Assessment to Improve Instruction." It provides a framework for the integral role of assessment in learning and teaching.

I. Classroom assessment
   A. Functions of classroom assessment
   B. Measurement and evaluation
       1. Formal and informal measurement
       2. The need for systematic assessment
   C. Validity: Making appropriate evaluation decisions
   D. Reliability: Consistency in measurement

■ *To help your students understand classroom assessment and concepts of validity and reliability:*
   1. **Introduce the topic by referring your students to the way you've assessed them in this class, which will be real and concrete for them. Describe the process by which it has evolved, its structure, and its evolution over time. While acknowledging that one function of assessment is to provide a basis for assigning grades, emphasize that your primary goal in assessment is to promote learning.**

   2. **Have the students identify some of the goals and results of effective assessment. Have them link their findings to topics they've studied in earlier chapters.**
       Among the goals and results the groups identify, the following might be included:
       .   **Provides feedback about learning progress (important in helping students form expectations about what content is important and which strategies are effective [Social cognitive theory is discussed in Chapter 6]). Also provides information that helps learners modify their existing schemas.**
       .   **Helps students understand the teacher's expectations.**

. Aids in task comprehension (one of the climate variables in the model for promoting learner motivation)

3. Have them identify a number of examples of evaluations that teachers make on a daily basis and the informal measurements on which those decisions are based. If the students have difficulty getting started, you may offer some examples of evaluations, such as decisions about:
   . which students to call on and when.
   . whether to conduct a learning activity in a whole-group or a small-group arrangement.
   . when to move from one learning activity to another.
   . how much time to give students in a small-group activity.
   . when to schedule a test, quiz, or performance assessment.

   As you discuss the results, emphasize that informal measurements are critical to the daily operation of the classroom, but they should be used with great caution as a primary basis for assigning grades.

4. Define validity and reliability and then have the students think about a number of the tests they've taken. (Remind them to avoid any discussion of specific instructors.) Have them offer some examples of course content, learning activities, and tests or other assessments. Discuss the extent to which the tests and other assessments were valid and/or reliable.

   (Since students sometimes feel tests are unfair, they are likely to be quite lively in this discussion.)

5. To help the students understand the concepts of validity and reliability display T 14.1 *"The Relationship Between Validity and reliability,"* which provides a way of visualizing the relationships between the two.

II. Traditional assessment
   A. Teachers' assessment patterns

   ■ *To help the students understand teachers' assessment patterns*:
   1. Display T 14.2 *"Teachers' Assessment Patterns"* which outlines some of the common assessment practices in schools. Ask the students why they believe these patterns exist.

   2. Display T 14.3 *"Characteristics of Teacher-Made Tests,"* which outlines the characteristics of teacher-made test items. Again, you might have the students discuss why they believe these characteristics exist.

   B. Valid test items
   C. Constructing valid test items: Instructional strategies
      1. Multiple choice items
         a. The stem
         b. Distracters
         c. Measuring higher level learning
      2. Matching items
      3. True-false items
      4. Completion items
      5. Essay items: Measuring complex outcomes
         a. Using rubrics

D.   Using commercially prepared test items

■ *The suggestions in this section are designed to help your students understand the characteristics of effective traditional assessments using different formats.*

1.   TM14.3 *"Guidelines for Preparing Multiple-Choice Items"* summarizes suggestions for preparing effective multiple-choice items.

2.   To review the concepts of measurement, evaluation, reliability, and validity, as well as provide students with some experience in assessing multiple choice items, have the students use the guidelines in TM 14.3 to assess the items on TM 14.2 *"Examples of Multiple-Choice Items."*

3.   The students should identify at least four problems with the first item. Among them should be:
     .   The stem doesn't present a clearly stated problem or question. The assassination of Ferdinand did precipitate the war, but economic problems and nationalism were also causes, so to suggest that choice c is *the* cause puts the learner in the position of trying to guess what the instructor wants.
     .   the correct answer is choice c.
     .   the correct answer is significantly shorter than the distracters.
     .   choice b is grammatically inconsistent with the stem.

     The students should find that the second and third items are effective based on the criteria.

     The students should also notice that the second and third items are interpretive exercises using a case study. (They will also notice that many of the test items that they've responded to on your tests and quizzes are interpretive exercises, which are intended to promote deeper understanding of the topics as well as higher-order and critical thinking.) TM 14.4 *"Interpretive Exercise With the Multiple-Choice Format"* provides another example of an interpretive exercise.

4.   Remind the students that, while popular, true-false and completion formats are generally considered to be weaker than multiple-choice and essay items, and they should be used with care.

5.   TM 14.5 *"Guidelines for Preparing and Scoring Essay Items"* offers suggestions for preparing effective essay items and scoring them as reliably as possible. T 14.4 *"Sample Rubric for Paragraph Structure"* illustrates a process for increasing the reliability of essay items.

     As with your multiple-choice and true-false items, having the students assess some of your essay items would be an effective way to help them understand and apply the information in this section.

6.   If you have access to some commercially prepared test items, have students assess the items according to the criteria suggested for the particular format.

7.   Remind students that teachers' goals and emphasis may not match those of the publisher, so they should use commercially prepared items with caution.

III. Alternative assessment
    A. Performance assessment
    B. Designing performance assessments: Instructional strategies
        1. Specifying the type of performance
        2. Selecting the focus of assessment
        3. Structuring the evaluation setting
        4. Designing evaluation procedures
        5. Performance evaluation strategies
    C. Portfolios: Involving students in alternative assessment
    D. Putting traditional and alternative assessment into perspective

■ *The suggestions in this section are designed to help your students understand the process of alternative assessment*

1. If you have chosen to assign one or more of the projects suggested at the introduction to this Instructor's Manual, use these projects as a basis for discussing the content in this section. For instance, having them prepare knowledge representations or complete a peer-taught lesson represent alternative assessments with a high degree of realism.

2. T 14.5 *"Designing Performance Assessments"* provides guidelines for designing performance assessments, and TM 14.7 *"Rating Scale for Content Representations"* illustrates a rating scale for the project that requires them to prepare content representations for a topic of their choice. If you have assigned this project, you might display the rating scale and definitions of values that you've used in assessing their work. TM 14.8 *"Definitions of Values for Rating Scale"* illustrates definitions for one of the dimensions in TM 14.7.

3. If you want to increase the emphasis on designing performance assessments, have students prepare performance assessments for a topic or set of topics.

4. Have the students identify an area of study, such as elementary math, middle school science, or secondary English and have them consider how they would design portfolio assessments for this area. Discuss the decisions involved in the design and implementation as a whole class.

IV. Effective assessment practices: Instructional strategies
    A. Planning for assessment
        1. Tables of specifications: Increasing validity through planning
    B. Preparing students for assessments
        1. Teaching test-taking strategies
        2. Reducing test anxiety
        3. Specific test-preparation procedures
    C. Administering assessments
    D. Analyzing results

■ *To help your students understand effective assessment practices:*

1. Display T 14.6 *"Effective Assessment Practices"* which outlines a framework for effective assessment. Then, again use your class as a model. If you have followed the suggestions made at the beginning of the Instructor's Manual, your class can serve as a model in several ways:
        . **You have given frequent announced quizzes.**
        . **You have specified the content of each quiz.**
        . **You have given them the chance to practice on items similar to those on the quizzes and tests by encouraging them to respond to the *Self-Help Quizzes*, the *Application***

Exercises, Margin Questions, and *Companion Website Self-Tests.*

- You have established positive expectations by encouraging them to study and suggesting that if they do, they will do well in your class.
- You have provided adequate time for them to complete each assessment.
- You have reminded them to focus on the quiz or test content as they try to respond.
- You have promptly returned the quizzes and tests and have discussed frequently missed items.

2. To increase students' understanding of these practices, have them link the practices to the content of other chapters. Some of the connections might include the following ideas:

- Giving frequent announced quizzes, specifying the content, and giving them adequate time to complete the quiz or test helps reduce test anxiety, and also aids in task comprehension.
- Providing practice puts them in an active role and helps them develop well-organized schemas for the content.
- Reminding them to focus on the content of the quiz helps reduce test anxiety by preventing the worry component from occupying working memory space.
- Discussing frequently missed items provides feedback which allows them to reorganize and elaborate their schemas.

E. Accommodating diversity in classrooms: Reducing bias in assessment
1. Being careful with wording in assessment items
2. Making provisions for non-native English speakers
3. Accommodating diversity in scoring

■ *To help your students understand the possibilities of bias in measurement:*
1. As you discuss your own test items, remind the students about your efforts to be careful with wording that might be a problem for non-native English speaking students.

2. If you have students in your class who are not proficient in English, you probably arrange to give them extra time to complete your assessments. You can use this as another example of your efforts to reduce bias in assessment.

V. Grading and reporting: The total assessment system
A. Designing a grading system
1. Formative and summative evaluation
2. Norm and criterion-referenced evaluation
3. Tests and quizzes
4. Alternative assessments
5. Homework
B. Assigning grades: Increasing learning and motivation
1. Raw points or percentages?

■ *To help your students understand grading and reporting:*
1. Display T 14.7 *"The Total Assessment System"* which outlines the features of a total system.

2. You might point out that most school districts specify criteria for grading, and most teachers use criterion-referenced systems.

3. You might ask students how norm referencing compares to criterion referencing and how these relate to their study of motivation in Chapters 10 and 11. They should point

out that a norm-referenced system tends to promote a performance-focused, rather than a learning-focused environment and an ego versus a task orientation. For these reasons, it is generally preferable to use a criterion-referenced system.

4. Remind the students of your rationale for the grading system you use in your class.

5. Point out that teachers tend to prefer a percentage system, because students and their parents understand and prefer it. Remind them that a percentage system can artificially increase the weight of assignments. (You might ask them to explain how this can happen.)

6. Emphasize that it is important for learners to understand the assessment system.

7. Ask them what variable in the Model for Promoting Student Motivation most closely relates to learners understanding the assessment system. (Task Comprehension).

C. Technology and learning: Using technology to improve assessment
   1. Planning and constructing tests
   2. Analyzing test data
   3. Maintaining student records
   4. Technology and portfolios

■ *To help your students understand how technology can improve the efficiency of assessment:*
   1. Have the students offer some examples of how technology can be used and how they can make the process of assessment more efficient.

   2. Describe your own use of technology in the assessment process.

DISCUSSION STARTERS

1. Does assessment increase, decrease, or have no affect on learning? On what evidence is your opinion based?

2. How does assessment affect the intrinsic motivation of learners? The extrinsic motivation of learners? On what evidence is your opinion based?

3. Is assessment overemphasized, underemphasized, or appropriately emphasized in today's schools? On what evidence is your opinion based?

4. Teachers, particularly at the elementary level, tend to rely heavily on commercially prepared test items? Why do you think this is the case? How appropriate is the practice of using commercially prepared items?

5. Would an ideal assessment system for your level or content area use the following types of items? If so, how would they be used?
   Traditional assessments
   • essay
   • multiple choice
   • short answer
   • true/false
   Alternative assessments
   • performance assessments

- portfolios

6. Is the emphasis on alternative assessment likely to increase or decrease in the future? Why do you think so?

7. Most teachers give grades based on district-mandated or suggested criteria, such as 94%-100% = A, 86-93 = B, etc.. How appropriate is this practice? Why do you think so?

8. You are asked to meet with parents to hand out report cards and explain the grades on them. What kinds of information would be most helpful in this process? How would you present it to parents?

9. How could portfolios be used in your content area or grade level to supplement other data sources? What would go in them? How would the contents be evaluated?

BACKGROUND READINGS

Airasian, P. (2001). *Classroom assessment: Concepts and Applications* (4th ed.). New York: McGraw-Hill. This book provides an up-to-date overview of the field of assessment.

Gronlund, N. (2003). *Assessment of student achievement* (7th ed.). Boston: Allyn & Bacon. A comprehensive look at assessment issues in the classroom.

Hambleton, R. (1996). Advances in assessment models, methods, and practices. In D. Berliner & R. Calfee (Eds.), *Handbook of educational psychology* (pp. 899–925). New York: Macmillan. This chapter provides an overview of assessment practices including both traditional and alternative assessment.

Linn, R., & Gronlund, N. (2000). *Measurement and evaluation in teaching* (8th ed.). Upper Saddle River, NJ: Prentice Hall. This classic text, by two of the leading figures in the field, provides a comprehensive description of the assessment process.

Stiggens, R. (2001). *Student-involved classroom assessment* (3rd ed.). Upper Saddle River, NJ: Prentice Hall. This text provides detailed descriptions of how to develop effective assessments with a learner-centered focus.

Venn, J. J. (2000). *Assessing students with special needs* (2nd ed.). Upper Saddle River, NJ: Merrill/Prentice Hall. Discusses the unique assessment challenges of assessing students with exceptionalities.

FEEDBACK FOR CONSTRUCTED RESPONSE AND DOCUMENT-BASED ANALYSIS QUESTIONS

Constructed Response Items_____

1. How well were Ron's curriculum and assessment aligned? Explain specifically. What could he have done to increase curricular alignment?

Ron's curriculum was out of alignment. His stated goal was, ". . . you'll all be able to use pronouns correctly in your writing." This goal was congruent with the second part of his assessment, which asked the students to write a passage in which pronoun cases were used correctly. However, his learning activity was behaviorist; it focused on the sentences in isolation rather than on writing, so it was not congruent with his goal and the second part of his assessment. To make his instruction congruent with his goal Ron needs to provide students with practice using pronouns correctly in their writing.

2. In the section on effective testing practices, we discussed preparing students for tests, administering tests, and analyzing results. How effectively did Ron perform each task? Describe specifically what he might have done to be more effective in these areas.

Effective preparation for testing involves giving students the opportunity to practice on test-like items that are similar to those they will encounter on the test itself. Ron's students only responded to the specific and isolated sentences and they didn't practice using pronouns in their writing.

The only problem that existed with his administration of the test was the fact that the students were pressed for time, and he may have increased the anxiety of test-anxious students by his repeated reminders of the amount of time remaining. Giving students more time to finish the exam would remedy this problem.

In discussing the test results, Ron again de-emphasized their writing in favor of the specific items, and his feedback was somewhat vague. Unquestionably, providing feedback for every student is very demanding, but he could have written a model response to which the students could have compared their own paragraphs.

3. Like most classes, Ron's class was composed of learners with diverse backgrounds. How effective was his teaching and assessment for these students?

Ron's instruction for learners with diverse backgrounds would have been more effective if he had made his instruction more concrete and meaningful. For example, he could have prepared a personalized written passage that included examples of pronoun cases, and in this way his content would have been more concrete and meaningful for his students.

Research indicates that learners with diverse backgrounds benefit from explicit test preparation procedures. Had Ron provided more test preparation practice, particularly with writing, his assessment would have been more effective and valid.

4. What were the primary strengths of Ron's teaching and assessment? What were the primary weaknesses? If you think Ron's teaching and assessment could have been improved on the basis of information in this chapter, what suggestions would you make? Be specific.

Ron used his time well, his instruction was interactive, he had a clear goal for his students, and he provided practice for his students with respect to properly placing the pronoun in specific sentences. These were the strengths of his instruction and assessment.

His primary weaknesses were the fact that his goal, learning activity, and assessment were out of alignment, he didn't provide as much practice for his students as he might have, especially with using pronouns in their writing, and he didn't discuss the test results as thoroughly as he might have.

Document-Based Analysis_____

DeVonne Lampkin had the following goal for one of her math lessons:

For students to understand equivalent fractions.

To measure students' attainment of this goal, she gave the following item:

The Jaguars soccer team won 16 out of the 24 games they played. The Dolphins soccer team won 14 of the 21 games they placed. Is the fraction of the games each team won the same, or is it different? Explain how you know.

On this item, Kevin answered, "The Jaguars won a larger fraction because they won more games."

Analyze DeVonne's item with respect to her goal. What does Kevin's response tell use about his understanding of equivalent fractions? Explain.

In answering this question, students would have to convert 16/24 and 14/21 to 2/3. This item gets at the idea of equivalent fractions tangentially and would have to be supplemented by other items that would allow the teacher to diagnose both conceptual and procedural difficulties with equivalent fractions. Kevin's response suggests he doesn't understand fractions in general nor the idea of equivalent fractions. Listening to student responses such as this provide teachers with opportunities to adapt instruction to the learning needs of students.

CLASSROOM EXERCISES

1. Karen Anderson gives a multiple-choice test to her biology students. She is careful to be sure her test is consistent with her goals. As it turns out, Karen inadvertently puts a clue in one of the items, so the students select the correct answer even though they don't understand the content. Is her test reliable? Is her test valid? Explain.

2. Greg Foster gives a multiple choice test to his biology students, and he is also careful to be certain that his test is consistent with his goals. As it turns out, Greg unintentionally writes the stem of one of the items in a misleading way, so that the students select a distracter rather than the correct answer, even though they understand the content measured on the item. Is Greg's test reliable? Is Greg's test valid? Explain.

3. Loretta Polanski is philosophically opposed to tests with her third graders on the grounds that it puts undue stress on them. She assigns grades based on their responses in class, arguing, "I call on all the students regularly, and I can tell from their answers whether or not they understand the content." Is Loretta's approach to measurement and evaluation reliable? Is it valid? Explain.

Eleanor Parker is emphasizing grammatically correct writing and expression of thought in writing with her students. She has begun using *portfolios*, where systematic collections of her students' work are placed for review and evaluation. She puts work samples in the portfolio at least three days a week, and she is careful to date the samples to help in assessing her students' progress. In examining her students' work, she checks for grammar, punctuation, spelling, and clear expression of thought, and she assigns grades on that basis.

4. Is Eleanor's behavior consistent with patterns identified by research; is she most likely an elementary teacher, a middle school teacher, or a high school teacher? Explain.

5. Are Eleanor's measurements reliable? Are they valid? Explain.

Four elementary teachers were discussing their handling of homework in their classes.

"They know they have to do it to do well on the tests," Jo Buck comments, "but I don't collect it or grade it."

"I don't grade it either, but I check to see if they did it, and they know they get a check mark in my grade book if they did it," Art Ames adds.

"It's a part of my grading system," Karen Warner continues. "I collect every assignment, score it, and record the scores."

"I spot check them," Lynn Peet adds. "They know it may or may not be collected, and I try to avoid falling into a pattern. I grade it and record the grades when I do collect it."

6. Based on research, which teacher's homework practice is *most* effective? Explain, using social cognitive theory as the basis for your explanation.

7. Based on research, which teacher's homework practice is *least* effective? Explain, again using social cognitive theory as the basis for your explanation.

8. Cal is in English Honors II as a 10th grader and is doing well, getting B's the first two grading periods-- missing A's by 2 percentage points each time. Joanne Wilkes, his English teacher, consistently commented on the good work Cal did on his writing assignments. Cal took the PSAT and but scored only in the 40th percentile on the verbal section. The results were shared with Joanne, since she is an English teacher.

Cal's mother continued to proofread his essays as she had done the first two grading periods, but Cal got a C the third grading period. "I'll do better. I can do it," Cal said to himself, but he also got a C the fourth grading period, and received a C for the year.

Based on the information in the case study, what is the most likely explanation for the decline in Jim's grades?

9. Look at the following test item.

Formative tests:
- a. are given at the beginning of instruction.
- b. are given at any time during instruction.
- c. are given at the end of instruction.
- d. are given when the teacher wants diagnostic information.

Based on guidelines for preparing multiple-choice items, write an assessment of the item.

FEEDBACK FOR CLASSROOM EXERCISES

1. Her test is reliable, but it isn't valid. In spite of the scores, Karen will get consistent results. However, since the students are able to get a correct answer without understanding the topic, the test doesn't actually measure the objectives, so it isn't valid. (Technically, the misleading item doesn't make the entire test invalid. It invalidates that particular items. When the test, per se, becomes invalid is a matter of judgment.)

2. The same explanation applies in Greg's case as applied in Karen's. Greg will get consistent results, so his test is reliable, but it isn't valid (or, at least that particular item is invalid).

3. Loretta's approach is neither reliable nor valid. Since she isn't getting responses to the same questions from all the students, she isn't getting consistent measurements, which makes her measurements unreliable. Unreliable measurements cannot be valid.

4. Eleanor is most likely an elementary teacher. Elementary teachers tend to use performance measures and samples of student work to a greater extent than do middle, junior high, and high school teachers.

5. Eleanor is making an effort to gather consistent information from all the students. Research indicates that these efforts can produce acceptable levels of reliability (although difficulties with reliability are quite common with performance measures). Based on the evidence we have, we would conclude that Eleanor has achieved an acceptable level of reliability. Her measurements are consistent with her goals, so they are also valid.

6. Karen's practice is most effective. If students do homework, they *expect* to be reinforced for doing it. The reinforcer could be as simple as credit for doing it, and better yet, having it scored and recorded.

7. Jo's practice is least effective. Again, If students do homework, they *expect* to be reinforced for doing it. The nonoccurrence of the expected reinforcer acts as a punisher, making it less likely that the students will make an effort to conscientiously do the homework if it isn't collected or scored.

8. It is likely that Joanne's perception of Cal's ability was adversely affected by his PSAT results. As a result, her expectations were lowered, and she responded to her perceptions and expectations in evaluating Cal's performance.

9. More information should be included in the stem, so a clear problem or question is presented. Also, the item measures mere recall.

CHAPTER 15: ASSESSMENT THROUGH STANDARDIZED TESTING

CHAPTER OVERVIEW

This chapter begins by describing the functions and types of standardized tests, including a brief history of intelligence tests, together with an examination of content, predictive, and construct validity. From there the chapter turns to a discussion of the teacher's role in standardized testing, descriptive statistics, the normal distribution, and an interpretation of standardized test results, including percentile ranks, stanines, grade equivalents, standard scores, and standard error of measurement. The chapter then examines some issues in standardized testing, such as minimum competency testing and standardized testing with alternative formats. The chapter closes with a discussion of standardized testing with diverse student populations and possible sources of test bias with those populations.

CHAPTER OBJECTIVES

- Describe different uses for standardized tests and explain how they influence educational decision making.

- Discuss the different types of standardized tests based on their educational use.

- Explain how different types of validity can be used to evaluate standardized tests.

- Discuss different issues involving standardized testing and explain how they influence classroom teachers.

- Explain how student diversity influences measurement validity and discuss strategies that teachers can use to minimize measurement bias.

TRANSPARENCIES

The transparencies exist in both acetate form and as PowerPoint slides.

T 15.1   David Palmer's achievement test report (Figure 15.1, p. 541)
T 15.2   Functions of standardized tests
T 15.3   Types of standardized tests
T 15.4   Types of validity for standardized tests
T 15.5   Normal distribution (Figure 15.4, p. 555)
T 15.6   Issues in standardized testing

TRANSPARENCY MASTERS

The transparency masters are included in this manual beginning on page 230.

TM 15.1   Principles for Using Standardized Tests Effectively
TM 15.2   Two Distributions of Scores
TM 15.3   Descriptive Statistics for the Two Distributions of Scores
TM 15.4   Interpreting Standardized Test Scores: An Application

CHAPTER OUTLINE

I. Standardized tests
    A. Functions of standardized tests
        1. Student assessment
        2. Diagnosis
        3. Selection and placement
        4. Program evaluation
        5. Accountability
    B. Types of standardized tests
        1. Achievement tests
        2. Diagnostic tests
        3. Intelligence tests
            a. A short history of intelligence tests
            b. The Stanford-Binet
            c. The Wechsler Scales
            d. Individual versus group intelligence tests
        4. Aptitude tests
    C. Evaluating standardized tests: Validity revisited
        1. Content validity
        2. Predictive validity
        3. Construct validity
    D. The teacher's role in standardized testing: Instructional strategies
            a. Test selection
            b. Preparing students
            c. Administering tests
            d. Interpreting results
II. Understanding and interpreting standardized test scores
    A. Descriptive statistics
        1. Frequency distributions
        2. Measures of central tendency
        3. Measures of variability
        4. The normal distribution
    B. Interpreting standardized test results
        1. Raw scores
        2. Percentiles
        3. Stanines
        4. Grade equivalents
        5. Standard scores
        6. Standard error of measurement
III. Issues in standardized testing
    A. Standards-based education and the accountability movement
    B. Testing teachers
    C. Cultural minorities and high-stakes tests
    D. Student diversity and test bias
        1. Bias in content
        2. Bias in testing procedures
        3. Bias in test use
    E. Eliminating bias in standardized testing: Instructional strategies
        1. Analyze test content
        2. Adapt testing procedures
        3. Use alternate assessment data sources

F.   Standardized testing with alternative formats
G.   Issues in standardized testing: Implications for teachers

PRESENTATION OUTLINE

Teaching suggestions in the outline will be marked with the symbol ■. In most cases, the suggested activities can be done individually and discussed as a whole group, or they can be done in small groups, and the small-group results can be discussed with the whole class. To be consistent with our understanding of knowledge construction, we recommend that you promote as much discussion–both in small groups and with the whole class–as possible.

I.   Standardized tests
  A.   Functions of standardized tests
    1.   Student assessment
    2.   Diagnosis
    3.   Selection and placement
    4.   Program evaluation
    5.   Accountability

■ *The purpose of this activity is to help students understand the characteristics of standardized tests.*

  1.   **Display T 15.1 "***David Palmer's Achievement Test Report***" and have students make at least three conclusions about the information in the report. (If T 15.1 is difficult to see because of the small print, you may have the students refer to Figure 15.1 on page 562 of their texts.) Remind them that PR stands for percentile rank, S stands for stanine, and GRADE EQUIV stands for grade equivalent. Discuss their findings.**

  2.   **Display T 15.2 *"Functions of Standardized Tests,"* which outlines the functions of standardized tests. After discussing David Palmer's standardized test results, have them relate the information on T 15.1 to the functions of standardized tests.**

  3.   **Have the students recall some of the standardized tests that they've taken. Most of them will have taken the SAT or the ACT as part of the college admissions process. You can then have them identify the function of these tests.**

  B.   Types of standardized tests
    1.   Achievement tests
    2.   Diagnostic tests
    3.   Intelligence tests
      a.   A short history of intelligence tests
      b.   The Stanford-Binet
      c.   The Wechsler Scales
      d.   Individual versus group intelligence tests
    4.   Aptitude tests

■ *The purpose of this activity is to help the students understand the characteristics of different types of standardized tests.*

  1.   **Display T 15.3 *"Types of Standardized Tests."* Have the students identify the type of test David Palmer took and the type of tests the SAT and ACT are.**

  2.   **Have students recall their experience with the sample intelligence test items to which they responded when you examined intelligence in Chapter 4. Then have them compare**

that experience to the functions and types of standardized tests. They will see that there is considerable overlap in the tests. For example, from their experience with the math problems on the sample intelligence test, they will see that items appearing on an intelligence test could also appear on an achievement test, and could even appear on a diagnostic test.

C. Evaluating standardized tests: Validity revisited
   1. Content validity
   2. Predictive validity
   3. Construct validity

■ *The purpose of this activity is to help students apply the concepts of content, predictive, and construct validity.*
   1. **Display T 15.4** *"Types of Validity for Standardized Tests."* **Discuss the descriptions and try to identify examples of each.**

D. The teacher's role in standardized testing: Instructional strategies
   a. Test selection
   b. Preparing students
   c. Administering tests
   d. Interpreting results

■ *The purpose of this activity is to help the students understand teachers' roles in the process of using standardized tests.*
   1. **Display TM 15.1** *"Principles for Using Standardized Tests Effectively."* **Point out that interpreting test results will be one of their most important roles, which will then lead to the next section of the chapter.**

II. Understanding and interpreting standardized test scores
   A. Descriptive statistics
      1. Frequency distributions
      2. Measures of central tendency
      3. Measures of variability
      4. The normal distribution

■ *The purpose of this activity is to help the students understand descriptive statistics.*
   1. **Display TM 15.2** *"Two Distributions of Scores"* **and have students compare the distributions of scores. Ask them to decide if the students in the second sample performed better or less well than the students in the first sample and provide a rationale for their answer. They will see that the comparisons are difficult, since the numbers of students are different.**

   2. **Have the plot a frequency distribution for the two classes and then predict whether or not the mean of the second sample will be higher than the mean of the first sample. Do the same with the standard deviation.**

3. **Have them calculate the mean, median, and mode for the two samples. Have the students estimate the standard deviation. (You may choose to have the students also calculate the standard deviation of the two samples.) Point out that these statistics help us "describe" the two samples.**

4. **Display TM 15.3 *"Descriptive Statistics for the Two Distributions of Scores."* Discuss the statistics, and again remind them that in actual standardized testing situations the samples will be much larger than those used for the purposes of illustration here.**

5. **Display T 15.5 *"Normal Distribution,"* and then ask students if the second class in TM 15.2 represents a normal distribution. Have them explain why or why not.**

6. **Have them examine both the measures of central tendency and the measures of variability. The mean, median, and mode of the second sample in TM 15.2 are the same, so in this regard the sample appears to have the characteristics of a normal distribution. However, a normal distribution has approximately 68% of the scores in the sample that fall within one standard deviation from the mean, whereas for the second class in TM 15.2 77% of the sample falls within this range. The class is not as "spread out" as is a normal distribution.**

B. Interpreting standardized test results
   1. Raw scores
   2. Percentiles
   3. Stanines
   4. Grade equivalents
   5. Standard scores
   6. Standard error of measurement

   ■ *The purpose of this activity is to help the students understand how to interpret standardized test results.*
   1. **Point out that interpreting standardized test results will be one of the most important roles that teachers have in using standardized tests.**

   2. **Display TM 15.4 *"Interpreting Standardized Test Scores: An Application"* and have students work to interpret the results of the problem. Have them explain their answers and discuss the results with the whole class.**

III. Issues in standardized testing
   A. Standards-based education and the accountability movement\
   B. Testing teachers
   C. Cultural minorities and high-stakes tests
   D. Student diversity and test bias
      1. Bias in content
      2. Bias in testing procedures
      3. Bias in test use
   E. Eliminating bias in standardized testing: Instructional strategies
      1. Analyze test content
      2. Adapt testing procedures
      3. Use alternate assessment data sources

F.   Standardized testing with alternative formats

G.   Issues in standardized testing: Implications for teachers

■ ***The purpose of this activity is to help students understand some of the issues involved in standardized testing.***

1. **Standards-based education and accountability are controversial topics. Have students work in groups, take a position with respect to the effectiveness of these movements, and have the groups present and defend their position. Have them predict whether or not the emphasis on accountability is likely to increase, and have them give reasons for their predictions.**

2. **Have the students discuss and/or debate the issues involved in standardized testing with alternative formats, i.e., using more authentic assessments with standardized testing. Again, you might have them take and defend a position regarding their predictions for the future of standardized testing with alternative formats.**

3. **Have the students again reflect on their experiences with the sample items that they responded to in the activity on intelligence testing in Chapter 4. Ask them how bias in measurement--particularly bias in content and bias in test result use--could exist in measurements similar to the ones they experienced. Discuss their reactions in a whole-group activity.**

DISCUSSION STARTERS

1. A great deal of criticism is being directed at education, the critics arguing that the nation's K-12 schools are doing an inadequate job of educating students for either the workplace or higher education. How much of this criticism is based on the results of standardized test scores? What are some other sources on which the criticisms are based?

2. You are responsible for explaining the results of a standardized achievement test to parents. What types of scores will be most useful to you? Least? Why?

3. You are explaining the same test results as in Question 2, but are working with the parents of students for whom English is a second language. What modifications would you have to make in your explanation?

4. What trends do you see in the future of standardized testing? Is the emphasis on standardized testing likely to increase or decrease in the next decade? Why do you think so?

5. What is the future of authentic assessment in standardized testing? Is the emphasis on authentic standardized testing likely to increase or decrease compared to the emphasis on "traditional" standardized testing? Why do you think so?

6. A great deal of emphasis has been placed on giving local districts and schools more autonomy. If the trend toward local control increases, how will standardized testing be influenced? Why do you think so?

7. Is emphasis on accountability likely to increase or decrease over the next decade? Why do you think so?

BACKGROUND READINGS

Amrein, A. L., & Berliner, D. C. (2002, March 28). *High-stakes testing, uncertainty, and student learning. Education Policy Analysis Archives, 10*(3). Available on-line at http://epaa.asu.edu/epaa/v10n18/ . A critical look at potential pitfalls with high-stakes testing.

Anastasi, A., & Urbina, S. (1997). *Psychological testing.* Upper Saddle River, NJ: Prentice-Hall. A classic; provides a definitive look at basic concepts in psychological testing.

Corno, L., Cronbach, L. J., Kupermintz, H., Lohman, D. F., Mandinach, E. B., Porteus, A. W., & Talbert, J. E. (2002). *Remaking the concept of aptitude; Extending the legacy of Richard E. Snow.* Mahwah, NJ: Erlbaum. An excellent overview of the history of aptitude testing.

Gronlund, N., & Linn, R. (2000). *Measurement and evaluation in teaching* (8th ed.). Upper Saddle River, NJ: Prentice Hall. This classic text by two of the leading figures in the field, provides a detailed examination of standardized testing and some of the issues involved.

Phye, G. D. (Ed.) (1997). *Handbook of classroom assessment: Learning, achievement, and adjustment.* San Diego: Academic Press. This excellent edited work covers a broad spectrum of assessment topics.

Venn, J. J. (2000). *Assessing students with special needs* (2nd ed.). Upper Saddle River, NJ: Merrill/Prentice Hall. Discusses basic principles of assessment in terms of students with special needs.

FEEDBACK FOR CONSTRUCTED RESPONSE AND DOCUMENT-BASED ANALYSIS QUESTIONS

Constructed Response Items_____

1. What type of standardized test would help Peggy determine the answer to her own question: "I don't know if this class is *really* doing better than last year, . . . or even my other classes this year."
   Standardized achievement tests are specifically designed to provide information about how much students learn in various content areas. To be useful in answering her question the standardized achievement test would have to be carefully aligned with her curriculum.

2. What type of validity would be a primary concern? How might Peggy answer the question about validity?
   Content validity, or the extent to which a standardized achievement test actually covers important content. This is essentially an issue of alignment.

3. One of Peggy's concerns was the background knowledge of her students: "I would say their background is weak." What type of standardized test might Peggy use to gather data related to this concern?
   Because of their focus on specific content, standardized diagnostic tests would be most useful here. Diagnostic tests assess more narrowly, but do so more thoroughly, thus providing the teacher with more in-depth information about specific topics.

4. In investigating the problems that her students were having in math, Peggy checked out their overall test scores from past standardized tests. What else might she have done?
   The more information that teachers gather in their decision-making, the better their decisions. Other possible sources of information include specific subtests within the standardized tests, previous grades in math classes, and observations and evaluations from previous teachers.

Document-Based Analysis_____

Examine the standardized test report for David Palmer, the student in the opening case study. The following are conclusions based on the results.

1. David answered 62% of the questions on the science subtest correctly.
2. Davis is better at reading than in math.
3. On the basis of his total battery score, David should be placed in fifth grade.
4. David is smarter than his peers in fourth grade.
5. David scored about as well as other fourth graders in math.

Decide which of the conclusions are valid and which are not. Explain why they are or are not in each instance.

1. *This conclusion is correct, because he answered 31 out of 50 questions on this subtest.*
2. *This conclusion is probably also correct because both his Grade Equivalent score and National Grade Percentile Bands were higher for his Total Reading than his Total Math score.*
3. *This is an incorrect conclusion. Despite the fact that his Grade Equivalent score for the total test battery was 5.1, this does not mean he should be placed in fifth grade. This is a common mistake made when using grade equivalent scores.*
4. *We don't know this for several reasons. First, this is an achievement test, not an intelligence or aptitude test. Second, his total test battery score was about 50th percentile. In every test there is a certain amount of measurement error, so we couldn't confidently conclude he was "smarter" than his peers. A third problem is we don't know what "peers" refers to. If it refers to national fourth grade peers, we might have some basis for comparison. However, we don't have information about his school's immediate peers' performance on the test.*
5. *Actually David scored slightly poorer than other fourth graders in math, as evidenced by his total math Grade Equivalent and National Grade Percentile Band scores. Note that the test was probably taken in the spring, which would explain the possible discrepancy between these two scores. If taken in the spring, the Grade Equivalent score should show 4.8 or 4.9, if the student is comparable to an average peer in the fourth grade.*

CLASSROOM EXERCISES

1. A class had the following scores on a quiz:

```
                        x
                        x   x
                    x   x   x
                x   x   x   x
            x   x   x   x   x   x
            x   x   x   x   x   x   x   x   x
        1   2   3   4   5   6   7   8   9   10
```

a. What is the mean for this quiz?

b. What is the mode for this quiz?

c. What is the median for this quiz?

2. A standardized test has a mean of 100 and a standard deviation of 10. Compute the *t scores*, *z scores*, and percentile for the following student scores on that test.

a. 110

b. 90

c. 130

d. 80

FEEDBACK FOR CLASSROOM EXERCISES

1. a. The mean is 5.84 (146/25).

   b. The mode, or most frequently occurring score is 6.

   c. The median, middle-point score, is also 6.

2. a. A score of 110 would result in a *z score* of 1, a *t score* of 60, and a percentile at approximately the 84th percentile.

   b. A score of 90 would result in a *z score* of -1, a *t score* of 40, and a percentile at approximately the 16th percentile.

   c. A score of 130 would result in a *z score* of 3, a *t score* of 70, and a percentile at approximately the 99th percentile.

   d. A score of 80 would result in a *z score* of -2, a *t score* of 30, and a percentile at approximately the 2nd percentile.

Transparency

Masters

Transparency Master 1.1   The INTASC Principles

Principle	Description
1. Knowledge of subject	Teachers understand the content they teach and can make the content meaningful for students.
2. Learning and human development	Teachers understand how children learn and develop, and they apply this information in their instruction.
3. Adapting instruction	Teachers understand how students differ in their approaches to learning and adapt instruction accordingly.
4. Strategies	Teachers understand and use a variety of instructional strategies to promote critical thinking and problem solving.
5. Motivation and management	Teachers create learning environments that encourage positive social interaction, active engagement in learning, and self-motivation.
6. Communic-ation skills	Teachers communicate clearly, their verbal and nonverbal messages are consistent, and they support classroom interaction.
7. Planning	Teachers plan instruction based upon knowledge of subject matter, students, the community, and curriculum goals.
8. Assessment	Teachers understand and use formal and informal assessment strategies to evaluate and ensure the continuous intellectual, social and physical development of the learner.
9. Commitment	Teachers are reflective practitioners who continually evaluate the effects of their choices and actions on others (students, parents, and other professionals in the learning community) and who actively seek out opportunities to grow professionally.
10. Partnership	Teachers foster relationships with school colleagues, parents, and agencies in the larger community to support students' learning and well-being.

Eggen/Kauchak
Educational Psychology: Windows on Classrooms, Sixth Edition

- Did I have a clear goal for this lesson? What was the specific goal?

- Was my goal important? How do I know?

- Was my learning activity consistent with my goal?

- What examples or representations would have made the lesson clearer for students?

- What could I have done to make the lesson more interesting for students?

- How do I know if the students understand what I taught? What would be a better way of finding out?

- Overall, what will I do differently to improve the lesson the next time I teach it?

Eggen/Kauchak
Educational Psychology: Windows on Classrooms, Sixth Edition

What Do These Descriptions Have in Common?

- Psychologists have learned that rumors emerge to explain confusing situations that are important to us and to relieve the tension of uncertainty. Their investigations suggest that highly anxious people spread rumors much more frequently than calm ones do, and rumors persist until the expectations that give rise to the uncertainty are fulfilled, or until the anxiety abates.

- The function of myth is to make sense of things that are not otherwise understandable.

- A sportswriter argues that sports are very important in our culture. They are one of the few things in life that have a conclusion. It is remedial medicine to attend sporting events -nine innings to a conclusion, 60 minutes to a conclusion, 15 rounds to a conclusion. America yearns for a world where the umpire says the man is out and it really is that way. As the umpire says, "He ain't anything until I call it."

Eggen/Kauchak
Educational Psychology: Windows on Classrooms, Sixth Edition

Read the following vignette and then describe in a paragraph how each of the following concepts, *equilibrium, organization, scheme, accommodation, assimilation, experience,* and *development* are illustrated in it.

You have learned to drive a car with an automatic transmission, and you're very comfortable driving a variety of cars.

Then, you are asked to help a friend move, and your friend asks you to drive her car to her new location as she drives a moving truck. However, the car has a stick shift, and you're very uncomfortable trying to drive it. Your friend helps you get started, and finally you're able to manage and you're now able to drive vehicles with both automatic transmissions and with stick shifts.

Sometime later, you help another friend move, and he has a pickup truck with a stick shift. Now, you're able to comfortably drive the pickup truck.

****

Feedback:

You have had a variety of *experiences* with driving cars having automatic transmissions, and you have *organized* those experiences into a "driving" *scheme*. Your scheme has helped you to achieve *equilibrium*. However, when you encountered the car with a stick shift your equilibrium was disrupted, and you were forced to *accommodate* your scheme. You modified your original driving scheme and constructed a new "driving-with-a-stick-shift" scheme, and your equilibrium was re-established. You were then able to *assimilate* the experience with the pickup truck into your "driving-with a-stick-shift" scheme. As a result of your added experience with driving vehicles having stick shifts, your driving ability is more fully developed than it was when you were only able to drive vehicles with automatic transmissions.

Eggen/Kauchak
Educational Psychology: Windows on Classrooms, Sixth Edition

Imagine that the following drawing is a balance with two blocks on it. The blocks are solids and cubes. Use the drawing to answer the questions that follow.

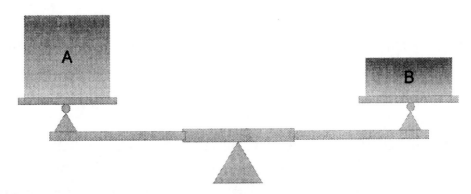

Select the best answer for each of the following items.

1. Block A is bigger than block B.
   a. True   b. False   c. We can't tell from the information that is provided.

2. Block A is heavier than block B.
   a. True   b. False   c. We can't tell from the information that is provided.

3. Block A is more dense than block B.
   a. True   b. False   c. We can't tell from the information that is provided.

4. Block A is made from a different substance than is block B.
   a. True   b. False   c. We can't tell from the information that is provided.

5. Suppose you blew up two identical balloons so that balloon 1 had the same volume as block A and balloon 2 had the same volume as block B. Balloon 1 would be heavier than balloon 2.
   a. True   b. False   c. We can't tell from the information that is provided.

Read the two examples below and identify the two concepts best illustrated in them. (The same two concepts are illustrated in each example.)

- A married woman called a "pop" psychologist on a radio call-in show to ask for advice. As she described it, her problem was as follows:

  She was upset that she couldn't get along with her mother-in-law, who was difficult and uncompromising. Her specific question was, "What could she do to make her mother-in-law be more reasonable?" During the course of the conversation, it was revealed that the woman and her husband were living in her mother-in-law's house, and further, they were living in the house rent free.

- A former NFL football player was caught dealing drugs. He was convicted of drug trafficking, and he served some time in jail. Upon being released, he commented at a press conference, "No one should ever have to go through what I went through."

****
*

Both people were *centering*–the woman on her disagreements with her mother-in-law, and the football player on the fact that he spent time in jail–and they were ignoring other salient facts, such as living rent free in her mother-in-law's house, and having dealt drugs. They also demonstrated remarkable *egocentrism*.

****

Eggen/Kauchak
Educational Psychology: Windows on Classrooms, Sixth Edition

The following principles can guide planning and implementation of instruction based on Piaget's work:

- Provide concrete experiences that represent abstract concepts and principles.

- Help students link the concrete representations to the abstract idea.

- Use social interaction to help students verbalize their developing understanding.

- Design learning experiences as developmental bridges to more advanced stages of development.

Eggen/Kauchak
Educational Psychology: Windows on Classrooms, Sixth Edition

Transparency Master 2.6   A Comparison of Piaget's and Vygotsky's Views of Knowledge Construction

	Piaget	Vygotsky
Goals	How is new knowledge created in all cultures?	How are the tools of knowledge transmitted in a specific culture?
Role of language	Aids in developing symbolic thought. Does not qualitatively raise the level of intellectual functioning	Is an essential mechanism for thinking, cultural transmission and self-regulation. Qualitatively raises the level of intellectual functioning
Social interaction	Provides a way to test and validate schemes	Provides an avenue for acquiring language and the cultural exchange of ideas
View of learner	Active in manipulating objects and ideas	Active in social contexts and interactions
Instructional implications	Design experiences to disrupt equilibrium	Provide scaffolding. Guide interaction

Eggen/Kauchak
Educational Psychology: Windows on Classrooms, Sixth Edition

The following principles can guide planning and implementation of instruction based on Vygotsky's work:

- Embed learning activities in a context that is culturally authentic.

- Create learning activities that involve students in social interactions.

- Encourage students to use language to describe their developing understandings

- Create learning activities that are in learners' zones of proximal development.

- Provide instructional assistance to promote learning and development.

- Provide concrete experiences that represent abstract concepts and principles.

Eggen/Kauchak
Educational Psychology: Windows on Classrooms, Sixth Edition

Type of Program	Advantage	Disadvantages
Maintenance bilingual programs: Instruction in native language and English	Maintains native culture, heritage, and language	Difficult to implement if a variety of languages are spoken.
Transitional bilingual programs: Use native language until English is proficient	Allows gradual transition to English	Possible communication problems between children and parents. Loss of home culture.
ESL Programs: Focus on mastery of English	Accommodates classes with a variety of native languages	Pull-out programs disrupt continuity. Communication problems similar to those in transitional programs.

"I want you in by 10," Ellen's dad says to her as she gets ready for her roller skating party, and then he turns back to his computer.

"Aww, Dad," Ellen protests. "The party isn't over 'till 11, and a bunch of parents will be there chaperoning.

"I said 10, Sweetheart."

"Gee, Dad, why."

"Ellen, remember that we've said no later than 10 on school nights."

"But, Dad, there's no school tomorrow. It's a teacher planning day."

"Ellen, I said 10. The discussion is over."

"Tell me about school," Tanya's dad says to her over dinner.

They talk for several minutes about school, social activities, and life in general.

"Now, when is your concert? I've sort of forgotten."

"Thursday," Tanya replies.

"Oh, yeah, . . . Remind me to call George and tell him I won't be able to meet him on Thursday," he says to Tanya's mother. "Tanya's concert is that night."

They finish dinner, and her dad finally says, "Better get started with your homework."

"Aww, Dad," Tanya grumbles.

"No, get going. . . . I'm working in here, so let me know if you get stuck on any of it, and I'll try and help you. . . . I want to see it when you're finished.

"Where's Jan?" Her dad asks her mother at 9:30 Thursday evening.

"She called after school and said she was going home with Christy," her mother responded.

"Didn't she say she had a test tomorrow? . . . When is she going to study?"

"She said she was fine, and besides she's not too crazy about biology. I know her grades aren't as good as they could be, but you're only young once."

Eggen/Kauchak
Educational Psychology: Windows on Classrooms, Sixth Edition

- Using modeling and explicit instruction to teach the kinds of social skills that you would like to see in your students

- Establish rules governing acceptable classroom behavior.

- Help students understand the rules by providing examples and guiding discussions.

- Have students practice social skills and provide feedback.

Eggen/Kauchak
Educational Psychology: Windows on Classrooms, Sixth Edition

Assumptions Involved in Erikson's Theory

1. People in general have the same basic needs.

2. The development of the ego or self occurs in response to those needs.

3. Development proceeds in stages.

4. Each stage is characterized by a psychosocial challenge, or *crisis*, that presents opportunities for development.

5. Different stages reflect differences in the motivation of the individual.

Corollaries Involved in Erikson's Theory

1. Although all people pass through all the stages, the rate and intensity may vary among individuals.

2. No one permanently resolves a crisis. Each conflict exists in some form throughout life but is at a critical period at its specific stage.

3. People do *not* remain at a certain stage if the crisis at that stage isn't positively resolved.

4. Less than ideal resolutions of crises at particular stages leave individuals with personality imperfections or "glitches."

5. The effectiveness of the conflict resolution at each stage determines the overall health of an individual's personality.

Eggen/Kauchak
Educational Psychology: Windows on Classrooms, Sixth Edition

Positive Resolution	**Negative Resolution**
1. Trust in themselves and others. Relaxed, optimistic and generous attitude.	See the world as inconsistent and threatening. See life as not predictable, and view good things as temporary.
2. Good sense and command of their will power. Feel free to be themselves.	Fear being exposed as inadequate. Attempt to hide their feelings of powerlessness.
3. Believe they know how the world works. Clear sense of what they want in life.	Fear of being inadequate and of making mistakes. Self-restrictive and sometimes overconscientious.
4. Relish achievement and like to tackle challenging tasks.	Feel inadequate, incapable, and estranged. Lack ambition.
5. Know who they are, what their goals are, and where they're going.	See conflict in who they are and what they would like to be.
6. Commit to partnerships and have the ethics to abide by the commitments-to same and opposite sex relationships.	Self-absorbed. Identity is too fragile to maintain the uncertainties of intimacy.
7. Concern for creation of better world. Focus on service to others.	Lack long-term goals and commitments. Live for short-term gratification.
8. Feel their lives have meaning and significance.	View life as filled with missed opportunities.

Eggen/Kauchak
Educational Psychology: Windows on Classrooms, Sixth Edition

- Communicate caring and genuine interest in all students.

- Maintain an authoritative interaction style.

- Reward autonomy and initiative in your students.

- Establish appropriately high expectations for all learners.

- Create learning activities in which students can succeed on tasks they view as challenging.

- Design grading systems that emphasize increasing competence and avoid competition.

Eggen/Kauchak
Educational Psychology: Windows on Classrooms, Sixth Edition

Three teachers were involved in a conversation in the faculty workroom during their lunch period.

"What are you doing?" Kevin asked Sue as she pored over some papers during their lunch period.

"I want to give these papers back, so the kids can figure out their bonus points."

"What ... what are you talking about?"

"I'm using a new system in my class," Sue continued. "Whenever I give a quiz, if the score is higher than their average, they get bonus points. That way they get rewarded for improving, regardless of their average. I told them that if they constantly improve, they can't fail.... It's working. I have kids studying that never tried before."

"I think you work too hard," Mary interjected. "All you do is work. You're the first one here in the morning, the last one out at night, and now you're working at lunch."

"Yeah, ... I know," Sue nodded, "But I worry about some of these kids. School has always been such a tough place for them. I'm afraid later on we'll lose them forever."

"I understand," Mary shrugged, "but I'm so tired. Jeff comes over and we talk until we're blue in the face. I care about him, but I just don't know ..."

"That's interesting," Kevin added. "My problems are a little different. Most of the kids are fine. It's just Karen and Andy. They will do what I ask them to do and no more. They're so afraid of making a mistake, but the work they do is always quite good, sometimes very good. It would be good to see them relax, go beyond the minimum and do some things on their own."

Based on the best evidence available in the case study and on Erikson's work, answer the following questions and in each case *provide the evidence on which your conclusions are based.*

1. What school level is this—elementary, middle, or secondary?

2. What is your estimate of Sue's age?

3. What is your estimate of Mary's age?

4. What stage of psychosocial development is best illustrated by Karen's and Andy's behaviors?

1. Based on Sue's concern for her students' success, the best estimate of the schools' level is elementary. At the elementary level, learners chronologically are faced with the challenge of industry versus inferiority. Success, challenge, and improvement of skills help contribute to a sense of industry.

2. Sue's behavior indicates she has positively resolved the generativity versus stagnation crisis. This is most characteristic of a person in middle adulthood, which could range from approximately the mid 30s to the mid 50s.

3. Mary is demonstrating behaviors characteristic of the intimacy versus isolation stage, which is characteristic of young adulthood, so somewhere in her 20s would be a reasonable estimate.

4. Karen and Andy indicate a lack of resolution of the initiative versus guilt stage of psychosocial development.

Eggen/Kauchak
Educational Psychology: Windows on Classrooms, Sixth Edition

Self-concept includes perceptions about our physical, social, and academic competence. It is a cognitive appraisal of the self in different areas. Self-esteem is an affective or emotional reaction to the self. Pintrich and Schunk (1996) observe:

> This distinction is often lost in the popular views of self-esteem, not just in schools but in many domains of life,.... For example, on many TV talk shows or in many popular self-help books, high self-esteem is offered as the major panacea for all individual problems. The basic argument is that poor or low self-esteem is the root of all problems, whether they be child abuse, spouse abuse, substance abuse, weight or body image problems, marital infidelity, delinquency, personal unemployment, criminality, learning problems, or just personal unhappiness and depression. Given this assumption, it then follows that increasing self-esteem will result in the remediation of these problems. As Lazarus (1991) notes, this logic leads people to believe that they will avoid these problems by rehearsing simple positive statements about the self (i.e., I'm a good person) or having others give them the same type of noncontingent positive feedback. Of course, any view this simplistic is absurd in the face of the complexity of these problems.

> The difficulty is that in U.S. schools today, many teachers do subscribe to this simplistic view, reflecting the emphasis it receives in our popular culture. Teachers are often afraid to say anything negative to students about their performance because they believe it will hurt the students' self-esteem. There are schools and classrooms that engage in self-esteem programs whereby children are asked to chant positive statements about themselves in order to enhance self-esteem. (pp. 312-313)

You are driving 67 miles per hour on an interstate highway. The posted speed limit is 55. You are traveling with the flow of traffic–you are being passed by about the same number of cars as you pass.

A highway patrol pulls you over and gives you a ticket for speeding. Upset, you protest that everyone else is driving the same speed.

"Look," the highway patrol responds. "I get sick of it when people do something wrong, and then they act like it's our fault when they get a ticket. My radar had you clocked at 67, and the speed limit clearly says 55."

You feel you've been dealt with unfairly.

1. Are you justified in feeling that you've been treated unfairly? Explain why you think so.

2. Is the highway patrol's position more, or less, justified than yours? Explain why you think so.

Eggen/Kauchak
Educational Psychology: Windows on Classrooms, Sixth Edition

"Listen, everyone.... I need to go to the office for a moment," Amanda Kellinger said as her students were completing a seat-work assignment. "You all have work to do, so work quietly on it until I get back."

The quiet shuffling of pencils and papers could be heard for a few moments, and then Gary whispered, "Psst, what math problems are we supposed to do?"

"Shh! No talking," Talitha said, pointing to the rules posted on the bulletin board.

"But he needs to know so he can do his homework," Krystal put in. "It's the evens on page 79."

"Who cares?" Dwain growled. "She's not here. She won't catch us."

Describe the moral reasoning Gary, Talitha, and Dwain each demonstrated.

Eggen/Kauchak
Educational Psychology: Windows on Classrooms, Sixth Edition

You have a boy named David in your class. He lives with his mother, a single parent of three. He has a job from 6 p.m. to midnight Sunday through Thursday. His mother needs his financial contribution to the family.

Dave's employers report that his work is very good; he is conscientious and reliable. They tell him he has a full-time job waiting for him beginning June 15, but company policy requires that all full-time employees be high school graduates, and they must fill the position by July 1.

Dave is performing poorly in your class, often putting his head down and sleeping through much of the period. You warn him repeatedly, and he listens, but his behavior hasn't changed.

Finally, after you warn him for the fourth time that he must "get going" to pass (and subsequently graduate from high school), he says, "Look, I have a job waiting for me after high school. This class has nothing to do with what I do on that job."

When you explain that he has to pass your class to graduate, his response is, "If you fail me, I can't get the job. You're screwing up my future."

He fails your final exam, and consequently doesn't have enough points to pass your class. (You have set up 60% as a minimum passing average, and he has a 51% average.)

Do you pass him or not?

Eggen/Kauchak
Educational Psychology: Windows on Classrooms, Sixth Edition

For the following items consider a teenager who is out with her friends. She has been directed by her parents to be in by midnight. She complies.

Which of Kohlberg's stages is best illustrated by each of the reasons stated below?

1. If I stay out, I'll be in big trouble with my parents.

2. Nobody's doing anything anyway, so I won't be missing anything.

3. My parents and I agreed that midnight was fair, and you can't go back on your agreements.

4. If I stay out, my parents will be worried.

5. It's the curfew, so I'll be in by midnight.

6. My friends have curfews, too, and they're going home then.

"Are you okay?" her mother asked as Melissa walked in the house after school.

"I feel really bad, Mom," Melissa answered softly. "We were working in a group, and Jessica said something sort of odd, and I said, 'That's dumb. Where did that come from?' . . . She didn't say anything for the rest of the time we did group work. She doesn't get really good grades, and I know saying something about her being dumb really hurt her feelings. I didn't intend to do it. It just sort of fell out."

"I know you didn't intend to hurt her feelings, Sweetheart. Did you tell her you were sorry?"

"No, when I realized it, I just sat there like a lump. I know how I'd feel if someone made me feel dumb."

"Tell you what," her mom suggested. "Tomorrow, you go directly to her, tell her you're very sorry, and that it won't happen again."

". . . Thanks, Mom. I'll do it as soon as I see her. . . . I feel a lot better."

1. Identify three emotions that Melissa demonstrated in her conversation with her mother.

•   Is Melissa' moral development higher or lower than it would have been if she hadn't experienced these emotions?

Eggen/Kauchak
Educational Psychology: Windows on Classrooms, Sixth Edition

Transparency Master 3.13 A Comparison of Character Education and Moral Education

	Character Education	Moral Education
Goals	Transmission of moral values	Development of moral reasoning capacities
	Translation of values into behavior	Decision making about moral issues
Instruction	Reading about and analyzing values	Discussion using moral dilemmas
	Practicing and rewarding good values	Moral perspectives are shared in discussions
Role of the teacher	Lecturer/advocate	Problem poser
	Role model	Facilitator
View of learner	Unsocialized citizen of the community needing moral direction and guidance	Undeveloped
		Constructor of increasingly complex moral structures

Eggen/Kauchak
Educational Psychology: Windows on Classrooms, Sixth Edition

- Model ethical thinking, behavior, and empathy in your interactions with students

- Use classroom management as a vehicle for promoting moral development.

- Encourage students to respect the perspectives of others.

- Use moral dilemmas as concrete reference points for discussions of moral issues.

- Encourage students to articulate and justify their moral positions in discussions.

Eggen/Kauchak
Educational Psychology: Windows on Classrooms, Sixth Edition

Transparency Master 4.1 Instructional Applications of Gardner's Multiple Intelligences

Dimension	Application
Linguistic	How can I get students to talk or write about the idea?
Logical/Mathematical	How can I bring in number, logic, and classification to encourage students to quantify or clarify the idea?
Spatial	What can I do to help students visualize, draw, or conceptualize the idea spatially?
Musical	How can I help students use environmental sounds, or set ideas into rhythm or melody?
Bodily Kinesthetic	What can I do to help students involve the whole body or to use hands-on experience?
Interpersonal	How can peer, cross-age, or cooperative learning be used to help students develop their interactive skills?
Intrapersonal	How can I get students to think about their capacities and feelings to make them more aware of themselves as persons and learners?
Naturalist	How can I provide experiences that require students to classify different types of objects and analyze their classification schemes?

Eggen/Kauchak
Educational Psychology: Windows on Classrooms, Sixth Edition

Transparency Master 4.2 Applying Analytic, Creative, and Practical Thinking in Different Content Areas

Content Area	Analytic	Creative	Practical
Math	Express the number 44 in base 2.	Write a test question that measures understanding of the Pythagorean theorem	How might geometry be useful in the construction area?
Language Arts	Why is *Romeo and Juliet* considered a tragedy	Write an alternative ending to *Romeo and Juliet* to make it a comedy.	Write a TV ad for the school's production of *Romeo and Juliet.*
Social Studies	In what ways were the Korean War and the Vietnam War similar and different	In hindsight, what could the United States have done differently in these two wars?	What lessons can we take away from these two wars?
Art	Compare and contrast the artistic styles of Van Gogh and Monet.	What would the Statue of Liberty look like if it were created by Picasso?	Create a poster for the student art show using the style of one of the artists studied.

Eggen/Kauchak
Educational Psychology: Windows on Classrooms, Sixth Edition

1. A learner who is labeled as a low achiever is likely to achieve a) *more than*, b) *about as much as*, or c) *less than* a learner of comparable ability who is not labeled as a low achiever.

    Why do you believe labeled students achieve as they do?

2. Students in low-ability groups tend to spend a) *more time,* b) *about the same amount of time,* or c) *less time* in on-task behaviors than do students in high-ability groups.

    Why do you believe that these patterns exist?

3. When teachers know that a student is labeled as a low-ability student, they tend to provide a) *more academic support (such as calling on them more often, and providing more academic feedback),* b) *about the same amount of academic support, or* c) *less academic support* than they provide for students who are not labeled as a low-ability student.

    Why do you believe that teachers behave this way?

4. Absenteeism in low-ability groups is a) *higher than, b) about the same as,* or c) *lower than* absenteeism in high-ability groups.

    Why do you believe these patterns exist?

Eggen/Kauchak
Educational Psychology: Windows on Classrooms, Sixth Edition

1. Within-class ability grouping creates organizational and logistical problems, because different groups have different lessons and assignments. Monitoring seatwork is difficult.

2. Placements are sometimes incorrectly made, and once a learner is placed in a low-ability group, the learner tends to remain there. Cultural minorities are underrepresented in high-ability classes.

3. Low-ability students are stigmatized, and their self-esteem and motivation tend to decrease.

4. Homogeneously grouped low-ability students achieve less than heterogeneously grouped students of similar ability.

Transparency Master 4.5 The Influence of SES on Learning

	High SES	Low SES
Basic needs and experiences	• Well nourished • Stable homes • Access to educational activities outside of school.	• Sometimes lack proper nourishment and medical care • Less stable homes • Transience • Homelessness • Lack access to learning experiences outside of school
Parental involvement	• Highly involved parents • Involvement in extracurricular activities • Interaction between parents and children • Parents explain causes of events, and demonstrate authoritative parenting styles	• Lower parental involvement • Low involvement in extracurricular activities • Little interaction between parents and children • Less elaborate interaction and authoritarian parenting styles
Attitudes and values	• Parents value and emphasize autonomy • High expectations	• Parents value conformity • Lower expectations

Eggen/Kauchak
Educational Psychology: Windows on Classrooms, Sixth Edition

- Demonstrate caring for all students by giving them your time and showing personal interest in them.

- Involve all students in learning activities as equally as possible.

- Use a variety of teaching methods to accommodate different cultural learning styles.

- Communicate that you value the contributions that all cultures can bring to school and society.

- Provide opportunities for students with different backgrounds to interact and work together.

Eggen/Kauchak
Educational Psychology: Windows on Classrooms, Sixth Edition

1. Stand by the door as your students come into class and greet as many of them by name as possible. Be sure that students who are not greeted one day are greeted the next.

2. Make it a point to make a periodic personal comment to individual students (such as a comment about their hair, clothes, incident at home, or extracurricular activity.)

3. Carefully monitor students' work and remind them immediately if some aspect of their work is missing or inadequate (such as a missing homework assignment).

4. Call students' parents or caregivers and solicit their help in making the school experience as positive as possible.

5. During learning activities, be sure you call on cultural minorities as often as you call on nonminorities.

6. During learning activities call on all students by name.

7. Use guided discovery methods to allow you to use *open-ended questions,* to promote *high levels of involvement,* and to *ensure success.*

8. Adopt and enforce rules that require students to treat you and each other with respect and courtesy.

Eggen/Kauchak
Educational Psychology: Windows on Classrooms, Sixth Edition

1. Boys are more likely to ask questions and make comments about ideas discussed in class. The differences increase as students move through school.

2. Boys are more likely to call out in class.

3. Teachers call on boys more often than they do girls.

4. Boys are more likely to conduct science demonstrations than are girls.

5. Girls are less likely to take non-required math and science courses than are boys.

6. Girls are less than half as likely as boys to pursue careers in engineering and physical and computer sciences.

7. Boys cut class more often than do girls.

8. Boys hold more part-time jobs than do girls.

9. Boys are less likely to take college preparatory courses than are girls.

10. Boys receive lower grades than girls and score lower than girls on measures of writing ability.

11. Women earn 53% of the bachelors and masters degrees in this country.

Eggen/Kauchak
Educational Psychology: Windows on Classrooms, Sixth Edition

- Communicate openly with students about gender issues and concerns.

- Eliminate gender bias in instructional activities.

- Present students with non-stereotypical role models.

Eggen/Kauchak
Educational Psychology: Windows on Classrooms, Sixth Edition

Characteristics of Schools That Promote Resilience

- **High and uncompromising academic standards**
  Mastery of content is emphasized, and passive
  attendance and mere completion of assignments are
  unacceptable.

- **Strong personal bonds between teachers and students**
  Teachers become the adults that refuse to let students
  fail, students feel connected to the schools, mutual
  respect between students and teachers is emphasized,
  and personal responsibility and cooperation are
  stressed.

- **Order and high structure**
  The school and classes are orderly and highly
  structured. Reasons for rules are emphasized, and
  rules and procedures are consistently enforced.

- **Participation in after-school activities**
  Activities such as clubs and athletics give students
  additional chances to interact with caring adults and
  receive reinforcement for achievement.

Eggen/Kauchak
Educational Psychology: Windows on Classrooms, Sixth Edition

- Create and maintain an orderly learning environment with predictable routines.

- Combine high expectations with frequent feedback about learning progress.

- Use teaching strategies that actively involve all students and promote high levels of success.

- Use high-quality examples that provide the background knowledge students need to learn new content.

- Stress student self-regulation and the acquisition of learning strategies.

Eggen/Kauchak
Educational Psychology: Windows on Classrooms, Sixth Edition

Transparency Master 4.12   Ethnicity and Computer Use

Ethnicity	School Use of Computer		Home Use of Computer	
	Grades 1–8	Grades 9–12	Grades 1–8	Grades 9–12
White	84%	72%	54%	61%
African American	72%	73%	21%	21%
Hispanic	68%	63%	19%	22%

Source: U.S. Department of Commerce, 1998

Household Income	School Use of Computer		Home Use of Computer	
	Grades 1–8	Grades 9–12	Grades 1–8	Grades 9–12
$15,000–$20,000	75%	67%	16%	21%
$35,000–$40,000	80%	70%	44%	46%
$75,000 or more	86%	72%	80%	81%

Source: U.S. Department of Commerce, 1998

Eggen/Kauchak
Educational Psychology: Windows on Classrooms, Sixth Edition

Learning Problem	*Characteristics*
Mental retardation	General subaverage intellectual functioning and a lack of adaptive skills (e.g., communication)
	• Failure to acquire basic learning strategies (e.g., maintaining attention, organizing new material)
	• May have low self-esteem
	• May require increased instructional support
Learning disabilities	Learning problems in reading, writing or math
	• Average to above average intelligence
	• Often perform very differently on IQ and achievement tests
	• May have low self-esteem
	• Symptoms may result in management problems
Behavioral disorders	Serious and persistent age-inappropriate behaviors
	• Externalizing behavior disorders can include hyperactivity, hostility, defiance, and uncooperativeness.
	• Internalizing behavior disorders can include social withdrawal and depression.

Eggen/Kauchak
Educational Psychology: Windows on Classrooms, Sixth Edition

1. Often connected with a learning disability

2. Characterized by:

   • Difficulty in concentrating and failure to finish tasks

   • Easy distractibility and failure to listen

   • Inordinate need for supervision

   • Impulsiveness

   • Frequent calling out in class and difficulty awaiting turns

3. Three subcategories:

   • Inattentive

   • Hyperactive-impulsive

   • Combined (includes characteristics of other two)

Eggen/Kauchak
Educational Psychology: Windows on Classrooms, Sixth Edition

Behavioral Management Strategies For Working With Students Having Behavioral Disorders

Strategy	Description and Example
Positive reinforcement	Rewarding positive behaviors Praising a student for behaving courteously
Replacement	Teaching appropriate behaviors Teaching students to express personal feelings instead of fighting
Extinction	Ignoring disruptive behaviors Ignoring a student who briefly talks out
Time out	Isolating a child for brief periods of time Having a child sit behind a file cabinet for ten minutes
Overcorrection	Requiring restitution beyond the damaging effects of the immediate behavior Requiring a child to return one of his own cookies in addition to the one he took from another student

Eggen/Kauchak
Educational Psychology: Windows on Classrooms, Sixth Edition

Disorder	Description	Example
Articulation disorders	Difficulty in producing certain sounds, including substituting, distorting, and omitting	'Wabbit' for rabbit 'Thit' for sit 'Onley' for lonely
Fluency disorders	Repetition of the first sound of a word (stuttering) and other problems in producing "smooth" speech	"Y, Y, Y, Yes'
Voice disorders	Problems with the larynx or air passageways in the nose or throat	High-pitched or nasal voice

Eggen/Kauchak
Educational Psychology: Windows on Classrooms, Sixth Edition

1. Holding the head in an awkward position when reading, or holding the book too close or too far away

2. Squinting and frequently rubbing the eyes

3. Tuning out when information is presented on the board

4. Constantly asking about classroom procedures, especially when information is on the board

5. Complaining of headaches, dizziness, or nausea

6. Having redness, crusting, or swelling of the eyes

7. Losing place on the line or page and confusing letters

8. Using poor spacing in writing or having difficulty in staying on the line

Eggen/Kauchak
Educational Psychology: Windows on Classrooms, Sixth Edition

1. Favoring one ear by cocking the head toward the speaker or cupping a hand behind the ear

2. Misunderstanding or not following directions, and exhibiting nonverbal cues (e.g., frowns or puzzled looks) when directions are given

3. Being distracted or seeming disoriented at times

4. Asking people to repeat what they just said

5. Poorly articulating words, especially consonants

6. Turning the volume of loud when listening to audio recordings, radio, or television

7. Showing reluctance to participate in oral activities

8. Having frequent earaches or complaining of discomfort or buzzing in the ears

Eggen/Kauchak
Educational Psychology: Windows on Classrooms, Sixth Edition

Instructional Adaptations to Help Students With Hearing Disabilities

- Supplement auditory presentations with visual information and hands-on experiences.

- Speak clearly and orient yourself so students can see your face.

- Minimize distracting noise.

- Check frequently for understanding.

Eggen/Kauchak
Educational Psychology: Windows on Classrooms, Sixth Edition

Learning Characteristics

1. Like to work alone

2. Are imaginative, like pretending

3. Are highly verbal and flexible in thinking

4. Are persistent, stay with tasks

5. Go beyond assignments

6. Are often bored with routine tasks

7. Are sometimes impulsive, with little interest in details

8. Achieve higher than regular students

Personal, Social, and Physical Characteristics

1. Are well-adjusted as children and adults

2. Have more hobbies than most other people

3. Read more books than most other people

4. Are healthier than the population as a whole

Eggen/Kauchak
Educational Psychology: Windows on Classrooms, Sixth Edition

Enrichment Options	Acceleration Options
1. Independent study and independent projects	1. Early admission to kindergarten and first grade
2. Learning centers	2. Grade skipping
3. Field trips	3. Subject skipping
4. Saturday programs	4. Credit by exam
5. Summer programs	5. College courses in high school
6. Mentors and mentorships	6. Correspondence courses
7. Simulations and games	7. Early admission to college
8. Small-group investigations	
9. Academic competitions	

Eggen/Kauchak
Educational Psychology: Windows on Classrooms, Sixth Edition

Roles for Teachers in Inclusive Classrooms

- Identifying students with exceptionalities

- Teaching students with exceptionalities content and cognitive skills

- Helping students with exceptionalities learn social skills

- Developing classmates' understanding and acceptance

Eggen/Kauchak
Educational Psychology: Windows on Classrooms, Sixth Edition

- Utilize the effective teaching practices that promote learning for all students.

- Provide additional instructional support.

- Design seatwork and homework activities to match the needs of students with exceptionalities.

- Adapt and supplement reading materials to meet the learning needs of students.

- Actively teach learning strategies.

- Implement plans for the social integration and growth of learners with exceptionalities.

Joan Hill, a fourth-grade teacher, has watched Lon Chu's work, and suspects that Lon, a native Chinese-speaking child whose parents immigrated from Taiwan, may have a learning exceptionality. He often turns in incomplete work, and his attention wanders. Joan calls his parents, but they are unable to provide much information. Joan contacts the school counselor and asks about the procedures for having Lon tested. In an effort to diagnose his possible exceptionality, an arrangement is made to give Lon the WISC-III, an individually administered intelligence test. Since Lon speaks competent English, and a Chinese language version of the test isn't available, the test is administered in English by a certified special education official. His I.Q. as measured by the test is 109, but he scores very low on the vocabulary section of the test. Lon's parents are called to a meeting, during which an individualized educational program for Lon is prepared collaboratively by Joan, the exceptional student specialist in the school, the school counselor, and Lon's parents. The IEP is immediately implemented to help Lon as much as possible. Part of the IEP calls for Lon being placed in a resource reading program for one hour a day. (He is mainstreamed the rest of the day.)

1. How effectively did Joan implement the "Prereferral Strategies in Identifying Students with Exceptionalities?" Cite specific evidence from the case study to defend your assessment.

2. Identify one violation of IDEA that was committed in diagnosing Lon's possible exceptionality. Identify a second possible violation.

3. Based on the evidence in the case study, what is Lon's exceptionality?

4. What other characteristic exists in Lon's case that teachers and school should keep in mind before concluding that a learner has an exceptionality?

Rod was feeling the "blahs," so he decided to reward himself with a Caribbean cruise. One evening he was involved in a casual conversation with Kim, a girl he had met, as Latin rhythms floated through the air. Their eyes accidently met, and he flushed and felt a sudden rush of emotion.

Now, whenever Rod hears Latin music, or even Reggae, he gets a feeling of excitement that he can't control. He doesn't react to rock music or jazz in the same way, however.

Eggen/Kauchak
Educational Psychology: Windows on Classrooms, Sixth Edition

1. Jennifer's parents have moved, and since she seems to be quite nervous about starting school in a new place, her dad takes her to school the first few days. She is secure when she is with him, but her heart "thumps" and tears well up in her eyes when he drops her off at school.

    Valdez Elementary, her new school, has a program for students like Jennifer. Teachers greet new students as they arrive and welcome them to the school. Mrs. Abbott, Jennifer's teacher, is at the door to greet Jennifer each morning for the first week when her father brings her to school. She puts her arm around Jennifer and chats with her dad as the three of them stand together near the door. Jennifer now seems quite comfortable when her dad leaves her with Mrs. Abbott.

2. Natasha is moving into the 6th grade in a middle school, and she is quite uneasy about leaving the security of the elementary school she attended for six years. In order to help her make the transition, Natasha's mother drives her to school the first few days. Natasha and her mother have a warm relationship and Natasha feels very secure when she is with her mother.

    In order to help new students ease the transition to the middle school, the teachers meet the students the first few days of school and help them find their way around. Natasha's mother drops her off the first day, and Natasha waves to her mother uneasily as she walks toward the school. Mrs. Rodriguez greets her at the entrance of the main building, smiles, touches her shoulder, and smiles reassuringly. Seeing the way Mrs. Rodriguez behaves, Natasha feels much better.

    Each day, Ms. Rodriguez greets Natasha with the same smile and reassuring manner. Now Natasha jumps out of the car and feels quite relaxed as she enters Mrs. Rodriguez's classroom.

Eggen/Kauchak
Educational Psychology: Windows on Classrooms, Sixth Edition

Explain the Students' and the Teachers' Behaviors in These Two Cases

1. After completing an assignment of 30 problems, one of Ann Johnson's students complains, "Man, Mrs. Johnson you sure do pile on the homework."

    "Yeah," another adds.

    "For sure," a third puts in.

    Several other members of the class chime in, adding to the comments of the first three.

    The next day Ann assigns 20 problems, and as soon as she is finished giving the assignment, the students respond, "Sheesh, Mrs. Johnson, giving homework must be your favorite thing to do."

    As Ann begins to give her homework assignment of 15 problems on the third day, the students protest, "I hope this isn't going to be another killer homework assignment."

2. "This test was impossible. The questions are always so tricky," Jim Gann's students comment as Jim finishes his discussion of a test that he just handed back. "And they're so long," they continue.

    Jim makes his next test easier and shorter, hoping his students will make fewer comments. He gives the test, scores it, and returns it.

    "Not again," the students react about halfway through the discussion. "Yeah, you must love to write tricky items, Mr. Gann," some others add.

    Jim then makes his third test still shorter, and he writes fewer application level items.

Eggen/Kauchak
Educational Psychology: Windows on Classrooms, Sixth Edition

What Do the Following Episodes Have in Common?

1. Mr. Jensen was having trouble keeping Sean in his seat. He then started giving Sean a token he could trade for privileges if he stayed in his seat for five minutes. He then required 7 minutes, later 10, and eventually Sean was able to stay in his seat for 20 minutes to earn his token.

2. Tasha would either hand in her math assignments incomplete or not start at all. Mrs. Yudin gave her a "practice point" for completing one problem. Later she had to complete two problems to get her practice point, and eventually she had to complete the assignment to get the point.

3. A junior high school English teacher wanted to increase the emphasis on writing in her class. Initially the students received points for everything they handed in. Later the essays needed to be more complete and better organized to receive the same number of points.

Eggen/Kauchak
Educational Psychology: Windows on Classrooms, Sixth Edition

What Reinforcement Schedule Is Illustrated in Each of the Following Examples?

1. "Your turn, David.... Please go ahead," Mrs. McLemore directs to the children gathered around her. After David has begun reading she gets up and circulates among the students doing seatwork, making comments and offering suggestions, and returning to the group just as David finishes his section. She repeats this process periodically.

2. When Mrs. Stahlman's students write particularly good responses to essay items, she will often write comments, such as, "Extremely well done. This was a clear and concise answer," near the students' response.

3. Mr. Lombardo, an algebra II teacher, assigns problems every night, and he collects them on Mondays and Thursdays. Mrs. Aschliman collects homework twice a week as well, sometimes on Mondays and Thursdays, but at other times Mondays and Tuesdays, Tuesdays and Wednesdays, or even Wednesdays and Thursdays. Both teachers give a quiz each Friday.

4. Mr. Lombardo often gives his students time to do their homework in class. Any students who finish before the end of the period are allowed to go to the back of the classroom and talk quietly to each other until the end of the period.

Eggen/Kauchak
Educational Psychology: Windows on Classrooms, Sixth Edition

Concept	Description	Example
Punishment	Being presented with something that decreases behavior	Student is told "Shh"
	Something is removed that decreases behavior	Student loses privileges that have been previously earned
Satiation	Reinforcer is overused to the point that it loses its potency	Teacher gives so many "Smiley faces" that they no longer affect student behavior
Extinction	Behavior decreases because it isn't being reinforced	Student stops raising her hand because teacher doesn't call on her

Eggen/Kauchak
Educational Psychology: Windows on Classrooms, Sixth Edition

- Treat students with respect and courtesy so that your classroom and school elicit positive emotions

- Create environmental antecedents that produce desired behaviors

- Reinforce students' efforts and increasing competence

- Establish clear standards for acceptable behavior

- Emphasize positive consequences (reinforcers) for meeting behavioral standards and use punishers only when reinforcers are ineffective

Eggen/Kauchak
Educational Psychology: Windows on Classrooms, Sixth Edition

Applied Behavioral Analysis

- Identify target behaviors

- Establish a baseline for the target behaviors

- Choose reinforcers and punishers (if necessary)

- Measure changes in the target behaviors

- Gradually reduce the frequency of reinforcers as behavior improves

Eggen/Kauchak
Educational Psychology: Windows on Classrooms, Sixth Edition

	Behaviorism	*Social Cognitive Theory*
Learning focus	Observable behavior	Observable behavior, mental representations, expectations, beliefs
Relationship between behavior and the environment	The environment influences behavior.	The environment, personal factors and behavior all influence each other.
Views of reinforcement and punishment	Reinforcement and punishment are direct causes of behavior.	Reinforcement and punishment cause people to form *expectations*. Reinforcement only works when learners are *aware* of what behaviors will be reinforced. Nonoccurrence of expected reinforcers act as punishers.

Eggen/Kauchak
Educational Psychology: Windows on Classrooms, Sixth Edition

You are driving 65 on the Interstate one evening, and you are suddenly passed by a sports car traveling at least 75.

A couple minutes later you see the sports car pulled over by the highway patrol. You immediately slow down.

Why do you slow down?

How would behaviorism explain you slowing down?

Eggen/Kauchak
Educational Psychology: Windows on Classrooms, Sixth Edition

"Greg, Natalie, please wait to be given permission before you speak out in class," Ms. Margossian directs two of her students as they whisper to each other in a class discussion. Greg and Natalie stop, and Christine, who has been looking at Ms. Margossian out of the corner of her eye as she whispers to Dawn, also stops.

1. Explain Greg's and Natalie's behavior.

2. Explain Christine's behavior using social cognitive theory.

3. In terms of modeling effects on behavior, which effect is best illustrated by Christine's behavior?

4. Suppose Ms. Margossian had said nothing to Greg and Natalie. What is the likely outcome for them, Christine, and the class as a whole? Explain.

1. *Greg and Natalie are being punished. Ms. Margossian "presented" them with her reprimand, and their behavior decreased.*

2. *Christine was vicariously punished. (She altered her behavior by observing the consequences for Greg and Natalie.)*

3. *Christine's inhibition about talking was increased. (The outcome was "increasing inhibitions.")*

4. *Being reprimanded for breaking rules is an expected consequence. Nonoccurrence of the reprimand—an intended punisher—could serve as a reinforcer and the misbehavior might increase.*

Eggen/Kauchak
Educational Psychology: Windows on Classrooms, Sixth Edition

290

According to a recent newspaper article, many people are reluctant to join fitness clubs because they're fearful that their overweight and out-of-shape bodies will look comical to the trim, fit, and athletic trainers they expect to see working there. As a result they continue to procrastinate about joining the clubs?

How can we explain their behavior based on social cognitive theory?

Eggen/Kauchak
Educational Psychology: Windows on Classrooms, Sixth Edition

A group of Southeast Asian immigrants from Vietnam have settled in the area around Mr. Brandao's school. The school finds that several of the immigrant children are very shy and reluctant to speak in class. Mr. Brandao decides to hold a session in which some older students come in and talk to the shy students and demonstrate how they speak up and participate. Chu, a Vietnamese American, tells the students that speaking up is easy and demonstrates raising his hand to speak and responding confidently to the teacher.

In a second session, Li, another Vietnamese immigrant who has been in the States for four years, tells the students he understands their shyness and that it was hard for him at first too, but he learned to do it. He then demonstrates attempts to volunteer answers in a role play situation.

In a third session, Yan, a Chinese American, tells the students that all you have to do is get used to the teachers. He then demonstrates confidence as he responds to the teacher in a role play situation.

Assessment of the effectiveness of the sessions reveals that the second session was most effective, the third session was least effective, and the first session was somewhere between the two.

Using social cognitive theory as a basis, provide a specific explanation for the results.

Li is the most similar to the students in the class, and on the basis of perceived similarity, he would be the most effective. In addition, Li demonstrates the characteristics of a coping model, whereas Chu demonstrated the characteristics of a mastery model. Yan is the least similar of the three, and he also demonstrated mastery characteristics.

Eggen/Kauchak
Educational Psychology: Windows on Classrooms, Sixth Edition

- Behave in ways you want students to imitate

- Enforce classroom rules and procedures fairly and consistently

- Capitalize on modeling effects and processes to promote learning

- Put students in modeling roles

- Capitalize on guests as role models when possible

Eggen/Kauchak
Educational Psychology: Windows on Classrooms, Sixth Edition

Different Types of Models

- A miniature representation of something, such as a model car or a globe

- Someone who poses for an artist

- Someone who displays merchandise

- Someone who displays behavior that is imitated (as was presented in Chapter 6)

A representation that allows us to visualize what we can't observe directly.

Eggen/Kauchak
Educational Psychology: Windows on Classrooms, Sixth Edition

1. Learners' writing often improves more rapidly if they are initially allowed to ignore handwriting quality, grammar, and spelling. (De La Paz & Graham, 1997; Graham, Berninger, Weintraub, & Schafer, 1998).

2. Students write better quality essays using word processors if their word processing skills are well developed. If not, handwritten essays are superior to those created on word processors (Roblyer, 2003) .

3. In spite of enormous staff development efforts to promote more sophisticated forms of instruction, lecture has always been the most common teaching strategy that exists (Cuban, 1984), and it likely continues to be the most used teaching technique.

4. Highly test anxious students are sometimes consumed with thoughts like , "I've never seen this stuff before," "I'm going to fail," "Where did this come from?" and so on.

5. Most teachers have a very powerful need to simplify their work, and experts have as much of what they do in the form of routines as possible.

Eggen/Kauchak
Educational Psychology: Windows on Classrooms, Sixth Edition

Sensory Memory

- Virtually unlimited capacity

- Retains exact copy of stimuli (information is "unprocessed")

- Holds information very briefly (a second or two)

Working Memory

- Depends on attention and perception

- The conscious part of our processing system

- Limited capacity

- Limited duration

- Receives information from both sensory memory and long-term memory

Long-Term Memory

- Depends on attention, perception, and encoding

- An unconscious part of our processing system

- Very large capacity (some experts believe virtually unlimited)

- Receives information only from working memory

Eggen/Kauchak
Educational Psychology: Windows on Classrooms, Sixth Edition

Finding similarities and differences and generalizing:
- "How are these alike?"
- "How are they different?"
- "What pattern do you see?"

Explaining:
- "Why?" (e.g., "Why do you suppose Mercury is so hot on one side and so cold on the other?")

Providing evidence:
- "How do you know?"
  Example: "How do you know that people's perceptions vary?"

  Evidence: Some people saw the young woman in the picture, whereas others saw the older woman.

Hypothesizing:
- "What would happen if?"
  Example: "What would happen if Mercury rotated on its axis as does the Earth?"
  Hypothesis: The temperature wouldn't vary so much. It would be very warm on all parts of the planet.

Eggen/Kauchak
Educational Psychology: Windows on Classrooms, Sixth Edition

With the hocked gems financing him, our hero defied all scornful laughter that tried to prevent his scheme. Your eyes deceive, he had said. An egg, not a table, correctly typifies this unexplored planet. Now three sturdy sisters sought proof. Forging along, sometimes through calm vastness, yet more often through turbulent peaks and valleys, days became weeks as the many doubters spread fearful rumors about the edge. At last, from nowhere welcome winged creatures appeared, signifying momentous success. (Dooling & Lachman, 1971)

Every Saturday night, four good friends get together. When Jerry, Mike, and Pat arrived, Karen was sitting in her living room writing some notes. She quickly gathered the cards and stood up to greet her friends at the door. They followed her into the living room but as usual they couldn't agree on exactly what to play. Karen's recorder filled the room with soft and pleasant music. Early in the evening, Mike noticed Pat's hand and the many diamonds. As the night progressed the tempo of play increased. Finally, a lull in the activities occurred. Taking advantage of this, Jerry pondered the arrangement in front of him. Mike interrupted Jerry's reverie and said, "Let's hear the score." They listened carefully and commented on their performance. When the comments were all heard, exhausted but happy, Karen's friends went home. (Anderson, Reynolds, Schallert, & Goetz, 1977)

Eggen/Kauchak
Educational Psychology: Windows on Classrooms, Sixth Edition

1.   You have seen a movie and you remember some of the details exactly. Sometime later you see the same movie again, and to your surprise some of the dialogue is not as you "remembered" it. Why might this happen?

2.   Three people are in a room discussing a mutual experience. One person "remembers" the event in a certain way, the second "remembers" it differently, and the third "remembers" it in a way that is different from either of the other two.

How is this event similar to the first one?

Why might the three people "remember" the experience differently?

You elaborated on the original information. You then retrieved your elaborated information, not the original. The elaborated information is in a different form from the original.

You may also have reorganized the original information, so that it now exists in a form that makes more sense to you than did the information in its original form.

Eggen/Kauchak
Educational Psychology: Windows on Classrooms, Sixth Edition

Three students were discussing the way they use the margin questions in their textbook to help them understand the content of the chapters.

"I read the questions very carefully, and then I ask myself how the question relates to the information in that part of the chapter," Stephanie offered. "After I do that, I look at the answer in the student study guide."

"I read the question carefully, and then I carefully read the answer in the student study guide," Dan added.

"I read the question in the margin, and then I write down an answer. After I've finished the answer I look at what they have in the student study guide," Leroy put in.

Which of the students is likely to learn the most from the margin notes? Explain.

While more than one factor is always operating in learning, based on this section of the chapter, Leroy is likely to learn the most. He puts himself in the most "active" role by writing an answer before looking at the feedback. Writing the answer requires at least two important decisions, such as: 1) deciding specifically to what information in the section of the chapter the question is related, and 2) deciding how to describe that relationship in writing (and actually doing the writing). These are active processes.

Dan is in the most "passive" role. He merely reads the questions and reads the feedback, which requires no decisions and minimal thinking on his part.

Eggen/Kauchak
Educational Psychology: Windows on Classrooms, Sixth Edition

Transparency Master 7.8   Types and Examples of Mnemonic Devices

Mnemonic	Description	Example
Method of loci	Learner combines imagery with specific locations in a familiar environment, such as the chair, sofa, lamp, and end table in a living room.	Student wanting to remember the first seven elements in order visualizes hydrogen at the chair, helium at the sofa, lithium at the lamp, and so on.
Peg-word method	Learner memorizes a series of "pegs" such as a simple rhyme like "one is bun" and "two is shoe," on which to-be-remembered information is hung.	A learner wanting to remember to get pickles and carrots at the grocery visualizes a pickle in a bun and carrot stuck in a shoe.
Link method	Learner visually links items to be remembered.	A learner visualizes *homework* stuck in a *notebook* which is bound to her *textbook*, *pencil*, and *pen* with a rubber band to remember to take the (italicized) items to class.
Key-word method	Learner uses imagery and rhyming words to remember unfamiliar words.	A learner remembers that *trigo* (which rhymes with tree) is the Spanish word for wheat by visualizing a sheaf of wheat sticking out of a tree.
First-letter method	Learner creates a word from the first letter of items to be remembered.	A student creates the word *Wajmma* to remember the first six presidents in order: Washington, Adams, Jefferson, Madison, Monroe, and Adams.

Eggen/Kauchak
Educational Psychology: Windows on Classrooms, Sixth Edition

FAMILY CIRCUS By Bil Keane

"I've got a new rocket launcher,
Grandma. I'll put the phone down
and show you how it works."

A kindergartner is sitting some distance away from the teacher
and is unable to hear the teacher give a set of directions. In a
different setting, a fifth grader is in the same situation.

How is the kindergartner likely to respond?
How is the fifth grader likely to respond?

Eggen/Kauchak
Educational Psychology: Windows on Classrooms, Sixth Edition

1. According to research, when teachers emphasize important points, learning increases. However, emphasizing too many topics decreases its positive effects. Explain the role of emphasis based on information processing. What concept from behaviorism can help us explain why emphasizing too many topics can detract from its effects?

2. Mrs. Stevens had written the following problems on the chalkboard for her second graders.

   43   21   19   36
   -8   -5   -3   -7

   As the children were copying the problems onto their papers, she emphasized, "Now remember that we first check to see if we must regroup before we subtract." When the students checked their answers, however, it appeared as if many of them hadn't "listened" to her directive. Explain why the students seemed not to have listened.

1. *Emphasis is an attention getter. However, from a behaviorist perspective, too much emphasis can lead to satiation.*

2. *In this case, Mrs. Stevens's students were receiving two types of information—verbal and visual—at the same time. Sensory memory is capable of simultaneously receiving the information, but her students were actively involved in the writing process, so the verbal information was lost from sensory memory before they attended to it.*

1. You have two math word problems on the overhead. Based on applications of information processing, which of the following is the most effective question? (a) "What is the first step in solving the problems?" (b) "How are these problems alike?" or (c) "How do we solve these problems?"

2. You call a friend, and her 7-year-old son answers. You tell him to be sure to tell his mother to call you. How likely is this to occur? Why? What could you do to help the 7-year-old? Answer the same question if her son were 10 years old?

1. *The most helpful (assuming there are similarities in the two problems) would be, "How are these problems alike?" This is an effective perception check.*

   (It also encourages students to consider the problems in a larger framework [e.g., time-distance problems, or percent mixture problems], which could activate both declarative and procedural knowledge related to the problems.)

2. *A seven-year-old is not likely to understand the limits of his or her memory (tends to not exercise metacognition) and consequently is not likely to write the number down. (So, you'd better tell him to do it.) The research on metamemory suggests a ten-year-old is much more likely to do this without prompting.*

Eggen/Kauchak
Educational Psychology: Windows on Classrooms, Sixth Edition

Read the following passage:

In 1367 Marain and the settlements ended a seven-year war with the Langurians and Pitoks. As a result of this war Languia was driven out of East Bacol. Marain would now rule Laman and other lands that had belonged to Languia. This brought peace to the Bacolian settlements. The settlers no longer had to fear attacks from Laman. The Bacolians were happy to be part of Marain in 1367. Yet a dozen years later, these same people would be fighting the Marish for independence, or freedom from United Marain's rule. (Beck & Mckeown, 1993, p. 2)

Now, make the following substitutions: In the passage replace Marain with Britain, Langurians with French, Pitoks with Indians, East Bacol with North America, and Laman with Canada. Also change the date to 1763.

Explain why the passage is more meaningful with the substitutions? This exercise illustrates an important idea or theme from this chapter. What is that important idea or theme?

The passage was more meaningful when you substituted the familiar countries for the unfamiliar ones, because you were able to use your understanding of the Revolutionary War and the events leading up to it to make sense of it. The important idea illustrated in the exercise is that background knowledge is critical in learning.

Joanne Hill has her second graders involved in an art activity, and she has a variety of colored paper on the shelves, in addition to paste, scissors, and other equipment.

"We are going to work together on our art projects today," she begins, "so this is a good chance for us to practice speaking clearly and being good listeners when we talk to each other." She pauses, then continues. "Why do we want to speak clearly, Tabatha?"

" ... So the person will understand what we say."

"Yes. Excellent, Tabatha. Now everybody think carefully and see if I speak clearly. Everyone ready?"

Mrs. Hill hesitates a few seconds and then says, "Please get me a piece of paper, Cathy.... Was that a clear message, class?"

The students think for a few seconds. Finally Ellen says, "Wouldn't it be better if you told Cathy what color of paper to get?"

"Yes. Good thinking, Ellen!"

She then moves on with the art activity.

To which aspect of the information processing model does Joanne's goal most closely relate?

Eggen/Kauchak
Educational Psychology: Windows on Classrooms, Sixth Edition

- Begin lessons with an attention getter.

- Check students' perceptions.

- Organize information to make it meaningful.

- Put students in active roles.

- Encourage elaboration by asking for examples.

- Provide practice to avoid overloading working memory.

- Model metacognition.

- Model metacognition.

Eggen/Kauchak
Educational Psychology: Windows on Classrooms, Sixth Edition

1.   The general direct of the Alps is straight up.

2.   Most of the houses in France are made of Plaster of Paris.

3.   Iron was discovered because someone smelt it.

4.   You can listen to thunder and tell how close you came to getting hit. If you don't hear it, you got hit, so never mind.

5.   Genetics explains why you look like your father, and if you don't why you should.

6.   Blood circulate through the body by flowing down one leg and up the other.

7.   The spinal column is a long bunch of bones. The head sits on the top, and you sit on the bottom.

Andrew, a seventh grader is talking to Sharon, his mom, about movie ratings, and she comments that X-rated movies are rarely seen anymore.

"They're just for old people anyway," Andrew comments.

"Where did you come up with that idea?" Sharon asked.

"Well," Andrew responded, "'G' movies are for little kids, 'PG-13' movies are for older kids, 'R' rated movies are for adults, so 'X' rated movies must be for old people."

Eggen/Kauchak
Educational Psychology: Windows on Classrooms, Sixth Edition

- What was Jenny's goal in the lesson?

- Describe the examples that Jenny used.

- How "good" was her example? Explain what made it "good" or not "good."

- Why did Suzanne and Tad "get it" in the interview but not in the lesson? Explain.

- Jenny probably didn't fully realize that Suzanne and Tad didn't "get it" in the lesson. What implications does this have for teaching?

- If Suzanne and Tad were given another problem to solve the next day, would they "get it?" Explain.

- What was the most significant aspect of the lesson and the interview that followed it? Explain.

Eggen/Kauchak
Educational Psychology: Windows on Classrooms, Sixth Edition

Feedback

- Jenny wanted the students to understand the principle that makes beams balance.

- Her examples were the actual beam balances.

- The examples were "good" because they *included all the information* the students needed to construct an understanding the principle. This is the essence of a high-quality example.

- Suzanne and Tad were more directly involved in social interaction in the interview than they were in the lesson.

- This suggests that assessment must be an integral part of the teaching-learning process. It is the way teachers determine the extent to which learners' constructions are valid.

- It is impossible to know without an assessment. They might revert back to their original thinking.

- While views will vary, a very significant aspect of the lesson was the fact that Suzanne heard three correct explanations for the problem–Molly's, Mavrin's, and Jenny's–yet her thinking at the beginning of the interview hadn't changed at all, as evidenced by her solution to the interviewer's first problem. This demonstrates that explanations don't work very well for many students.

Eggen/Kauchak
Educational Psychology: Windows on Classrooms, Sixth Edition

- Provide a variety of examples and other representations of content.

- Connect content to the real world.

- Be skeptical of explanations.

- Promote high levels of interaction

- Make assessment an integral part of the teaching-learning process

Eggen/Kauchak
Educational Psychology: Windows on Classrooms, Sixth Edition

- Identifying a question or problem

- Forming an hypothesis to answer the question or solve the problem

- Gathering data to test the hypothesis

- Drawing conclusions from the data

- Generalizing on the basis of the conclusions

Eggen/Kauchak
Educational Psychology: Windows on Classrooms, Sixth Edition

Characteristic	Description
Grouping	Students are placed in small groups (typically 2 to 5).
Goals	Clearly stated goals direct the groups' activities.
Social Interaction	Discussion and student-student interaction are emphasized.
Positive Interdependence	Learners must depend on each other to reach the goals.

Characteristic	**Description**
Grouping	Approximately equal numbers of minority and non-minority students, boys and girls, and high and low achievers should exist in each group.
Training	Learners should be trained to be supportive and helpful as they work with their teammates.
Learning Tasks	Learning tasks should be designed so that team members must depend on each other for reaching the goals of the learning activity.
Monitoring	The teacher must carefully monitor the groups as they work.

Eggen/Kauchak
Educational Psychology: Windows on Classrooms, Sixth Edition

Chapter	Examples of Concepts
Chapter 2	Preoperations Zone of Proximal Development Scaffolding Holophrases
Chapter 3	Crisis Industry vs. Inferiority Moral Dilemma Self-concept
Chapter 4	Intelligence Ability grouping Cultural Inversion At Risk
Chapter 5	Behavior Disorder IEP Hyperactivity Inclusion
Chapter 6	Negative Reinforcement Conditioned Stimulus Vicarious Learning Symbolic Modeling
Chapter 7	Attention Perception Rehearsal Encoding

Eggen/Kauchak
Educational Psychology: Windows on Classrooms, Sixth Edition

1. The sun revolves around the earth.

2. Living things are things that move and grow (so clouds, for example, are living things).

3. Green plants take in their food from outside sources, just as animals do.

4. We (in the Northern Hemisphere) are closer to the sun in the summer than we are in the winter.

5. It is much colder in Europe than it is in the United States.

6. Trees are not living things.

7. Any moving object has a force acting on it. (A thrown ball, for example, continues to have a forward force acting on it even after it leaves the thrower's hand.)

8. The Great Lakes are salty.

9. Negative reinforcement decreases behavior.

10. Frogs are reptiles.

11. Whales are fish.

12. Spiders are insects.

Eggen/Kauchak
Educational Psychology: Windows on Classrooms, Sixth Edition

- Provide a wide enough variety of examples to prevent learners from undergeneralizing about the concept.

- Use non-examples to prevent students from overgeneralizing about the concept.

- Sequence the examples beginning with the most typical and ending with those least familiar.

- Help students with schema construction by linking the concept to related concepts.

Eggen/Kauchak
Educational Psychology: Windows on Classrooms, Sixth Edition

1.   You're baking cookies and you run out of flour. There is a supermarket one block from your house.

2.   You're going to visit friends in a city 350 miles away. They would like you to be there for dinner that evening at 7:00 p.m. Since the trip is interstate highway all the way, you believe you can average 60 miles/hour on the road, but you'll probably make four 15-minute stops on the trip. What time do you need to leave in the morning to make it to your friends' house at the desired time?

3.   You are the chair of a committee, which has been given the task of examining the science curriculum for your school. You're not making much progress, because the people seem to be spending most of their time bickering with each other about unrelated issues.

4.   Your car has over 100,000 miles on it. It is running okay, but you know that it is going to need some costly work done on it before too long.

5.   Jerome, one of your students, consistently comes to your class without his book. He needs it for many of the activities you conduct.

6.   You're going out to eat, but you only have $5.00 in cash with you. You check your bank balance and see that you have $380 in your checking account.

A druggist has 20 grams of a 15% alcohol solution but he needs a 10% solution. He looks around and finds that he has some 6% solution. He throws up his hands in frustration. What should he do now?

The Problem:

How many grams of the 6% solution should the druggist add to the 20 grams of the 15% solution to create a 10% solution?

$$.15 (20) + .06(n) = .10(20 + n)$$

$$3 + .06n = 2 + .10n$$

$$3 - 2 + .06n - .06n = 2 - 2 + .10n - .06n$$

$$3 - 2 = .10n - .06n$$

$$1 = .04n$$

$$\frac{1}{.04} = \frac{.04n}{.04}$$

$$n = 25 \text{ grams}$$

- Present problems in real-world contexts

- Capitalize on social interaction

- Provide scaffolding for novice problem solvers

- Teach general problem-solving strategies

Eggen/Kauchak
Educational Psychology: Windows on Classrooms, Sixth Edition

P	Preview	Survey headings to understand how the material is organized.
Q	Question	Create elaborative questions as you survey the content.
R	Read	Read the material, and try to answer the elaborative questions as you're reading.
R	Reflect	Create and try to answer additional elaborative questions after you've finished reading the passage.
R	Recite	Summarize what you've read, and relate the passage to other passages you've read.
R	Review	Reread parts of the passage for which you were unable to ask or answer your questions.

****

P	Preview	Preview chapter outlines and headings in text.
Q	Question	Respond to the margin questions. Create additional questions.
R	Read	Read the chapter. Use questions as guidelines.
R	Reflect	See how the teachers in the case studies apply the chapter content in their teaching.
R	Recite	Complete the application exercises and quizzes in the study guide and on the companion website.
R	Review	Review the case studies, margin questions, and application exercises.

- Describe the strategy and explain why it is useful.

- Explicitly teach the strategy by modeling its use.

- Model metacognition by describing their thinking as they work through the strategy

- Provide opportunities for students to practice the strategy in a variety of contexts.

- Provide feedback as students practice.

Eggen/Kauchak
Educational Psychology: Windows on Classrooms, Sixth Edition

- Use rewards for tasks that are not initially intrinsically interesting.

- Base rewards on the quality of the work, not mere participation in an activity.

- Use rewards to communicate increasing competence.

Eggen/Kauchak
Educational Psychology: Windows on Classrooms, Sixth Edition

Suzanne loves going to art galleries and museums. Whenever she is in a city she hasn't visited before, she checks to see what kind of galleries and museums they have.

Suzanne is also a symphony patron. She attends a concert presented by the full symphony, a chamber group, or some other performance nearly once a month.

Based on this information and Maslow's work, which of the following is the most accurate statement?

a. Suzanne feels a sense of belonging with her family and friends.
b. Suzanne is a self-actualized person.
c. Suzanne's intellectual achievement needs have been met.
d. We don't have enough evidence in the example to allow us to make a conclusion about Suzanne's needs.

Based on Maslow's work, choice a is the most accurate statement. We don't have enough information to make a conclusion about whether or not Suzanne is self-actualized (choice b). Growth needs are never "met" (choice c). The information in the example illustrates "aesthetic appreciation," which is a growth need. According to Maslow, in order to be at the growth needs, the deficiency needs must have been met, which implies that choice a is the most accurate statement.

- Treat students as people first and students second.

- Provide students with unconditional positive regard by separating their behaviors from their intrinsic worth.

- Create safe and orderly classrooms where students believe they can learn, and they are expected to do so.

- Consider teaching–learning experiences from students' points of view.

Eggen/Kauchak
Educational Psychology: Windows on Classrooms, Sixth Edition

A small jar filled with sand is sitting on a board that is floating in a tub of water. The jar is sealed so no sand can escape and no water can leak in. The jar weighs 200 grams and has a volume of 40 ml.

The jar is then taken off the board, put into the water, and allowed to sink to the bottom. The board is left in the water.

With the jar at the bottom of the tub, is the water level higher, lower, or the same as it was when the jar was sitting on the board? Explain.

Eggen/Kauchak
Educational Psychology: Windows on Classrooms, Sixth Edition

Which of the Following Are Effective and Which Are Ineffective Goals?

1. To get a B+ or better in this class.

2. To answer each of the margin questions for the chapters and write a brief explanation for the answer.

3. To score at least 80% on all the quizzes and tests.

4. To respond to each of the practice quizzes in the student study guide and explain the answer in each case.

5. To respond in writing to each of the application exercises in the student study guide.

6. To understand why I get the wrong answer for any item I miss on the quizzes or tests.

The effective goals are 2, 4, and 5. They are specific,, immediate, moderately difficult,, and learning focused. In contrast, goals 1 and 3 are performance oriented, and goal 6 isn't specific. To understand why you got a wrong answer, for example, you might talk to your instructor and get an explanation. Talking to your instructor about the items you miss would be an effective goal.

Four 9th graders are discussing the results of a test that has just been returned to them.

"How'd you do, Bob?" Anne asked.

"Terrible," Bob answered somewhat sheepishly. "I just can't do this stuff. I'm no good at writing the kind of essays she wants. . . I suck on this stuff. I'll never get it."

"I didn't do so hot either," Anne replied, "but I knew I wouldn't. I just didn't study hard enough. I knew I was going to be in trouble. I won't let that happen again."

"Unbelievable!" Armondo added. "I didn't know what the heck was going on, and I got a B. I don't think she read mine."

"I got a C Billy shrugged. "Not bad considering how much I studied. I couldn't get into it for this test."

1. Which student is most likely to feel guilty?

2. Which student is most likely to feel shame or embarrassment?

3. Which student's motivation is most likely to increase in the future?

4. Explain why Billy would emphasize that he didn't study.

5. Explain why—in spite of the fact that he did well on the test—Armondo's attribution isn't desirable.

6. Suppose Billy increases his effort and does well on the next test. Which of the following is the better response?

A. Well done Billy. You're getting good at this stuff aren't you.
B. Well done Billy. Your hard work is paying off isn't it.

1. Which student is most likely to feel guilty?
Since she can control her effort Anne is most likely to feel guilty about not studying.

2. Which student is most likely to feel shame or embarrassment?
Bob is attributing his failure to lack of ability, which he viewed as uncontrollable.

3. Which student's motivation is most likely to increase in the future?
With increased effort, Anne can expect success in the future, so her motivation is most likely to increase.

4. Explain why Billy will emphasize that he *didn't* study.
Billy is attempting to preserve the perception of high ability by pointing out that he was able to get an acceptable grade without studying.

5. Explain why—in spite of the fact that he did well on the test—Armondo's attribution isn't desirable.
Armondo attributes his success to luck, over which he has no control. Since he isn't in control of how lucky he will be in the future, his motivation isn't likely to increase.

6. Suppose Billy increases his effort and does well on the next test. Which of the following is the better response?

A. Well done Billy. You're getting good at this stuff aren't you.
B. Well done Billy. Your hard work is paying off isn't it.
Since perception of high ability is important to Billy, suggesting that his ability (competence) is increasing is a more desirable response than suggesting that his hard work is paying off (which he may believe is an indicator of low ability).

Eggen/Kauchak
Educational Psychology: Windows on Classrooms, Sixth Edition

- Attempt to increase learner self-efficacy by modeling efficacy and providing evidence of accomplishment.

- Encourage internal attributions for successes and controllable attributions for failures.

- Emphasize the utility value of increased skills.

- Promote student interest by modeling your own interest, personalizing content, providing concrete examples, involving students, and offering choices.

- Emphasize learning and social responsibility goals, effective strategies, and metacognition.

Eggen/Kauchak
Educational Psychology: Windows on Classrooms, Sixth Edition

A teacher is circulating around the class while the students are involved in a homework activity. The teacher stops near Jerome, who appears to be having a bit of difficulty with a problem, but she says nothing. She stops near Leroy and comments, "Let me give you a hint," and makes a suggestion, even though Leroy had not asked for help and seems to be making progress, although the progress is somewhat slow.

The teacher stops near Anthony, who has made a mistake, and smiles, "Now, that's a very good try. Here, let me show you how to solve the problem."

What message is the teacher sending each student about their ability? What attributions is she subtly and unconsciously encouraging?

Graham (1991) suggests that when teachers praise students for a "good try," express pity, or offer unsolicited help, they subtly communicate that the students have low ability, and it increases the likelihood that the students will attribute failure to lack of ability. Even young students perceive students who are offered unsolicited help as being lower in ability than those not offered help (Graham & Barker, 1990).

"The ... pertinent question for blacks is whether their own history of academic failure makes them more likely to be the targets of sympathetic feedback from teachers and thus the recipients of low-ability cues." (Graham, 1991, p. 28)

Eggen/Kauchak
Educational Psychology: Windows on Classrooms, Sixth Edition

- Use assessments that increase intrinsic motivation.

- Reinforce increasing competence instead of compliance or mere participation in an activity.

- Create classroom environments and learning activities that give students as much control as possible.

- Design learning activities that challenge learners' existing understanding and skills.

- When possible, begin learning activities with events that are inconsistent with learners existing understanding and beliefs.

- Treat students with unconditional positive regard and communicate that you are committed to their learning.

Eggen/Kauchak
Educational Psychology: Windows on Classrooms, Sixth Edition

You are skilled at the computer keyboard. You've had a great deal of practice, and you can type rapidly with relatively few errors. You're applying for a job in which typing skills are important, and you want the job badly. You have to take a timed test as part of the job application process. Are you likely to perform better, poorer, or similar to your performance when you work at the keyboard at home? Explain.

You're taking a difficult test involving a considerable amount of higher-order thinking. You are struggling with several of the questions, and the instructor announces, "Just a reminder; everyone has to be finished in five minutes." Is the announcement likely to increase, decrease, or have no effect on your performance on the test? Explain.

You're in the process of learning to play golf. You have a lot of problems with your putting; you can't seem to get comfortable with it, but you continue to practice. You then go on an outing with some of your competitive friends. They want to bet on each hole, so you reluctantly agree. You are near the end of the outing and have to sink a four-foot putt to win. Are you more likely, less likely, or similarly likely to sink the putt than you would be when you practice? Explain.

There is likely to be anxiety in each case. However, research indicates that anxiety increases performance on well-practiced tasks and decreases performance on new or difficult tasks. As a result, your performance is likely to increase in the first case but decrease in the other two.

Eggen/Kauchak
Educational Psychology: Windows on Classrooms, Sixth Edition

- Model effort attributions and personal improvement, and de-emphasize competition and ability.

- Emphasize incremental rather than entity views of intelligence.

- Give students the opportunity to practice exercises similar to those they'll encounter on assessments.

- Assess frequently, announce all assessments, and give students ample time to complete assessment activities.

Two students are discussing the way they study for their educational psychology course.

Selena says, "First, I carefully read the italicized definitions of the bold-faced concepts. Then, I highlight the examples in the book and I try to figure out how the example fits the definition."

"I highlight the definition," Terri responds. "Then I try to memorize it."

"But," Selena returns uncertainly, "all the quizzes are application. Just memorizing the definitions won't work."

"Yeah, I guess," Terri shrugs. "What else do you do?"

"Well, I have a little chart. I do all the practice quiz stuff in the study guide, and I check to see how many I got right and how well I understood them. Then, I do the practice quiz on the Website. . . . Then, if I'm confused, I go in and see my instructor."

"You do that before every quiz?"

"Yeah. I have my little chart on the practice quizzes, and it's sort of fun to keep track of how many I really understand."

Eggen/Kauchak
Educational Psychology: Windows on Classrooms, Sixth Edition

- Emphasize the relationship between accepting responsibility and learning.

- Solicit student input in the process of establishing class procedures that include student responsibility.

- Help students understand responsibility by treating it as a concept and link consequences to actions.

- Model responsibility, a learning focus, and metacognition, and guide students as they initially set goals.

- Provide concrete mechanisms to help students monitor and assess goal achievement.

- Strive to believe in yourself and your capability of getting all students to learn.

- Model responsibility, effort, and interest in the topics you're teaching.

- Demonstrate commitment to your students' learning by spending personal time with them.

- Maintain appropriately high expectations for all students.

Eggen/Kauchak
Educational Psychology: Windows on Classrooms, Sixth Edition

- Establish rules and procedures that create and maintain a safe, orderly learning environment.

- Clearly describe expectations and the reasons for studying particular topics.

- Attempt to link topics to students' personal lives.

- Establish and maintain high levels of student involvement in learning activities.

- Provide specific and detailed feedback on student work.

Eggen/Kauchak
Educational Psychology: Windows on Classrooms, Sixth Edition

- **State rules positively.**

- **Minimize the number of rules.**

- **Solicit student input.**

- **Emphasize rationales for rules.**

- **Teach rules as concepts.**

- **Monitor rules throughout the school year.**

Eggen/Kauchak
Educational Psychology: Windows on Classrooms, Sixth Edition

Transparency Master 12.2 Sample Classroom Procedures

Elementary School Classrooms

Student Behavior	Sample Expectations
Using worktables	Worktables are cleaned and materials stored in appropriate places at teacher signal.
Using bathroom and drinking fountain	Students always go to the bathroom and drinking fountain before entering the classroom.
Having access to pencil sharpener	Students sharpen two pencils after they've put their books on their desk or table.
Changing groups	Students go to their desks and begin assigned seatwork. The next group comes to the table.
Lining up for lunch and other transitions	Students quietly line up against the classroom wall transitions when the teacher calls their row.

Middle, Junior High, and Secondary Classrooms

Student Behavior	Sample Expectations
Using worktables	Worktables are cleaned and materials stored in appropriate places at teacher signal.
Using bathroom and drinking fountain	Students always go to the bathroom and drinking fountain before entering the classroom.
Having access to pencil sharpener	Students sharpen two pencils after they've put their books on their desk or table.
Changing groups	Students go to their desks and begin assigned seatwork. The next group comes to the table.
Lining up for lunch and other transitions	Students quietly line up against the classroom wall transitions when the teacher calls their row.

Eggen/Kauchak
Educational Psychology: Windows on Classrooms, Sixth Edition

I put each of their names, as well as my own, on a cubby hole in a storage place on the wall of my room. I did a very short worksheet myself and literally walked it over and put it in my storage spot, thinking aloud as I went. "Hmm, I'm finished with my worksheet. . . . What do I do now? . . . I need to put it in my cubby hole. If I don't put it there, my teacher can't check it, so it's very important. . . . Now, I start on the next assignment."

Then, I gave each of them the worksheet, directing them to take it to their file, quietly and individually, as soon as they were finished. After we had done one, I asked them why we did that, and we spent several minutes discussing the reasons for taking the finished work to their cubby hole immediately, not touching or talking to anyone as they move from and back to their desks, and starting right back to work. Then I gave them another, asked them what they were going to do and why, and had them do it. We then spent a few more minutes talking about what might happen if we didn't put papers where they belong. I asked them whether they had ever lost anything and how this was similar.

Now, we have a class meeting nearly every day, just before we leave for the day. During the meeting we give each other compliments, and offer suggestions for improving our classroom. Some people might be skeptical about whether or not first graders can handle meetings like this, but they can. This is also the way I help them keep the procedures fresh in their minds.

Vicki Williams is organizing her handouts on the first day of class. Her eighth graders come into the room; some take their seats while others mill around talking in small groups. As the bell rings, she looks up and says over the hum of the students, "Everyone take your seats, please," and she turns back to finish organizing her materials.

Donnell Alexander is waiting at the door for her eighth-grade class and also has prepared handouts. As the students come in, she smiles and says, "Take your seats quickly, please. You'll find your name on the desk. The bell is going to ring in less than a minute, and everyone must be at their desk and quiet when it does. Please read the handout while you're waiting." She is standing at the front of the room surveying the class as the bell rings. When it stops, Donnell begins, "Good morning, everyone."

Eggen/Kauchak
Educational Psychology: Windows on Classrooms, Sixth Edition

Sharon Van Horn

Fort Caroline Elementary School   Phone 745-4904 (School)   221-9044 (Home)

Let's see a good report!

Name _____

Week _____

Comments _____

Grade [ ] _____

✓ = did well on the task

X = had problems with the task

Study Skills

	Mon.	Tues.	Wed.	Thurs.	Fri.
Completes homework					
Completes classwork					
Follows directions					
Listens to instructions					
Makes wise use of time & works well on own					

Personal Development—Counts two

	Mon.	Tues.	Wed.	Thurs.	Fri.
Follows classroom rules					
Follows school rules					
Respects the rights of others & gets along with classmates					

0–Xs = A,   1–2 Xs = B   3–4 Xs = C,   5 or more Xs = D

Parent's Signature _____

Eggen/Kauchak
Educational Psychology: Windows on Classrooms, Sixth Edition

Which of the Following Are Aligned?

Stated Goal	Learning Activity
1. To be able to apply the strategy SQ4R in individual study	Instructor describes and explains the meaning of each of the steps in SQ4R.
2. To understand the concept "density"	Instructor demonstrates calculation of density problems using the formula $d = m/v$ (density = mass/volume). Learners solve a series of problems using the formula.
3. To understand dynamics of Civil War, causes of the War, and why the North won	Instructor explains the term "sectionalism," describes Lincoln, examines the advantage for both the North and South, and provides some information on reconstruction. Has the students write an essay on the meaning of the term "indivisible."
4. To write using proper punctuation and grammar	Teacher and learners analyze a series of exercises, such as "Please come with Karen and (I, me) to the store."
5. To understand what products are "best buy"	Learners go to supermarkets and write down the size or weight of several products together with their cost. They calculate the cost per unit.

Eggen/Kauchak
Educational Psychology: Windows on Classrooms, Sixth Edition

Traditional Measurement Formats	Alternative Measurement Formats
True-false	Specific performance task
Multiple choice	Timed trial
Matching	Exhibition of work
Fill in the blank	Reflective journal entry
Short, open-ended answer	Open-ended oral presentation
Paragraph response to specific question	Oral response to specific question
Paragraph response to open-ended question	Collaborative group project
Essay	Audio visual presentation
	Debate
	Simulation

Eggen/Kauchak
Educational Psychology: Windows on Classrooms, Sixth Edition

1. The cause of World War I was the:
    a. increase in economic problems in several European countries that made living quality difficult for the people.
    b. Germany had become very aggressive and appeared to be poised to attack France.
*   c. assassination of Archduke Ferdinand.
    d. spirit of nationalism that had increased significantly in Europe at about that time.

You are conducting a discussion with your class on Wednesday, and in the process you call on 20 of the 30 students in your class. Of the 20 you call on, you remember that all but four answered correctly and you were able to get acceptable answers from three of those four by prompting them. You decide that the class understands the content, so you plan to move on to the next topic on Thursday.

2. Of the following, concluding that the class understands the material best illustrates:
    a. a formal measurement.
    b. an informal measurement.
*   c. an evaluation.
    d. an assessment system.

3. Which of the following best describes your conclusion?
    a. It is reliable but not valid.
    b. It is both reliable and valid.
*   c. It is unreliable and therefore invalid.
    d. It is invalid and therefore unreliable.

Eggen/Kauchak
Educational Psychology: Windows on Classrooms, Sixth Edition

- Present one clear problem in the stem of the item.

- Make all distracters plausible to the uninformed.

- Vary the position of the correct choice randomly, and be careful to avoid overusing choice *c.*

- Avoid similar wording in the stem and the correct choice.

- Avoid phrasing the correct choice in more technical terms than distracters.

- Keep the correct answer and the distracters similar in length. A longer or shorter answer should usually be a distracter.

- Avoid using absolute terms, such as *always* or *never* in a distracter.

- Keep the stem and the distracters grammatically consistent.

- Avoid using two distracters with the same meaning.

- Emphasize *negative wording* if it is used.

- Use "none of the above" with care, and avoid "all of the above" as a choice.

Eggen/Kauchak
Educational Psychology: Windows on Classrooms, Sixth Edition

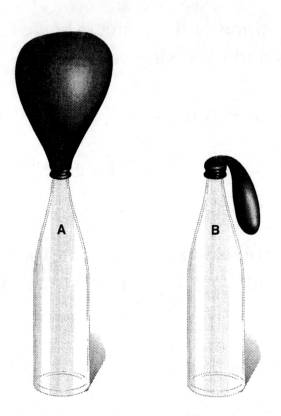

Look at the drawings above. They represent two identical soft drink bottles covered with identical balloons sitting side-by-side on a table. Bottle A was then heated. Which of the following is the most accurate statement?

  a. The density of the air in Bottle A is greater than the density of the air in Bottle B.

*b. The density of the air in Bottle A is less than the density of the air in Bottle B.

  c. The density of the air in Bottle A is equal to the density of the air in Bottle B.

  d. We don't have enough information to compare the density of the air in Bottle A to the density of the air in Bottle B.

- Elicit higher order thinking by using such terms as *explain* and *compare*. Have students defend their responses with facts.

- Write a model answer for each item. This can be used both for scoring and for providing feedback.

- Require all students to answer all items. Allowing students to select particular items prevents comparisons and detracts from reliability.

- Prepare criteria for scoring in advance.

- Score all students' answers to a single item before moving to the next item.

- Score all responses in a single sitting if possible. This increases reliability.

- Score answers without knowing the identity of the student. This helps reduce the influence of past performance and expectations.

- Develop a model answer complete with points, and compare a few students' responses to it, to see if any adjustments are needed in the scoring criteria.

Eggen/Kauchak
Educational Psychology: Windows on Classrooms, Sixth Edition

- Specify clearly the type of performance you are trying to assess.

- Decide whether processes or products are the primary focus of your assessment efforts.

- Structure the evaluation setting, balancing realism with pragmatic concerns.

- Design evaluation procedures with clearly identified criteria.

Eggen/Kauchak
Educational Psychology: Windows on Classrooms, Sixth Edition

Each of the following items is rated according to the following scale:
4 = excellent; 3 = good; 2 = fair; 1 = poor;   0 = nonexistent.

4   3   2   1   0   1. Examples are of high quality.

4   3   2   1   0   2. Examples provide adequate variety.

4   3   2   1   0   3. Examples are in context or are
                             applied to a new context.

4   3   2   1   0   4. Presenters provide an effective
                             rationale for the choice of examples.

Eggen/Kauchak
Educational Psychology: Windows on Classrooms, Sixth Edition

Definitions of Values:

Dimension 1.   Examples are of high quality.

Rating   Definition

4   All the information learners need to understand the topic
           exists in each of the representations. The characteristics
           of the concept are observable in the examples if a concept
           is being represented, and the relationship is observable in
           each of the examples if a principle, generalization, or
           academic rule is represented.

3   All the information learners need to understand the topic is
           represented in the examples. Not all the information exists
           in each example, but does exist in the combination of the
           examples. The characteristics or relationships are
           observable in the examples.

2   Some of the information the learners need to understand
           the topic can be observed from the combination of the
           examples, and the rest of the information can be inferred
           from the examples.

1   Some of the information the learners need to understand
           the topic can be observed or inferred in the examples.

0   The examples provide little or no information that learners
           need to understand the topic. The information is
           presented in the abstract.

Eggen/Kauchak
Educational Psychology: Windows on Classrooms, Sixth Edition

- Carefully examine tests to ensure that test content matches learning goals.

- Prepare students so that test performance accurately reflects what they know and can do.

- Administer tests in ways that allow valid comparisons and maximize student performance.

- Communicate results to students and their caregivers to help them make wise educational decisions.

Eggen/Kauchak
Educational Psychology: Windows on Classrooms, Sixth Edition

Transparency Master 15.2 Two Distributions of Scores

Class #1	50	Class #2	48
	49		47
	49		47
	48		47
	47		45
	47		45
	46		44
	46		44
	45		43
	45		43
	45		43
	44		43
	44		43
	44		42
	44		42
	43		42
	42		42
	41		41
	41		40
	40		40
	40		40
	39		35
	39		
	38		
	37		
	37		
	36		
	35		
	34		
	34		
	33		

Eggen/Kauchak
Educational Psychology: Windows on Classrooms, Sixth Edition

Class #1

Mean = 42

Median = 43

Mode = 44

Standard deviation = 4.8

Class #2

Mean = 43

Median = 43

Mode = 43

Standard deviation = 2.9

Eggen/Kauchak
Educational Psychology: Windows on Classrooms, Sixth Edition

The mean on an 80-item standardized test is 48, the standard deviation is 6, and the standard error is 3. Jessica scores a 59 on the test, Luis scores a 54, and Steve scores a 49.

Assume the sample size for the test is very large, so the results approximate a normal distribution.

Answer the following questions:

1. What is the approximate percentile ranking for each student?

2. What is the approximate stanine for each student?

3. What is each student's T-score?

4. We said that Jessica scored a 59 on the test. What kind of score do we call the 59?

5. Think about the learners' true scores on the test, and decide which of the following is the most valid conclusion?
    a. Jessica's true score *is* higher than both Luis's and Steve's, and Luis's *is* higher than Steve's.
    • Jessica's true score *might be* higher than Luis's, it *is* higher than Steve's, and Luis's *is* higher than Steve's.
    • Jessica's true score is higher than both Luis's and Steve's, and Luis's *might be* higher than Steve's.
    d. Jessica's true score *might be* higher than Luis's, it *is* higher than Steve's, and Luis's *might be* higher than Steve's.

Explain your answers.

MEDIA GUIDE

to Accompany

Educational Psychology: Windows on Classrooms
Sixth Edition

TABLE OF CONTENTS

INTRODUCTION

The twelve videotapes and CD-ROM that accompany *Educational Psychology: Windows on Classrooms* present a number of *cases* designed as instructional supplements to increase your teaching effectiveness. The segments on the tapes demonstrate the application of selected concepts and practices described in various chapters. The CD-ROM provides opportunities for your students to directly experience educational psychology concepts through technology.

ABOUT THE VIDEOS

Table 1 provides an overview of the videos available with this text. The video segments present "real" teachers performing unrehearsed lessons in actual school settings, and you can use them to capitalize on the benefits of case-based instruction. Because they are unrehearsed, they represent reality rather than perfection, and there are instances in each segment where the teaching could be improved. This can be used to your advantage with your students by asking them to evaluate the lesson on a 5 or 10 point scale, justifying their evaluations. Discussions of possible alternatives for improving the instruction in each case are often animated and sometimes heated, resulting in high levels of involvement from students.

Table 1:   Overview of Video Package for Eggen and Kauchak

Title	Description
Looking Through Classroom Windows: Integrated Video Cases I & II	These two videos contain 12 segments that directly correspond to written cases at the beginning and end of chapters.
Concepts in Classrooms 1 & 2	These two videos contain 10 segments focusing on specific concepts from the text such as cognitive development, improving transfer, personalizing content, and essential teaching skills.
Insights into Learning (3) Using Balance Beams in Fourth Grade (Chapter 8 Opening Case) Designing Experiments in Seventh Grade (Chapter 8 Opening Case) Finding Area in Elementary Math (Chapter 9 Closing Case)	These three videos provide an in-depth examination of three of the lessons contained in the Looking Through Classroom Windows: Integrated Video Cases. Each includes an extended look at the lesson (approximately 25 minutes), post-lesson interviews with focal students (approximately 20 minutes), and a teacher interview (approximately 15 minutes).
Windows on Classrooms: Video Case Studies (1)	This video consists of four 15-minute lesson segments: 1) Properties of Air in First Grade Science, 2) Climate, Geography and Economics in Junior High Social Studies, 3) Graphing in Second Grade Math, and 4) The Scarlet Letter in a High School English Class. These 15-minute segments also appear in Looking Through Classroom Windows: Integrated Video Cases I and II. In addition, there are 4 longer (approximately 25-30 minutes) lesson videos on these same topics, with the same titles, and following by approximately 15-minute teacher interview segments.

Educational Psychology Video Package: Videos I and II	These two tapes contain 11 segments focusing on a number of topics: e.g., measuring cognitive and moral development, cooperative learning, lecture discussion, and teaching for learner diversity.
A Private Universe	This 18-minute segment focuses on a high school student's misconceptions about science. Interviews and classroom segments provide insights into how hard it is to change student misconceptions.
Double Column Addition: A Teacher Uses Piaget's Theory	This 20-minute video shows a second grade teacher using questioning and problem-posing to help her students understand adding and subtracting two digit numbers

We anticipate that most instructors will prefer to show individual segments as the different topics are covered, rather than an entire videotape at one time. To do so you only need to rewind the tape to its beginning, set the tape counter to zero and then fast forward the counter to the correct number. You may not end up at the exact starting point, but you should be close. A blue screen is used between segments, so this will tell you that you are "in the ball park.."

LOOKING THROUGH CLASSROOM WINDOWS: INTEGRATED VIDEO CASES

These two tapes contain twelve segments that correspond to the opening and closing cases in eight different chapters in the text. Three of these lesson segments are new; 9 aren't. We have repackaged them together to make it easier for you to show them as you cover different chapters. The tape topics, the content that they focus on, and chapter locations are found in Table 2.

Table 2 Looking Through Classroom Windows: Integrated Video Cases: Topics and Location

Topic	Grade	Content Focus	Chapter and Location
Demonstrating Knowledge in Classrooms	K, 7th, 10th,11th	Teacher knowledge	1–Closing case Tape 1, 0-14:00
Properties of Air in First Grade Science	1st	Cognitive development	2–Closing case Tape 1, 14:28-28:16
The Scarlet Letter in a High School English Class	12th	Information processing	7-Closing case Tape 1, 28:46-37:20
Constructing Understanding: Instructional Applications	4th	Constructing understanding	8-Opening case Tape 1, 37:50-46:55
Designing Experiments in Seventh Grade	7th	Constructing understanding	8-Closing case Tape 1, 47:29-1:12:35
Finding Area in Elementary Math	5th	Problem solving	9-Opening case Tape 1, 1:13:06-1:23:45
Graphing in Second Grade Math	2nd	Complex cognitive processes	9-Closing case Tape 2, 0-14:20

Studying Arthropods in Fifth Grade	5th	Motivation in the classroom	11-Opening case Tape 2, 14:51-27:58
Writing Effective Paragraphs	5th	Motivation in the classroom	11-Closing case Tape 2, 28:25-41:40
Improving Instruction: Essential Teaching Skills	7th	Essential teaching skills	13-Opening case Tape 2, 42:00-55:44
Climate, Geography, Economics in Junior High Social Studies	9th	Essential teaching skills	13-Closing case Tape 2, 56:14-1:10:24
Using Assessment to Improve Instruction	5th	Assessing learning	14-Opening case Tape 2, 1:10:55-1:26:09

Because these twelve episodes exist in both written and video form, you have options that don't exist if they were in video or written form alone.
Some of these options include:

- You can introduce the chapter with the video case and have students discuss it. The discussion will give you some insight into their current understanding of chapter content. This process is consistent with constructivist views of learning; using students' current understanding as a guide to your instruction. As students study the chapter they can then refer to the written version of the case to remind them of specifics of the case.

- You can show the video episodes after you've completed your study of each chapter. In using the video cases in this way, discuss with students how the teachers in the episodes applied chapter concepts in their teaching. After viewing each video case, students can refer to the written case for specific aspects of the lesson they want to review.

- After studying the chapter you may choose to have students *read, discuss and analyze* the written case. Show the video case to allow students to see the episode in its authentic context and see if their analyses change because of contextual factors.

CONCEPTS IN CLASSROOMS

Concepts in Classrooms, in two tapes, contains ten segments designed to illustrate important concepts in educational psychology. All of the segments are from real classrooms; they have been edited from other videos in this package to focus on specific topics. The average length of time for each segment is about nine minutes, providing you with flexibility to use them as you see fit.

INSIGHTS INTO LEARNING

These three tapes contain three lessons as well as student and teacher interviews following the lessons. Each tape is approximately 60 minutes long and contains a 25-30 minute lesson, a 15-20 minute student interview and a

10-15 interview with the teacher. These tapes provide insights into learning by following four focal students both in the lesson and after. The student interviews use instructional tasks similar to those in the lesson to provide your educational psychology students with opportunities to analyze learning, transfer, and retention as it occurs in realistic classroom environments.

These videotapes are also integrated into the text and can be used in conjunction with the following chapters:

Chapter 8 *Using Balance Beams in Fourth Grade.* Chapter Opening Case
Chapter 8 *Designing Experiments in Seventh Grade*: Chapter Closing Case
Chapter 9 *Finding Area in Elementary Math:* Chapter Opening Case

Windows on Classrooms

The video segments that appear in Windows on Classrooms also appear in Integrated Cases I and II. If you have Looking Through Classroom Windows: Integrated Video Cases I and II, you do not need this video as the cases are the same. The running time for each of these episodes is approximately 15 minutes: The episodes are:

Chapter 2:	*Properties of Air in First-Grade Classroom Science*
Chapter 13:	*Climate, Geography and Economics in Junior High Social Studies*
Chapter 9:	*Graphing in Second-Grade Math*
Chapter 7:	*The Scarlet Letter in a High School English Class*

USING THE VIDEO SEGMENTS AS CASES IN EDUCATIONAL PSYCHOLOGY

Cases have been used as teaching aides in a number of disciplines ranging from medicine to business to teacher education. In educational psychology they can be used in at least three ways:

1)   To increase student involvement and motivation

2)   To help students' develop problem-solving and cooperative learning skills

3)   To provide concrete examples of abstract ideas embedded in realistic classroom settings (Merseth & Lacey, 1993)

   The increasing popularity of case-based pedagogy can be linked to developments in cognitive psychology which document the importance of student involvement in problem solving tasks that are embedded in realistic contexts (Bruning, Schraw, & Ronning, 1999). Cases are one way of presenting realistic, contextualized, problems (Harrington, 1996; Mostert, 1996).
   Cases can also effectively illustrate abstract ideas. Shulman (1993) compares cases to manipulatives in math instruction, providing concrete representations of events and abstractions, and allowing opportunities for analysis of experience.
   Research supports this instructional promise. Hmelo (1995) found that students exposed to cases provided more elaborate and comprehensive explanations of problems than did students exposed to traditional, teacher-centered instruction.

Morine-Dershimer (1993) found that opportunities to analyze cases in small groups led to more complex processing of information about the case and increased application of principles than did teacher-led discussions. Additional research indicates that cases can stimulate the development of expertise in teachers (Copeland & Decker, 1995). Collectively, these studies suggest that cases help students learn to process information in deep, meaningful ways.

References

Bruning, R., Schraw, G., & Ronning, R. (1999). *Cognitive psychology & instruction (3rd Ed.)*. Englewood Cliffs, NJ: Prentice Hall.

Copeland, W., & Decker, D. (1995, April). *Video cases and the development of meaning making in preservice teachers.* Paper presented at the Annual Meeting of the American Educational Research Association, San Francisco.

Harrington, H. (1996, April). *Learning from cases.* Paper presented at the annual meeting of the American Educational Research Association, New York.

Hmelo, C. (1995, April). *The effect of problem-based learning on the early development of medical expertise.* Paper presented at the Annual Meeting of the American Educational Research Association, San Francisco.

Merseth, K., & Lacey, C. (1993). *Weaving stronger fabric: The pedagogical promise of hypermedia case methods in teacher education.* Teaching & Teacher Education, *9*(3), 283-299.

Morine-Dershimer, G. (1993, April). *What's in a case--and what comes out?* Paper presented at the Annual Meeting of the American Educational Research Association, Atlanta.

Mostert, M. (1996, April). *Cognitive aspects of case-based teaching.* Paper presented at the annual meeting of the American Educational Research Association, New York.

Shulman, L. (1993, April). *Roles for cases in courses and programs.* Paper presented at the Far West Laboratory Conference on Case-Based Teaching, Tahoe, CA.

ABOUT THE SIMULATIONS IN EDUCATIONAL PSYCHOLOGY

Your students will have access to a CD-ROM compact disk when they purchase Educational Psychology: Windows on Classrooms, 6th edition. Contained in this CD-ROM are four interactive simulations that allow your students to experiment with educational psychology concepts. Boxed References within the text refer to these simulations, which occur in the following chapters in the text:

- Chapter 2   The Pendulum Experiment
- Chapter 3   Assessing Moral Responses
- Chapter 7   Bartlett's Ghosts
- Chapter 9   Intuitive Physics
- Chapter 14   Assessment in the Balance

Suggestions for using these simulations can be found in Section III of this Media Guide.

MEDIA GUIDE ORGANIZATION

Each video segment is described individually on the following pages. The segments are presented in three parts: *"Before You Begin, " "Instructional Resources,"* and *"Feedback for Questions for Discussion and Analysis."* In each *"Instructional Resources"* section is a transparency master entitled *"Questions for Discussion and Analysis."* In addition, a rating scale to assess the lesson is included for some of the segments to assist your students in focusing on relevant aspects of the lesson.

Before You Begin

Before You Begin briefly summarizes the content of the segment and identifies the text topic, chapter, and pages to which the segment most closely relates.

Instructional Resources

The resources in this section suggests the use of certain transparencies and transparency masters from the *Transparency Package* (overhead acetates), the *Instructor's Manual*, and transparency masters created especially for this guide. All video episodes have accompanying transparency masters for *"Questions for Discussion and Analysis"* and some also include a rating scale that encourages students to evaluate the effectiveness of the instructor in the episode.

Please note that in using the analysis questions on the transparency masters, you have several options: 1) You can display the questions prior to viewing the lesson and ask students to think about them as they view the segment; 2) You can view a portion of the segment, stop the tape and discuss one or more of the questions; or 3) You can show the entire segment, and discuss the questions afterward. The questions can also be reworded as statements in a rating scale which you can use to provide a quantitative assessment of the teacher's and the lesson's effectiveness.

Feedback for Questions for Discussion and Analysis

To help wrap up your class discussions of the video episodes and assess student answers to *"Questions for Discussion and Analysis"*, we have provided feedback for these questions, responses designed to help you guide your students in the analysis of the episode. As with all discussion questions, differences in opinion will exist. Our feedback is intended to provide perspective. Hopefully it will aid you as you guide your students in their discussion and analysis of the case.

You may choose to ignore or use these responses according to your professional judgement.

Good luck! We sincerely hope the videos enrich your instruction.

Looking Through Classroom Windows: Integrated Video Cases, Tape 1 (0-14:00)
Segment #1: Demonstrating Knowledge in Classrooms

BEFORE YOU BEGIN (Note: This 14 minute segment appears in written form at the end of Chapter 1.)

Lesson Summary

This segment contains parts of four lessons, each illustrating a different kind of teacher knowledge. In the first part, Rebecca Atkins, a kindergarten teacher, illustrates General Pedagogical Knowledge as she interacts with her children about planting a garden. In the second part, Richard Nelms, a middle school teacher, illustrates Knowledge of Learners and Learning while teaching the concept of symmetry to his seventh graders. In the third part, Didi Johnson, a tenth grade chemistry teacher, illustrates Pedagogical Content Knowledge as she presents Charles Law to her students. In the fourth part, Bob Duchaine, an American History teacher, illustrates Knowledge of Content in a lesson on the Viet Nam War.

INSTRUCTIONAL RESOURCES

Transparencies (From the Transparency Package)

T1.3   Knowledge Needed for Expert Teaching

Transparency Masters (From the Instructor's Manual)

TM 1.2   Questions for Reflective Teaching

Transparency Masters (In this Media Guide)

Questions for Discussion and Analysis

Feedback for "Questions for Discussion and Analysis"

Questions for Discussion and Analysis: Demonstrating Knowledge in Classrooms

1. How did the kindergarten teacher display evidence of General Pedagogical Knowledge in her lesson?

2. What aspects of Knowledge of Learners and Learning were evident in the middle school science teacher's lesson on symmetry?

3. How was Pedagogical Content Knowledge illustrated in the lesson on Charles' Law?

4. Evaluate the lesson on the Viet Nam War in terms of General Pedagogical Knowledge, Knowledge of Learners and Learning, and Pedagogical Content Knowledge.

**Feedback for "Questions for Discussion and Analysis" for
Demonstrating Knowledge in Classrooms**

1. General Pedagogical Knowledge involves an understanding of instruction and management that transcends specific topics. Rebecca knew that students need a warm, nurturant environment to learn. She also understood basic principles of management and the need to actively involve her students through questioning that linked new content to their existing background knowledge.

2. Knowledge of Learners and Learning focuses on general principles of learning and development. Richard Nelms understood the need for concrete examples, which are important for all learners, but especially younger ones, such as his middle school students. He also recognized the need to actively involve his students through questioning.

3. Pedagogical Content Knowledge involves knowing how to represent abstract ideas in learnable ways. The science teacher did this in several ways. First, she began her lesson with a demonstration that provided a concrete frame of reference for students. She also modeled correct solutions on the board.

4. Though the history teacher was quite knowledgeable in terms of content, his lesson was lacking in other respects. First, he lectured to them, which generally violates principles of learning and development. He also failed to convert abstract ideas into concrete examples, a key element of Pedagogical Content Knowledge. His management was good, which is one component of General Pedagogical Knowledge. However, he failed to use a variety of instructional strategies in his teaching.

Looking Through Classroom Windows: Integrated Video Cases
Tape 1 (14:28-28:16)
Segment #2: Properties of Air in First Grade Science

BEFORE YOU BEGIN (Note: This 15 minute case study appears in written form at the end of Chapter 2.)

Lesson Summary

Jenny Newhall, a first grade teacher at Jesse Types Elementary School, is beginning a science unit on the properties of air. Jenny begins by reviewing the five senses and asking student how they know if something is "real." After discussing how the five senses help us understand objects such as a spoon or chair, Jenny asks, "Is air real?" Though most students nod, Jenny can tell by their puzzled looks that they aren't quite sure.

Jenny then calls the class's attention to a fish tank and empty glass. Jenny asks them to predict what would happen to the inside of the glass if she places it in the water upside down. A controversy ensues; some say the inside will get wet and others contend that it will stay dry. She has a student come up to feel the inside of the glass both before and after placing it in the water, and to her surprise (and dismay) he reports that it was dry before but wet after. The class is puzzled but not surprised.

Jenny then takes a roll of paper towels next to her chair and asks students to predict what will happen if she places a paper towel up in the glass and again puts it in the water upside down. Again student opinions differ. When the paper towel comes out dry Jenny asks for an explanation. After several attempts, one student suggests that the air has kept the water out. Jenny proceeds to demonstrate with the glass under the water allowing bubbles to escape and asks students to explain the bubbles. With some prompting the class agrees that air is real. Jenny then has students experiment in small groups with water, clear glasses and paper towels.

INSTRUCTIONAL RESOURCES

Transparencies (From the Transparency Package)

T 2.1 Factors Influencing Human Intellectual Development

T 2.4 Piaget's Stages and Characteristics

T 2.6 The Zone of Proximal Development

Transparency Masters (From the Instructor's Manual)

TM 2.1 The Drive for Equilibrium

TM 2.3 Measuring Thinking

Transparency Masters (In this Media Guide)

Questions for Discussion and Analysis

Rating Scale: Science Instruction in a First-Grade Classroom

Feedback for "Questions for Discussion and Analysis"

Questions for Discussion and Analysis: Properties of Air in First-Grade Science

1. How effective was Jenny's lesson from a developmental perspective? Specifically, why was it important to use the: a) water, b) clear glass, c) paper towels, and d) learning centers?

2. Rather than teacher demonstration, Jenny could have begun the lesson with students exploring the materials on their own. What are the advantages and disadvantages of this alternative?

3. Samantha placed her hand up into the glass and said, "It's wet on the outside, but dry on the inside," but Terry continued to assert, "It's wet!" How effectively did Jenny respond? What other alternatives might she have pursued? What advantages and disadvantages exist with these alternatives?

4. How effectively did Jenny utilize social interaction in her lesson? What instructional purpose did this social interaction serve?

5. How effective was the instruction in this lesson?

Rating Scale for
Properties of Air in First-Grade Science

Rate the effectiveness of the teacher on each of the following dimensions using the following scale:

5 = Excellent
4 = Very good
3 = Good
2 = Fair
1 = Poor
0 = No evidence available

1. The developmental
   effectiveness of the lesson   0 1 2 3 4 5

2. Responding to student   0 1 2 3 4 5
   disagreements

3. Utilizing social interaction   0 1 2 3 4 5

4. Overall lesson effectiveness   0 1 2 3 4 5

Feedback for "Questions for Discussion and Analysis" for Properties of Air in First-Grade Science

1. Jenny's students were first graders, and based on their responses, they were at Piaget's Preoperational Stage of Development. Learners at this stage are dominated by their perceptions; what they perceive is indeed real for them. Concrete experiences are essential if learning is to be meaningful for children at this stage of development.

   Because it is invisible, the physical reality of air is a difficult concept for first graders. The water was important in the lesson because it allowed students to see air bubbles, which are concrete. The transparent glass allowed students to see the air/water line inside it. The paper towel also provided concrete evidence that something (air) was keeping the water out, since the towel remained dry. From a developmental perspective the learning center activities were a critical component of the lesson. They allowed students to experiment with the ideas in a personal hands-on way.

2. One alternative to Jenny's introducing the lesson with a teacher-centered demonstration would be to begin the lesson with student exploration at the learning centers. The advantage of this approach is that it would allow each student to individually experiment with the water and the glasses and paper towels. Disadvantages are organization and the focus of the lesson; organizing individual student exploration, particularly with first graders, can be demanding.

3. When Samantha placed her hand up the glass and said, "It's wet on the outside, but dry on the inside," Terry continued to assert, "It's wet!" Jenny responded by saying "Uh, oh! We have two differing opinions. We've got to find out how to solve this problem," and then said, "Let's dry this glass off and start again. Only this time we're going to put a paper towel in the glass. Now if water goes in the glass what is the paper towel going to look like?"

   This approach lies at an approximate middle point on a continuum ranging from essentially "teacher-centered" at one end to totally "learner-centered" at the other. At the teacher-centered end of the continuum a teacher might say, "No, Terry feel again. It's really dry." The advantage of this approach is that it saves time and establishes a critical aspect of the lesson. The disadvantage is that it frames the teacher as the ultimate authority and the center of knowledge. The message this sends to students about the legitimacy of their own knowledge and beliefs and their role in knowledge construction is potentially damaging.
       An alternative at the other end of the continuum would be for the teacher to say, "Hmm, we have a disagreement here. How could we resolve it?" This places greater responsibility on students and provides opportunities for them to develop their problem solving abilities. The disadvantage from a content perspective is that this approach usually takes more time. Teaching involves trade-offs such as these; being aware of their options allows teachers to make professional decisions based on their best judgment.

4. Social interaction encourages students to put their own ideas into words and allows them to compare their ideas with others. Jenny encouraged this by guiding students with her questioning as they constructed their understanding. Her questions encouraged students to think about the content, put their ideas

into words, and compare their ideas with others. Jenny was careful not to offer too many explanations of her own or impose her ideas onto the class. The overall effect of this questioning was to communicate to students that their ideas were valued and important and that it was their responsibility to make sense of what they were observing.

5. Overall, Jenny's lesson was quite effective. Her goals were clear, the learning activity was aligned with the goals, she was well organized and used her time well, students were orderly yet involved, and the information was meaningful to them. She also promoted higher-order thinking with first graders.

   Her lesson was effective for another reason. One of the most important factors in fostering learner development is *experience*, and the students acquired a great deal of experience in this lesson. Even if they didn't actually reach the content goal of the lesson, i.e., truly "get" the idea that air takes up space, they acquired a great deal of experience which will make later study more meaningful. This is the essence of developmentally effective instruction.

Looking Through Classroom Windows: Integrated Video Cases
Tape 1 (28:46-37:20)
Segment #3: *The Scarlet Letter* in a High School English Class

BEFORE YOU BEGIN (Note: This 9 minute segment appears in written form at the end of Chapter 7)

Lesson Summary

Sue Southam is a high school English teacher at Highland High School in Salt Lake City, Utah. The lesson takes place in a class that has been reading different American works of fiction. The class is focusing on Nathaniel Hawthorne's *The Scarlet Letter,* and in previous sessions the class has discussed the setting for the novel and its heroine, Hester Prynne.

In this session Sue is attempting to help students understand the character of Reverend Dimmesdale, the secret father of Hester's illegitimate child. She begins by briefly reviewing the book and then asks students how they know that Dimmesdale is the father of the child. After some discussion, she asks students to create a portrait or picture of Dimmesdale in their writing journals. Following this assignment she asks students to pretend they are directing a film and asks them to suggest whom they might cast in Dimmesdale's character.

After discussing students' suggestions, Sue reads a scene from the book in which the Reverend Dimmesdale, in front of the whole congregation, exhorts Hester to identify the father of the child and her illegitimate lover. Following this passage, she assigns half the class to be "Hesters" and half to be "Dimmesdales" and asks them to record their feelings line-by-line during Dimmesdale's speech. She then breaks the students into groups of four with two "Hesters" and two "Dimmesdales" in each and asks them to role play the characters, responding to each other's reactions.

After the small groupwork Sue brings them back together and the class discusses their reactions in a whole-group setting. Students can't decide whether Dimmesdale is a tragic character to be pitied or a cowardly one to be scorned.

INSTRUCTIONAL RESOURCES

Transparencies (From the Transparency Package)

T 7.2 An Information Processing Model

T 7.3 Limitations of Working Memory

Transparency Masters (From the Instructor's Manual)

TM 7.4 Questions that Promote Deep Processing of Information

TM 7.5 Background Knowledge and Encoding

TM 7.6 Elaborating on Past Experiences

TM 7.7 Active and Passive Study Strategies

Transparency Masters (In this Media Guide)

Questions for Discussion and Analysis

Rating Scale: *The Scarlet Letter* in a High School English Class

Feedback for "Questions for Discussion and Analysis"

Questions for Discussion and Analysis:
The Scarlet Letter in a High School English Class

1. How effectively did Sue incorporate cognitive learning principles in her lesson?

2. Research indicates that active student involvement increases learning.

   a) How effectively did Sue promote student involvement in her lesson?

   b) What strategies did she use to involve the students?

3. The meaningfulness of new content can be thought of as the number of connections that can be made between the new information and students' background knowledge.

   a) How effective was Sue in making the information meaningful for her students?

   b) What strategies did she use to make Dimmesdale's character meaningful for learners?

4. How effectively did Sue incorporate small groupwork into her lesson?

5. How effective was the instruction in this lesson?

Rating Scale for
The Scarlet Letter in a High School English Class

Rate the effectiveness of the teacher on each of the following dimensions using the following scale:

5 = Excellent
4 = Very good
3 = Good
2 = Fair
1 = Poor
0 = No evidence available

1. Incorporating cognitive learning principles   0   1   2   3   4   5

2. Promoting student involvement   0   1   2   3   4   5

3. Making the information meaningful   0   1   2   3   4   5

4. Incorporating small groupwork   0   1   2   3   4   5

5. Overall lesson effectiveness   0   1   2   3   4   5

Feedback for "Questions for Discussion and Analysis" for
The Scarlet Letter **in a High School English Class**

1. Cognitive learning theories are based upon four principles: 1) learners' active attempts to understand experience, 2) new understanding depends on previous knowledge, 3) learners construct understanding, and 4) learning involves a change in mental structures. Sue's goal was for her students to interpret Dimmesdale's character, which would involve a change in her students' mental structures. She built upon previous knowledge by continuously asking students to refer to the text, which they had read, and by asking questions that encouraged students to recall previous lessons.

    Sue encouraged student knowledge construction with respect to Dimmesdale's character by asking students to construct a verbal or pictorial portrait of Dimmesdale and by casting this character in a movie. She also helped the students construct an understanding of the novel's characters by asking them to get inside the minds of the two main characters during Dimmesdale's speech to Hester. This was followed by role playing in small groups and general discussion by the class as a whole. During their discussion students shared their perspectives and were encouraged to reconcile them with the perspectives of others.

2. Sue did a good job of involving students in the lesson as they wrestled with their understanding of Dimmesdale's character. She did this in several ways. She solicited their ideas and opinions in a whole-group discussion. She also encouraged individual students to construct a personnel portrait of Dimmesdale in their learning logs. This was followed by each student individually interpreting Dimmesdale's speech from either a Dimmesdale or Hester Prynne perspective. Role playing these characters' reactions provided another opportunity for student involvement. In each instance students were actively involved in trying to make sense of a complex character in a potentially difficult novel.

3. In her lesson, Sue was effective in actively encouraging students to personally understand and interpret Dimmesdale's character. To promote meaningful learning, Sue asked students to interpret the character from their personal perspectives, rather than discussing the character in abstract terms. Sue presented students with several tasks, including creating a concrete portrait of the character, casting him in a movie, perspective taking during the speech, and role playing. The combination of all these strategies allowed students to individually construct a view of Dimmesdale that was meaningful to them.

4. Sue's groupwork was quite effective. Effective groupwork has four characteristics: a) clear directions, b) a relatively short, specific time period, c) a required written product, and d) teacher monitoring. Her directions were clear, providing a clear content focus for their activities. While Sue didn't require a written product, their group discussions were based on information they had put their logs a few minutes before, and she kept the group activity relatively short. Finally, as students worked in groups she circulated around the room, clarifying directions, answering questions and providing encouragement.

5. The overall effectiveness of Sue's lesson might generate considerable discussion. She was well organized and used her time well, students were orderly yet involved, and the information was meaningful to them. Her stated goal was for students to interpret Dimmesdale's character, and they did, so the learning activity was aligned with her goal.

    However, this lesson raises a number of questions. For example, are all interpretations of Dimmesdale's character equally valid? If not, how do we know which is more valid than another? Is one interpretation of Hawthorne's intent in writing the novel any more valid than another? If all interpretations are equally valid, what is accomplished in the lesson, and how do we know if we've accomplished it? Does this matter? What kind of understanding of character development did the students construct? Questions such as these raise interesting issues about the purposes of instruction and teachers' beliefs.

Looking Through Classroom Windows: Integrated Video Cases
Tape 1 (37:50-46:55)
Segment #4: Constructing Understanding: Instructional Applications

BEFORE YOU BEGIN
(Note: This 9-minute segment appears in written form at the beginning of Chapter 8)

Lesson Summary

Jenny Newhall, a fourth grade teacher, wants her students to know how to solve problems involving a balance beam and weights. Jenny starts by dividing students into groups and giving each group of students a balance beam and weights. She begins the lesson by directing each group to put 4 weights 8 places or notches from the center on the right hand side and 1 weight 2 places from the center on the left side. She then asks each student in the different groups to come up with as many different ways to balance the beam without moving the original weights. After students work for awhile on their individual solutions they then share them with other members of their group and test the different solutions out on the balance beam.

Different students in the focal group offer different solutions.
- One suggests adding three to the 10 place and explains it in this way (3 x 10 + 2 x 1 = 8 x 4).
- A second suggests adding 5 to the 6 place and explains it in this way (6 x 5 + 2 x 1 = 8 x 4).
- A third student suggests adding a 3 to the 10 place and justifies by noting there will then be 4 on each side. This same student also suggests adding 2 weights to the 10 and 1 on the 6.

When Jenny visits this group she encourages students to share their thinking. Two of the students understand the logic behind balancing the beam (i.e. number x distance) while two others believe that the number of weights alone (without consideration of their distance from the center) determine whether the beam will balance.

The whole class then discusses the solutions the different groups produced. Jenny encourages students to use number sentences like, 8 x 4 = 32 = (10 x 3) + 2 = 32 to explain their answers.

Jenny then asks the groups to generate different solutions to balancing a beam that has one weight 2 places from the center on the left and three weights five from the center and 1 weight 6 from the center on the right. As students share their answers it is evident that many still don't understand the length x weight principal needed to solve the problem.

INSTRUCTIONAL RESOURCES

Transparencies (from the Transparency Package)

T2.8   The Zone of Proximal Development

T2.9   Scaffolding Tasks in Three Zones of Proximal Development

T8.3 Characteristics of Constructivism

T9.4   A General Problem-Solving Model

Transparency Masters (from the Instructor's Manual)

TM2.6 A Comparison of Piaget's and Vygotsky's Views of Knowledge Construction

TM 8.3 Constructing Understanding of Balance Beams

TM 8.4 Principles of Instruction for Applying Constructivism in Classrooms

Transparency Masters (In this Media Guide)

Questions for Discussion and Analysis

Rating Scale: Using Balance Beams in Fourth Grade

Feedback for "Questions for Discussion and Analysis"

Questions for Discussion and Analysis: Constructing Understanding: Instructional Applications

1. How effectively did Jenny incorporate the following characteristics of constructivism in her lesson?
    a. Learners constructing their own understanding
    b. New learning depending on current understanding
    c. Learning facilitated by social interaction
    d. Authentic learning tasks

2. When some of the students in the small group didn't understand the weight x distance principle, Jenny didn't directly intervene, instead encouraging group members to work out differences. What are the advantages and disadvantages of this approach?

3. How effective was the lesson in using cooperative learning to facilitate learning?

4. From an overall perspective how effective was the instruction in this lesson?

Rating Scale for
Constructing Understanding:
Instructional Applications

Rate the effectiveness of the lesson on each of the following dimensions using the following scale:

5 = Excellent
4 = Very good
3 = Good
2 = Fair
1 = Poor
0 = No evidence available

1. Constructivism

   a. Learners constructing their own understanding   0 1 2 3 4 5

   b. New learning depending on current understanding   0 1 2 3 4 5

   c. Learning facilitated by social interaction   0 1 2 3 4 5

   d. Authentic learning tasks   0 1 2 3 4 5

2. Overall lesson effectiveness   0 1 2 3 4 5

**Feedback for "Questions for Discussion and Analysis" for
Constructing Understanding: Instructional Applications**

1a. Learners Constructing their own Understanding

From the dialogue in the lesson it was apparent that several members of the group were actively struggling with the content. In terms of the zone of proximal development, Molly and Drexel were beyond it, understanding the principle involved. Suzanne's struggle with the content and her wavering suggested that she was in the zone. Tad's reticence to participate makes it difficult to tell exactly where he was.

1b. New Learning Depending on Current Understanding

It was obvious from the lesson that the four students in the focal group started from different places. What is unclear is what this starting point was. Had the problems been simpler (e.g. using just one weight on one side) would Suzanne and Tad been able to participate? This is valuable information that would have allowed Jenny to design her instruction more effectively.

1c. Learning Facilitated by Social Interaction

Social interaction was a major influence in the lesson. Though more evident in the student interviews which occurred after the lesson, the exchange of ideas and perspectives had a major influence on Suzanne and Tad's thinking.

1d. Authentic Learning Tasks

Having access to the balance beam and being able to ultimately test their solutions on the beam was a major motivational part of the lesson. The power of concrete manipulatives was evident when the group arrived at a (correct) solution but when they tried it out on the beam and it didn't work because the beam malfunctioned. Several of the students were willing to discard the abstract, logical solution they had developed in favor of the concrete, visible balance beam.

2. This question cuts to the very center of one of the constructivist dilemmas--how much should teachers intervene to guide learning and how much should students be allowed to wander around on their own? Two factors influenced the effectiveness of Jenny's decision to ask questions and not intervene directly. One was the presence of the balance beam which could provide students with feedback about the accuracy of their solutions. The second factor was the presence of several students in the group who understood the principle involved and could share their knowledge with the others. In the absence of these two factors greater teacher intervention would have been necessary.

3. There was student diversity in the group, which facilitated learning. In addition, students were given a clear and specific learning task, a specified amount of time to complete it , and were required to produce a product.

4. While generally effective, the lesson could have been improved in several ways. The lesson might have incorporated more opportunities for students to experiment with the balance beam with simpler problems. This would have provided an experiential base for students and allowed Jenny to gain insights into the background knowledge students brought to the task. In addition, the initial tasks given to students might have been simplified to provide positive learning experiences for students who were experiencing difficulties. Finally, some type of structured summary at the end of the lesson would have provided closure to the lesson and helped students who were still floundering resolve some of their doubts and confusion.

Looking Through Classroom Windows: Integrated Video Cases
Tape 1 (47:29-1:12:35)
Segment #5: Designing Experiments in Seventh Grade

BEFORE YOU BEGIN (Note: This 25-minute segment appears in written form at the end of Chapter 8.)

Lesson Summary

Scott Sowell, a seventh grade science teacher at Kirby Smith Middle School is trying to teach his students how to control variables within an inquiry oriented lesson. The class has been introduced to the topic of controlling variables but is still struggling with it.

Scott begins the lesson by demonstrating a simple pendulum, explaining frequency as the number of swings in a certain time period. When he asks for possible factors that might influence the frequency of a pendulum the class offers length, weight, and the angle of release. Scott then asks the class, in small groups, to design experiments to ascertain which of these variables influences the frequency of a pendulum. (In reality only the length influences the frequency; weight and height have no effect.)

The video then focuses on a focal group of students attempting to design experiments to test these different variables. Using a ring stand, string, and paper clip weights the group conducts one test. After noting the results the group does a second test, both shortening the string and making the weight heavier. After counting for a fixed period of time they conclude that a shorter string makes the pendulum go faster. Scott visits the group and asks which variable caused the change. Different students voice different opinions, some claiming it was the change in weight, others the change in length. Scott encourages them to think about why they can't come to a firm conclusion.

The group designs a third experiment, this time changing only the length and keeping the weight and angle constant. Again Scott intervenes, encouraging them to think systematically about their results and the influence of each of the three variables.

In the next two experiments the group keeps length constant but changes both weight and height and comes up with the same frequency. Scott again asks them to think about the logic of their design.

When Scott pulls the different groups together to report their findings, the class concludes (incorrectly) that each of the variables influences the frequency. To counter this conclusion Scott then does repeated tests at the front of the room, changing one variable and keeping the others constant. Scott writes these conclusions on the board and asks the class what they learned about controlling variables. Wensley, one of the students from the focal group, offers, "Each time you do a different part of the experiment, only change one of the variables."

INSTRUCTIONAL RESOURCES

Transparencies (From the Transparency Package)

T 2.4 Piaget's Stages and Characteristics

T 2.8 The Zone of Proximal Development

T 8.3 Characteristics of Constructivism

Transparency Masters (From the Instructor's Manual)

TM 2.6   A Comparison of Piaget's and Vygotsky's Views of knowledge Construction

TM 8.4   Principles of Instruction for Applying Constructivism in Classrooms

TM 8.5   Steps in Inquiry Instruction

Transparency Masters (In this Media Guide)

Questions for Discussion and Analysis (Lesson)

Rating Scale: Designing Experiments in Seventh Grade

Feedback for "Questions for Discussion and Analysis"

Questions for Discussion and Analysis: Designing Experiments in Seventh Grade

1. To what extent did the lesson incorporate constructivist principles?

2. How effectively was groupwork incorporated in the lesson?

3. How effectively did the lesson use inquiry strategies to promote higher-order thinking?

4. From an over-all perspective, how effective was the lesson?

Rating Scale for
Designing Experiments in Seventh Grade

Rate the effectiveness of the lesson on each of the following dimensions using the following scale:

5 = Excellent
4 = Very good
3 = Good
2 = Fair
1 = Poor
0 = No evidence available

1. Applying constructivist principles in instruction   0 1 2 3 4 5

2. Incorporating groupwork in instruction   0 1 2 3 4 5

3. Using inquiry to promote higher-order thinking   0 1 2 3 4 5

4. Overall lesson effectiveness   0 1 2 3 4 5

**Feedback for "Questions for Discussion and Analysis" for
Designing Experiments in Seventh Grade**

1. In evaluating the lesson in terms of constructivism we use its four major
   characteristics as a frame of reference.
   - Learners construct their own understanding: The hands-on activities allowed
     students to both experiment with pendulums and experience inquiry first hand.
   - New learning depends on current understanding: This was clearly illustrated
     by the fits and starts the group took as it was attempting to learn to control
     variables. Through his questioning Scott attempted to get the group to wrestle
     with the logic of their conclusions.
   - Learning is facilitated by social interaction: The small groups provided an
     effective vehicle for students to share and compare their ideas with each other.
   - Meaningful learning occurs within authentic learning tasks: This characteristic
     was addressed in two ways. In introducing pendulums Scott asked for
     everyday examples. In addition, students were able to actually experiment with
     their own pendulum.

2. Effective groupwork has the following characteristics:
   - Goals direct the groups' activities.
   - Social interaction is emphasized.
   - Learners must depend on each other to reach the goals.
     We saw these features in Scott's lesson. His students' goal was to determine
     how length, weight, and angle affected the frequency of a simple pendulum; a
     great deal of interaction took place in the groups; and learners collaborated in
     designing, implementing, and interpreting the experiment.

3. Scott's students were involved in an inquiry activity, which typically includes
   the following steps:
   - Identifying a question or problem
   - Forming an hypothesis to answer the question or solve the problem
   - Gathering data to test the hypothesis
   - Drawing conclusions from the data
   - Generalizing on the basis of the conclusions
     During the lesson Scott's students were presented with the problem of
     determining how the length, weight, and angle affect the frequency of a simple
     pendulum. While the problem could have been presented more generally, such
     as, "What influences the frequency of a simple pendulum?", Scott chose to
     narrow the problem to make it more manageable for the students.
     In Scott's lesson, the students didn't form hypotheses; instead they moved
     directly to gathering data. Understanding and applying the processes needed
     to gather meaningful data were the lesson's primary goals; understanding the
     relationships between length, weight, angle, and frequency were secondary.
     This emphasis on process is characteristics of inquiry activities (Eggen &
     Kauchak, 2001; Kauchak & Eggen, 1998). Conclusions and generalizations
     were made both in small groups and as part of the whole-class discussion.
     Again, much of the discussion focused on the process of controlling variables.

4. From an over-all perspective, Scott's lesson was quite effective. Students were
   actively involved in a hands-on inquiry activity. Scott provided enough focus to
   provide structure for the lesson but still placed most of the responsibility for
   learning on students. Classroom interaction, both in small and large groups,

was good, providing opportunities for students to share and compare their differing perspectives.

The lesson could have been improved in several ways. One was to make the process of inquiry more explicit to students. While students went through most of the inquiry steps they were probably unaware of them or the logic behind them. A short introduction at the beginning and a summary wrap-up at the end focusing on the process of inquiry would help learners understand the inquiry process better.

The second area of improvement would be to explicitly deal with the topic of controlling variables. During the lesson students in the focal group had problems with this process. Scott might have dealt with this through a short introduction at the beginning or a brief discussion of the problem when the class discussed their disparate results.

BEFORE YOU BEGIN (Note: This 11-minute segment appears in written form at the beginning of Chapter 9.)

Lesson Summary

Laura Hunter, a fifth grade teacher at Bennion Elementary, is trying to teach students about area by involving them in a problem solving lesson. Laura begins by posing the following problem, "The principal is planning to recarpet the classroom and needs to know how much carpeting to order." The complexity of the problem is increased by the fact that the room is irregularly shaped and that the linoleum part of the room will not be carpeted.

To help students in their problem solving Laura displays an overhead with the five-step problem solving model described in Chapter 8. Breaking students into groups of four, she has each group identify the problem. The camera follows a focal group of four students that will be interviewed later. After reporting back to the whole class, each group then is responsible for measuring a different part of the room. They report back to a group who is coordinating measurements and constructing a diagram of the whole room.

Laura then asks each group to select a strategy to find the carpeted area of the room. Two strategies emerge. One is to find the total area of the room and subtract out the linoleum or non-carpeted parts of the room. The other is to compute the area of a rectangle within the carpeted area and then add on additional, irregularly shaped carpeted sections.

After selecting and implementing their strategies different groups report back to the whole class. The class discusses not only the different problem solving strategies but also interpersonal problems within the groups.

In evaluating their results the class finds that the answers generated by the different groups differ and the class discusses why. Laura asks for suggestions about ways to make the answers more accurate and students suggest starting with common numbers and using the same strategies.

INSTRUCTIONAL RESOURCES

Transparencies (From the Transparency Package)

T 2.8 Zone of Proximal Development

T 8.3 Characteristics of Constructivism

T 9.4 A General Problem-Solving Model

T 9.5 Expert-Novice Differences in Problem Solving Ability

T 9.6 Helping Learners Become Better Problem Solvers

T 9.9 Factors Affecting the Transfer of Learning

Transparency Masters (From the Instructor's Manual)

TM 9.4 Cases That Are and Are Not Problems

TM 9.6 Principles of Instruction for Developing Problem Solving Ability

Transparency Masters (In this Media Guide)

Questions for Discussion and Analysis (Lesson)

Rating Scale: Finding Area in Elementary Math

Feedback for "Questions for Discussion and Analysis"

Questions for Discussion and Analysis: Finding Area in Elementary Math

1. How effective was Laura's lesson in teaching the concept of area?

2. How effective was Laura's lesson in teaching problem solving?

3. How effective was the lesson in terms of the following dimensions of constructivism: learners constructing their own understanding, and authentic learning tasks?

4. How effectively did Laura utilize social interaction in her lesson?

5. From an overall lesson perspective, how effective was Laura's instruction?

Rating Scale for
Finding Area in Elementary Math

Rate the effectiveness of the lesson on each of the following dimensions using the following scale:

   5 = Excellent
   4 = Very good
   3 = Good
   2 = Fair
   1 = Poor
   0 = No evidence available

1. The effectiveness of the lesson in teaching the concept area   0 1 2 3 4 5

2. The effectiveness of the lesson in teaching problem solving   0 1 2 3 4 5

3. The effectiveness of the lesson in incorporating:

    a. learners constructing their own understanding   0 1 2 3 4 5

    b. authentic learning task   0 1 2 3 4 5

    c. social interaction   0 1 2 3 4 5

4. Overall lesson effectiveness   0 1 2 3 4 5

**Feedback for "Questions for Discussion and Analysis" for
Finding Area in Elementary Math**

1. The key to teaching concepts effectively is a large number of examples to illustrate abstract ideas. Laura began the lesson by reviewing the examples the class had discussed yesterday--the perimeter and area of a playground. The rest of the lesson contained two examples. The first was a brief mention of the use of linoleum tiles as area units. The other was the extended problem of finding area of the carpeted part of the room.

    Judging from students' comments, both during and after the lesson, the concepts of perimeter and area were not clear in their minds. The effectiveness of the lesson from a concept learning perspective could have been enhanced by including more examples of area early in the lesson. This might include a mini-lesson on finding area of a simple geometric shape or a discussion of the use of tiles as an area unit.

2. Learning to problem solve is enhanced when teachers:
    *   capitalize on social interaction
    *   present problems in meaningful contexts
    *   provide practice in problem finding
    *   provide scaffolding
    *   teach general problem solving strategies.

    Laura's lesson effectively used small groupwork to capitalize on social interaction. The problem she posed to the class was concrete, authentic and meaningful to learners. The lesson did not provide practice in problem finding. Different forms of teacher scaffolding used were the diagram of the class, and her interactions with different groups as she circulated around the room. Laura attempted to teach general problem solving strategies by using the five-step problem solving model to frame the lesson. The effectiveness of using this model (in terms of transfer) would have been increased if she had encouraged students to apply it to a different problem.

3. The lesson was effective from these two constructivist perspectives. By framing the lesson in terms of carpeting their own room, students were provided with an authentic learning task that was meaningful to them. By actually allowing them to measure the room and work in groups on the measurements in the diagram the students were able to wrestle with constructing their own understanding.

4. This was probably one of the strengths of the lesson. Students worked in small groups to: 1) discuss the problem, 2) measure the room, 3) select and implement a strategy, and 4) evaluate the strategy they used and the answer they got. In addition, Laura encouraged students to reflect on the effectiveness of the interaction in their groups.

5. We would rate the lesson about a 4+. In terms of strengths the lesson was framed with a meaningful, authentic task; students were actively involved in problem solving, Laura used a model to teach problem solving, and students were encouraged to reflect back on their strategy, answer, and effectiveness as group members.

    Two areas of improvement might include providing students with more concept examples of area before asking them to utilize the concept to problem solve, and providing additional practice with the problem solving model to promote transfer.

BEFORE YOU BEGIN (Note: This 15 minute segment appears in written form at the end of Chapter 9.)

Lesson Summary

Suzanne Brush is a second grade teacher at Webster Elementary School in St. Augustine, Florida. This lesson was conducted in late March and had been preceded by some discussion of using graphs to represent number quantities.

Suzanne begins the lesson by explaining that she is planning a party for the class and needs to know what kinds of jelly beans she should buy. After some discussion the class agrees that one way to find out would be to give each student a sample of different kinds of jelly beans and have each student vote for their favorite. Suzanne then gives a bag containing seven different-flavored jelly beans to each student and asks them to choose their favorite. After the tasting, Suzanne asks students how they could organize this information. After considerable discussion they arrive at the idea of graphing the information by having each student place a colored cardboard rectangle in the appropriate column of the graph.

After each student "votes," Suzanne encourages students to begin interpreting the graph by asking questions such as, "What does the graph tell us?" Suzanne encourages students to analyze the graphed information by asking questions that require them to compare the information in the columns (the numbers of students choosing each color). Suzanne then asks them to pose similar problems of their own. As students discuss theirs and others' problems, Suzanne emphasizes student understanding of their problem solving strategies by repeatedly asking "How did you get that?" To provide additional practice with problem solving, Suzanne then assigns students to different learning center activities where they work in small groups to apply their problem solving and graphing strategies to new problems.

INSTRUCTIONAL RESOURCES

Transparencies (From the Transparency Package)

T 9.4 A General Problem-Solving Model

T 9.6 Helping Learners Become Better Problem Solvers

T 9.8 Elements of Critical Thinking

T 9.9 Factors Affecting the Transfer of Learning

Transparency Masters (From the Instructor's Manual)

TM 9.4 Cases That Are and Are Not Problems

TM 9.6 Principles of Instruction for Developing Problem Solving Ability

(In this Media Guide)

Questions for Discussion and Analysis

Rating Scale: Graphing in Second Grade Math

Feedback for "Questions for Discussion and Analysis"

Questions for Discussion and Analysis: Graphing in Second-Grade Math

1. How effective was Suzanne's lesson from a developmental perspective?

2. How effectively did Suzanne involve the students in her lesson?

3. How effective was Suzanne's lesson for promoting transfer?

4. How effective was the instruction in the lesson?

Rating Scale for
Graphing in Second-Grade Math

Rate the effectiveness of the teacher on each of the following dimensions using the following scale:
- 5 = Excellent
- 4 = Very good
- 3 = Good
- 2 = Fair
- 1 = Poor
- 0 = No evidence available

1. The developmental effectiveness of the lesson   0   1   2   3   4   5

2. Involving students in the lesson   0   1   2   3   4   5

3. Promoting transfer   0   1   2   3   4   5

4. Overall lesson effectiveness   0   1   2   3   4   5

**Feedback for "Questions for Discussion and Analysis" for
Graphing in Second-Grade Math**

1. The lesson was effective from both a Piagetian and a Vygotskyan perspective. From a Piagetian point of view, Suzanne provided a concrete problem that was meaningful to students. In solving the problem each student was personally involved in tasting, voting, and representing the information. As students constructed the graph, they could see in a concrete way how their vote influenced the shape of the graph and the final results.

   From a Vygotskyan perspective, the lesson was effective in encouraging student dialogue about their problem solving strategies, and Suzanne provided the guidance of a "more knowledgeable other" in the entire process. Most students appeared to be in the zone of proximal development, and Suzanne helped them make progress through the zone.

   An interesting question for discussion might be whether or not Suzanne was too teacher-centered and directive. The optimal amount of teacher direction in teaching problem solving is open to debate.

2. Students were actively involved throughout the lesson. All students tasted the jelly beans, voted for their favorite flavors, and indicated their preferences on the graph. Many of the students were involved in the discussion of the problem and the strategy for solving it, and all students were involved in the work at the centers.

3. Transfer is enhanced by the depth of student understanding, the variety and quality of learning experiences, and by the different contexts in which learners' experiences are embedded. Suzanne promoted depth of understanding and provided quality learning experiences by directly involving students in solving a problem that was meaningful to them. Learning and transfer were further enhanced by allowing students to see how their personal "vote" influenced the shape of the graph and by discussing the information in the graph from different points of view. Finally, transfer was enhanced by student involvement in the different learning centers which provided different contexts for gathering and graphing information.

4. While teaching is a complex process, and it is difficult to provide an overall lesson evaluation, we have found this question effective for promoting discussions. Students' comments offer insights into their beliefs about teaching and learning and their understanding of effective instruction.

   Suzanne was generally very effective in the lesson. She made the learning meaningful by embedding problem solving in a question about people's preferences in jelly beans, which was an authentic task for second graders. The lesson began with a motivating problem (planning a party) that asked students to assist in the design and data gathering. Each student was actively involved in tasting, voting, and indicating their preferences on the graph, which helped them see the connection between the data gathering process and abstract numerals. Suzanne helped them develop a deeper understanding of gathering and graphing information by having them do similar activities in their learning centers.

   An additional strength of the lesson was the interaction that occurred both between teacher and students and the students with each other. Through effective questioning, Suzanne encouraged students to analyze and discuss the data they were gathering. She also encouraged students to explain the logic behind their answers, placing greater emphasis on understanding than on mechanics.

   Two possible criticisms of the lesson might be the amount of teacher direction and the extent to which the lesson focused on strategies. Teacher judgment is always involved in deciding how much to structure a lesson and how much the teacher should "steer" the lesson toward a desired outcome. Pure constructivists argue for student autonomy and opportunities to learn through trial and error. Others suggest that the practical need to maintain lesson focus and meet lesson goals must prevail. A second way that the lesson might be improved is through more emphasis on problem solving strategies per se. For example, at the end of the lesson Suzanne might have increased the emphasis on students' reflection on the process of problem solving, what they learned about it, and how the process could be improved.

Looking Through Classroom Windows: Integrated Video Cases
Tape 2 (14:51-27:58)
Segment #2: Studying Arthropods in Fifth Grade

BEFORE YOU BEGIN (Note: This 13 minute segment appears in written form at the beginning of Chapter 11.)

DeVonne Lampkin, a fifth grade teacher at Abbott Park Elementary in Jacksonville, Florida, wants her students to understand the essential characteristics of arthropods. She begins the lesson by reviewing other major animal groups and then shows the class a lobster and asks for observations. Through prompting she identifies the three essential characteristics of arthropods: hard outer covering (exoskeleton), three-part body, and segmented legs.

Using these characteristics as criteria, DeVonne then has the class analyze the following positive and negative examples: cockroach, clam, and Mrs. Sapp, the school principal. Next, she distributes whole shrimp and has the students in small groups analyze these.

INSTRUCTIONAL RESOURCES

Transparencies (From the Transparency Package)

T 1.3 Knowledge Needed for Expert Teaching

T 7.8 Making Information Meaningful

T 8.3 Characteristics of Constructivism

T 9.1 Theories of Concept Learning

Transparency Masters (From the Instructor's Manual)

TM 7.4 Questions That Promote Deep Processing of Information

TM 8.4 Principles of Instruction for Applying Constructivism in Classrooms

TM 9.3 Principles of Instruction for Promoting Concept Learning

Transparency Masters (In this Media Guide)

Questions for Discussion and Analysis

Rating Scale: Studying Arthropods in Fifth Grade

Feedback for "Questions for Discussion and Analysis"

Questions for Discussion and Analysis: Studying Arthropods in Fifth Grade

1. How effectively did DeVonne deal with student background knowledge?

2. Analyze DeVonne's classroom in terms of the following teacher characteristics: personal teaching efficacy, enthusiasm, and caring.

3. Analyze DeVonne's classroom in terms of the following climate variables: order and safety, success, challenge, and task comprehension.

4. Analyze DeVonne's lesson in terms of the following instructional variables: introductory focus, personalization, involvement, and feedback.

5. From an overall perspective, how effective was the instruction in this lesson?

Rating Scale for
Studying Arthropods in Fifth Grade

Rate the effectiveness of the teacher on each of the following dimensions using the following scale:
   5 = Excellent
   4 = Very good
   3 = Good
   2 = Fair
   1 = Poor
   0 = No evidence available

1. Dealing with student background Knowledge   0 1 2 3 4 5

2. Teacher characteristics   0 1 2 3 4 5

3. Climate variables   0 1 2 3 4 5

4. Instructional variables   0 1 2 3 4 5

5. Overall lesson effectiveness   0 1 2 3 4 5

**Feedback for "Questions for Discussion and Analysis" for
Studying Arthropods in Fifth Grade**

1. DeVonne dealt with students' background knowledge by beginning the lesson with review questions about the major animal groups. In addition, her use of concrete examples minimized the need for student knowledge about the animals she used as positive and negative examples.

2. While all these teacher characteristics are inferential, we can conjecture about them based on evidence in the video. DeVonne seemed to have high personal teaching efficacy; she had a clear goal and worked hard to help students reach that goal. She was quite enthusiastic; she walked around the room, gestured, and interacted frequently with students. She seemed to genuinely care about her students; she had a gentle, but warm way of interacting with students.

3. Even though the class was quite excited during the lesson, DeVonne was able to maintain an orderly classroom that was conducive to learning. She promoted success through her questions and prompting, and through the use of concrete examples. She provided challenge by asking students to classify new examples and explain their classification. Throughout the lesson students were clear about the learning task at hand.

4. DeVonne used a lobster for introductory focus. She might have used it earlier to provide a motivational pull into the lesson. She used personalization when she asked them if their legs were segmented and when she asked them to categorize the principal. She used involvement both through her interactive questioning and through small group work. She provided feedback continually during her questioning.

5. From a motivation perspective the lesson was effective. Students were actively engaged in the less, and the concrete examples provided opportunities for students to construct a concept of arthropod. DeVonne might have used additional positive and negative examples to help them construct a better concept of arthropod. In addition, she might have used small groups earlier to more actively involve all students.

BEFORE YOU BEGIN (Note: This 13 minute segment appears in written form at the end of Chapter 11.)

DeVonne Lampkin, a fifth grade teacher at Abbott Park Elementary in Jacksonville, Florida, was working on her students' writing skills. She wanted them to be able to write effective expository paragraphs.

She began by reviewing the following criteria for an effective paragraph: topic sentence, four or five supporting sentences that related to the topic sentence, and correct grammar, punctuation, and spelling. She then showed a positive and negative example of an effective paragraph on the overhead and asked the class to analyze, using the criteria they had discussed. Next she walked them through writing an effective paragraph, using the following topic sentence, "Basketball is a sport played by both girls and boys."

Then she had each student write his or her own paragraph on a topic of their choice. When they were done she had them put these on a transparency, and the class critiqued several, using the criteria they had discussed earlier.

INSTRUCTIONAL RESOURCES

Transparencies (From the Transparency Package)

T 1.3 Knowledge Needed for Expert Teaching

T 8.3 Characteristics of Constructivism

T 9.7 Characteristics of Effective Strategy Users

Transparency Masters (From the Instructor's Manual)

TM 7.14   Principles of Instruction for Applying Information Processing in Classrooms

TM 8.4   Principles of Instruction for Applying Constructivism in Classrooms

Transparency Masters (In this Media Guide)

Questions for Discussion and Analysis

Rating Scale: Writing Effective Paragraphs

Feedback for "Questions for Discussion and Analysis"

Questions for Discussion and Analysis: Writing Effective Paragraphs

1. What type of knowledge was being taught?

2. How well did DeVonne use instructional scaffolding during her lesson?

3. How motivating was the lesson from these three perspectives?

   a) Teacher characteristics

   b) Climate variables

   c) Instructional variables

4. Analyze DeVonne's lesson in terms of the following instructional variables: introductory focus, personalization, involvement, and feedback.

5. What could she have done to improve the overall effectiveness of the lesson?

Rating Scale for
Writing Effective Paragraphs

Rate the effectiveness of the teacher on each of the following dimensions using the following scale:

5 = Excellent
4 = Very good
3 = Good
2 = Fair
1 = Poor
0 = No evidence available

1. Lesson introduction and review   0 1 2 3 4 5

2. Presentation/description of skill   0 1 2 3 4 5

3. Guided practice   0 1 2 3 4 5

4. Independent practice   0 1 2 3 4 5

5. Overall effectiveness of lesson   0 1 2 3 4 5

Feedback for "Questions for Discussion and Analysis" for
Writing Effective Paragraphs

1. Learning to write effective paragraphs is a form of procedural knowledge.

2. Scaffolding provides instructional support to learners as they progress through the zone of proximal development. DeVonne assisted her students in several ways: 1) she reviewed at the beginning of the lesson, 2) she showed a positive and negative example and discussed these, 3) she assisted the class in writing a whole-class paragraph, and 4) she used questioning to assist the class's analysis of each other's paragraphs.

3. She was generally strong in terms of teacher motivational characteristics; she was caring and enthusiastic, and communicated that all could and should learn. Her classroom was a motivating learning environment. Students understood what was expected of them, they were challenged, most succeeded, and the classroom management was good. One issue is whether students felt safe standing up while their work was being critiqued.

4. She didn't use introductory focus at the beginning of the lesson, but the paragraphs she displayed provided effective focus during the lesson. All students were involved, both in writing their own paragraphs and analyzing others'. She achieved some degree of personalization through allowing each to select their own topic and feedback was continuous.

5. She might have started the lesson by displaying a paragraph and asking if it was effective. Also, safety could be enhanced by having the paragraphs evaluated anonymously. Finally, she could have provided more practice with feedback by having students trade papers and critique each others'. She could have collected these and graded them herself to provide quality control and additional feedback.

Looking Through Classroom Windows: Integrated Video Cases
Tape 2 (42:00-55:44)
Segment #4: Improving Instruction: Essential Teaching Skills

BEFORE YOU BEGIN: (Note: This 14 minute segment appears in written form at the beginning of Chapter 13.)

Lesson Summary

Scott Sowell, a seventh grade science teacher, wants his students to understand Bernoulli's principle, the physical law that explains why airplanes can fly. He begins by reviewing the concept of force and reminds students that when opposing forces meet, movement occurs in the direction of the one of greater magnitude.

To illustrate Bernoulli's principle he first has his students blow over the top of a piece of paper. Then he has students blow between two pieces of paper held closely together. Finally, he places a ping pong ball in a funnel and blows out; surprisingly, the ball remains in the funnel. On the board he reviews each of these experiments, in each case asking students where the force was greater. To conclude the lesson, he introduces the term, "Bernoulli's principle."

INSTRUCTIONAL RESOURCES

Transparencies (From the Transparency Package)

T 13.4 Essential Teaching Skills

T 13.5 Characteristics of Effective Praise

T 13.6 Characteristics of Effective Questioning

Transparency Masters (From the Instructor's Manual)

TM 7.4 Questions That Promote Deep Processing of Information

TM 7.14 Principles of Instruction for Applying Information Processing in Classrooms

TM 8.4 Principles of Instruction for Applying Constructivism in Classrooms

Transparency Masters (In this Media Guide)

Questions for Discussion and Analysis

Rating Scale: Improving Instruction: Essential Teaching Skills

Feedback for "Questions for Discussion and Analysis"

Questions for Discussion and Analysis:
Improving Instruction: Essential Teaching Skills

1. What are essential teaching skills and why are they important to teachers?

2. Which of the essential teaching skills were clearly illustrated in this lesson?

3. How effective was the lesson from a motivational perspective?

Rating Scale for
Improving Instruction:
Essential Teaching Skills

Rate the effectiveness of the teacher on each of the following dimensions using the following scale:

5 = Excellent
4 = Very good
3 = Good
2 = Fair
1 = Poor
0 = No evidence available

1. Introduction to lesson

0 1 2 3 4 5

2. Examples

0 1 2 3 4 5

3. Questioning

0 1 2 3 4 5

4. Review and closure

0 1 2 3 4 5

5. Overall effectiveness of lesson

0 1 2 3 4 5

1. Essential skills are the abilities that all teachers should have to promote learning. They are important to teachers because they form a basic repertoire of strategies that are foundational to other teaching strategies.

2. The essential teaching skills that were most prominent in the lesson were:

- Positive Attitudes: Scott had positive expectations for his students and treated them with respect.
- Effective Organization: Scott's lesson was well organized. He started on time, had materials prepared in advance, and used classroom routines effectively.
- Clear Communication: Scott's communication used precise terminology (which he illustrated with examples), connected discourse, transition signals, and emphasis.
- Focus: The lesson was clearly focused on Bernoulli's Principle.
- Feedback: Through his questioning, Scott provided informative feedback to the class.
- Questioning: In his questioning, Scott strived for equitable distribution, used prompting, and practiced wait time.
- Review and Closure: At the beginning of the lesson Scott reviewed the concept of force and at the end he used the diagrams on the board to summarize the various activities.

3. The lesson was effective from several perspectives. Scott used introductory focus to attract students' attention. He also actively involved students through hands-on activities and questioning. There were also elements of challenge and surprise.

Looking Through Classroom Windows: Integrated Video Cases
Tape 2 (56:14-1:10:24)
Segment #5: **Climate, Geography and Economics in Junior High Social Studies**

BEFORE YOU BEGIN (Note: This 15 minute segment appears in written form at the end of Chapter 13.)

Lesson Summary

Judy Holmquist, a ninth-grade geography teacher at Lakeside Junior High School in Orange Park, Florida, is beginning a unit on the different climate regions of the United States. To introduce students to the unit she assigns them to four different groups to investigate the influence of geography on four states--Florida, California, New York and Alaska. Each group is responsible for describing one of these states in terms of geography, economy, ethnic composition and future issues. When students have completed their investigation Judy assists them in placing the information into a matrix; the states along the vertical axis and the dimensions--geography, economy, ethnic composition, and future issue along the top.

Judy begins the lesson by asking students to find a partner and identify three similarities and differences between states in terms of geography. After several minutes Judy calls the class back together and asks the groups to share their conclusions with the whole class, in the process writing their findings on the board. She then asks the groups to do the same with the "Economy" column, listing similarities and differences among the states. After discussing the economic similarities and differences Judy asks the class to compare the two columns and explain connections between them. Finally, she has the students summarize their findings by making generalizations about the influence of climate on economics in different regions.

INSTRUCTIONAL RESOURCES

Transparencies (From the Transparency Package)

T 13.4   Essential Teaching Skills

T 13.5   Characteristics of Effective Praise

T 13.6   Characteristics of Effective Questioning

Transparency Masters (From the Instructor's Manual)

TM 7.4 Questions That Promote Deep Processing of Information

TM 7.14 Principles of Instruction for Applying Information Processing in Classrooms

TM 8.4 Principles of Instruction for Applying Constructivism in Classrooms

Transparency Masters (In this Media Guide)

Questions for Discussion and Analysis

Rating Scale: Climate, Geography and Economics in Junior High Social Studies

Feedback for "Questions for Discussion and Analysis"

Questions for Discussion and Analysis: Climate, Geography and Economics in Junior High Social Studies

1. To what extent did Judy apply constructivist principles in her teaching?

2. How effectively did Judy use groupwork in her lesson?

3. How effectively did Judy promote higher-order thinking in her lesson? What could she have done to increase the emphasis on higher-order thinking.

4. How effective was Judy in promoting learning in her lesson?

Rating Scale for
Climate, Geography and Economics in
Junior High Social Studies

Rate the effectiveness of the teacher on each of the following dimensions using the following scale:

  5 = Excellent
  4 = Very good
  3 = Good
  2 = Fair
  1 = Poor
  0 = No evidence available

1. Applying constructivist principles in   0 1 2 3 4 5
   instruction

2. Incorporating groupwork in   0 1 2 3 4 5
   instruction

3. Promoting higher-order thinking   0 1 2 3 4 5

4. Overall lesson effectiveness   0 1 2 3 4 5

Feedback for "Questions for Discussion and Analysis" for
Climate, Geography and Economics in Junior High Social Studies

1. Constructivist approaches to instruction are based on the idea that learners "construct" their own understanding rather than having it delivered to them by teachers or written materials. Guided discovery approaches to instruction are consistent with constructivist views of learning. Judy's instruction incorporated elements of guided discovery. For example, students identified similarities and differences in the geography and economy of the four regions, and, with Judy's guidance they developed explanations for the differences. This approach is consistent with constructivism.

   Judy also encouraged active student "meaning-making" by having students gather their own information and by helping them interpret these data through her questioning. The fact that she designed her lesson to include Florida as one of the states ensured that her students would have a personal and concrete frame of reference for comparing the different states. She also used social interaction effectively in both large and small group instruction to encourage students to verbalize their own ideas and compare them to others'.

2. Judy's groupwork was quite effective. Effective groupwork has four characteristics: a) clear directions, b) a relatively short, specific time period, c) a required written product, and d) teacher monitoring. Her directions were clear, providing a clear content focus for their activities. In addition, she identified what the product should be--three written similarities and differences, and clearly specified the time limits for the task. Finally, as students worked in groups she circulated around the room, clarifying directions, answering questions and providing encouragement.

3. Higher-order thinking involves the use of cognitive strategies that help us efficiently and accurately process information. These include basic processes such as comparing and contrasting, identifying relevant and irrelevant information, inferring, and explaining. Students become proficient at these processes by using them in specific classroom learning activities and by being able to see how they apply across the curriculum.

   Judy promoted the development of thinking skills in her students by designing learning activities that directly integrated them into her teaching. Students were asked to find similarities and differences between states in terms of both geography and economics and then were asked to explain connections between these two concepts. Her effectiveness in teaching higher-order thinking was also promoted by small groupwork in which all students were provided opportunities to practice these skills and by social interaction that encouraged students to articulate their conclusions.

   The effectiveness of her instruction could have been improved by explicit attempts to make students aware of the thinking skills they were using. For example, when students concluded that climate influences the economy, Judy might have asked them to specifically identify data in the chart that supported that conclusion. In addition she might have called students' attention to the process itself, i.e., how we use inferences based on data to form conclusions. This makes thinking skills overt and visible, allowing students to understand the cognitive processes involved.

4. Overall, Judy's lesson was effective. Her goals were clear, the learning activity was aligned with the goals, she was well organized and used her time well, students were orderly yet involved, and the information was meaningful to them.

   The primary way the lesson could have been improved would be to increase the emphasis on higher-order thinking based on the information in the matrix. This could have been accomplished by asking more questions that called for explanations and hypotheses. For example Judy asked the following questions that called for explanations:
   - Why do they all have fishing?
   - Why do they all have forestry?
   - What does this tell us about their climate?

413

- Why do we have the citrus industry in California and Florida?

She could have asked many more questions of this type, and questions that called for hypothetical thinking, such as, "Suppose global warming becomes a reality. How might that affect the economy of each region?"

She might also have made the lesson more student centered by asking students to generate their own questions about the information in the chart. This would have taken little additional effort on her part, and with practice the students would become quite adept with the process.

BEFORE YOU BEGIN (Note: This 15 minute segment appears in written form at the beginning of Chapter 14.)

Lesson Summary

DeVonne Lampkin, a fifth grade teacher at Abbott Park Elementary in Jacksonville, Florida, is beginning a unit on fractions. To assess her students' understanding of the topic she administers a pretest. The pretest told her that her students basically understood the concept of fractions, could add them when the denominators were alike, but had difficulties when the denominators were different. So she designed her first lesson to focus on equivalent fractions.

To begin the lesson she passed out chocolate bars divided into 12 parts and, through questioning, helped students see that 1/4 = 3/12, 6/12 = ½, and 8/12 = 2/3. As the lesson continued she went to the board and showed how to do these problems with numbers.

To assess learning progress DeVonne assigned and graded homework. Her students' work told her that some were still having problems with equivalent fractions. So, she designed a second hands-on activity using cars and streets divided into different fractional parts to further illustrate equivalent fractions. A test after the lesson told her that the lesson was successful.

INSTRUCTIONAL RESOURCES

Transparencies (From the Transparency Package)

T 14.1   The Relationship Between Validity and Reliability

T 14.2   Teachers' Assessment Patterns

T 14.3   Characteristics of Teacher-made Tests

T 14.6   Effective Assessment Practices

Transparency Masters (From the Instructor's Manual)

TM 14.1 Traditional and Alternative Measurement Formats

Transparency Masters (In this Media Guide)

Questions for Discussion and Analysis

Rating Scale: Using Assessment to Improve Instruction

Feedback for "Questions for Discussion and Analysis"

Questions for Discussion and Analysis:
Using Assessment to Improve Instruction

1. Analyze DeVonne's actions using the concepts measurement and evaluation.

2. Evaluate the quality of the pretest that DeVonne gave.

3. Using the concepts of alignment and validity evaluate the quality of DeVonne's first lesson.

4. Evaluate the quality of the homework that DeVonne gave.

5. How effective were the two lessons from an instructional perspective?

Rating Scale for
Using Assessment to Improve Instruction

Rate the effectiveness of the teacher on each of the following dimensions using the following scale:

    5 = Excellent
    4 = Very good
    3 = Good
    2 = Fair
    1 = Poor
    0 = No evidence available

1. Quality of pretest   0 1 2 3 4 5

2. Overall quality of first lesson   0 1 2 3 4 5

3. Quality of homework   0 1 2 3 4 5

4. Overall quality of second lesson   0 1 2 3 4 5

Feedback for "Questions for Discussion and Analysis" for
Using Assessment to Improve Instruction

1. DeVonne used several measurements to gather information about her students. The pretest gathered information about what they knew prior to the lessons. Homework provided information about what they took from the first lesson, and her test gathered information about cumulative learning progress after the two lessons. On the basis of this information she made a number of evaluations, or decisions, about learning progress.

2. From the items that we saw we can infer that the pretest was valid because it allowed her to make accurate decisions about her students' instructional needs. We don't have sufficient information to comment on reliability.

3. Two of DeVonne's important sub-goals were for her students to understand equivalent fractions and be able to add fractions with unlike denominators. The pretest provided her with valid information about her students' capabilities in regards to these two goals, which allowed her to construct a lesson that was aligned with these goals.

4. Again, from the items we saw, we can infer that the homework was valid because it allowed her to make decisions about her two goals: understanding equivalent fractions and adding fractions with unlike denominators. On the basis of the information provided by thee homework she designed a second lesson targeting these goals. We don't have sufficient information to comment on reliability.

5. The lessons were effective because both provided hands-on experiences with equivalent fractions. They could have been improved by her making a closer connection between the manipulatives and number symbols. For example, when they were finding that 4/8 = ½ with both the candy and cars she could have written this on the board and shown how equivalent fractions are numerically derived.

CONCEPTS IN CLASSROOMS
(CONTENT OVERVIEW)

TAPE ONE

Segment	Counter Reading

1. Examining Cognitive Development: Analyzing Learner Differences   00:00:00
   - Conservation tasks
   - Properties of air in first grade
   - Balance beams in 4th grade

2. Constructing Understanding: Instructional Applications   00:07:52
   - Balance beams in 4th grade
   - Interview with a group of 4 students

3. Promoting Encoding: Putting Students in Active Roles   00:17:11
   - Hands-activity with 1st graders on properties of air
   - Whole-group and hands-on activities on graphing in 2nd grade
   - Hands-on activity on problem-solving in 5th grade
   - Whole-group activity on geography and economy in 9th grade

4. Organizing Information: Applying Dual-Coding Theory   00:25:15
   - Outline–a history teacher introducing the Vietnam War
   - Matrix–a geography teacher examining the relationships between geography and economy
   - Drawing–life science examining different types of worms
   - Schematic–fifth grade teacher introducing problem solving

5. Improving Transfer: Applications in Classrooms   00:31:40
   - Fifth grade–transfer of problem solving abilities
   - Seventh grade–transfer of ability to control variables

Tape Two

6. Improving Learner Motivation: Introductory Focus   00:45:01
   - First grade–Using baking soda and vinegar to introduce using our senses
   - Seventh grade–Using a 20-meter length of tape measure to introduce parasites
   - Chemistry–Using a demonstration illustrating heat and expansion to introduce Charles's Law

7. Personalizing Content: Increasing Learner Motivation   00:53:18
   - Second grade–Determining the class's favorite jelly bean flavor to introduce graphing
   - Seventh grade–Using a student from the class to illustrate the concept of symmetry
   - Twelfth grade–Putting themselves in the characters of the novel *The Scarlet Letter*.

8. Improving Instruction: Essential Teaching Skills   01:03:44
   7th grade teacher teaches Bernoulli's Principle and attempts to demonstrate:

- Positive attitudes
- Effective organization
- Clear communication
- Lesson focus
- Informative feedback
- Skilled questioning
- Review and closure

9. Involving Students: Discovery Learning   01:17:42
   A 4th grade teacher guides a class to discover the characteristics of Haiku poetry

10. Assessing Background Knowledge: Questioning Strategies   01:27:55
    - A kindergarten teacher determines how much the children know about seeds and soil.
    - A first grade teacher assesses children's understanding of what scientists do

BEFORE YOU BEGIN

This 8-minute segment focuses on cognitive development from three perspectives. In the first segment traditional conservation tasks are used to illustrate Piagetian stages. In the next two segments the effects of students centering on perceptually prominent aspects of instruction are illustrated in two classroom vignettes.

This segment is designed to be used with Chapter 2, with particular emphasis on Piaget's Theory of Cognitive Development.

INSTRUCTIONAL RESOURCES

Transparencies (From the Transparency Package)

T 2.1 Factors Influencing Human Intellectual Development

T 2.2 Principles of Development and Examples

T 2.3 Maintaining Equilibrium Through the Process of Adaptation

Transparency Masters (From the Instructor's Manual)

TM2.1 The Drive For Equilibrium

TM2.3 Measuring Thinking

Transparency Masters (In this Media Guide)

Questions for Discussion and Analysis

Feedback for "Questions for Discussion and Analysis"

Questions for Discussion and Analysis:
Segment #1: Examining Cognitive Development:
Analyzing Learner Differences

1. What do students' responses in the interview tell us about the Piagetian stages of development they are in?

2. How effective was Jenny's lesson on air from a developmental perspective? Specifically, why was it important to use the: a) water, b) clear glass, c) paper towels, and d) learning centers?

3. How effectively did Jenny incorporate constructivist learning principles in her lesson on air? What could she have done to make the lesson more constructivist in its orientation? What advantages and disadvantages exist in making it more constructivist?

4. In the balance beam lesson, when some of the students in the small group didn't understand the weight x distance principles, Jenny didn't directly intervene, instead encouraging group members to work out differences. What are some advantages and disadvantages of this approach?

**Feedback for "Questions for Discussion and Analysis" for
Segment #1: Examining Cognitive Development: Analyzing Learner Differences**

1. Learners who center on salient physical aspects of a task rather than logical ones are at Piaget's Preoperational stage. Students at higher levels, such as Concrete or Formal Operational can mentally reverse operations and think logically about operations.

2. Jenny's students were first graders, and based on their responses, they were at Piaget's Preoperational Stage of Development. Learners at this stage are dominated by their perceptions; what they perceive is indeed real for them. Concrete experiences are essential if learning is to be meaningful for children at this stage of development.

   Because it is invisible, the physical reality of air is a difficult concept for first graders. The water was important in the lesson because it allowed students to see air bubbles, which are concrete. The transparent glass allowed students to see the air/water line inside it. The paper towel also provided concrete evidence that something (air) was keeping the water out, since the towel remained dry. From a developmental perspective the learning center activities were a critical component of the lesson. They allowed students to experiment with the ideas in a personal hands-on way.

3. Constructivist approaches to instruction are based on the idea that learners "construct" their own understanding rather than having it delivered to them by teachers or written materials. Teachers facilitate the knowledge construction process by embedding new content in meaningful learning tasks and by encouraging individual students to share their evolving thoughts with each other.

   Jenny was careful in her lesson not to impose her beliefs on her students. She provided them with concrete experiences that allowed them to construct their own meaning from the demonstration. Using water, a transparent glass, and paper towels, together with asking students to predict what would happen when she placed the glass underwater, provided her students with an authentic learning task that promoted interaction among students.

   One alternative to Jenny's introducing the lesson with a teacher-centered demonstration would be to begin the lesson with student exploration at the learning centers. The advantage of this approach is that it would allow each student to individually experiment with the water and the glasses and paper towels. Disadvantages are organization and the focus of the lesson; organizing individual student exploration, particularly with first graders, can be demanding.

4. This question cuts to the very center of one of the constructivist dilemmas--how much should teachers intervene to guide learning and how much should students be allowed to wander around on their own? Two factors influenced the effectiveness of Jenny's decision to ask questions and not intervene directly. One was the presence of the balance beam which could provide students with feedback about the accuracy of their solutions. The second factor was the presence of several students in the group who understood the principle involved and could share their knowledge with the others. In the absence of these two factors greater teacher intervention would have been necessary.

BEFORE YOU BEGIN

This 9-minute segment explores constructivism through a short instructional segment followed by interviews with four students. The segment illustrates how individual differences and background knowledge can influence the process of knowledge construction.

This segment is designed to be used with Chapter 2 and 7, with particular emphasis on constructivism.

INSTRUCTIONAL RESOURCES

Transparencies (From the Transparency Package)

T 2.8 The Zone of Proximal Development

T 8.1 Suzanne's Thinking about Balance Beams

T 8.3 Characteristics of Constructivism

T 8.4 Suggestions for Classroom Practice

Transparency Masters (In this Media Guide)

Questions for Discussion and Analysis

Transparency Masters (From the Instructor's Manual)

TM 8.3 Constructing Understanding of Balance Beams

TM 8.4 Principles of Instruction for Applying Constructivism in Classrooms

Feedback for "Questions for Discussion and Analysis"

Questions for Discussion and Analysis
Segment #2: Constructing Understanding: Instructional Applications:

1. How effectively did Jenny incorporate the following characteristics of constructivism in her lesson?
    a. Learners constructing their own understanding
    b. New learning depending on current understanding
    c. Learning facilitated by social interaction
    d. Authentic learning tasks

2. During the lesson describe the different students in terms of the zone of proximal development.

3. Using constructivism, explain Tad's and Suzanne's progress during the interview.

Feedback for "Questions for Discussion and Analysis" for
Segment #2: Constructing Understanding: Instructional Applications

1a. Learners Constructing their own Understanding
     From the dialogue in the lesson it was apparent that several members of the group were actively struggling with the content. In terms of the zone of proximal development, Molly and Drexel were beyond it, understanding the principle involved. Suzanne's struggle with the content and her wavering suggested that she was in the zone. Tad's reticence to participate makes it difficult to tell exactly where he was.

1b. New Learning Depending on Current Understanding
     It was obvious from the lesson that the four students in the focal group started from different places. What is unclear is what this starting point was. Had the problems been simpler (e.g. using just one weight on one side) would Suzanne and Tad been able to participate? This is valuable information that would have allowed Jenny to design her instruction more effectively.

1c. Learning Facilitated by Social Interaction
     Social interaction was a major influence in the lesson. Though more evident in the student interviews which occurred after the lesson, the exchange of ideas and perspectives had a major influence on Suzanne and Tad's thinking.

1d. Authentic Learning Tasks
     Having access to the balance beam and being able to ultimately test their solutions on the beam was a major motivational part of the lesson. The power of concrete manipulatives was evident when the group arrived at a (correct) solution but when they tried it out on the beam and it didn't work because the beam malfunctioned. Several of the students were willing to discard the abstract, logical solution they had developed in favor of the concrete, visible balance beam.

2.   Molly and Drexel understood the principle and were beyond the zone of proximal development. Tad and Suzanne were within it as evidenced by their progress during the interview.

3.   During the lesson and interview Tad and Suzanne were attempting to construct their own understanding of how the balance beam worked based on their current understanding. The balance beam provided an authentic task, and social interaction, during both the lesson and interview, provided instructional scaffolding.

BEFORE YOU BEGIN

This 8-minute segment illustrates different ways that instructors can encourage active learning through whole group and individual hands-on instructional activities.

This segment is designed to be used with Chapter 7, with particular emphasis on meaningful encoding and activity.

INSTRUCTIONAL RESOURCES

Transparencies (From the Transparency Package)

T 7.2 An Information Processing Model

T 7.8 Making Information Meaningful

Transparency Masters (From the Instructor's Manual)

TM 7.3 Characteristics of the Memory Stores

TM 7.4 Questions that Promote Deep Processing of Information

TM 7.5 Background Knowledge and Encoding

TM 7.6 Elaborating on Past Experiences

TM 8.4 Principles of Instruction for Applying Constructivism in Classrooms

Transparency Masters (In this Media Guide)

Questions for Discussion and Analysis

Feedback for "Questions for Discussion and Analysis"

Questions for Discussion and Analysis:
Segment #3: Promoting Encoding:
Putting Students in Active Roles

Analyze the four lessons in terms of constructivism.

A. Properties of Air

B. Graphing in Second Grade

C. Problem Solving in Fifth Grade

D. Social Studies in Ninth Grade

Feedback for "Questions for Discussion and Analysis" for
Segment #3: Promoting Encoding: Putting Students in Active Roles

A. Properties of Air

Jenny was careful in her lesson not to impose her beliefs on her students. She provided them with concrete experiences that allowed them to construct their own meaning from the demonstration. Using water, a transparent glass, and paper towels, together with asking students to predict what would happen when she placed the glass underwater, provided her students with an authentic learning task that promoted interaction among students.

One alternative to Jenny's introducing the lesson with a teacher-centered demonstration would be to begin the lesson with student exploration at the learning centers. The advantage of this approach is that it would allow each student to individually experiment with the water and the glasses and paper towels. Disadvantages are organization and the focus of the lesson; organizing individual student exploration, particularly with first graders, can be demanding.

Social interaction encourages students to put their own ideas into words and allows them to compare their ideas with others. Jenny encouraged this by guiding students with her questioning as they constructed their understanding. Her questions encouraged students to think about the content, put their ideas into words, and compare their ideas with others. Jenny was careful not to offer too many explanations of her own or impose her ideas onto the class. The overall effect of this questioning was to communicate to students that their ideas were valued and important and that it was their responsibility to make sense of what they were observing.

B. Graphing in Second Grade

Students were actively involved throughout the lesson. All students tasted the jelly beans, voted for their favorite flavors, and indicated their preferences on the graph. Many of the students were involved in the discussion of the problem and the strategy for solving it, and all students were involved in the work at the centers.

The lesson was effective from both a Piagetian and a Vygotskyan perspective. From a Piagetian point of view, Suzanne provided a concrete problem that was meaningful to students. In solving the problem each student was personally involved in tasting, voting, and representing the information. As students constructed the graph, they could see in a concrete way how their vote influenced the shape of the graph and the final results.

From a Vygotskyan perspective, the lesson was effective in encouraging student dialogue about their problem solving strategies, and Suzanne provided the guidance of a "more knowledgeable other" in the entire process. Most students appeared to be in the zone of proximal development, and Suzanne helped them make progress through the zone.

An interesting question for discussion might be whether or not Suzanne was too teacher-centered and directive. The optimal amount of teacher direction in teaching problem solving is open to debate.

C. Problem Solving in Fifth Grade

The lesson was effective from these two constructivist perspectives. By framing the lesson in terms of carpeting their own room, students were provided with an authentic learning task that was meaningful to them. By actually allowing them to measure the room and work in groups on the measurements in the diagram the students were able to wrestle with constructing their own understanding.

429

Social interaction was also a strength in the lesson. Students worked in small groups to: 1) discuss the problem, 2) measure the room, 3) select and implement a strategy, and 4) evaluate the strategy they used and the answer they got. In addition, Laura encouraged students to reflect on the effectiveness of the interaction in their groups.

D. Social Studies in Ninth Grade

Guided discovery approaches to instruction are consistent with constructivist views of learning. Judy's instruction incorporated elements of guided discovery. For example, students identified similarities and differences in the geography and economy of the four regions, and, with Judy's guidance they developed explanations for the differences. This approach is consistent with constructivism.

Judy also encouraged active student "meaning-making" by having students gather their own information and by helping them interpret these data through her questioning. The fact that she designed her lesson to include Florida as one of the states ensured that her students would have a personal and concrete frame of reference for comparing the different states. She also used social interaction effectively in both large and small group instruction to encourage students to verbalize their own ideas and compare them to others'.

BEFORE YOU BEGIN

This 6-minutes segment explores applications of dual coding theory to instructional practice. Outlines, matrices, drawings, and schematics are used to help learners organize information in meaningful ways.

This segment is designed to be used with Chapter 7, with particular emphasis on meaningful encoding, organization, and dual coding theory.

INSTRUCTIONAL RESOURCES

Transparencies (From the Transparency Package)

T 7.2 An Information Processing Model

T 7.8 Making Information Meaningful

Transparency Masters (From the Instructor's Manual)

TM7.3 Characteristics of the Memory Stores

TM7.4 Questions that Promote Deep Processing of Information

Transparency Masters (In this Media Guide)

Questions for Discussion and Analysis

Feedback for "Questions for Discussion and Analysis"

Questions for Discussion and Analysis:
Segment #4: Organizing Information:
Applying Dual-Coding Theory

1. Three of the lessons were focused on a particular type of content. What was this content and how did it differ from the fourth lesson?

2. Why were the lessons effective in terms of dual coding theory?

3. What else did all four teachers do to ensure meaningful encoding of information?

Feedback for "Questions for Discussion and Analysis" for
Segment #4 Organizing Information: Applying Dual Coding Theory

1. All the lessons except the problem solving one focused on organized bodies of knowledge.

2. The lessons were effective in terms of dual coding theory because they provided a graphic way of organizing information. This allows students to encode and store this information in two forms – verbal and pictorial or graphic. This also allows students to use imagery to remember and retrieve the information.

3. All four teachers used questioning to encourage students to form logical links between information.

BEFORE YOU BEGIN

This 13-minute segment uses two instructional episodes and subsequent student interviews to explore the process of transfer.

This segment is designed to be used with Chapter 9, with particular emphasis on transfer.

INSTRUCTIONAL RESOURCES

Transparencies (From the Transparency Package)

T 9..9   Factors Affecting the Transfer of Learning

Transparency Masters (In this Media Guide)

Questions for Discussion and Analysis

Feedback for "Questions for Discussion and Analysis"

Questions for Discussion and Analysis:
Segment #5: Improving Transfer:
Applications in Classrooms

1. What evidence was there that transfer occurred between the carpeting and plywood problems? Was this general or specific transfer: What did the interviewer do to promote transfer?

2. What did the circle problem tell about the students' understanding of area? Was this an example of general of specific transfer?

3. What elements of transfer were illustrated in the student interview on controlling variables?

4. In Chapter 7, we described generative knowledge as knowledge that can be used to interpret new situations and inert knowledge as knowledge that exists in isolated pieces. How could these concepts be used to explain the students' ability to control variables before and after the lesson?

**Feedback for "Questions for Discussion and Analysis" for
Segment #5 Improving Transfer: Applications in Classrooms**

1. The students, with instructional scaffolding from the interviewer, were able to see similarities between the carpeting triangle and the plywood triangle. This was an instance of specific transfer which probably occurred due to similarities between the two learning situations. Note that even though the two learning situations were only separated by several minutes and both involved the area of triangles, the students still needed help. Transfer is not easy.

2. Students' responses to the circle problem suggested that their understanding of area was developing. While they didn't know the formula, with the squared paper as a scaffold, they were able to visualize the circle as an area problem. While this was still specific transfer, it required more of a transfer leap than the triangle.

3. This is a complex question. One interpretation of students' ability to successfully design the pendulum problem was that this was just retention and did not involve transfer. However, recall that in the lesson the focal group never successfully designed this experiment and it wasn't until the end of the lesson that Scott explained the logic behind it. Because of this we consider their design of the pendulum experiment in the interview to be an instance of specific transfer. Their ability to design the dog food experiment was an example of more general transfer.

4. Before the lesson the concept of controlled variables was inert; students weren't able to relate it to the problem at hand. After the lesson during the interview this knowledge was generative, in that students were able to use it to think about and design new experiments.

BEFORE YOU BEGIN

This 8-minute segment illustrates how different forms of introductory focus can be used to draw learners into lessons and increase motivation.

This segment is designed to be used with Chapter 7, with particular emphasis on attention as well as Chapter 11 and introductory focus.

INSTRUCTIONAL RESOURCES

Transparencies (From the Transparency Package)

T 7.6   Strategies for Attracting Attention

T 11.2   A Model for Promoting Student Motivation

Transparency Masters (In this Media Guide)

Questions for Discussion and Analysis

Feedback for "Questions for Discussion and Analysis"

Questions for Discussion and Analysis:
Segment #6 Improving Learner Motivation: Introductory Focus

1. What is introductory focus and why is it important?

2. How were the different forms of introductory focus similar and different?

3. How effective were the different forms of introductory focus from a learning perspective? From a motivational perspective?

**Feedback for "Questions for Discussion and Analysis" for
Segment #6 Improving Learner Motivation: Introductory Focus**

1. Introductory focus attracts student attention and provides a conceptual framework for the lesson. It is important because attention is the beginning point of information processing.

2. Each of the examples of introductory focus were similar in that they used a concrete, sensory event to focus students' attention. They differed in the way they did this. The science lesson on senses used surprise, an effective motivational technique. The seventh grade science lesson used personalization and active involvement. The chemistry lesson used a sensory focus to help students understand the principle.

3. All were effective from a learning perspective because they concretely illustrated the central idea of the lesson. All were effective from a motivational perspective because they drew students into the lesson and provided sensory focus during the lesson that helped students see the relationship of abstract ideas to the real world.

Concepts In Classrooms:
Tape Two
Segment #7: Personalizing Content:
Increasing Learner Motivation (Tape Two, 53:18 - 1:03:44)

BEFORE YOU BEGIN

This 8-minute segment examines different ways that personalization can be used to motivate learners and involve them in lessons.

This segment is designed to be used with Chapters 10 and 11, with particular emphasis on introductory focus, personalization, and involvement.

INSTRUCTIONAL RESOURCES

Transparencies (From the Transparency Package)

T 11.1 Comparisons of Learning-Focused and Performance-Focused Classrooms

T 11.2 A Model for Promoting Student Motivation

Questions for Discussion and Analysis

Questions for Discussion and Analysis:
Segment #7: Personalizing Content:
Increasing Learner Motivation

1. What is personalization and why is it an effective motivational strategy?

2. How did each of the teachers integrate personalization into their lessons?

3. What other motivational elements were important in these lesson?

Feedback for "Questions for Discussion and Analysis" for
Segment #7: Personalizing Content: Increasing Learner Motivation

1. Personalization attempts to make topics meaningful by using intellectually or emotionally relevant examples. It is an effective motivational strategy because it: 1) encourages students to personally relate to content, 2) increases meaningfulness by providing a concrete frame of reference for the students and, 3) actively involves students in the lesson.

2. Sue Brush in the math lesson used planning for a class party as the motivational framework for her lesson. The science teacher used one student at the front of the room to personalize the concept of symmetry. Sue Southam, the English teacher, had students role play characters in *The Scarlet Letter.*

3. In each of the lessons the teachers displayed personal motivating characteristics such as enthusiasm, caring, and positive expectations. In addition, positive climate variables like order and safety, success, task comprehension, and challenge existed. In addition, all lessons also included introductory focus, involvement, and feedback.

Concepts in Classrooms:
Tape Two
Segment#8: Improving Instruction:
Essential Teaching Skills (Tape Two, 1:03:44 - 1:17:42)

BEFORE YOU BEGIN

This 14-minute segment analyzes how essential teaching skills, like lesson focus and feedback, are integrated into a 7th grade science lesson.

This segment is designed to be used with Chapter 13, Creating Productive Learning Environments: Principles of Instruction, with particular emphasis on essential teaching skills.

INSTRUCTIONAL RESOURCES

Transparencies (From the Transparency Package)

T 13.4 Essential Teaching Skills

T 13.5 Characteristics of Effective Praise

T 13.6 Characteristics of Effective Questioning

Transparency Masters (From the Instructor's Manual)

TM 7.4 Questions That Promote Deep Processing of Information

TM 7.14 Principles of Instruction for Applying Information Processing in Classrooms

TM 8.4 Principles of Instruction for Applying Constructivism in Classrooms

Transparency Masters (In this Media Guide)

Questions for Discussion and Analysis

Feedback for "Questions for Discussion and Analysis"

Questions for Discussion and Analysis:
Segment #8: Improving Instruction:
Essential Teaching Skills

1. What are essential teaching skills and why are they important to teachers?

2. Which of these essential teaching skills were clearly illustrated in this lesson?

3. How effective was the lesson from a motivational perspective?

Feedback for "Questions for Discussion and Analysis" for
Segment #8 Improving Instruction: Essential Teaching Skills

1. Essential skills are the abilities that all teachers should have to promote learning. They are important to teachers because they form a basic repertoire of strategies that are foundational to other teaching strategies.

2. The essential teaching skills that were most prominent in the lesson were:

   • Positive Attitudes: Scott had positive expectations for his students and treated them with respect.
   • Effective Organization: Scott's lesson was well organized. He started on time, had materials prepared in advance, and used classroom routines effectively.
   • Clear Communication: Scott's communication used precise terminology (which he illustrated with examples), connected discourse, transition signals, and emphasis.
   • Focus: The lesson was clearly focused on Bernoulli's Principle.
   • Feedback: Through his questioning, Scott provided informative feedback to the class.
   • Questioning: In his questioning, Scott strived for equitable distribution, used prompting, and practiced wait time.
   • Review and Closure: At the beginning of the lesson Scott reviewed the concept of force and at the end he used the diagrams on the board to summarize the various activities.

3. The lesson was effective from several perspectives. Scott used introductory focus to attract students' attention. He also actively involved students through hands-on activities and questioning. There were also elements of challenge and surprise.

Concepts in Classrooms:
Tape Two
Segment #9: Involving Students:
Discovery Learning (Tape Two, 1:17:42 - 1:27:55)

BEFORE YOU BEGIN

This 10-minute segment describes a 4th grade language arts lesson focusing on Haiku poetry. Through guided discovery the teacher helps students identify essential characteristics of Haiku poetry. This tape is designed to be used with Chapter 8, Constructing Understanding, with the topic, Guided Discovery.

INSTRUCTIONAL RESOURCES

Transparencies (From the Transparency Package)

T 13.4 Essential Teaching Skills

T 13.5 Characteristics of Effective Praise

T 13.6 Characteristics of Effective Questioning

Transparency Masters (From the Instructor's Manual)

TM 8.4 Principles of Instruction for Applying Constructivism in Classrooms

TM 9.3 Principles of Instruction for Promoting Concept Learning

Transparency Masters (In this Media Guide)

Questions for Discussion and Analysis

Feedback for "Questions for Discussion and Analysis"

Questions for Discussion and Analysis:
Segment #9 Involving Students:
Discovery Learning

1. What is discovery learning and how does it relate to constructivism?

2. What are similarities and differences between unstructured and guided discovery?

3. Which type of discovery lesson was this – unstructured or guided – and how effective was the lesson?

**Feedback for "Questions for Discussion and Analysis" for
Segment #9: Involving Students: Discovery Learning**

1. Discovery learning is an instructional strategy that provides information they can use to construct understanding. It is a form of constructivist learning because the teacher assist students in constructing meaning from the data provided.

2. Both unstructured and guided discovery place students at the center of learning, asking or requiring them to make sense of information. In unstructured discovery learners are left to their own resources to form conclusions; in guided discovery the teacher aids the knowledge construction process by providing data and through interactive questioning.

3. This lesson was an example of guided discovery because the teacher played a central role in arranging the data (the Haiku poems) and using questioning to guide students to the essential characteristics of these poems. The lesson was effective from several perspectives: focus, organization, social interaction, clear communication, and feedback. Placing students in an active role in writing their own Haiku poems was one of the strengths of the lesson.

BEFORE YOU BEGIN

This 12-minute segment illustrates how interactive questioning strategies in both a kindergarten and first grade classroom can be used to enhance learning and motivation.

This segment is designed to be used with Chapter 7, Cognitive Views of Learning, with particular emphasis on meaningful encoding as well as Chapter 13, Creating Productive Learning Environments: Instructional Strategies, with particular emphasis on questioning.

INSTRUCTIONAL RESOURCES

Transparencies (From the Transparency Package)

T 7.2 An Information Processing Model

T 13.4 Essential Teaching Skills

T 13.5 Characteristics of Effective Praise

T 13.6 Characteristics of Effective Questioning

Transparency Masters (From the Instructor's Manual)

TM 7.4 Questions That Promote Deep Processing of Information

TM 7.5 Background Knowledge and Encoding

Transparency Masters (In this Media Guide)

Questions for Discussion and Analysis

Feedback for "Questions for Discussion and Analysis"

Questions for Discussion and Analysis:
Segment #10: Assessing Background Knowledge: Questioning Strategies

1. What is background knowledge and why is it important for learning?

2. What are some different ways that teachers can assess learners' background knowledge?

3. How effective were the teachers in their questioning strategies?

Feedback for "Questions for Discussion and Analysis" for
Segment #10 Assessing Background Knowledge:
Questioning Strategies

1. Background knowledge is lesson-specific information stored in students' long term memory. Background knowledge influences basic processes like attention, perception, encoding, and perception. It is essential to learning because it helps link new information to existing learner schemas.

2. Teachers can pre-test, give a seatwork assignment, discuss topics informally with students, or use systematic questioning to assess and activate student background knowledge.

3. The teachers displayed a number of characteristics of effective questioning. They attempted equitable distribution and often elaborated on students' responses. Classroom climate was also positive, being both warm and orderly. The teacher might have increased their wait time and also might have been more systematic in involving all students.

Insights Into Learning: Constructing Understanding
Instructional Applications
Using Balance Beams in Fourth Grade

BEFORE YOU BEGIN
(Note: This lesson appears in written form at the beginning of Chapter 8.)

This 60-minute tape contains three segments:
- A 23-minute lesson focusing on a fourth grade classroom learning how to mathematically balance a balance beam (0 - 23:00)
- A 17-minute interview with four students after the lesson (23:00 - 40:00)
- An 18-minute interview with the teacher about the lesson (40:00 - 57:40)

Lesson Summary (0 - 23:00)

Jenny Newhall, a fourth grade teacher, wants her students to know how to solve problems involving a balance beam and weights. Jenny starts by dividing students into groups and giving each group of students a balance beam and weights. She begins the lesson by directing each group to put 4 weights 8 places or notches from the center on the right hand side and 1 weight 2 places from the center on the left side. She then asks each student in the different groups to come up with as many different ways to balance the beam without moving the original weights. After students work for awhile on their individual solutions they then share them with other members of their group and test the different solutions out on the balance beam.

Different students in the focal group offer different solutions.
- One suggests adding three to the 10 place and explains it in this way ($3 \times 10 + 2 \times 1 = 8 \times 4$).
- A second suggests adding 5 to the 6 place and explains it in this way ($6 \times 5 + 2 \times 1 = 8 \times 4$).
- A third student suggests adding a 3 to the 10 place and justifies by noting there will then be 4 on each side. This same student also suggests adding 2 weights to the 10 and 1 on the 6.

When Jenny visits this group she encourages students to share their thinking. Two of the students understand the logic behind balancing the beam (i.e. number x distance) while two others believe that the number of weights alone (without consideration of their distance from the center) determine whether the beam will balance.

The whole class then discusses the solutions the different groups produced. Jenny encourages students to use number sentences like, $8 \times 4 = 32 = (10 \times 3) + 2 = 32$ to explain their answers.

Jenny then asks the groups to generate different solutions to balancing a beam that has one weight 2 places from the center on the left and three weights five from the center and 1 weight 6 from the center on the right. As students share their answers it is evident that many still don't understand the length x weight principal needed to solve the problem.

Student Interview Summary (23:00 - 40:00)

This interview follows the focal students introduced in the lesson and investigates what kinds of understandings they took away from the lesson. The interview, which occurred immediately after the lesson, begins with the interviewer asking individual students to devise as many solutions to balancing a beam that has 4 weights 3 spaces away from the center. Students are asked to both draw and explain their solutions. Despite participating in the lesson some students want to just count the number of weights on each side, ignoring their distance from the center.

Initially Tad and Suzanne have a rudimentary understanding that weights placed further from the center exert more force but are unable to verbalize this in a formula. The interviewer then asks the group to balance this problem:

$$3 \times 3 + 2 \times 5 = 1 \times 2 + 2 \times 1 + ?$$

Molly and Drexel are able to verbalize a solution but Tad and Suzanne aren't sure.

Returning to the original problem ($4 \times 3 = ?$), the interviewer asks for a solution and Molly proposes $4 \times 3 = 8 \times 1 + 4 \times 1$. Tad, when asked to explain this solution, is able to describe the logic behind it. Drexel offers this solution: $4 \times 3 = 1 \times 2 + 1 \times 10$. Suzanne is able to explain it, using both number and placement.

Teacher Interview Summary (40:00 - 57:40)

The interview begins with Jenny describing problem solving as a primary goal for the lesson. In commenting on the lesson Jenny was surprised at the diversity of her students in terms of their knowledge of balance beams and their ability to engage in group problem solving. After viewing a segment of the interview showing Suzanne focusing on number and ignoring length, the interview focuses on Suzanne and Tad's inability to use the principle. Jenny offers that part of the problem may be automaticity and suggests additional, simpler experiences with the balance beam. The interview then focuses on the role of social interaction in learning. Jenny and the interviewer explore different hypotheses about why Tad and Suzanne were able to understand the principle during the interview, but not the lesson. The interview concludes with Jenny describing various alternate assessment procedures.

INSTRUCTIONAL RESOURCES

Transparencies (from the Transparency Package)

T2.8   The Zone of Proximal Development

T8.3 Characteristics of Constructivism

T9.4   A General Problem-Solving Model

Transparency Masters (from the Instructor's Manual)

TM 2.6 A Comparison of Piaget's and Vygotsky's Views of Knowledge Construction

TM 8.3 Constructing Understanding of Balance Beams

TM 8.4 Principles of Instruction for Applying Constructivism in Classrooms

Transparency Masters (In this Media Guide)

Questions for Discussion and Analysis (Lesson)

Questions for Discussion and Analysis (Student Interview)

Rating Scale: Using a Balance Beam in Fourth Grade

Feedback for "Questions for Discussion and Analysis"

Questions for Discussion and Analysis: Using Balance Beams in Fourth Grade

From the Lesson

1. How effectively did Jenny incorporate the following characteristics of constructivism in her lesson?
   a.   Learners constructing their own understanding
   b.   New learning depending on current understanding
   c.   Learning facilitated by social interaction
   d.   Authentic learning tasks

2. When some of the students in the small group didn't understand the weight x distance principle, Jenny didn't directly intervene, instead encouraging group members to work out differences. What are the advantages and disadvantages of this approach?

3. How effective was the lesson in using cooperative learning to facilitate learning?

4. From an overall perspective how effective was the instruction in this lesson?

Questions for Discussion and Analysis:
Using Balance Beams in Fourth Grade:
The Student Interview

1. Which students understood the balance beam principle at the beginning of the interview? The end? How do you know?

2. During the lesson describe the different students in terms of the zone of proximal development.

3. How might we explain Suzanne's initial solution using the Piagetian concept of centering?

4. Explain Tad's and Suzanne's progress during the interview using social cognitive theory.

5. Using constructivism, explain Tad's and Suzanne's progress during the interview.

Rating Scale for
Using Balance Beams in Fourth Grade

Rate the effectiveness of the lesson on each of the following dimensions using the following scale:

    5 = Excellent
    4 = Very good
    3 = Good
    2 = Fair
    1 = Poor
    0 = No evidence available

1. Constructivism

    a. Learners constructing their own understanding   0 1 2 3 4 5

    b. New learning depending on current understanding   0 1 2 3 4 5

    c. Learning facilitated by social interaction   0 1 2 3 4 5

    d. Authentic learning tasks   0 1 2 3 4 5

2. Overall lesson effectiveness   0 1 2 3 4 5

**Feedback for "Questions for Discussion and Analysis" for
Using Balance Beams in Fourth Grade**

From the Lesson

1a. Learners Constructing their own Understanding

From the dialogue in the lesson it was apparent that several members of the group were actively struggling with the content. In terms of the zone of proximal development, Molly and Drexel were beyond it, understanding the principle involved. Suzanne's struggle with the content and her wavering suggested that she was in the zone. Tad's reticence to participate makes it difficult to tell exactly where he was.

1b. New Learning Depending on Current Understanding

It was obvious from the lesson that the four students in the focal group started from different places. What is unclear is what this starting point was. Had the problems been simpler (e.g. using just one weight on one side) would Suzanne and Tad been able to participate? This is valuable information that would have allowed Jenny to design her instruction more effectively.

1c. Learning Facilitated by Social Interaction

Social interaction was a major influence in the lesson. Though more evident in the student interviews which occurred after the lesson, the exchange of ideas and perspectives had a major influence on Suzanne and Tad's thinking.

1d. Authentic Learning Tasks

Having access to the balance beam and being able to ultimately test their solutions on the beam was a major motivational part of the lesson. The power of concrete manipulatives was evident when the group arrived at a (correct) solution but when they tried it out on the beam and it didn't work because the beam malfunctioned. Several of the students were willing to discard the abstract, logical solution they had developed in favor of the concrete, visible balance beam.

2. This question cuts to the very center of one of the constructivist dilemmas--how much should teachers intervene to guide learning and how much should students be allowed to wander around on their own? Two factors influenced the effectiveness of Jenny's decision to ask questions and not intervene directly. One was the presence of the balance beam which could provide students with feedback about the accuracy of their solutions. The second factor was the presence of several students in the group who understood the principle involved and could share their knowledge with the others. In the absence of these two factors greater teacher intervention would have been necessary.

3. There was student diversity in the group, which facilitated learning. In addition, students were given a clear and specific learning task, a specified amount of time to complete it , and were required to produce a product.

4. While generally effective, the lesson could have been improved in several ways. The lesson might have incorporated more opportunities for students to experiment with the balance beam with simpler problems. This would have provided an experiential base for students and allowed Jenny to gain insights into the background knowledge students brought to the task. In addition, the initial tasks given to students might have been simplified to provide positive learning experiences for students who were experiencing difficulties. Finally, some type of structured summary at the end of the lesson would have provided closure to the lesson and helped students who were still floundering resolve some of their doubts and confusion.

From the Interview

1. Molly and Drexel understood the weight and length principle and were able to verbalize it in explaining their solutions. Suzanne had the mistaken idea that only number counted. Tad was not very confident in explaining his understanding.

2. Molly and Drexel understood the principle and were beyond the zone of proximal development. Tad and Suzanne were within it as evidenced by their progress during the interview.

3. Suzanne was centering on the number of weights on each side while disregarding their distance. This is understandable as number is more salient than distance.

4. Social cognitive theory focuses on the effects of observation on learning. Tad and Suzanne were able to hear and observe Molly and Drexel's answers and able to reproduce similar ones in subsequent problems.

5. During the lesson and interview Tad and Suzanne were attempting to construct their own understanding of how the balance beam worked based on their current understanding. The balance beam provided an authentic task, and social interaction, during both the lesson and interview, provided instructional scaffolding.

Insights Into Learning:
Finding Area in Elementary Math

BEFORE YOU BEGIN (Note: This lesson appears in written form at the beginning of Chapter 9.)

This 60-minute tape contains three segments:

- A 24.5-minute lesson focusing on a fifth grade classroom attempting to find the area of a carpeted area in their classroom. (0-24:30)
- A 22-minute interview with four students after the lesson. (24:30-46:00)
- A 10-minute interview with the teacher about the lesson. (46:00-56:30)

Lesson Summary (0 - 24:30)

Laura Hunter, a fifth grade teacher at Bennion Elementary, is trying to teach students about area by involving them in a problem solving lesson. Bennion Elementary is an inner city school serving a diverse student population. The class has been introduced to the concepts of perimeter and area but is still struggling with them.

Laura begins by posing the following problem, "The principal is planning to recarpet the classroom and needs to know how much carpeting to order." The complexity of the problem is increased by the fact that the room is irregularly shaped and that the linoleum part of the room will not be carpeted.

To help students in their problem solving Laura displays an overhead with the five-step problem solving model described in Chapter 8. Breaking students into groups of four, she has each group identify the problem. The camera follows a focal group of four students that will be interviewed later. After reporting back to the whole class, each group then is responsible for measuring a different part of the room. They report back to a group who is coordinating measurements and constructing a diagram of the whole room.

Laura then asks each group to select a strategy to find the carpeted area of the room. Two strategies emerge. One is to find the total area of the room and subtract out the linoleum or non-carpeted parts of the room. The other is to compute the area of a rectangle within the carpeted area and then add on additional, irregularly shaped carpeted sections.

After selecting and implementing their strategies different groups report back to the whole class. The class discusses not only the different problem solving strategies but also interpersonal problems within the groups.

In evaluating their results the class finds that the answers generated by the different groups differ and the class discusses why. Laura asks for suggestions about ways to make the answers more accurate and students suggest starting with common numbers and using the same strategies.

Student Interview Summary (24:30 - 46:00)

The purpose of the interview with the focal group of students introduced in the lesson is to investigate the kinds of understandings taken away from the lesson. The interview occurred only hours after the lesson. To investigate near transfer the interview begins with a problem called, "We forgot the closet," which asks students to find the carpeted area of an irregularly shaped rectangle. Despite the similarity to the problem in the lesson, students struggle, confusing perimeter and area.

460

The next problem asks students to find the amount of plywood needed to cover the end of a house. It requires them to compute the area of a rectangle, subtract out windows and doors and then add on the triangle-shaped gabled end under the roof. (The class has not discussed how to find the area of a triangle.) With some prompting, students are able to find the area of the triangle by considering it to be half of a square.

A third problem asks students to divide up a piece of poster board by computing the area of parts of a rectangle comprised of smaller rectangles and triangles. To do this students must disassemble the rectangle into its parts.

Finally, students are asked to compute the area of a circle, something that they haven't discussed in class before. With some prompting by the interviewer and scaffolding from paper lined with squares, they explain how to estimate the area using the squared paper.

Teacher Interview Summary (46:00 - 56:30)

The interview begins with Laura explaining her goals for the lesson and describing the kinds of activities her students had experienced in working with area. The interview cuts to an early part of the lesson when students had problems differentiating perimeter from area which Laura explains in terms of lack of experience in computing area. Then the interview cuts to the student interview where students struggle again with these concepts even after the lesson. Laura discusses this in terms of a lack of concrete experiences with area. The final part of the interview focuses on the importance of student interactions for learning.

INSTRUCTIONAL RESOURCES

Transparencies (From the Transparency Package)

T 2.8   Zone of Proximal Development

T8.3   Characteristics of Constructivism

T 9.4   A General Problem-Solving Model

T 9.5   Expert-Novice Differences in Problem Solving Ability

T 9.6   Helping Learners Become Better Problem Solvers

T 9.9   Factors Affecting the Transfer of Learning

Transparency Masters (From the Instructor's Manual)

TM 8.4 Principles of Instruction for Applying Constructivism in Classrooms

TM 9.4 Cases That Are and Are Not Problems

TM 9.6 Principles of Instruction for Developing Problem Solving Ability

Transparency Masters (In this Media Guide)

Questions for Discussion and Analysis (Lesson)

Questions for Discussion and Analysis (Student Interview)

Rating Scale: Finding Area in Elementary Math

Feedback for "Questions for Discussion and Analysis"

Questions for Discussion and Analysis: Finding Area in Elementary Math

From the Lesson

1. How effective was Laura's lesson in teaching the concept of area?

2. How effective was Laura's lesson in teaching problem solving?

3. How effective was the lesson in terms of the following dimensions of constructivism: learners constructing their own understanding, and authentic learning tasks?

4. How effectively did Laura utilize social interaction in her lesson?

5. From an overall lesson perspective, how effective was Laura's instruction?

Questions for Discussion and Analysis: Finding Area in Elementary Math

From the Student Interview

1. What do the students' response to the carpeting problem tell you about how well the students understand the concept of area?

2. What different types of instructional scaffolding did the interviewer use to help the students solve the carpeting problem?

3. What evidence was there that transfer occurred between the carpeting and plywood problem? Was this general or specific transfer? What did the interviewer do to promote transfer?

4. In terms of the poster board problem, were students in the zone of proximal development? How can we tell?

5. What did the circle problem tell about the students' understanding of area? Was this an example of general or specific transfer?

Rating Scale for
Finding Area in Elementary Math

Rate the effectiveness of the lesson on each of the following dimensions using the following scale:

5 = Excellent
4 = Very good
3 = Good
2 = Fair
1 = Poor
0 = No evidence available

1. The effectiveness of the lesson in teaching the concept area

0 1 2 3 4 5

2. The effectiveness of the lesson in teaching problem solving

0 1 2 3 4 5

3. The effectiveness of the lesson in incorporating:

a. learners constructing their own understanding

0 1 2 3 4 5

b. authentic learning task

0 1 2 3 4 5

c. social interaction

0 1 2 3 4 5

4. Overall lesson effectiveness

0 1 2 3 4 5

**Feedback for "Questions for Discussion and Analysis" for
Finding Area in Elementary Math**

From the Lesson

1. The key to teaching concepts effectively is a large number of examples to illustrate abstract ideas. Laura began the lesson by reviewing the examples the class had discussed yesterday--the perimeter and area of a playground. The rest of the lesson contained two examples. The first was a brief mention of the use of linoleum tiles as area units. The other was the extended problem of finding area of the carpeted part of the room.

    Judging from students' comments, both during and after the lesson, the concepts of perimeter and area were not clear in their minds. The effectiveness of the lesson from a concept learning perspective could have been enhanced by including more examples of area early in the lesson. This might include a mini-lesson on finding area of a simple geometric shape or a discussion of the use of tiles as an area unit.

2. Learning to problem solve is enhanced when teachers:
    *   capitalize on social interaction
    *   present problems in meaningful contexts
    *   provide practice in problem finding
    *   provide scaffolding
    *   teach general problem solving strategies.

    Laura's lesson effectively used small groupwork to capitalize on social interaction. The problem she posed to the class was concrete, authentic and meaningful to learners. The lesson did not provide practice in problem finding. Different forms of teacher scaffolding used were the diagram of the class, and her interactions with different groups as she circulated around the room. Laura attempted to teach general problem solving strategies by using the five-step problem solving model to frame the lesson. The effectiveness of using this model (in terms of transfer) would have been increased if she had encouraged students to apply it to a different problem.

3. The lesson was effective from these two constructivist perspectives. By framing the lesson in terms of carpeting their own room, students were provided with an authentic learning task that was meaningful to them. By actually allowing them to measure the room and work in groups on the measurements in the diagram the students were able to wrestle with constructing their own understanding.

4. This was probably one of the strengths of the lesson. Students worked in small groups to: 1) discuss the problem, 2) measure the room, 3) select and implement a strategy, and 4) evaluate the strategy they used and the answer they got. In addition, Laura encouraged students to reflect on the effectiveness of the interaction in their groups.

5. We would rate the lesson about a 4+. In terms of strengths the lesson was framed with a meaningful, authentic task; students were actively involved in problem solving, Laura used a model to teach problem solving, and students were encouraged to reflect back on their strategy, answer, and effectiveness as group members.

    Two areas of improvement might include providing students with more concept examples of area before asking them to utilize the concept to problem solve, and providing additional practice with the problem solving model to promote transfer.

From the Interview:

1. Their responses suggest that they still don't have a clear idea of area, confusing it at times with perimeter.

466

This became clear when they thought that three square feet equaled one square yard.

2. The interviewer provided several types of scaffolding. First, he drew a diagram that helped them visualize the closet as a rectangle. Then he prompted them to see that the small internal rectangle was similar to the larger one. Finally, he helped them visualize the triangle as a half-square.

3. The students, with instructional scaffolding from the interviewer were able to see similarities between the carpeting triangle and the plywood triangle. This was an instance of specific transfer which probably occurred due to similarities between the two learning situations. Note that even though the two learning situations were only separated by several minutes and both involved the area of triangles, the students still needed help. Transfer is not easy.

4. All of the students were in the zone of proximal development, but some needed more assistance than others. For example, Gunjan was able to solve the problem with only minor prompting from the interviewer, while Olga required additional help from her peers.

5. Students' responses to the circle problem suggested that their understanding of area was developing. While they didn't know the formula, with the squared paper as a scaffold, they were able to visualize the circle as an area problem. While this was still specific transfer, it required more of a transfer leap than the triangle.

Insights Into Learning:
Designing Experiments in Seventh Grade

BEFORE YOU BEGIN (Note: This lesson appears in written form at the end of Chapter 8.)

This 60-minute tape contains three segments:
- A 25-minute lesson focusing on a seventh grade science classroom doing an experiment on a pendulum.(0-24:55)
- A 15-minute interview with four students after the lesson.(24:55-40:20)
- A 19-minute interview with the teacher about the lesson.(40:20-59:00)

Lesson Summary (0-24:55)

Scott Sowell, a seventh grade science teacher at Kirby Smith Middle School is trying to teach his students how to control variables within an inquiry oriented lesson. Kirby Smith Middle School is an inner city school that serves a diverse student population. The class has been introduced to the topic of controlling variables but is still struggling with it.

Scott begins the lesson by demonstrating a simple pendulum, explaining frequency as the number of swings in a certain time period. When he asks for possible factors that might influence the frequency of a pendulum the class offers length, weight, and the angle of release. Scott then asks the class, in small groups, to design experiments to ascertain which of these variables influences the frequency of a pendulum. (In reality only the length influences the frequency; weight and height have no effect.)

The video then focuses on a focal group of students attempting to design experiments to test these different variables. Using a ring stand, string, and paper clip weights the group conducts one test. After noting the results the group does a second test, both shortening the string and making the weight heavier. After counting for a fixed period of time they conclude that a shorter string makes the pendulum go faster. Scott visits the group and asks which variable caused the change. Different students voice different opinions, some claiming it was the change in weight, others the change in length. Scott encourages them to think about why they can't come to a firm conclusion.

The group designs a third experiment, this time changing only the length and keeping the weight and angle constant. Again Scott intervenes, encouraging them to think systematically about their results and the influence of each of the three variables.

In the next two experiments the group keeps length constant but changes both weight and height and comes up with the same frequency. Scott again asks them to think about the logic of their design.

When Scott pulls the different groups together to report their findings, the class concludes (incorrectly) that each of the variables influences the frequency. To counter this conclusion Scott then does repeated tests at the front of the room, changing one variable and keeping the others constant. Scott writes these conclusions on the board and asks the class what they learned about controlling variables. Wensley, one of the students from the focal group, offers, "Each time you do a different part of the experiment, only change one of the variables."

Student Interview Summary (24:55-40:20)

The interview begins with the interviewer asking the students to provide three conclusions about the experiment they just finished. Jonathan offers length as a variable that effects pendulum frequency. Wensley concludes that the angle doesn't influence frequency. Page offers that weight has no effect on frequency. The interviewer challenges this last conclusion and asks the students to design an experiment that will prove this. Collectively the group designs an experiment in which angle and length are controlled (kept constant) and weight is varied by changing the number of clips. Through probing, the interviewer encourages students to explain the logic behind this experiment. They are successful.

To test for transfer the interviewer poses another problem; finding out which dog food is best for helping dogs grow. Each student is asked to think about the experiment before offering a plan. The interviewer first asks students how they're going to decide this. They all volunteer, "By designing an experiment." With probing and scaffolding the students identify the kind of food as the independent variable, and amount of food, time of feeding, kind of dog, age of dog, and exercise as controlled variables.

Teacher Interview Summary (40:20-59:00)

The teacher interview begins with Scott describing his goals for the lesson, which include learning how to design experiments as well as understanding how a pendulum operates. Scott then explains that his students have had two prior lessons on scientific method (inquiry); one was a lecture on the topic, the other was a whole-class experiment involving factors that influenced growth of plants. Because of these experiences, and based on their performance in the lesson, Scott concluded that his students knew the terms "controlled," "independent" and "dependent" variables but didn't know how to apply them. A short clip from the lesson showing the students changing two variables at the same time verifies this.

When asked to explain the lack of transfer after the first (plant) lesson and their new ability to control variables after the pendulum experiment, Scott conjectures that the difference was due to lack of hands-on, first-hand experiences.

The problem of experimental error is mentioned and Scott explains how impulsiveness causes students to jump at conclusions, rather than systematically gathering lots of data. He proposes additional demonstrations to deal with this.

The interview returns to the end of the lesson where Scott demonstrated that angle doesn't influence the frequency. The issue of time and the ineffectiveness of the earlier activity in teaching content arises. Scott concludes that the hands-on trial and error learning that occurred in the groups was essential for their learning. Scott mentions confusion and frustration as potential problems in constructivist activities.

The interview concludes with the topic of assessment. Scott suggests an additional problem/experiment to assess their understanding of scientific method. When he did this using paper and pencil measures he found that his students understood the specific content of the lesson (factors influencing the frequency of a pendulum) better than the process itself.

INSTRUCTIONAL RESOURCES

Transparencies (From the Transparency Package)

T 2.4   Piaget's Stages and Characteristics

T 2.8   The Zone of Proximal Development

T 8.3   Characteristics of Constructivism

Transparency Masters (From the Instructor's Manual)

TM 2.6 A Comparison of Piaget's and Vygotsky's Views of Knowledge Construction

TM 8.4 Principles of Instruction for Applying Constructivism in Classrooms

TM 8.5 Steps in Inquiry Instruction

Transparency Masters (In this Media Guide)

Questions for Discussion and Analysis (Lesson)

Questions for Discussion and Analysis (Student Interview)

Rating Scale: Designing Experiments in Seventh Grade

Feedback for "Questions for Discussion and Analysis"

Questions for Discussion and Analysis: Designing Experiments in Seventh Grade

From the Lesson

1. How effectively did the lesson incorporate student-centered learning in the lesson? What aspects of the lesson were learner-centered? What aspects were teacher-centered?

2. To what extent did the lesson incorporate constructivist principles?

3. How effectively was groupwork incorporated in the lesson?

4. How effectively did the lesson use inquiry strategies to promote higher-order thinking?

5. From an over-all perspective, how effective was the lesson?

Questions for Discussion and Analysis: Designing Experiments in Seventh Grade

From the Student Interview

1. What elements of transfer were illustrated in the student interview?

2. What evidence from the interview suggests that the students understood the process of controlling variables?

3. How did the design of the dog food experiment relate to the process of inquiry?

4. Describe the process of controlling variables from a Piagetian perspective.

5. Using constructivism and the zone of proximal development, explain the difference between students' ability to control variables during the lesson and during the interview.

6. In Chapter 7, we described generative knowledge as knowledge that can be used to interpret new situations and inert knowledge as knowledge that exists in isolated pieces. How could these concepts be used to explain the students' ability to control variables before and after the lesson?

Rating Scale for
Designing Experiments in Seventh Grade

Rate the effectiveness of the lesson on each of the following dimensions using the following scale:
- 5 = Excellent
- 4 = Very good
- 3 = Good
- 2 = Fair
- 1 = Poor
- 0 = No evidence available

1. Utilizing student-centered approaches   0 1 2 3 4 5
   to learning

2. Applying constructivist principles in
   instruction   0 1 2 3 4 5

3. Incorporating groupwork in instruction
                                           0 1 2 3 4 5

4. Using inquiry to promote higher-order
   thinking   0 1 2 3 4 5

5. Overall lesson effectiveness   0 1 2 3 4 5

Feedback for "Questions for Discussion and Analysis" for
Designing Experiments in Seventh Grade

From the Lesson

1. Learner-centered instruction has two major characteristics: students at the center of the learning process and teaching for understanding. By providing hands-on experiences and allowing students to work and dialogue in small groups, Scott encouraged students to be at the center of the learning process. In addition, his interventions with the focal group encouraged students to wrestle with and make sense of the data. This encouraged deep processing and illustrated teaching for understanding.

2. In evaluating the lesson in terms of constructivism we use its four major characteristics as a frame of reference.
    *   Learners construct their own understanding: The hands-on activities allowed students to both experiment with pendulums and experience inquiry first hand.
    *   New learning depends on current understanding: This was clearly illustrated by the fits and starts the group took as it was attempting to learn to control variables. Through his questioning Scott attempted to get the group to wrestle with the logic of their conclusions.
    *   Learning is facilitated by social interaction: The small groups provided an effective vehicle for students to share and compare their ideas with each other.
    *   Meaningful learning occurs within authentic learning tasks: This characteristic was addressed in two ways. In introducing pendulums Scott asked for everyday examples. In addition, students were able to actually experiment with their own pendulum.

3. Effective groupwork has the following characteristics:
    *   Goals direct the groups' activities.
    *   Social interaction is emphasized.
    *   Learners must depend on each other to reach the goals.
        We saw these features in Scott's lesson. His students' goal was to determine how length, weight, and angle affected the frequency of a simple pendulum; a great deal of interaction took place in the groups; and learners collaborated in designing, implementing, and interpreting the experiment.

4. Scott's students were involved in an inquiry activity, which typically includes the following steps:
    *   Identifying a question or problem
    *   Forming an hypothesis to answer the question or solve the problem
    *   Gathering data to test the hypothesis
    *   Drawing conclusions from the data
    *   Generalizing on the basis of the conclusions
        During the lesson Scott's students were presented with the problem of determining how the length, weight, and angle affect the frequency of a simple pendulum. While the problem could have been presented more generally, such as, "What influences the frequency of a simple pendulum?", Scott chose to narrow the problem to make it more manageable for the students.
        In Scott's lesson, the students didn't form hypotheses; instead they moved directly to gathering data. Understanding and applying the processes needed to gather meaningful data were the lesson's primary goals; understanding the relationships between length, weight, angle, and frequency were secondary. This emphasis on process is characteristics of inquiry activities (Eggen & Kauchak, 2001; Kauchak & Eggen, 1998). Conclusions and generalizations were made both in small groups and as part of the whole-class discussion. Again, much of the discussion focused on the process of controlling variables.

5. From an over-all perspective, Scott's lesson was quite effective. Students were actively involved in a hands-on inquiry activity. Scott provided enough focus to provide structure for the lesson but still placed

most of the responsibility for learning on students. Classroom interaction, both in small and large groups, was good, providing opportunities for students to share and compare their differing perspectives.

The lesson could have been improved in several ways. One was to make the process of inquiry more explicit to students. While students went through most of the inquiry steps they were probably unaware of them or the logic behind them. A short introduction at the beginning and a summary wrap-up at the end focusing on the process of inquiry would help learners understand the inquiry process better.

The second area of improvement would be to explicitly deal with the topic of controlling variables. During the lesson students in the focal group had problems with this process. Scott might have dealt with this through a short introduction at the beginning or a brief discussion of the problem when the class discussed their disparate results.

From the Interview

1. This is a complex question. One interpretation of students' ability to successfully design the pendulum problem was that this was just retention and did not involve transfer. However, recall that in the lesson the focal group never successfully designed this experiment and it wasn't until the end of the lesson that Scott explained the logic behind it. Because of this we consider their design of the pendulum experiment in the interview to be an instance of specific transfer. Their ability to design the dog food experiment was an example of more general transfer.

2. The students were able to design the experiment and cautioned the interviewer about varying both length and weight when he tried to increase weight by connecting another paper clip at the end.

3. Inquiry is an instructional strategy designed to teach students to attack problems in a scientific manner. It has five steps: 1) identify the question, 2) form a hypotheses, 3) gather data, 4) draw conclusions, and 5) generalize on the basis of the conclusions. In the interview the interviewer identified the question, and the students designed the data-gathering procedures. Forming hypotheses, drawing conclusions and generalizing were missing.

4. Piaget described development in terms of stages. The formal operational stage usually occurs during early adolescence and includes the ability to understand the logic behind controlling variables.

5. During the lesson students were in the zone of proximal development and the activities, Scott's interventions, and group interaction helped them understand the process of controlling variables. During the interview the students as a group were able to successfully design experiments with assistance from each other and prompting from the interviewer. Two interesting questions remain: 1) could each of the students do this alone, and 2) could the students do this without the scaffolded prompting of the interviewer?

6. Before the lesson the concept of controlled variables was inert; students weren't able to relate it to the problem at hand. After the lesson during the interview this knowledge was generative, in that students were able to use it to think about and design new experiments.

Windows on Classrooms
Segment #1: Properties of Air in First-Grade Science

BEFORE YOU BEGIN (Note: This 15 minute lesson appears in written form at the end of Chapter 2.)

Lesson Summary

Jenny Newhall, a first grade teacher at Jesse Tynes Elementary School, is beginning a science unit on the properties of air. Jesse Tynes is a medium-sized elementary school that serves a lower-middle class population.

Jenny begins by reviewing the five senses and asking student how they know if something is "real." After discussing how the five senses help us understand objects such as a spoon or chair, Jenny asks, "Is air real?" Though most students nod, Jenny can tell by their puzzled looks that they aren't quite sure.

Jenny then calls the class's attention to a fish tank and empty glass. Jenny asks them to predict what would happen to the inside of the glass if she places it in the water upside down. A controversy ensues; some say the inside will get wet and others contend that it will stay dry. She has a student come up to feel the inside of the glass both before and after placing it in the water, and to her surprise (and dismay) he reports that it was dry before but wet after. The class is puzzled but not surprised.

Jenny then takes a roll of paper towels next to her chair and asks students to predict what will happen if she places a paper towel up in the glass and again puts it in the water upside down. Again student opinions differ. When the paper towel comes out dry Jenny asks for an explanation. After several attempts, one student suggests that the air has kept the water out. Jenny proceeds to demonstrate with the glass under the water allowing bubbles to escape and asks students to explain the bubbles. With some prompting the class agrees that air is real. Jenny then has students experiment in small groups with water, clear glasses and paper towels.

INSTRUCTIONAL RESOURCES

Transparencies (From the Transparency Package)

T 2.1   Factors Influencing Human Intellectual Development

T 2.4   Piaget's Stages and Characteristics

T 2.8   The Zone of Proximal Development

Transparency Masters (From the Instructor's Manual)

TM 2.1 The Drive for Equilibrium

TM 2.3   Measuring Thinking

TM 2.5 Principles of Instruction for Applying Piaget's Theory in Classrooms

TM 8.4 Principles of Instruction for Applying Constructivism in Classrooms

Transparency Masters (In this Media Guide)

Questions for Discussion and Analysis

Rating Scale: Properties of Air in First-Grade Science

Feedback for "Questions for Discussion and Analysis"

Questions for Discussion and Analysis:
Properties of Air
In First-Grade Science

1. How effective was Jenny's lesson from a developmental perspective? Specifically, why was it important to use the: a) water, b) clear glass, c) paper towels, and d) learning centers?

2. How effectively did Jenny incorporate constructivist learning principles in her lesson? What could she have done to make the lesson more constructivist in its orientation? What advantages and disadvantages exist in making it more constructivist?

3. Samantha placed her hand up the glass and said, "It's wet on the outside, but dry on the inside," but Terry continued to assert, "It's wet!" How effectively did Jenny respond? What other alternatives might she have pursued? What advantages and disadvantages exist with these alternatives?

4. How effectively did Jenny utilize social interaction in her lesson? What instructional purpose did this social interaction serve?

Rating Scale for
Properties of Air in First-Grade Science

Rate the effectiveness of the teacher on each of the following dimensions using the following scale:

5 = Excellent
4 = Very good
3 = Good
2 = Fair
1 = Poor
0 = No evidence available

1. The developmental effectiveness of   0 1 2 3 4 5
   the lesson

2. Incorporating constructivist   0 1 2 3 4 5
   principles in the lesson

3. Responding to student   0 1 2 3 4 5
   disagreements

4. Utilizing social interaction   0 1 2 3 4 5

5. Overall lesson effectiveness   0 1 2 3 4 5

**Feedback for "Questions for Discussion and Analysis" for
Properties of Air in First-Grade Science**

1. Jenny's students were first graders, and based on their responses, they were at Piaget's Preoperational Stage of Development. Learners at this stage are dominated by their perceptions; what they perceive is indeed real for them. Concrete experiences are essential if learning is to be meaningful for children at this stage of development.

   Because it is invisible, the physical reality of air is a difficult concept for first graders. The water was important in the lesson because it allowed students to see air bubbles, which are concrete. The transparent glass allowed students to see the air/water line inside it. The paper towel also provided concrete evidence that something (air) was keeping the water out, since the towel remained dry. From a developmental perspective the learning center activities were a critical component of the lesson. They allowed students to experiment with the ideas in a personal hands-on way.

2. Constructivist approaches to instruction are based on the idea that learners "construct" their own understanding rather than having it delivered to them by teachers or written materials. Teachers facilitate the knowledge construction process by embedding new content in meaningful learning tasks and by encouraging individual students to share their evolving thoughts with each other.

   Jenny was careful in her lesson not to impose her beliefs on her students. She provided them with concrete experiences that allowed them to construct their own meaning from the demonstration. Using water, a transparent glass, and paper towels, together with asking students to predict what would happen when she placed the glass underwater, provided her students with an authentic learning task that promoted interaction among students.

   One alternative to Jenny's introducing the lesson with a teacher-centered demonstration would be to begin the lesson with student exploration at the learning centers. The advantage of this approach is that it would allow each student to individually experiment with the water and the glasses and paper towels. Disadvantages are organization and the focus of the lesson; organizing individual student exploration, particularly with first graders, can be demanding.

3. When Samantha placed her hand up the glass and said, "It's wet on the outside, but dry on the inside," Terry continued to assert, "It's wet!" Jenny responded by saying "Uh, oh! We have two differing opinions. We've got to find out how to solve this problem," and then said, "Let's dry this glass off and start again. Only this time we're going to put a paper towel in the glass. Now if water goes in the glass what is the paper towel going to look like?"

   This approach lies at an approximate middle point on a continuum ranging from essentially "teacher-centered" at one end to totally "learner-centered" at the other. At the teacher-centered end of the continuum a teacher might say, "No, Terry feel again. It's really dry." The advantage of this approach is that it saves time and establishes a critical aspect of the lesson. The disadvantage is that it frames the teacher as the ultimate authority and the center of knowledge. The message this sends to students about the legitimacy of their own knowledge and beliefs and their role in knowledge construction is potentially damaging.

   An alternative at the other end of the continuum would be for the teacher to say, "Hmm, we have a disagreement here. How could we resolve it?" This places greater responsibility on students and provides opportunities for them to develop their problem solving abilities. The disadvantage from a content perspective is that this approach usually takes more time. Teaching involves trade-offs such as these; being aware of their options allows teachers to make professional decisions based on their best judgment.

4. Social interaction encourages students to put their own ideas into words and allows them to compare their

480

ideas with others. Jenny encouraged this by guiding students with her questioning as they constructed their understanding. Her questions encouraged students to think about the content, put their ideas into words, and compare their ideas with others. Jenny was careful not to offer too many explanations of her own or impose her ideas onto the class. The overall effect of this questioning was to communicate to students that their ideas were valued and important and that it was their responsibility to make sense of what they were observing.

5. Overall, Jenny's lesson was quite effective. Her goals were clear, the learning activity was aligned with the goals, she was well organized and used her time well, students were orderly yet involved, and the information was meaningful to them. She also promoted higher-order thinking with first graders.

Her lesson was effective for another reason. One of the most important factors in fostering learner development is *experience*, and the students acquired a great deal of experience in this lesson. Even if they didn't actually reach the content goal of the lesson, i.e., truly "get" the idea that air takes up space, they acquired a great deal of experience which will make later study more meaningful. This is the essence of developmentally effective instruction.

Segment #2: Climate, Geography and Economics in Junior High Social Studies

BEFORE YOU BEGIN (Note: This 15 minute segment is the second on this tape and appears at about 15 minutes into the tape. This lesson appears in written form at the end of Chapter 13.)

Lesson Summary

Judy Holmquist is a ninth-grade geography teacher at Lakeside Junior High School in Orange Park, Florida. Lakeside is a large suburban junior high that serves a lower-middle to middle class student population. Judy has 27 students in her second period geography class.

Judy is beginning a unit on the different climate regions of the United States. To introduce students to the unit she assigns them to four different groups to investigate the influence of geography on four states--Florida, California, New York and Alaska. Each group is responsible for describing one of these states in terms of geography, economy, ethnic composition and future issues. When students have completed their investigation Judy assists them in placing the information into a matrix; the states along the vertical axis and the dimensions--geography, economy, ethnic composition, and future issue along the top.

Judy begins the lesson by asking students to find a partner and identify three similarities and differences between states in terms of geography. After several minutes Judy calls the class back together and asks the groups to share their conclusions with the whole class, in the process writing their findings on the board. She then asks the groups to do the same with the "Economy" column, listing similarities and differences among the states. After discussing the economic similarities and differences Judy asks the class to compare the two columns and explain connections between them. Finally, she has the students summarize their findings by making generalizations about the influence of climate on economics in different regions.

INSTRUCTIONAL RESOURCES

Transparencies (From the Transparency Package)

T 13.4 Essential Teaching Skills

T 13.5 Characteristics of Effective Praise

T 13.6 Characteristics of Effective Questioning

Transparency Masters (From the Instructor's Manual)

TM 7.4 Questions That Promote Deep Processing of Information

TM 7.14 Principles of Instruction for Applying Information Processing in Classrooms

TM 8.4 Principles of Instruction for Applying Constructivism in Classrooms

Transparency Masters (In this Media Guide)

Questions for Discussion and Analysis

Rating Scale: Climate, Geography and Economics in Junior High Social Studies

Feedback for "Questions for Discussion and Analysis"

482

Questions for Discussion and Analysis: Climate, Geography and Economics in Junior High Social Studies

1. To what extent did Judy apply constructivist principles in her teaching?

2. How effectively did Judy use groupwork in her lesson?

3. How effectively did Judy promote higher-order thinking in her lesson? What could she have done to increase the emphasis on higher-order thinking.

4. How effective was Judy in promoting learning in her lesson?

Rating Scale for
Climate, Geography and Economics
in Junior High Social Studies

Rate the effectiveness of the teacher on each of the following dimensions using the following scale:

5 = Excellent
4 = Very good
3 = Good
2 = Fair
1 = Poor
0 = No evidence available

1. Applying constructivist principles in instruction   0   1   2   3   4   5

2. Incorporating groupwork in instruction   0   1   2   3   4   5

3. Promoting higher-order thinking   0   1   2   3   4   5

4. Overall lesson effectiveness   0   1   2   3   4   5

Feedback for "Questions for Discussion and Analysis"for
Climate, Geography and Economics in Junior High Social Studies

1. Constructivist approaches to instruction are based on the idea that learners "construct" their own understanding rather than having it delivered to them by teachers or written materials. Guided discovery approaches to instruction are consistent with constructivist views of learning. Judy's instruction incorporated elements of guided discovery. For example, students identified similarities and differences in the geography and economy of the four regions, and, with Judy's guidance they developed explanations for the differences. This approach is consistent with constructivism.

    Judy also encouraged active student "meaning-making" by having students gather their own information and by helping them interpret these data through her questioning. The fact that she designed her lesson to include Florida as one of the states ensured that her students would have a personal and concrete frame of reference for comparing the different states. She also used social interaction effectively in both large and small group instruction to encourage students to verbalize their own ideas and compare them to others'.

2. Judy's groupwork was quite effective. Effective groupwork has four characteristics: a) clear directions, b) a relatively short, specific time period, c) a required written product, and d) teacher monitoring. Her directions were clear, providing a clear content focus for their activities. In addition, she identified what the product should be--three written similarities and differences, and clearly specified the time limits for the task. Finally, as students worked in groups she circulated around the room, clarifying directions, answering questions and providing encouragement.

3. Higher-order thinking involves the use of cognitive strategies that help us efficiently and accurately process information. These include basic processes such as comparing and contrasting, identifying relevant and irrelevant information, inferring, and explaining. Students become proficient at these processes by using them in specific classroom learning activities and by being able to see how they apply across the curriculum.

    Judy promoted the development of thinking skills in her students by designing learning activities that directly integrated them into her teaching. Students were asked to find similarities and differences between states in terms of both geography and economics and then were asked to explain connections between these two concepts. Her effectiveness in teaching higher-order thinking was also promoted by small groupwork in which all students were provided opportunities to practice these skills and by social interaction that encouraged students to articulate their conclusions.

    The effectiveness of her instruction could have been improved by explicit attempts to make students aware of the thinking skills they were using. For example, when students concluded that climate influences the economy, Judy might have asked them to specifically identify data in the chart that supported that conclusion. In addition she might have called students' attention to the process itself, i.e., how we use inferences based on data to form conclusions. This makes thinking skills overt and visible, allowing students to understand the cognitive processes involved.

4. Overall, Judy's lesson was effective. Her goals were clear, the learning activity was aligned with the goals, she was well organized and used her time well, students were orderly yet involved, and the information was meaningful to them.

    The primary way the lesson could have been improved would be to increase the emphasis on higher-order thinking based on the information in the matrix. This could have been accomplished by asking more questions that called for explanations and hypotheses. For example Judy asked the following questions that called for explanations:
    - Why do they all have fishing?
    - Why do they all have forestry?
    - What does this tell us about their climate?

485

• Why do we have the citrus industry in California and Florida?

She could have asked many more questions of this type, and questions that called for hypothetical thinking, such as, "Suppose global warming becomes a reality. How might that affect the economy of each region?"

She might also have made the lesson more student centered by asking students to generate their own questions about the information in the chart. This would have taken little additional effort on her part, and with practice the students would become quite adept with the process.

Windows on Classrooms
Segment#3: Graphing in Second-Grade Math

BEFORE YOU BEGIN (Note: This is the third 15 minute segment on this tape and appears at about 30 minutes. This lesson appears in written form at the end of Chapter 9.)

Lesson Summary

Suzanne Brush is a second grade teacher at Webster Elementary School in St. Augustine, Florida. The school, located in a lower to lower middle class neighborhood, serves a variety of students from different ethnic backgrounds. Suzanne has 25 students of varying ability in her class. This lesson was conducted in late March and had been preceded by some discussion of using graphs to represent number quantities.

Suzanne begins the lesson by explaining that she is planning a party for the class and needs to know what kinds of jelly beans she should buy. After some discussion the class agrees that one way to find out would be to give each student a sample of different kinds of jelly beans and have each student vote for their favorite. Suzanne then gives a bag containing seven different-flavored jelly beans to each student and asks them to choose their favorite. After the tasting, Suzanne asks students how they could organize this information. After considerable discussion they arrive at the idea of graphing the information by having each student place a colored cardboard rectangle in the appropriate column of the graph.

After each student "votes," Suzanne encourages students to begin interpreting the graph by asking questions such as, "What does the graph tell us?" Suzanne encourages students to analyze the graphed information by asking questions that require them to compare the information in the columns (the numbers of students choosing each color). Suzanne then asks them to pose similar problems of their own. As students discuss theirs and others' problems, Suzanne emphasizes student understanding of their problem solving strategies by repeatedly asking "How did you get that?" To provide additional practice with problem solving, Suzanne then assigns students to different learning center activities where they work in small groups to apply their problem solving and graphing strategies to new problems.

INSTRUCTIONAL RESOURCES

Transparencies (From the Transparency Package)

T 9.4   A General Problem-Solving Model

T 9.5   Expert-Novice Differences In Problem Solving Ability

T 9.6   Helping Learners Become Better Problem Solvers

T 9.8   Elements of Critical Thinking

T 9.9   Factors Affecting the Transfer of Learning

Transparency Masters (From the Instructor's Manual)

TM 8.4 Principles of Instruction for Applying Constructivism in Classrooms

TM 9.4   Cases That Are and Are Not Problems

TM 9.6 Principles of Instruction for Developing Problem Solving Ability

Transparency Masters (In this Media Guide)

Questions for Discussion and Analysis

Rating Scale: Graphing in Second Grade Math

Feedback for "Questions for Discussion and Analysis"

Questions for
Discussion and Analysis:
Graphing in Second-Grade Math

1. How effective was Suzanne's lesson from a developmental perspective?

2. How effectively did Suzanne involve the students in her lesson?

3. How effective was Suzanne's lesson for promoting transfer?

Rating Scale for
Graphing in Second-Grade Math

Rate the effectiveness of the teacher on each of the following dimensions using the following scale:

5 = Excellent
4 = Very good
3 = Good
2 = Fair
1 = Poor
0 = No evidence available

1. The developmental effectiveness of the lesson　　0 1 2 3 4 5

2. Involving students in the lesson　　0 1 2 3 4 5

3. Promoting transfer　　0 1 2 3 4 5

4. Overall lesson effectiveness　　0 1 2 3 4 5

Feedback for "Questions for Discussion and Analysis" for
Graphing in Second-Grade Math

1. The lesson was effective from both a Piagetian and a Vygotskyan perspective. From a Piagetian point of view, Suzanne provided a concrete problem that was meaningful to students. In solving the problem each student was personally involved in tasting, voting, and representing the information. As students constructed the graph, they could see in a concrete way how their vote influenced the shape of the graph and the final results.

    From a Vygotskyan perspective, the lesson was effective in encouraging student dialogue about their problem solving strategies, and Suzanne provided the guidance of a "more knowledgeable other" in the entire process. Most students appeared to be in the zone of proximal development, and Suzanne helped them make progress through the zone.

    An interesting question for discussion might be whether or not Suzanne was too teacher-centered and directive. The optimal amount of teacher direction in teaching problem solving is open to debate.

2. Students were actively involved throughout the lesson. All students tasted the jelly beans, voted for their favorite flavors, and indicated their preferences on the graph. Many of the students were involved in the discussion of the problem and the strategy for solving it, and all students were involved in the work at the centers.

3. Transfer is enhanced by the depth of student understanding, the variety and quality of learning experiences, and by the different contexts in which learners' experiences are embedded. Suzanne promoted depth of understanding and provided quality learning experiences by directly involving students in solving a problem that was meaningful to them. Learning and transfer were further enhanced by allowing students to see how their personal "vote" influenced the shape of the graph and by discussing the information in the graph from different points of view. Finally, transfer was enhanced by student involvement in the different learning centers which provided different contexts for gathering and graphing information.

4. While teaching is a complex process, and it is difficult to provide an overall lesson evaluation, we have found this question effective for promoting discussions. Students' comments offer insights into their beliefs about teaching and learning and their understanding of effective instruction.

    Suzanne was generally very effective in the lesson. She made the learning meaningful by embedding problem solving in a question about people's preferences in jelly beans, which was an authentic task for second graders. The lesson began with a motivating problem (planning a party) that asked students to assist in the design and data gathering. Each student was actively involved in tasting, voting, and indicating their preferences on the graph, which helped them see the connection between the data gathering process and abstract numerals. Suzanne helped them develop a deeper understanding of gathering and graphing information by having them do similar activities in their learning centers.

    An additional strength of the lesson was the interaction that occurred both between teacher and students and the students with each other. Through effective questioning, Suzanne encouraged students to analyze and discuss the data they were gathering. She also encouraged students to explain the logic behind their answers, placing greater emphasis on understanding than on mechanics.

    Two possible criticisms of the lesson might be the amount of teacher direction and the extent to which the lesson focused on strategies. Teacher judgment is always involved in deciding how much to structure a lesson and how much the teacher should "steer" the lesson toward a desired outcome. Pure constructivists argue for student autonomy and opportunities to learn through trial and error. Others suggest that the practical need to maintain lesson focus and meet lesson goals must prevail. A second way that the lesson might be improved is through more emphasis on problem solving strategies per se. For example, at the end of the lesson Suzanne might have increased the emphasis on students' reflection on the process of problem solving, what they learned about it, and how the process could be improved.

Windows on Classrooms
Segment #4: *The Scarlet Letter* in a High School English Class

BEFORE YOU BEGIN (Note: This 15 minute segment is the fourth on this tape, approximately 45 minutes into the tape. This lesson appears in written form at the end of Chapter 7)

Lesson Summary

Sue Southam is a high school English teacher at Highland High School in Salt Lake City, Utah. Highland is a large (2,200 students) high school located in a major western metropolitan area. The lesson takes place in a class that has been reading different American works of fiction. The class is focusing on Nathaniel Hawthorne's *The Scarlet Letter,* and in previous sessions the class has discussed the setting for the novel and its heroine, Hester Prynne.

In this session Sue is attempting to help students understand the character of Reverend Dimmesdale, the secret father of Hester's illegitimate child. She begins by briefly reviewing the book and then asks students how they know that Dimmesdale is the father of the child. After some discussion, she asks students to create a portrait or picture of Dimmesdale in their writing journals. Following this assignment she asks students to pretend they are directing a film and asks them to suggest whom they might cast in Dimmesdale's character.

After discussing students' suggestions, Sue reads a scene from the book in which the Reverend Dimmesdale, in front of the whole congregation, exhorts Hester to identify the father of the child and her illegitimate lover. Following this passage, she assigns half the class to be "Hesters" and half to be "Dimmesdales" and asks them to record their feelings line-by-line during Dimmesdale's speech. She then breaks the students into groups of four with two "Hesters" and two "Dimmesdales" in each and asks them to role play the characters, responding to each other's reactions.

After the small groupwork Sue brings them back together and the class discusses their reactions in a whole-group setting. Students can't decide whether Dimmesdale is a tragic character to be pitied or a cowardly one to be scorned.

INSTRUCTIONAL RESOURCES

Transparencies (From the Transparency Package)

T 7.2   An Information Processing Model

T 7.3   Limitations of Working Memory

T 7.8   Making Information Meaningful

Transparency Masters (From the Instructor's Manual)

TM 7.3 Questions that Promote Deep Processing of Information

TM 7.4 Background Knowledge and Encoding

TM 7.6 Elaborating on Past Experiences

TM 7.7 Active and Passive Study Strategies

Transparency Masters (In this Media Guide)

Questions for Discussion and Analysis

Rating Scale: *The Scarlet Letter* in a High School English Class

Feedback for "Questions for Discussion and Analysis"

Questions for Discussion and Analysis:
The Scarlet Letter in a High School English Class

1. How effectively did Sue incorporate constructivist learning principles in her lesson?

2. Research indicates that active student involvement increases learning.

    a) How effectively did Sue promote student involvement in her lesson?

    b) What strategies did she use to involve the students?

3. The meaningfulness of new content can be thought of as the number of connections that can be made between the new information and students' background knowledge.

    a) How effective was Sue in making the information meaningful for her students?

    b) What strategies did she use to make Dimmesdale's character meaningful for learners?

4. How effectively did Sue incorporate small groupwork into her lesson?

Rating Scale for
The Scarlet Letter in a High School English Class

Rate the effectiveness of the teacher on each of the following dimensions using the following scale:

    5 = Excellent
    4 = Very good
    3 = Good
    2 = Fair
    1 = Poor
    0 = No evidence available

1. Incorporating constructivist learning principles   0 1 2 3 4 5

2. Promoting student involvement   0 1 2 3 4 5

3. Making the information meaningful   0 1 2 3 4 5

4. Incorporating small groupwork   0 1 2 3 4 5

5. Overall lesson effectiveness   0 1 2 3 4 5

Feedback for "Questions for Discussion and Analysis" for
The Scarlet Letter **in a High School English Class**

1. Constructivist approaches to instruction are based on the idea that learners "construct" their own understanding rather than having it delivered to them by teachers or written materials. Teachers facilitate the knowledge construction process by embedding new content in meaningful learning tasks and by encouraging individual students to share their evolving thoughts with each other.

    Sue encouraged student knowledge construction with respect to Dimmesdale's character by asking students to construct a verbal or pictorial portrait of Dimmesdale and by casting this character in a movie. She also helped the students construct an understanding of the novel's characters by asking them to get inside the minds of the two main characters during Dimmesdale's speech to Hester. This was followed by role playing in small groups and general discussion by the class as a whole. During their discussion students shared their perspectives and were encouraged to reconcile them with the perspectives of others.

2. Sue did a good job of involving students in the lesson as they wrestled with their understanding of Dimmesdale's character. She did this in several ways. She solicited their ideas and opinions in a whole-group discussion. She also encouraged individual students to construct a personnel portrait of Dimmesdale in their learning logs. This was followed by each student individually interpreting Dimmesdale's speech from either a Dimmesdale or Hester Prynne perspective. Role playing these characters' reactions provided another opportunity for student involvement. In each instance students were actively involved in trying to make sense of a complex character in a potentially difficult novel.

3. In her lesson, Sue was effective in actively encouraging students to personally understand and interpret Dimmesdale's character. To promote meaningful learning, Sue asked students to interpret the character from their personal perspectives, rather than discussing the character in abstract terms. Sue presented students with several tasks, including creating a concrete portrait of the character, casting him in a movie, perspective taking during the speech, and role playing. The combination of all these strategies allowed students to individually construct a view of Dimmesdale that was meaningful to them.

4. Sue's groupwork was quite effective. Effective groupwork has four characteristics: a) clear directions, b) a relatively short, specific time period, c) a required written product, and d) teacher monitoring. Her directions were clear, providing a clear content focus for their activities. While Sue didn't require a written product, their group discussions were based on information they had put their logs a few minutes before, and she kept the group activity relatively short. Finally, as students worked in groups she circulated around the room, clarifying directions, answering questions and providing encouragement.

5. The overall effectiveness of Sue's lesson might generate considerable discussion. She was well organized and used her time well, students were orderly yet involved, and the information was meaningful to them. Her stated goal was for students to interpret Dimmesdale's character, and they did, so the learning activity was aligned with her goal.

    On the other hand, this lesson raises a number of questions. For example, are all interpretations of Dimmesdale's character equally valid? If not, how do we know which is more valid than another? Is one interpretation of Hawthorne's intent in writing the novel any more valid than another? If all interpretations are equally valid, what is accomplished in the lesson, and how do we know if we've accomplished it? Does this matter? What kind of understanding of character development did the students construct? Questions such as these raise interesting issues about the purposes of instruction and teachers' beliefs.

Educational Psychology Video Package, Video I (Overview)

Video I

Total Length: 137:41 Minutes

Segment	Chapter(s)	Running Time
1. Piaget & Kohlberg	2	13:50
2. Cognitive Strategies	7, 8, 9	21:30
a. Learning To Question (Kindergarten)		3:50
b. Reciprocal Teaching (7th Grade)		8:00
c. SQ4R (College)		8:20
3. Cooperative Learning	8	12:50
4. Classroom Management	12	30:20
5. Lecture Discussion	7	14:30
6. Classrooms in Action	12, 13	40:00
a. English (Résumés & Job Applications)		8:45
b. American History (Vietnam War)		13:00
c. Chemistry (Charles Law)		17:20

The segments for this videotape consist of the following:

SEGMENT SUMMARIES

SEGMENT #1: PIAGET AND KOHLBERG (CHAPTERS 2 & 3)

This 14-minute segment illustrates teachers conducting six different tasks with learners of different ages. It demonstrates characteristics of preoperational and concrete operational thinking in students.

SEGMENT #2: COGNITIVE STRATEGIES (CHAPTER 9)

This 21-minute segment exists in three parts. The first illustrates a kindergarten teacher helping her students develop reading readiness skills by asking questions about a story she is reading. In the second part, a seventh-grade teacher describes and models *Reciprocal Teaching*. The third part illustrates a university instructor explaining the comprehensive study strategy *SQ4R* to a group of college students.

SEGMENT #3: COOPERATIVE LEARNING (CHAPTER 8)
Cooperative learning in the form of Student Teams Achievement Divisions (STAD) with a seventh grade math class is illustrated in this 13-minute segment.

SEGMENT #4: CLASSROOM MANAGEMENT (CHAPTER 12)
This 30-minute segment illustrates different classroom management strategies with a second-grade class. In the first of three parts, the teacher is establishing rules on the first day of class. The second part, occurring one week later, illustrates the teacher reviewing and reinforcing her rules, and the third part illustrates a "typical" school day eight weeks later.

SEGMENT #5: THE LECTURE-DISCUSSION MODEL (CHAPTER 7)
This 15-minute segment contains excerpts from a lesson on the Civil War taught to a fifth-grade class using lecture-recitation.

SEGMENT #6: CLASSROOMS IN ACTION
This 40-minute segment illustrates three secondary teachers in different content area classrooms. The first episode shows an English teacher discussing effective job applications and résumés with her students. In the second episode, a social studies teacher is presenting information on the Vietnam War, and a chemistry teacher demonstrates Charles Law in the third episode. Lecture-discussion and direct instruction are the primary methods of instruction.

Educational Psychology Video Package: Video I
Segment #1: Piaget and Kohlberg

BEFORE YOU BEGIN

This 14-minute segment shows a teacher conducting several Piagetian tasks with students of different ages.

Task 1:   The interviewer asks a 6-year-old to pretend that a customer orders a pizza. She says that the pizza person asks if he wants it cut into four or eight pieces. The child is told that the customer responds, '. . . four pieces, because I couldn't eat eight." The interviewer asks the child if the answer makes sense.

The interviewer repeats the task with an 11 ½-year-old.

Task 2:   The interviewer gives the 6-year-old two equal balls of clay. The child confirms that they are equal and is then asked to flatten one of the balls into a pancake shape. The interviewer asks the child if the two pieces now have the same amount of clay.

The interviewer repeats the task with a 7-year-old and a 12-year-old.

Task 3:   The interviewer shows the 6-year-old two identical beakers with the same amount of water in each. The child is then asked to pour the liquid from one beaker into a larger beaker and is asked if the two beakers now contain the same amount of liquid.

The task is repeated with the 11 ½-year-old.

Task 4:   The interviewer shows the 6-year-old two rows of five coins each, has the child confirm that the two rows have the same number of coins, and then spreads the coins apart in one of the rows. She then asks the child if the number of coins is the same.

The interviewer repeats the task with the 12-year-old.

Task 5:   The interviewer tells the six-year-old that she has 10 puppies and wants to find out which of two kinds of dog food will make the puppies grow faster. She asks the child to describe an experiment to answer the question.

The interviewer repeats the task with the 7-year-old and the 11 ½-year-old.

Task 6:   The teacher describes a moral dilemma involving whether or not it is acceptable to cheat if a boy is required to work the night before a test, making it impossible for him to study. She presents the dilemma to each of the four students (the 6, 7, 11 ½ and 12-year-old).

The first five tasks of the segment can be effectively used with *Piaget's Theory of Intellectual Development* in Chapter 2. The 6th task is intended to be used with *Kohlberg's Theory of Moral Development* in Chapter 3.

INSTRUCTIONAL RESOURCES

Transparencies (From the Transparency Package)

INSTRUCTIONAL RESOURCES

Transparencies (From the Transparency Package)

T 2.1   Factors Influencing Human Intellectual Development

T 2.4   Piaget's Stages and Characteristics

T 3.6   Kohlberg's Stages of Moral Development

Transparency Masters (From the Instructor's Manual)

TM 2.1 The Drive For Equilibrium

TM 2.3 Measuring Thinking

TM 2.5 Principles of Instruction for Applying Piaget's Theory in Classrooms

TM 2.6 A Comparison of Piaget's and Vygotsky's Views of Knowledge Construction

TM 3.8 Moral Reasoning on the Interstate

TM 3.10 A Classroom Dilemma

(In this Media Guide)

Questions for Discussion and Analysis

Feedback for "Questions for Discussion and Analysis"

Questions for Discussion and Analysis :
Segment #1: Piaget & Kohlberg

1. How does the thinking of the six-year-old in the episodes illustrate centration, nontransformation, and irreversibility?

2. What stage of reasoning is required to respond "accurately" to each of the first five tasks?

3. Into what Level and Stage of moral reasoning is the 6-year-old's thinking best classified in the sixth task?

4. Some critics argue that children's performances on conservation tasks depend on how well they understand the problem as described by the teacher or interviewer. Identify any examples in the episodes where the teacher's questions to the children could have been misleading. How could the question in each case be improved?

5. Construct an answer to the sixth task that would reflect postconventional thinking.

**Feedback for "Questions for Discussion and Analysis" for
Segment #1: Piaget & Kohlberg**

1. The six-year-old child focuses on only one aspect of the event, such as the height of the water (Task 3). Also, the child doesn't mentally record the process of the liquid being poured from one beaker to the other, and is unable to mentally describe the process begin reversed (the liquid going back from the larger to the smaller beaker.)

2. The first four tasks require concrete operations. The fifth task requires formal operations (control of variables).

3. He is at Stage 1 (Punishment and Obedience) of Level I (Preconventional Level). (Note to instructors: The information on the tape is described inaccurately. Preconventional, Conventional, and Postconventional are described as "Stages," and they should be described as "Levels.")

4. In the third task we're not sure if the child understands the question. The teacher asks, "Now, is there the same amount of water here than in here" [pointing at the beakers]. The child responds, "This one is taller," and the teacher doesn't follow up with a clarifying question, such as, "Yes it is taller, but are the amounts the same."

    In the fourth task the teacher--after spreading out the coins in one row--asks, "Is there the same amount of pennies in this row as this row or are they different?" It would be easy for a young child to center on the part of the question ". . . or are they different?" and not react to the number, particularly since the teacher never used the word "number" in any of her questions. The child follows up by saying, "And that one is bigger" [pointing to the longer row], and the teacher responds, "And that one is bigger why?" A better question could be, "Yes, this row is longer, but is the *number of coins the same or different in each row?*"

    The moral dilemma is long and totally verbal. It is unlikely that the young children understood the dilemma, instead centering on the question, "Is it OK to cheat?"

    It should be noted, however, that the older children responded differently in spite of the way the questions were asked.

5. A postconventional response would require a statement about cheating that would involve a principle. This could be described in a variety of ways, such as breaking the social contract between people (Stage 5) or not cheating because it would break the Golden Rule (Stage 6).

502

Educational Psychology Video Package: Video I
Segment #2: Cognitive Strategies

BEFORE YOU BEGIN

This 21-minute segment exists in three episodes, each featuring a different age group involved in the learning and application of cognitive strategies. The segment can be most effectively used with Chapter 9, "The Strategic Learner" with particular emphasis on *Study Strategies*.

The three parts of the segment appear as follows:

In the first episode: "Kindergarten: Learning to Question," the teacher reads a story to students and, through questioning, discusses the story with them. The teacher's goal is to develop students' reading readiness skills by:
- thinking about the story and its characters
- asking questions about the story
- predicting what will happen next in the story
- relating events to personal experiences.

In the second episode: "Seventh Grade: Reciprocal Teaching," the teacher and a group of six seventh-graders are reading a story about General George Armstrong Custer. The teacher then models the steps in the comprehensive study strategy: "Reciprocal Teaching." The segment also shows one of the students operating in the role of the teacher as the strategy is used.

In the third segment: "College: SQ4R," a college instructor outlines the steps in the study strategy: "SQ4R" with his class. The students are then given a short assignment in which they are directed to use the strategy. The *"Group Exercises for SQ4R"* transparency master that is provided as an **INSTRUCTIONAL RESOURCES** can be located in the Transparency Masters created for this section of the Media Guide.

INSTRUCTIONAL RESOURCES

Transparencies (From the Transparency Package)

T 9.7   Characteristics of Effective Strategy Users

T 9.8   Elements of Critical Thinking

Transparency Masters (From the Instructor's Manual)

TM 9.7   Utilizing SQ4R With This Text

TM 9.8   Principles of Instruction for Developing Strategic Learning

Transparency Masters (In this Media Guide)

Questions for Discussion and Analysis

Rating Scale "Cognitive Strategies"

Group Exercises for SQ4R

Feedback for "Questions for Discussion and Analysis"

Questions for Discussion and Analysis:
Segment #2: Cognitive Strategies

Kindergarten: Learning to Question

1. To what extent was the teacher's activity congruent with her goals?

2. Assess the teacher's pattern of interaction with her students. Could she have done anything to improve the quality of the interaction? If so, what?

Seventh Grade: Reciprocal Teaching

3. To what extent was the teacher's activity congruent with her goals?

4. How effectively did the teacher teach the strategy? What is the teacher's role when the students use the strategy? How well did the teacher in this episode fulfill that role?

College: SQ4R

5. Assess the teacher's effectiveness in teaching the study strategy: "SQ4R." What was effective about his activity? What could he have done to improve the learning activity?

Rating Scale for
Segment #2: Cognitive Strategies

Rate the effectiveness of the teacher on each of the following dimensions using the following scale:

5 = Excellent
4 = Very good
3 = Good
2 = Fair
1 = Poor
0 = No evidence available

Kindergarten: Learning to Question

1. The teacher's activity was congruent
   with her goals.   0 1 2 3 4 5

2. The teacher's patterns of interaction
   with her students was effective.   0 1 2 3 4 5

Seventh Grade: Reciprocal Teaching

3. The teacher's activity was congruent
   with her goals.   0 1 2 3 4 5

4. Assess the teacher's effectiveness
   in implementing each of the following steps:

a.	Summarizing	0 1 2 3 4 5
b.	Questioning	0 1 2 3 4 5
c.	Clarifying	0 1 2 3 4 5
d.	Predicting	0 1 2 3 4 5

College: SQ4R

5. The instructor's activity was congruent with his goal.   0 1 2 3 4 5

6. Assess the teacher's effectiveness in implementing each of the following steps:

a.	Survey	0 1 2 3 4 5
b.	Question	0 1 2 3 4 5
c.	Read	0 1 2 3 4 5
d.	Reflect	0 1 2 3 4 5
e.	Recite	0 1 2 3 4 5
f.	Review	0 1 2 3 4 5

GROUP EXERCISES for SQ4R

1. Break your class into groups of 6-9 students. Give each of the groups a story or article, assign one person in each group to be the teacher, and have the groups practice the strategy: "Reciprocal Teaching" on one of the paragraphs in the story or article. After one round, have a different student operate in the role of teacher. Conduct 3-4 rounds.

2. Model "SQ4R" for the students. Then have them practice the strategy as individuals with a portion of the story or article for 10-15 minutes.

3. After completing the experience with both "Reciprocal Teaching" and "SQ4R," conduct a whole-group discussion. In the process you may want to ask some of the following questions:

   Which of the strategies was easier to learn?

   Which strategy resulted in greater comprehension of the information you read? Why do you think so?

   Which strategy was more motivating for you? Why do you think so?

   Would you use one or the other or both of the strategies with your own students? Why or why not?

Feedback for "Questions for Discussion and Analysis" for
Segment #2: Cognitive Strategies

Kindergarten: Learning to Question

1. Her goal and activity were not congruent. Her goal was to help students develop their reading readiness skills by: thinking about the story, asking questions about the story, predicting what would happen next in the story, and relating events in the story to their personal lives. The students asked no questions about the story, and there was little evidence of the students predicting or relating the story's events to their personal experiences. Instead, the activity was directed toward the comprehension of terms based on their context in the story. While this is a perfectly appropriate activity, it isn't consistent with the intent of the activity.

2. The students primarily gave group responses that were usually a repeat of what the teacher had already said. While sometimes difficult, it would have been better to get at least some responses from the students as individuals. Since the goal was for students to learn cognitive strategies, the interaction would also have been more effective if the teacher had asked the students to predict what they thought might happen next in the story and also ask them about any personal experiences that might relate to the story, such as, "Suppose your mother says to you, 'Don't muck about in your room.' What do you think she means by that?"

Seventh Grade: Reciprocal Teaching

3. The goal and learning activity were essentially congruent. She wanted students to understand "Reciprocal Teaching," and her learning activity was directed at that goal.

4. The teacher's activity was quite effective. She explained the steps in "Reciprocal Teaching," and she then modeled the strategy with the students. This was followed by having one of the students operate in the role of the teacher.

    An additional teacher role is to monitor the process and give the students feedback about their progress. We have no evidence one way or the other about how well the teacher fulfilled her role.

College: SQ4R

5. The effective aspects of the activity were the clarity of the description of "SQ4R" and the fact that students were given the opportunity to practice on their own. However, the learning activity was essentially a lecture in which each of the steps in "SQ4R" was merely described. Then the students were asked to practice on their own. The learning activity would have been improved if the instructor had modeled the strategy with students using a sample from their texts. This should then have been followed with opportunities for student practice with feedback. Lack of teacher modeling and student practice and feedback detracted from the effectiveness of the activity. In effect, the activity was out of alignment with the goal.

508

Educational Psychology Video Package: Video I
Segment #3: Cooperative Learning

BEFORE YOU BEGIN

This 13-minute segment features the use of Student Teams Achievement Divisions (STAD)--a cooperative learning strategy--with a seventh-grade math class. The segment begins by explaining the rationale for STAD and then shows the following scenes:

- Conventional Instruction - Conventional independent practice where students work alone on seatwork assignments is illustrated.
- Cooperative Learning Components - The principles on which STAD are based are presented. These are:
  - Group Rewards
  - Individual Accountability
  - Equal Opportunity for Success
- Planning Activities - The scene shows the teacher preparing exercises and worksheets for students to use when they work as teams.
- Forming Teams - The class is organized into 4-5 member STAD teams in this scene.
- Teaching Team Etiquette/Ground Rules - This scene illustrates the teacher's efforts to help the groups develop skills in cooperation and groupwork.
- Teaching the Lesson - This short scene illustrates the teacher developing the concept of estimation.
- Beginning Cooperative Learning Activities - The students join their groups. They work together by quizzing the tutoring one another. It is explained that team scores are determined on the basis of how much individual members improve, rather than on absolute scores.
- Administering the Unit Test - In this scene the teacher--about a week later--gives a unit test, which is taken individually.
- Scoring Tests - The teacher scores the test and computes improvement points for each student.
- Computing Team Points - Team points are computed and associated rewards are determined.
- Recognizing Team Accomplishments - In this scene the teacher identifies gold and silver medalists, hands out certificates of award to team members, and notes that the students have earned free time for their accomplishments.

The segment can be used most effectively with *Cooperative Learning* in Chapter 8.

INSTRUCTIONAL RESOURCES

Transparencies (From the Transparency Package)

T 8.3   Characteristics of Constructivism

Transparency Masters (From the Instructor's Manual)

TM 8.6 Characteristics of Cooperative Learning

TM 8.7 Capitalizing on Diversity with Cooperative Learning

Transparency Masters (In this Media Guide)

Questions for Discussion and Analysis

Feedback for "Questions for Discussion and Analysis"

Questions for Discussion and Analysis:
Segment #3: Cooperative Learning

1. What advantages does the group activity in cooperative learning have over traditional seatwork?

2. What strategies could the teacher in the video have used to ensure diversity in the cooperative learning groups?

3. On what view of learning is the awarding of improvement points as presented in the Media Guide based?

4. For teaching what kind of content is STAD probably most easily applied? Provide a rationale for your answer.

5. For what content areas would STAD be most easily applied? Provide a rationale for your answer.

6. The video segment demonstrated that it is possible for all groups to win a gold medal. How was this accomplished?

Feedback for "Questions for Discussion and Analysis" for
Segment #3: Cooperative Learning

1. There are several advantages. First, students aren't working alone, instead being actively involved with other students. This is especially important for poorly motivated students. Students also get immediate feedback in terms of their work. Also, students have opportunities to explain concepts and skills to other students, which has benefits to both the explainer and the student being taught.

2. In terms of group composition, the teacher could have placed equal numbers of high and low ability students, males and females, and students from different ethnic groups on different teams. During training, she could have stressed the importance of all students contributing and then followed through with monitoring to ensure that this occurred.

3. On what view of learning is the awarding of improvement points as presented in the Media Guide based?

   The awarding of improvement points is as follows:

Perfect paper	30
> 10 above	30
0-10 above	20
1-10 below	10
> 10 below	0

   This system is based on behaviorism, which for some people is somewhat controversial.

4. Because worksheets with convergent answers can be more easily prepared for concepts and the application of principles, rules, and generalizations, applying STAD with these content forms is probably easier than for teaching organized bodies of knowledge.

5. Because there is more skill development in areas such as math, language arts, and some parts of science, STAD is probably more applicable with them than it is in areas such as social studies.

6. The medal award is based on the average improvement of the group, and the groups don't compete with each other.

511

Educational Psychology Video Package: Video I
Segment #4: Classroom Management

BEFORE YOU BEGIN

This approximately 25-minute segment exists in three parts. The first--a 3-minute episode--demonstrates a second grade teacher on the first day of school establishing rules for her class. The brief second part (about 2 minutes) illustrates the teacher reinforcing her rules about a week later, and the third part--the remainder of the segment-illustrates the teacher monitoring and enforcing her rules during four typical instructional activities.

Before the four activities in the third part are presented, the following questions are displayed on the screen.
1. Is the teacher's orientation more positive than negative?
2. Does she demonstrate "smoothness" and "withitness"?
3. Does she use the least disruptive interventions?
4. Are her management techniques effective overall? Why or why not?

Students are asked to think about and respond to these questions as they view the video.

The four learning activities occur as follows:
- Reading Groups (9:00 a.m.): In this episode (about 4 minutes long) the teacher works with one reading group while the rest of the class does seatwork. We see her simultaneously conduct the reading groups and monitor students doing seatwork.
- Language Arts (10:30 a.m.): During this approximately 5-minute episode the teacher conducts a whole-group activity on identifying nouns.
- Math (12:30 p.m.): During this episode of about 7 minutes, the teacher conducts a brief whole-class activity on math facts and then makes the transition to seatwork. She uses negative reinforcement at one point (threatens the students with loss of playground time if they aren't quiet and on-task).
- Writing (1:45 p.m.): In this 3-minute episode, the teacher begins the writing period by applying the Premack Principle (using the more preferred activity--coloring--as a reinforcer for producing good quality writing). She then passes out papers and offers suggestions about correctly writing letters.

The segment is designed to be used with Chapter 12, Creating Productive Learning Environments, with particular emphasis on *planning for effective classroom management*, *rules and procedures*, and *dealing with misbehavior*.

INSTRUCTIONAL RESOURCES

Transparencies (From the Transparency Package)

T 12.1 Planning For an Orderly Classroom

T 12.2 Learner Characteristics Affecting Classroom Management

T 12.3 Guidelines For Preparing Rules

T 12.9 An Intervention Continuum

Transparency Masters (From the Instructor's Manual)

TM 12.2   Sample Classroom Procedures

Transparency Masters (In this Media Guide)

Questions for Discussion and Analysis

Ms. Riley's Rules

Additional Questions to Consider

Feedback for "Questions for Discussion and Analysis"

Questions for Discussion and Analysis:
Segment #4: Classroom Management

1. Assess the teacher's rules according to the criteria for effective rules described in the text.

2. Describe the physical environment of the teacher's classroom. What aspect of the environment might make managing the students a bit difficult.

3. Discuss the teacher's characteristics. Does she demonstrate caring, firmness, and democracy? Provide a rationale for your answer.

4. The first episode indicates at least two important characteristics of effective management. What are they?

5. What did the teacher do in her language arts activity to maintain student involvement?

6. Do the students appear less attentive in their writing lesson than in the other lessons? If so, what might be a reason?

7. The teacher used at least two concepts from behaviorism extensively in managing her students. What are these concepts?

8. If the students were 7th graders, would the teacher's strategies need to change to be effective?

MS. RILEY'S RULES

1. Follow directions.

2. Be polite.

3. Obey safety rules.

4. Come to class prepared with supplies and homework.

5. Work quietly and independently using self-control.

Additional Questions to Consider for
Segment #4: Classroom Management

1. Is the teacher's orientation more positive than negative?

2. Does she demonstrate "smoothness" and "withitness"?

3. Does she use the least disruptive interventions?

4. Are her management techniques effective overall? Why or why not?

Feedback for "Questions for Discussion and Analysis" for
Segment #4: Classroom Management

1. Her rules meet the criteria. While a rule such as, "Be Polite" is general, it appeared that she gave examples of the rule, thereby clarifying it. Her other rules were stately clearly, with the exception of the phrase "self-control" for which we have no evidence one way or the other in the segment. She only has five rules, and they are stated positively. She provided rationales for rules by discussing in detail the need for them, which also provided the students with opportunities for input. (The students didn't have actual input into the creation of the rules themselves.)

2. The major problem with her physical environment is the fact that her class is large, which is out of her control. The students are close together, which increases the likelihood of distractions.

3. The climate in the classroom appeared to be positive, suggesting a caring teacher. She also used "desists" in a positive way, but followed through to be certain that they complied, which suggests firmness. The combination of the two are characteristic of a democratic teacher.

4. Among the characteristics is the fact that she established classroom rules, and began the process the very first day of school, so her management patterns for the year were established from the first day.

5. She used a "thumbs up, thumbs down" technique to get responses from all the students.

6. It was nearing the end of the day, and students were probably getting tired.

7. She used positive reinforcement in the form of praise, and she used vicarious reinforcement in the form of statements such as, "You should see Ricky being so polite. Thank you, Ricky, for not disturbing the rest of the class," and "This whole table group has their English books out and their folders open." (The individuals or group she refers to are serving as models as well.)

8. She would need to reduce her extensive use of group praise and vicarious reinforcement to prevent satiation with older students. A stronger appeal to self-responsibility and personal initiative would be needed.

Educational Psychology Video Package: Video I
Segment #5: Lecture Discussions

BEFORE YOU BEGIN

This segment is approximately 15 minutes long. It shows excerpts from a 50-minute lesson on the Civil War, taught to a fifth-grade class using a lecture-discussion strategy. The segment is designed to be used with the content of Chapter 7. The segment can be used as a basis for assessing the teacher's behavior with respect to the following topics:

Topic	Chapter
Encoding: Making connections in long-term memory	7
Schema production: Acquiring integrative declarative knowledge	7
Essential teaching skills	13

INSTRUCTIONAL RESOURCES

Transparencies (From the Transparency Package)

T 7.2   An Information Processing Model

T 13.4   Essential Teaching Skills

T 13.6   Characteristics of Effective Questioning

Transparency Masters (From the Instructor's Manual)

TM 7.3 Characteristics of the Memory Stores

TM 7.4 Questions that Promote Deep Processing of Information

TM 7.5 Background Knowledge and Encoding

TM 7.14 Principles of Instruction for Applying Information Processing in Classrooms

Transparency Masters (In this Media Guide)

Questions for Discussion and Analysis

Rating Scale: Lecture Discussions

Feedback for "Questions for Discussion and Analysis"

Questions for Discussion and Analysis:
Segment #5: Lecture Discussions

1. What type of content was the teacher teaching?

2. What strategy did the instructor use?

3. How well did the teacher utilize her allocated time.

4. How well did the teacher promote meaningfulness in her lesson?

5. How effectively did the teacher demonstrate each of the following essential teaching skills?
   Use of Time:
   Organization:
   Communication:
   Focus:
   Feedback:
   Monitoring:
   Questioning:
   Review and Closure:

6. How clearly did the teacher demonstrate one or more lecture-discussion cycles.

7. How effective was this lesson from a constructivist perspective?

Rating Scale for
Segment #5: Lecture Discussions

Rate the effectiveness of the teacher on each of the following dimensions using the following scale:
- 5 = Excellent
- 4 = Very good
- 3 = Good
- 2 = Fair
- 1 = Poor
- 0 = No evidence available

1. The teacher used her time efficiently.   0 1 2 3 4 5

2. The teacher made the content meaningful to the students.   0 1 2 3 4 5

3. The teacher effectively demonstrated essential teaching skills.

Organization:	0 1 2 3 4 5
Clear language:	0 1 2 3 4 5
Connected discourse:	0 1 2 3 4 5
Introductory Focus:	0 1 2 3 4 5
Sensory Focus:	0 1 2 3 4 5
Review and Closure:	0 1 2 3 4 5
Questioning:	0 1 2 3 4 5

4. The teacher clearly demonstrated one or more lecture-discussion cycles.   0 1 2 3 4 5

Feedback for "Questions for Discussion and Analysis" for
Segment #5: Lecture Discussions

1. An organized body of knowledge. Note how the presentation combined facts, concepts and generalizations into a connected body of information.

2. Lecture-discussion is characterized by intermittent questions to clarify points and ascertain student comprehension.

3. She began her lesson on time, and what materials she used were available and ready. The students were generally engaged. We saw only a few instances of inattentiveness. We have little evidence about the students' level of success, so we don't know about academic learning time.

4. She could have done a much better job in this regard. She had little observable organization in the lesson. The content could have been made more meaningful with a visual form of organization, such as a matrix or hierarchy. There was no evidence of elaboration in the lesson. The students were relatively active in the question and answer portion of the lesson.

5. Organization: Managerially, she was well organized. The lesson started promptly, her map was ready, and students quickly made the transition from seatwork to the activity. Conceptually, the lesson covered too much content which was only loosely connected.

   Communication: She gave an effective transition signal at the beginning of the lesson, and her language was clear. We have little evidence of emphasis. Her primary problem was a lack of a systematic thread in the lesson, i.e., her discourse was scrambled. She dealt with the topics of sectionalism, slavery, President Lincoln, The Civil War, and Reconstruction all in the same lesson without links between the different topics. As a result, it is unlikely that the information became meaningful for the students.

   Focus: Her initial lesson objectives provided a form of introductory focus. She could have better capitalized on introductory focus by putting the lesson in the context of a problem or question, such as factors leading to the Civil War, why slavery existed in the South but not the North, or why the North won the War. A form of conceptual organization, such as a hierarchy or matrix would have significantly improved her sensory focus.

   Feedback: We have little evidence of feedback other than her general responses to student answers.

   Monitoring: While evidence of monitoring was not extensive, she appeared to be aware of students' behaviors, for example, she noticed that one of the boys wasn't sitting with his chair flat on the floor.

   Review and
   Closure: There was little evidence of either review or closure in the lesson. The discussion ended rather abruptly, and she then gave students the assignment of an essay to write in class. The assignment was related to the discussion in only a general way. She then gave a homework assignment, which asked the students to respond to a very abstract concept, which again was only related to the lesson in a general way.

Questioning: She asked a variety of questions. However, they were directed primarily to volunteers, and she did little prompting when a student was unable to answer.

6. The lecture-discussion cycles lacked clarity. In a typical lecture-discussion cycle, the teacher presents information for a brief period and then asks questions directly related to the information to check the extent to which students comprehend the information . The relationship between information presentation and comprehension monitoring wasn't clear in this lesson.

7. Other than specific examples describing how the slaves would subvert the plantation owners, the lesson was conducted largely in the abstract. Also, there was little evidence of sequencing from concrete to abstract thinking in the discussion.

Educational Psychology Video Package: Video I
Segment #6: Classrooms in Action

BEFORE YOU BEGIN

The three episodes on this 40-minute segment illustrate instruction as it typically occurs in secondary school classrooms. As such, the episodes can be effectively used to give your students practice in analyzing and assessing teaching behaviors and teachers' ability to apply principles of learning and motivation.

Episode #1: Letters of Application and Resume Writing

In the first episode--about 9 minutes long--an English teacher is discussing the characteristics of a good letter of application, what should go in a résumé and how people should act in a job interview. The segment can be used as a basis for assessing the teacher's behavior with respect to the following topics:

Topic	Chapter
Meaningful Encoding: Making connections in long-term memory	7
Acquiring Procedural Knowledge	7
Acquiring Integrative Declarative Knowledge	7
Concept Learning	9
Essential teaching skills	13

INSTRUCTIONAL RESOURCES

Transparencies (From the Transparency Package)

T 7.2   An Information Processing Model

T 13.4   Essential Teaching Skills

T 13.6   Characteristics of Effective Questioning

Transparency Masters (From the Instructor's Manual)

TM 7.3 Characteristics of the Memory Stores

TM 7.4 Questions that Promote Deep Processing of Information

TM 7.5 Background Knowledge and Encoding

TM 7.14 Principles of Instruction for Applying Information Processing in Classrooms

TM 8.4 Principles of Instruction for Applying Constructivism in Classrooms

Transparency Masters (In this Media Guide)

Questions for Discussion and Analysis

Rating Scale "Letters of Application"

Feedback for "Questions for Discussion and Analysis"

QUESTIONS FOR DISCUSSION AND ANALYSIS:
Segment #6: Classrooms in Action
Episode #1: Letters of Application and Résumé Writing

1. What type of content was the teacher teaching?

2. What strategy did she use?

3. What were the primary strengths and weaknesses of the lesson?

4. How well did the teacher promote meaningfulness in her lesson?

5. How effectively did the teacher demonstrate each of the following essential teaching skills?

   Organization:
   Communication:
   Focus:
   Feedback:
   Monitoring:
   Review and Closure:
   Questioning:

6. How effective was this lesson from a constructivist perspective?

Rating Scale for Segment #6: Classrooms in Action
Episode #1: Letters of Application and Résumé Writing

Rate the effectiveness of the teacher on each of the following dimensions using the following scale:
5 = Excellent, 4 = Very good, 3 = Good, 2 = Fair, 1 = Poor, 0 = No evidence available

1. The teacher used Lecture-Discussion effectively.   0 1 2 3 4 5

2. The teacher made the content meaningful to the students.   0 1 2 3 4 5

3. The teacher used high-quality examples.   0 1 2 3 4 5

4. The teacher effectively demonstrated essential teaching skills.

    Organization: 0 1 2 3 4 5
    Clear language: 0 1 2 3 4 5
    Connected discourse: 0 1 2 3 4 5
    Introductory Focus: 0 1 2 3 4 5
    Sensory Focus: 0 1 2 3 4 5
    Review and Closure: 0 1 2 3 4 5
    Questioning: 0 1 2 3 4 5

5. The lesson demonstrated application of constructivist principles.   0 1 2 3 4 5

**Feedback for "Questions for Discussion and Analysis" for
Segment #6: Classrooms in Action
Episode #1: Letters of Application and Résumé Writing**

1. She was teaching what amounted to concepts--the concept of an effective letter of application, the concept of an effective résumé, and the concept of effective behavior in an interview. As students practiced each, procedural skill learning would be involved.

2. Lecture-discussion.

3. The strengths of the lesson were her interactions with students. She was positive and enthusiastic. The lesson would have been substantially improved if she had shown the students an example of a good letter of application compared to a poor letter of application, and a good and poor résumé, asking students to analyze differences.

4. Examples would have made the lesson much more meaningful for the students. There was little evidence of elaboration or organization, and the students were more passive than active in the lesson.

5. Organization: We don't know whether or not the lesson began promptly, and she used no materials other than the chalkboard. The activity was partially congruent with the implied goal of learning to write effective letters of application and resumes in that they learned about characteristics of effective letters, but never put these into practice.

   Communication: Her language was clear and precise, and the discourse was connected. There was no evidence of emphasis or transition signals.

   Focus: Her introductory focus was weak; she merely announced that they were discussing letters of application. She gave no introduction that would draw students into the lesson.

      Her sensory focus could have been dramatically improved by having an example of an effective letter of application to look at during the course of the lesson, or two--one good and one bad--for students to analyze.

   Feedback: There was a minimum of responding, so feedback was limited.

   Monitoring: There was little evidence of monitoring.

   Review and
   Closure: She summarized what they discussed as a review.

   Questioning: She displayed few of the effective questioning behaviors. She didn't ask many questions, and those that were asked were not directed to individuals. There was little evidence of wait-time and no need for prompting was evident.

6. The lesson was conducted primarily in the abstract. As noted earlier, a concrete example of a résumé, letters of application or a role-played interview would have helped considerably.

Educational Psychology Video Package: Video I
Segment #6: Classrooms in Action
Episode #2: The Vietnam War

In the second episode--about 13 minutes long--a social studies teacher is beginning a discussion of the Vietnam War. The segment can be used as a basis for assessing the teacher's behavior with respect to the following topics:

Topic	Chapter
Meaningful Encoding: Making connections in long-term memory	7
Acquiring Procedural Knowledge	7
Acquiring Declarative Knowledge	7
Essential teaching skills	13

INSTRUCTIONAL RESOURCES

Transparencies (From the Transparency Package)

T 7.2 An Information Processing Model

T 7.3 The Limitations of Working Memory

T 13.4 Essential Teaching Skills

T 13.6 Characteristics of Effective Questioning

Transparency Masters (From the Instructor's Manual)

TM 7.3 Characteristics of the Memory Stores

TM 7.4 Questions that Promote Deep Processing of Information

TM 7.5 Background Knowledge and Encoding

TM 7.6 Elaborating on Past Experiences

TM 7.14 Principles of Instruction for Applying Information Processing in Classrooms

Transparency Masters (In this Media Guide)

Questions for Discussion and Analysis

Rating Scale "The Vietnam War"

Feedback for "Questions for Discussion and Analysis"

**QUESTIONS FOR
DISCUSSION AND ANALYSIS:
Segment #6: Classrooms in Action
Episode #2: The Vietnam War**

1. What type of content was the teacher teaching?

2. What procedure did he use?

3. What were the primary strengths and weaknesses of the lesson?

4. How well did the teacher promote meaningfulness in his lesson?

5. How effectively did the teacher demonstrate each of these essential teaching skills?

   Organization:
   Communication:
   Focus:
   Feedback:
   Monitoring:
   Review and Closure:
   Questioning:

6. How is this lesson similar to and different from the lesson on writing letters of application?

**Rating Scale for
Segment #6: Classrooms in Action
Episode #3: The Vietnam War**

Rate the effectiveness of the teacher on each of the following dimensions using the following scale:
5 = Excellent, 4 = Very good, 3 = Good, 2 = Fair, 1 = Poor
0 = No evidence available

1. The teacher used Lecture-Discussion
   effectively.   0 1 2 3 4 5

2. The teacher made the content   0 1 2 3 4 5
   meaningful to students.

3. The teacher effectively demonstrated
   essential teaching skills.

   Organization: 0 1 2 3 4 5
   Clear language: 0 1 2 3 4 5
   Connected discourse: 0 1 2 3 4 5
   Introductory Focus: 0 1 2 3 4 5
   Sensory Focus: 0 1 2 3 4 5
   Review and Closure: 0 1 2 3 4 5
   Questioning: 0 1 2 3 4 5

4. The lesson demonstrated application of
   constructivist principles.   0 1 2 3 4 5

Feedback for "Questions for Discussion and Analysis" for
Segment #6: Classrooms in Action
Episode #3: The Vietnam War

1. He was beginning a discussion of the Vietnam War, which is an organized body of knowledge. However, the episode primarily illustrated the presentation of facts. Presumably they would be incorporated into an organized body of knowledge as the unit on the Vietnam War progressed.

2. Primarily lecture, with some small elements of lecture-discussion.

3. The strengths of the lesson were in his manner. He was pleasant, enthusiastic, and knowledgeable about his content. The major weakness of the lesson was that he used lecture as his primary teaching strategy which put the students in an almost totally passive mode.

4. The map drawn on the chalkboard provided a form of organization. Otherwise, he did little to promote meaningfulness in the lesson. The biggest problem was the lack of activity on the part of students.

5. Organization: We don't know whether or not the lesson began promptly, and he used no materials other than the chalkboard. The activity was an introduction to the topic of the Vietnam War.

    Communication: His language was clear and precise, and the discourse was connected. His communication skills were generally very good.

    Focus: His introductory focus was limited. He merely began by announcing that they would be studying the Vietnam War.

    His map on the chalkboard provided adequate sensory focus. A map putting Vietnam in the larger context of Asia, or the world, would have improved his sensory focus.

    Feedback: Since lecture was the teaching technique, little opportunity for feedback existed.

    Monitoring: Little evidence of monitoring appeared in the lesson.

    Review and
    Closure: Little evidence of review or closure existed.

    Questioning: Again, since lecture was the teaching strategy, few questions were asked. He demonstrated virtually none of the effective questioning skills we look for in teachers.

6. 1) The primary difference is in the type of content taught. The English teacher taught concepts and procedural skills, while this teacher was teaching facts [leading to an organized body of knowledge]. 2) The English teacher had taught some aspects of writing letters of application as evidenced by her questions, while this teacher was introducing his unit. The English teacher was more interactive in her teaching, involving more students in the lesson.

Educational Psychology Video Package: Video I
Segment #6: Classrooms in Action
Episode #3: Charles Law

In this 16-minute episode a chemistry teacher teaches Charles Law and the procedure for finding temperature and volume when conditions change. The segment can be used as a basis for assessing the teacher's behavior with respect to the following topics:

Topic	Chapter
Meaningful Encoding: Making connections in long-term memory	7
Acquiring Procedural knowledge	7
Acquiring Declarative Knowledge	7
Discovery Learning	8
Concept Learning	9
Essential teaching skills	13

INSTRUCTIONAL RESOURCES

Transparencies (From the Transparency Package)

T 7.2 An Information Processing Model

T 13.4 Essential Teaching Skills

T 13.6 Characteristics of Effective Questioning

Transparency Masters (From the Instructor's Manual)

TM 7.3 Characteristics of the Memory Stores

TM 7.4 Questions that Promote Deep Processing of Information

TM 7.5 Background Knowledge and Encoding

TM 7.14 Principles of Instruction for Applying Information Processing in Classrooms

TM 8.4 Principles of Instruction for Applying Constructivism in Classrooms

Transparency Masters (In this Media Guide)

Questions for Discussion and Analysis

Rating Scale: "Charles's Law"

Feedback for "Questions for Discussion and Analysis"

QUESTIONS FOR
DISCUSSION AND ANALYSIS:
Segment #6: Classrooms in Action
Episode #3: Charles Law

1. What type of content was the teacher teaching?

2. What strategy did she use?

3. Assess her application of the direct instruction model. Were all of the phases present? If so, how well did she apply each phase?

4. How well did the teacher promote meaningfulness in her lesson?

5. How effectively did the teacher demonstrate each of the essential teaching skills?
    Organization:
    Communication:
    Focus:
    Feedback:
    Monitoring:
    Review and Closure:
    Questioning:

6. How effective was this lesson from a learner-centered perspective?

Rating Scale for
Segment #6: Classrooms in Action
Episode #3: CHARLES LAW

Rate the effectiveness of the teacher on each of the following dimensions using the following scale:
5 = Excellent, 4 = Very good, 3 = Good, 2 = Fair, 1 = Poor
0 = No evidence available

1. The teacher used the Direct-Instruction Model effectively.

Introduction and Review	0 1 2 3 4 5
Presentation	0 1 2 3 4 5
Guided Practice	0 1 2 3 4 5
Independent Practice	0 1 2 3 4 5

2. The teacher made the content meaningful to the students.   0 1 2 3 4 5

3. The teacher used high-quality examples. 0 1 2 3 4 5

4. The teacher effectively demonstrated essential teaching skills.

Organization:	0 1 2 3 4 5
Clear language:	0 1 2 3 4 5
Connected discourse:	0 1 2 3 4 5
Introductory Focus:	0 1 2 3 4 5
Sensory Focus:	0 1 2 3 4 5
Review and Closure:	0 1 2 3 4 5
Questioning:	0 1 2 3 4 5

5. Overall effectiveness of lesson   0 1 2 3 4 5

Feedback for "Questions for Discussion and Analysis" for
Segment #6: Classrooms in Action
Episode #3: Charles Law

1. As the name "Charles Law" implies, she taught a law (principle). She then moved to the procedures for calculating temperatures and volumes, which is a procedural skill.

2. Direct instruction was the primary mode. (The presentation phase of her direct instruction was lecture-discussion.) There was a brief episode of guided discovery as the students formed the statement of Charles Law based on her demonstration.

3. Each phase was present. She first reviewed kinetic theory as a context for understanding Charles Law, she demonstrated the law [with her balloons and water], and she then moved on to the procedure for finding temperatures and pressures.

4. This was one of the weakest aspects of the lesson. The problem was that the lesson existed primarily at a knowledge and memorization level. For example, the students memorized the procedure for solving the problems, and the problems all existed in the abstract. Her review promoted elaboration, and the students were quite active throughout the lesson.

5. Organization: She was well organized. She began her demonstration, then moved on to another part of the lesson, and then moved back to her demonstration when the changes were observable.

    Communication: Her language was clear and precise, and the discourse was connected. There was little evidence of emphasis or transition signals.

    Focus: Her introductory focus was quite good. She began with a review which served as a beginning point for the rest of her lesson.

                      Her demonstration was an excellent form of sensory focus. Her examples on the chalkboard provided adequate sensory focus as she taught the procedural skill.

    Feedback: She presumably gave students feedback as she monitored their seatwork.

    Monitoring: She questioned students during the lesson to assess comprehension. Also, she monitored the students as they did their seat work.

    Review and
    Closure: She provided a clear and concise review of Charles Law.

    Questioning: Her questioning was quite good. The primary improvement that she could have made would have been to direct questions to individuals by name. Since the students were able to answer, no evidence of prompting existed.

6. The lesson was effective but almost totally teacher-centered. Other than the concrete demonstration of Charles Law, there was little about the lesson that was learner-centered. It could have been initially conducted as a guided discovery, and the problems could have been made more meaningful by making them more personalized. For example, room temperature and the temperature inside a refrigerator could have been used together with common volumes, such as the volumes of measuring cups (which are now commonly graduated both in English and metric units). In addition, she might have used think-pair-share to more actively involve all students.

Educational Psychology Video Package, Video II (Overview)

Video II
   Total Length: 92 Minutes

	Segment	Chapter(s)	Running Time
I.	Teaching for Learner Diversity	2-5, 7-9, 13	27 min.
2.	Reflecting on the Multiple Roles of Teaching	1, 12,13	21 min.
3.	Essential Teaching Skills	13	18 min.
4.	Involving Students Through Groupwork	8	17 min.
5.	Teaching Whole Language	2	10 min.

SEGMENT SUMMARIES

SEGMENT #1: TEACHING FOR LEARNER DIVERSITY
This 27-minute segment shows a first grade teacher using students' background knowledge to develop concepts and reading skills. It contains an interactive questioning section, student book reports and a short play.

SEGMENT #2: REFLECTING ON THE MULTIPLE ROLES OF TEACHING
This 21-minute segment follows an experienced fifth grade teacher through a typical school day and captures her planning, evaluating, and interacting with students. The teacher is shown arranging her classroom to support learning, testing and grading, planning for instruction, using a variety of teaching strategies, and meeting with a parent. It concludes with an interview in which the teacher reflects about her teaching.

SEGMENT #3: ESSENTIAL TEACHING SKILLS
This 18-minute segment shows a junior high science teacher using lecture-discussion to teach about the worm family.

SEGMENT #4: INVOLVING STUDENTS THROUGH GROUPWORK
In this three-part, 17-minute segment we see teachers using groupwork in three different ways. In the first part a sixth grade teacher has students work in groups to answer textbook questions. In the second, a junior high science teacher uses groupwork to help students learn about the life cycle of a sheep liver fluke and how to use mnemonic devices to remember information. In the third part the same science teacher uses groupwork to teach problem solving and higher order thinking skills.

SEGMENT #5: TEACHING WHOLE LANGUAGE
In this ten and a half minute segment a first grade teacher uses elements of whole language teaching to develop her students' language skills. Choral reading, learning centers, student writing and peer-reading are featured.

Educational Psychology Video Package: Video II
Segment #1: Teaching for Learner Diversity

BEFORE YOU BEGIN

This 27-minute segment illustrates how a first grade teacher uses a variety of instructional strategies to develop and build upon her students' background knowledge. In the first segment, which lasts 11 minutes, the teacher uses a whole language approach to develop vocabulary and build concepts. Through interactive questioning the teacher builds on students' background knowledge about planting a garden.

Student book reports are the central focus of the second segment. As two students talk about the books they've read about pets, the teacher skillfully involves the rest of the class through questions and problems.

In the third segment we see students role playing and acting in a little play based upon a book that the class has previously read. Again the teacher does an excellent job of making connections between words and abstract ideas and the concrete experiences of the play.

The segment can be used to illustrate ideas in the following chapters:

Topic	Chapter
Background Knowledge: A Source of Diversity	2
Learner Differences	4
Impact of Diversity on Information Processing	7
Teacher Characteristics and Motivation	11

INSTRUCTIONAL RESOURCES

Transparencies (From the Transparency Package)

T 2.1 Factors Influencing Human Intellectual Development

T 2.3 Maintaining Equilibrium Through the Process of Adaptation

T 4.1 Sources of Learner Individuality

T 11.2   A Model for Promoting Student Motivation

Transparency Masters (From the Instructor's Manual)

TM 4.6   Principles of Instruction for Culturally Responsive Teaching

TM 4.7   Making Students Feel Welcome in School

TM 4.8   Gender Differences in the Classroom

TM 4.11 Principles of Instruction for Teaching Students Placed At Risk

TM 7.5   Background Knowledge and Encoding

Transparency Masters (In this Media Guide)

Questions for Discussion and Analysis

Feedback for "Questions for Discussion and Analysis"

1. How effectively did the teacher use the following strategies?
   a. Concrete examples
   b. Personalization
   c. Teacher-student interaction
   d. Student-student interaction

2. How effectively did the teacher implement the following characteristics of whole language?
   a. Use of language to think about and describe experiences
   b. Use of language to communicate with others
   c. Use of language across the curriculum

3. How effectively did the teacher use the following strategies to accommodate background diversity?
   a. Assessing student background knowledge
   b. Providing background experiences
   c. Using experiences of students to augment others

4. How well did the teacher utilize the following motivational components?
   a. Enthusiasm
   b. Caring
   c. Expectations

5. How well did the teacher implement the following characteristics of effective questioning?
   a. Frequency
   b. Equitable distribution
   c. Prompting
   d. Wait-time

**Feedback for "Questions for Discussion and Analysis" for
Segment #2: Teaching for Learner Diversity**

1. *Concrete examples*   The pictures in the books as well as the props in the play provided concrete examples. The teacher also encouraged students to recall their own experiences in working in gardens.

   Personalization   The teacher asked students to recall their experiences in planting gardens as well as their experiences with their hamster.

   Teacher-student interaction   The questioning sessions provided considerable amounts of teacher- student interaction.

   Student-student interaction   Though this interaction was one-to-one, the book reports provided opportunities for student-student interaction.

2. *Use of language to think about and describe experiences*

   The teacher did an excellent job of encouraging students to think about their own experiences in working in gardens.

   Use of language to communicate with others

   The teacher capitalized on this when she made the book reports interactive and when she translated the book they had read into a play.

   Use of language across the curriculum

   At several points in the lesson on plants she encouraged students to recall information from their science lessons.

3. *Assessing student background knowledge*

   The teacher did this through her interactive questioning.

   Providing background experiences

   She did this through the play and the pictures in the book. It appeared to be adequate.

   Using experiences of students to augment others

   The teacher encouraged students to share their experiences about gardens and pets.

4. *Enthusiasm*   The teacher had a positive, enthusiastic manner.

   Caring   Through both verbal and nonverbal channels the teacher exhibited a warm interpersonal style.

   Expectations   Though this wasn't explicitly stated, the teacher appeared to have positive expectations for all students.

5. *Frequency*   During the first two sessions she used a large number of questions.

Equitable distribution	At several points in the presentation the teacher consciously tried to involve more students.
Prompting	This may have been the teacher's only major weakness. At several times she responded with a "No" rather than taking the time to elicit a better student response.
Wait-time	Most of her questions were convergent and required little wait-time.

Educational Psychology Video Package: Video II
Segment #2: Reflecting on the Multiple Roles of Teaching

BEFORE YOU BEGIN

This 21-minute segment explores the multiple roles of teaching from an elementary teacher's perspective. Divided into two segments, the first part of this video contains a number of segments capturing the teacher during planning, instruction, management and assessment. In the second segment the teacher talks about the way she plans to meet learner needs, how she plans and implements instruction for total student growth and strategies she uses to involve parents in the learning process. The segment can be used in a number of ways to stimulate students' thinking on the following topics:

Topic	Chapter
Teaching in the Real World	1
Classroom Management	12
Planning for Instruction	13
Instruction	13
Assessing Classroom Learning	14

INSTRUCTIONAL RESOURCES

Transparencies (From the Transparency Package)

T 12.1 Planning For An Orderly Classroom

T 12.2 Learner Characteristics Affecting Classroom Management

T 12.3 Guidelines For Preparing Rules

T 13.4 Essential Teaching Skills

T 13.6 Characteristics of Effective Questioning

T 14.2 Teachers' Assessment Patterns

T 14.3 Characteristics of Teacher-Made Test Items

Transparency Masters (From the Instructor's Manual)

TM 12.2   Sample Classroom Procedures

Transparency Masters (In this Media Guide)

Questions for Discussion and Analysis

Feedback for "Questions for Discussion and Analysis"

QUESTIONS FOR DISCUSSION AND ANALYSIS:
Segment #2: Reflecting on The Multiple Roles of Teaching

1. How many different roles did the teacher display in this segment?

2. What other roles do teachers perform that weren't explicitly highlighted in this segment?

3. What multiple roles did the teacher perform in terms of management?

4. How many different types of instruction were captured on the video?

5. What kinds of different educational goals did the teacher either teach for or discuss?

**Feedback for "Questions for Discussion and Analysis" for
Segment #2: Reflecting on the Multiple Roles of Teaching**

1. The segment focused primarily on planning, management, instruction, and assessment.

2. Some additional roles might include motivation, accommodating individual differences, teaching students with exceptionalities, and professional leadership at the school and district level.

3. In addition to the interactive aspects of planning, the teacher also planned for management, the logistics of learning materials, and the physical environment.

4. The teacher used whole group instruction, cooperative learning, one-to-one instruction and role playing.

5. In addition to cognitive skills the teacher also focused on self-concept and self-esteem, social and group interaction skills, and the development of independent learning and problem solving skills.

Educational Psychology Video Package: Video II
Segment #3: Essential Teaching Skills

BEFORE YOU BEGIN

This 18-minute segment focuses on a junior high biology teacher discussing different worm phyla. Through questioning and learning aides the teacher involves the class in the learning activity.

This segment can be most effectively used with the section *Essential Teaching Skills* of Chapter 13.

INSTRUCTIONAL RESOURCES

Transparencies (From the Transparency Package)

T 13.4   Essential Teaching Skills

T 13.6   Characteristics of Effective Questioning

Transparency Masters (From the Instructor's Manual)

TM 7.4 Questions That Promote Deep Processing of Information

Transparency Masters (In this Media Guide)

Questions for Discussion and Analysis

Feedback for "Questions for Discussion and Analysis"

QUESTIONS FOR
DISCUSSION AND ANALYSIS:
Segment #3: Essential Teaching Skills

1. To what extent did the teacher exhibit the following essential teaching attitudes?
   a. High Efficacy
   b Democratic

2. Evaluate the teacher's organization in terms of:
   a. Starting on Time
   b. Preparing Materials in Advance
   c. Established Routines

3. Identify examples of the following different types of focus:
   a. Introductory Focus
   b. Sensory Focus

4. Evaluate the teacher in terms of the following questioning dimensions:
   a. Frequency
   b. Equitable Distribution
   c. Prompting

**Feedback for "Questions for Discussion and Analysis" for
Segment #3: Essential Teaching Skills**

1. In terms of efficacy, the teacher did a good job of accepting student answers, and used praise and time effectively. Though we only have indirect evidence, the classroom appeared democratic.

2. The teacher was well prepared in terms of learning materials and aids.

3. *Introductory Focus*   The teacher used introductory focus when he asked the students to go to the window to tell what they saw. He followed this with the question, "Why would Charles Darwin say that worms are one of the most important creatures?"

    Sensory Focus   The lesson was quite effective with respect to sensory focus. Different forms of sensory focus include the examples of different types of symmetry, the three diagrams on the board representing different worm phyla, and the ribbon that illustrated potential lengths of tapeworms.

4. *Frequency*   The teacher asked a large number of questions which encouraged students' active involvement.

    Equitable Distribution   The teacher seemed to make a concerted effort to call on and involve a large number of students.

    Prompting   Most of his questions were answered correctly the first time. One instance of prompting occurred when students couldn't provide an adequate definition of radial symmetry. The teacher prompted, "What is the starfish doing?"

Educational Psychology Video Package: Video II
Segment #4: Involving Students Through Groupwork

BEFORE YOU BEGIN

In this 17-minute segment we see students involved in groupwork in three different ways. In the first segment (about 5 minutes), a sixth grade teacher uses group activities to help students master content and learn to work together. In the second segment (about 5.5 minutes), a junior high science teacher uses student groups to learn the reproductive cycle of the sheep liver fluke and to teach students how to develop mnemonic devices to remember information. In the third segment (about 6.5 minutes), the same science teacher uses small groups to teach higher order thinking skills and problem solving by asking different groups to come up with creative solutions to the problem of breaking the sheep liver fluke's parasitic cycle. The segment can be used in a number of ways to stimulate students' thinking on the following topics:

Topic	Chapter
Cooperative Learning	8
Motivation in the Classroom	11
Essential Teaching Skills	13

INSTRUCTIONAL RESOURCES

Transparencies (From the Transparency Package)

T 1.1   Comparisons of Learning-Focused and Performance-Focused Classrooms

T 11.2   A Model for Promoting Student Motivation

T 13.4   Essential Teaching Skills

T 13.6   Characteristics of Effective Questioning

Transparency Masters (From the Instructor's Manual)

TM 8.4 Principles of Instruction for Applying Constructivism in Classrooms

TM 8.6 Characteristics of Cooperative Learning

TM 8.7 Capitalizing on Diversity with Cooperative Learning

Transparency Masters (In this Media Guide)

Questions for Discussion and Analysis

Feedback for "Questions for Discussion and Analysis"

547

QUESTIONS FOR
DISCUSSION AND ANALYSIS:
Segment #4: Involving Students Through Groupwork

1. How well did the teachers in the three episodes follow these guidelines for implementing effective groupwork activities?
   a. Training Students on Simple Tasks
   b. Provide a Clear and Specific Task
   c. Require a Product
   d. Monitor Group Progress

2. How did the goals for the three activities differ?

3. Which of the three kinds of activities would be easiest to implement? Hardest? Why?

4. How were these activities different from:
   a. Peer Tutoring
   b. Discussions

Feedback for "Questions for Discussion and Analysis" for
Segment #4: Involving Students Through Groupwork

1. *Training Students on Simple Tasks*
   We don't have any evidence regarding pre-training other than to infer from student behavior that it occurred.

   Provide a Clear and Specific Task
   The teachers in all three segments provided clear, specific tasks that the groups were to accomplish.

   Require a Product
   All three segments had clearly identifiable products. In the first it was the answers to the twenty questions; in the second it was the mnemonic device; and in the third it was the solution to the problem of breaking the parasitic cycle.

   Monitor Group Progress
   All three teachers circulated around the room and used this time to work with students in the groups.

2. The teacher in the first segment was focusing on content acquisition and used the activity as a motivational tool. The teacher in the second segment used the activity to teach study skills--how to create a mnemonic device to remember the life cycle of the sheep liver fluke. The teacher in the third segment used the activity to develop students' thinking and problem solving skills.

3. The first type of activity would be easiest to implement because students already know how to answer questions from a book. The major skill the teacher worked on in this segment was interpersonal skills and group problem solving. Probably the hardest to implement would be the third; this involved open-ended problem solving which required both knowledge of the content domain (the life cycle of the sheep liver fluke), as well as knowledge of problem solving strategies.

4. *Peer Tutoring*
   In peer tutoring there are typically convergent answers, with one student acting as teacher and the other as tutee. The first segment came closest here didn't involve peer teaching per se.

   Discussions
   Discussions are typically open-ended activities that build on previous knowledge. The third segment comes closest to a discussion; it builds on previous content knowledge and poses a focused, but open-ended problem.

549

Educational Psychology Video Package: Video II
Segment #5: Teaching Whole Language

BEFORE YOU BEGIN

This 10 and a half minute segment shows a first grade teacher using a variety of instructional strategies to develop students' language and help them learn to read. The first section begins with the teacher building on students' background knowledge by asking them about their favorite foods. Then the class is involved in the choral reading of a patterned book. The teacher reads the first part of each page and the class responds with the second part.

After the choral reading students break off into several related activities. In one, students listen to a tape of the story just read as they follow along in their own books. In another activity, students write stories about their own favorite foods. In a third activity students read to each other out of the same book.

The segment can be used in a number of ways to stimulate students' thinking on the following topics:

Topic	Chapter
Language Development	2
Motivation in the Classroom	11
Essential Teaching Skills	13

INSTRUCTIONAL RESOURCES

Transparencies (From the Transparency Package)

T 2.1   Factors Influencing Human Intellectual Development

T 2.8   The Zone of Proximal Development

T 10.1 Extrinsic and Intrinsic Motivation

T 10.2 A Model for Promoting Student Motivation

T 11.1 Comparisons of Learning-Focused and Performance-Focused Classrooms

T 13.4 Essential Teaching Skills

T 13.6 Characteristics of Effective Questioning

Transparency Masters (From the Instructor's Manual)

TM 2.6 A Comparison of Piaget's and Vygotsky's Views of Knowledge Construction

TM 2.7 Principles of Instruction for Applying Vygotsky's Theory in Classrooms

TM 8.4 Principles of Instruction for Applying Constructivism in Classrooms

Transparency Masters (In this Media Guide)

Questions for Discussion and Analysis

Feedback for "Questions for Discussion and Analysis"

QUESTIONS FOR DISCUSSION AND ANALYSIS
Segment #5: Teaching Whole Language

1. Which of the following theories of language development were most congruent with the teaching and learning activities in the segment? Least?
   a. Behaviorist Theory
   b. Social Cognitive Theory
   c. Psycholinguistic Theories

2. To what extent did the lesson segment illustrate the following characteristics of whole language?
   a. Use of language to describe experiences
   b. Use of language to communicate with others
   c. Use of language across the curriculum

3. How well did the teacher demonstrate or facilitate the following variables from the Model for Promoting Student Motivation?
   a. Enthusiasm
   b. Caring
   c. Success
   d. Personalization
   e. Involvement

4. How well did the teacher demonstrate the following essential teaching skills?
   a. Organization
   b. Focus
   c. Monitoring
   d. Questioning

**Feedback for "Questions for Discussion and Analysis" for
Segment #5: Teaching Whole Language**

1. Probably the theory that is most congruent with the activities is social cognitive theory, which emphasizes learning through observation and modeling. By listening to and observing others use language students develop their own language abilities. Also, the teacher used a good deal of praise and positive reinforcement in her verbal interactions with students, which is congruent with behaviorist theories. We have little evidence about psycholinguistic theories which posit an innate language acquisition device.

2. The teacher did an effective job at the beginning of the lesson to activate students' background knowledge by asking them to describe their favorite foods. In terms of communicating with others, she also had them write about their favorite foods. The tape segment didn't contain specific attempts to create bridges across the curriculum (except in art in which they drew pictures of their favorite food), but these could easily be made in areas like science, health and social studies.

3. *Enthusiasm*   The teacher demonstrated positive levels of enthusiasm.

   Caring   The emotional tone of the classroom appeared very warm. You may wish to ask students to identify specific teacher behaviors that communicated warmth and caring. Some might include: eye contact, smiling, body stance, calling on students by names, accepting student responses, and the silent cheer at the end of the choral reading.

   Success   By using open-ended questions (e.g. "What is your favorite food?") the teacher promoted both involvement and success.

   Personalization   The teacher achieved this by asking for students' favorite foods and by allowing them to write about these foods later on.

   Involvement   This was a particular lesson strength. Students were involved during choral reading, while listening to tapes, during writing and reading their "stories" and through interactive reading.

4. *Organization*   The teacher was well organized. Materials were available and ready to use and students had a variety of activities to keep them busy.

   Focus   The lesson had excellent focus. The teacher used the larger framework of favorite foods to link together all the separate activities.

   Monitoring   The teacher also did a good job here. The best explicit example came when she circulated around to check on students' writing progress.

   Questioning   The best example of this occurred at the beginning of the segment. She used an open-ended question to involve a large number of students, accepting all reasonable answers and prompting to obtain more specific responses.

A PRIVATE UNIVERSE

This 18-minute video focuses on misconceptions and how they can persist even after instruction. The video opens on a graduation ceremony at Harvard University. Graduates are asked simple questions related to astronomy. They are asked why we have different seasons of the year and why the moon has different phases. The students and faculty members interviewed offer incorrect explanations for these phenomena despite having college degrees and in some instances extensive experience in science and even astronomy-related fields. The scene then shifts to a nearby Cambridge high school, where ninth graders who have initially had little or no instruction related to the two phenomena in question offer answers similar to those of Harvard students. The video then focuses on one especially capable ninth grade girl both before and after instruction on these topics. Although the student shows improved understanding after instruction, questions that probe into her reasoning reveal that she still holds on to many of her prior misconceptions.

DOUBLE-COLUMN ADDITION:
A TEACHER USES PIAGET'S THEORY

This 20-minute video focuses on Dr. Constance Kamii's applications of Piaget's theory to learning math. Children in a second-grade class are assisted through interactive questioning to develop cognitive strategies for adding and subtracting two-digit numbers. Instead of directly teaching such strategies the teacher helps the children construct their own strategies by posing problems, asking for possible solutions, and encouraging class discussion of different approaches. The students develop a variety of creative strategies for adding and subtracting two-digit numbers, many of which reflect a true conceptual understanding of place value in two-digit numbers.

SIMULATIONS IN EDUCATIONAL PSYCHOLOGY

Accompanying each copy of *Educational Psychology: Windows on Classrooms is* a CD-ROM compact disk, *Simulations in Educational Psychology.* The CD allows students to experience first-hand several virtual activities, places the experiments in a theoretical context, and helps students draw implications for educational practice. An optional "Educational Research" track, connected with four of the simulations, allows students to explore research and read a journal article or book chapter related to the topic in question. Each simulation is designed to stand on its own and be self-explanatory.

There are five simulations on this CD-ROM:
- The Pendulum Experiment
- Assessing Moral Reasoning
- Bartlett's Ghosts
- Intuitive Physics
- Assessment in the Balance

Using The Simulations In Your Class

Each CD-ROM simulation is identified in the text by a boxed feature, "Using Technology in Your Study of Educational Psychology," which appears in Chapters 2, 3, 7, and 14 and in *Learning in the Content Areas* on the Companion Website.. Once inside the CD-ROM students will be instructed how to use it and directed to the next learning activity.

Each simulation ends with two options: "Opportunities for Learning: Educational Psychology," which examines classroom applications of the content or "Opportunities for Learning: Further Exploration, Educational Research." Depending on your students' background and expertise you can direct them to click on one of two options.

1. (*If you want to introduce basic concepts in research and basic categories of research studies*) When they reach the frame entitled `Further Exploration,' they should click the `Educational Research' button to read a short discussion about concepts and categories related to educational research. When they reach the frame `Reading the Article,' click the `Home' button to exit the program.

2. (*If your students have had some background in reading and analyzing research reports*) When they reach the frame entitled `Further Exploration,' click the `Educational Research' button to read a brief review of basic concepts in educational research. Then they read and analyze a research article about the topic of that simulation. (Note: Depending on the degree of students' knowledge about research methods, you may want them to respond only to a subset of the nine questions the CD poses about the article.)

If all students have access to a computer printer, you might also ask that they click the "Print Report" button before clicking the "Home" button and bring their report to the next class session for discussion.

The Pendulum Experiment (Chapter 2)

This simulation allows students to "experiment" with a virtual pendulum. They can manipulate one or more of three variables (height of release, weight, and length), and the computer keeps an ongoing record of the oscillation rates that result. An explanation of the role that the ability to separate and control variables plays in Piaget's theory of cognitive development is presented. Implications for classroom practice are presented. The simulation relates to the following topics:

- Chapter 2, Piaget's Theory of Intellectual Development
- Chapter 2, Using Technology to Develop Formal Thinking
- Chapter 9, Misconceptions and Conceptual Change

The simulation exists in five sections.

Introduction: Provides an overview of the problem and identifies height of release, weight, and length as possible variables influencing oscillation rate.

Laboratory: In this section students experiment with the three variables. In the design of their experiment students are asked to:

- Form a hypothesis (By selecting one or more variables to test)
- Design an experiment (By selecting levels or units within each variable)
- Run the experiments (The simulation provides immediate results)
- Analyze results (which appear in a table).

Reflection and Debrief: Students are asked to analyze what they did. The following text appears to help them in this process:

Did you test each hypothesis in a systematic fashion? A student capable of formal operational thinking separates and controls variables, testing one at a time while holding all others constant. For example, if you were testing the hypothesis that weight makes a difference, you might have tried different weights while keeping constant the length of the arm and the height of release. Similarly, if you hypothesized that the length of the arm was a critical factor, you might have varied the length of the arm while continuing to use the same weight and releasing the pendulum from the same height. If you carefully separated and controlled the variables that you considered, then you would have come to the correct conclusion: Only length affects a pendulum's rate of oscillation.

Opportunities for Learning: Educational Implications: This section has three parts:

- A short discussion of the role of controlling variables in Piaget's Theory of Cognitive Development.
- Three student scenarios taken from Tape Five, *Insights Into Learning: Designing Experiments in Seventh Grade* (parts of this lesson can also be found in *Concepts in Classrooms: Segment 5: Improving Transfer: Applications in Classrooms.*
- Three teaching cases:
  1. Given what you have learned from this CD and from the discussion of Piaget in the text, describe what you might do as Maria's teacher when she says, "We found out that the shorter it is and the heavier it is, the

faster it goes." For example, would you tell her that the group's conclusion is incorrect? If so, what would you say or do next? Explain why you would do this.

2. A high school science teacher asks students in a chemistry lab to find out whether water boils faster when more heat is applied. He gives them the equipment they need and shows them how to use it safely, but provides no additional guidance about how to approach the task. Is this appropriate instructional practice? Explain.

3. Mr. Harvey decides to introduce the scientific method to his fourth-grade class. He explains what the scientific method is and writes this list on the board:

1. Form hypothesis.
2. Design experiment to test hypothesis.
3. Carry out experiment.
4. Observe results.
5. Draw conclusion about hypothesis.

He then explains the importance of designing an experiment such that only one variable varies at a time, while all others remain constant. Considering the characteristics and capabilities of these children from Piaget's point of view, Mr. Harvey has assumed the fourth graders can do at least two things that in fact they probably cannot do. What two crucial capabilities necessary for understanding his lecture do his students probably not yet have? Justify your answer in a short paragraph.

Opportunities for Learning: Educational Research: This option contains a series of frames that discuss basic concepts in educational research (*variable, independent variable, dependent variable, hypothesis*) and several types of research *(historical, qualitative, descriptive, correlational, causal-comparative, experimental)* and a research article related to children's ability to separate and control variables:

Pulos, S., & Linn, M. C. (1981). Generality of the controlling variables scheme in early adolescence. *Journal of Early Adolescence, I, 36-37.*

Students are then asked to respond to the following:

1. State the purpose of the study.
2. What is the independent variable?
3. What is the dependent variable?
4. Describe the sample used.
S. Describe the procedures.
6. Describe the method of analysis.'
7. Describe the results of the study.
8. State the major conclusions.
9. Classify the study-what type of study is it?

Discussion Questions: (See the boxed feature in Chapter 2)

Assessing Moral Reasoning (Chapter 3)

This simulation first presents a moral dilemma that a teacher might face and asks students to decide what the teacher should do and why. It then describes Kohlberg's theory of moral development and illustrates how people at different stages might respond to Kohlberg's classic "Heinz dilemma." Then students are provided opportunities to analyze and score responses to moral dilemmas. The simulation relates to the following topics:

- Chapter3, Kohlberg's theory of moral development
- Chapter3, The moral education versus character education debate.

The simulation exists in four sections:

Introduction. The following situation is presented to illustrate a *moral dilemma:*

> Ms. Cole, an outstanding veteran social studies teacher, specializes in constitutional issues and has raised concerns about her school district's drug testing policy. She has always told her students to follow their conscience when faced with unjust laws. She has recently become the target of a police search-a police dog is alleged to have smelled marijuana in the teacher's car ashtray. Ms. Cole is required to take a mandatory drug test within 48 hours. Since she believes the policy is unconstitutional, she must decide whether to practice what she preaches and refuse to take the drug test or to ignore her conscience and submit to the test. Ms. Cole is one year away from retirement and will lose her job and pension if she refuses to take the test.

> Should the teacher take the drug test? Explain why you think the teacher should or should not take the drug test.

The nature of moral dilemmas is described, and Kohlberg's stage theory of moral reasoning is introduced.

(Assessment Lab): Students are presented with Kohlberg's classic "Heinz dilemma"and nine responses are shown to illustrate reasoning at different stages of moral development. (Kohlberg's Stage 6 is omitted due to its lack of empirical support.) Students then evaluate different responses to three other dilemmas, including the "drug test" dilemma presented above and these "cheating" and "software copying" dilemmas:

> Bruce finds out that some of his classmates obtained the answers to an exam before taking it. He [should/should not] report the cheating because ....

> Mr. Collins is told about some software that will help several of his students improve their understanding of an important math concept. The school administration claims there is no money for the software, even considering the software company's educational discount. The person who told Mr. Collins about the software offers to make him an illegal copy for him to use in his classroom. He [should/should not] accept the free

software because ....

Opportunities for learning: Educational implications. Strategies for promoting moral development are presented, along with the following three issues/problems:

1. Imagine that you teach third grade and that each year all the third grade classes at your school have an annual food drive for the homeless. Over the years, the school has discovered that the food drive is much more successful if prizes are offered for those who bring in the most food. Using Kohlberg's theory, explain why this might be so. Is this likely to be an effective strategy to motivate secondary students to help the homeless? Again using Kohlberg's theory, explain why or why not. If you feel it would not be the most effective motivation strategy with secondary students, offer a strategy that you think might be more effective.

2. Students' moral development is affected not only by their family and friends, but by their school experiences as well. Whether you intend to or not, you will undoubtedly be teaching your students moral values as well as academic content. With this in mind, describe the types of experiences that, according to researchers and theorists, are likely to help students develop morally. In your discussion, identify three different factors that promote moral development.

3. Identify a moral issue that may arise either within a specific content area you will be teaching or within the general classroom situation. Explain what you, as a teacher, might specifically do to promote moral growth as you deal with the issue you just identified.

Opportunities for learning: Educational research. Students (1) read about alternative approaches to assessing moral reasoning and have a firsthand experience with one approach, and /or (2) read and analyze a research article related to assessment of moral reasoning:

Basinger, K. S., Gibbs, J. C., & Fuller, D. (1995). Context and the measurement of moral judgment. *International Journal of Behavioral Development, 18, 537-556.*

Students are then asked to respond to the following:

1. State the purpose of the study.
2. What is the independent variable?
3. What is the dependent variable?
4. Describe the sample used.
5. Describe the procedures.
6. Describe the method of analysis.
7. Describe the results of the study.
8. State the major conclusions.
9. Classify the study-what type of study is it?

Discussion Questions: (See the boxed feature in Chapter 3)

Bartlett's Ghosts (Chapter 7)

This simulation, based on studies conducted by F. C. Bartlett in 1932, explores the impact of background knowledge and expectations on how students perceive an ambiguous reading passage and what they remember from this experience. Students read Bartlett's classic story "War of the Ghosts" and then recall what they can remember of the story. They compare their own version against the original and record omissions, transformations, and additions. Also included are a brief theoretical discussion of schema theory and implications for classroom practice. The simulation relates to the following topics:

- Chapter 7   Perception, Encoding, and the Impact of Diversity on Information Processing
- Chapter 8   Constructivism
- Chapter 9   Misconceptions and Conceptual Change.

The simulation exists in four sections.

War of the Ghosts. A brief passage introduces Bartlett's story, which students are asked to read and then type as much of the story as they can remember. Then they are given the following overview of Bartlett's original experiment.

Bartlett first ran this experiment in 1913. After participants wrote their versions of the "War of the Ghosts," he compared them to the original story. As you would expect, participants' versions omitted, changed, or added details.

But what was novel about Bartlett's approach was his focus on what he called the "effort after meaning," rather than on the accuracy of recall. He theorized that an individual's mental "schemas"-organized bodies of knowledge about specific objects and events would influence what was remembered. Details that did not fit into a person's schemas would be forgotten or transformed into something more familiar. People might add details not in the original because their existing schemas, activated by reading the story, provided details consistent with the meaning of the story.

Of course, different people read different meanings into the story, so Bartlett asked participants to share some of their thoughts after they completed the recall task. He then attempted to explain the omissions, transformations, and additions based on each individual's mental schemas.

Analysis Lab. Students then analyze their own stories for omissions, transformations, and additions. Following their analysis, they read about their errors due to existing schemas and the constructive nature of memory.

Opportunities for learning: Educational implications. In this section students read about schema theory and analyze the following scenarios:

1. Mr. Goldberg's class has already learned that insects have three body parts and six legs. Then he says, "Let's take a look at a picture of a wasp. See? It has all the parts that insects have, so it must be an insect." Given

what you have just learned, is this an effective strategy?

2. Wendy sees a picture of a house and then later tries to draw the house from memory. She draws a chimney on the house, even though the house in the picture had no chimney. .

3. As a third-grade teacher begins to read *Black Beauty* to her class, eight-year-old Casey pictures the main character-a horse-with a shiny coat, a flowing mane, and long black tail.

4. Although no one has ever told her so, Joyce insists that Democrats are better than Republicans because a democracy is the best kind of government to have and the Democrats believe in democracy.

Opportunities for learning: Educational research. In this section students: (1) analyze two stories that Bartlett's original subjects produced and/or (2) read and analyze the following research article on knowledge construction:

Bransford, J. D., & Johnson, M. K. (1972). Contextual prerequisites for understanding: Some investigations of comprehension and recall. *Journal of Verbal Learning and Verbal Behavior, II,* 717-726.

Students are then asked to respond to the following:

1. State the purpose of the study.
2. What is the independent variable?
3. What is the dependent variable?
4. Describe the sample used.
5. Describe the procedures.
6. Describe the method of analysis.
7. Describe the results of the study.
8. State the major conclusions.
9. Classify the study-what type of study is it?

Discussion Questions: (See the boxed feature in Chapter 7)

Intuitive Physics (*Learning in the Content Areas* on the Companion Website)

This simulation investigates how student misconceptions about science content are formed and influence subsequent cognitive processes. Students are asked to predict the path that an object will take when it: (a) is pushed over the edge of a cliff, (b) is carried along a conveyor belt and reaches the end of the belt, and (c) is carried by a flying airplane and then released. Students receive feedback about the path that the object will actually take in each instance, and relevant principles of physics are described. The resistance of student misconceptions to change is discussed, and recommendations for promoting conceptual change are presented. The simulation relates to the following topics:

- Chapter 7: Encoding, and Impact of Diversity on Information Processing
- Chapter 8: Constructivism
- Chapter 9: Transfer

- Learning in the Content Areas: Found on Companion Website and Student Study Guide

The simulation exists in five sections.

Identifying Beliefs About Motion. Students are given several illustrations related to the physical motion of moving objects such as a ball pushed off the edge of a cliff, and are given the following explanation.

In 1687, Sir Isaac Newton published his theories on gravity and motion. Three hundred years later, we still rely on his theories to calculate the motion of objects. The power of a theory is its ability to ignore irrelevant features and focus on underlying principles. When you apply Newton's theory to these two problems, you ignore how the ball was put into motion. All that matters is that an object continues to move in a straight line unless acted upon by external forces, such as gravity and air resistance. Whether the ball was pushed, shot from a cannon, carried by a conveyor belt or a person makes no difference. Since the Newtonian view is not distracted by this irrelevant aspect of the two problems, it results in the same (correct) prediction each time. Two identical objects traveling at the same speed will trace the same path (falling to the earth due to the influence of gravity and air resistance), regardless of how they achieved that speed.

Prior to Newton, scientists believed that a person throwing an object imparted a force, often called an "impetus," that stayed with the object even after it left the grasp of the thrower. Someone holding an impetus view may believe that a force, or impetus, is imparted to the pushed or propelled ball but NOT the carried ball, and therefore, predict different paths for the cliff and the conveyor situations.

Then students read about common student misconceptions about "impetus" and are provided with several examples of student explanations that reflect this misconception. Students learn that the "impetus" misconception is common even among students who have studied physics in high school or college; they also read examples of student statements that reflect the misconception.

Transfer task. Students are then asked to predict the path of an object dropped from a plane. After students make a prediction, the correct answer-a path identical to that in the cliff and conveyor problems-is shown in an animated fashion.

Debrief. The persistence of student misconceptions is discussed, and several teaching strategies for addressing students' misconceptions are described.

Opportunities for learning: Educational implications. Principles related to conceptual change are presented, and students are asked to respond to the following questions and to compare their responses with those that an expert might recommend:

1. Imagine that you have to teach a lesson to middle school children on what causes the seasons. Given what you have learned from the rolling ball problem and from the discussion of how to promote conceptual change, how might you start the lesson? (1) Describe what you would do in specific terms.

For example, if you decide to start the lesson by showing students a diagram, describe the diagram (e.g.. the diagram would show the earth, tilted on its axis revolving around the sun). And (2) explain why you have chosen to start in this way (e.g., giving the students a concrete representation of the reason we have seasons will help the students "see" the concept we are discussing).

2. What would you do next? Again, be specific and explain why you have chosen this step.

3. How and when would you assess what students have learned? Again, be specific and explain why you have chosen this step.

Opportunities for learning: Educational research. In this section, students (1) read a brief passage about how research about misconceptions can guide teaching practice, and/or (2) read and analyze the following book chapter about student misconceptions:

McCloskey, M. (1983). Naive theories of motion. In D. Gentner & A. L. Stevens (Eds.), *Mental* models. Hillsdale, NJ: Erlbaum.

Students are then asked to respond to the following:

1.   State the purpose of the study.
2.   What is the independent variable?
3.   What is the dependent variable?
4.   Describe the sample used.
S.   Describe the procedures.
6.   Describe the method of analysis.
7.   Describe the results of the study.
8.   State the major conclusions.
9.   Classify the study-what type of study is it?

Discussion Questions: (See the boxed feature in Learning in the Content Areas on the Companion Website)

ASSESSMENT IN THE BALANCE (Chapter 14)

This simulation allows students to examine children's reasoning about problems involving beam balances and gives them hands-on practice with both performance and paper-pencil assessment tasks. In the first part of the simulation, students construct a variety of beam balance problems and see how four different children (William, Marta, Chrys, and Ravi) solve each problem; your students' task is to form and test hypotheses about the mental model each child is using while reasoning about the problems. Later, students examine and analyze three classroom artifacts: a kindergartner's attempt to write the numbers 1-20, a fourth grader's science lab report, and a seventh grader's English essay. Students are asked to reflect on the assessment activities they have completed, and general guidelines for classroom assessment are offered.

The simulation relates to the following chapters:

Chapter 14: Assessing Classroom Learning
Chapter 15: Assessment Through Standardized Testing

Detailed Description

The simulation has three parts:

Part I: Assessment in the Balance (Frames 3-24) explores how teachers can make inferences about students' mental models by posing beam balance problems. In the first part, the general nature of beam balance problems is described, but at this point no information about how to solve such problems is given. Students are urged to look beyond the particular answers that children give and to consider the reasoning that underlies their answers. By looking at the responses of four focal students, the reader learns that three things are important for adequately assessing students' performance:

Content knowledge: In our beam balance example, you yourself needed to understand how the balances works.

Mental models: You needed to understand different ways in which someone can think about how the balance works.

Problem construction: You needed to be able to construct problems that would assess and differentiate the ways in which your four students came up with their answers.

Four possible mental models of a beam balance are described:
1. Some children focus exclusively on weight.
2. Others begin to consider distance, but only under limited   circumstances.
3. Students who always consider distance and weight may not know what to do when distance is greater on one side and weight is greater on the other.
4. Some students know that the downward force, or "torque," on one side is equal to the weight times the distance from the fulcrum. They use this formula to compare the torque on each side and determine which side, if either, will tilt down.

Video clips are presented in which three children solve beam balance problems in a classroom, and students are asked to draw inferences about the children's mental models. At the end of Part I students look at the nature of assessment more generally, and assessment is described as having three primary purposes:

- It can promote students' learning.
- It can promote the development of self-regulation skills.
- It can help teachers determine whether instructional goals have been achieved.

Part II

Kindergarten: Numbers contains an analysis of three artifacts. A kindergartner writes the numbers 1-20. Students type notes regarding conclusions they can draw from these numbers. They are then asked if, in their assessment, they considered each of the following in their analysis:

- Knowledge of the correct order of different numbers
- Knowledge about right-left and top-bottom orientation
- Eye-hand coordination

After reexamining the artifact with these characteristics in mind, they compare their own analysis with that of an expert and are asked to reflect on why the child might have made the errors he did. They also consider how the assessment task might be used for each of the three purposes of assessment introduced in Part I.

Grade 4: Lab Report: A fourth grader has written a lab report about his group's dissection of a cow's eye. Students read the report and draw preliminary conclusions about the child's knowledge and abilities. They are then asked if they considered each of the following in their analysis:

- Knowledge about how vision works
- Knowledge about the anatomy of the eye
- Ability to follow directions
- Written language skills
- Handwriting and/or eye-hand coordination

After reexamining the lab report with these characteristics in mind, they compare their own analysis with that of an expert and look more closely at what the report reveals about the child's knowledge of science, spelling, and sentence structure. They consider how the report might be helpful for the three purposes of assessment presented in Part I.

Grade 7: English essay: A seventh grader has written an argumentative essay. After conducting an initial evaluation, students are asked if they considered each of the following in their analysis:

- Choice of a particular position on the issue
- Use of three reasons or sources of evidence in support of the position
- Clear, in-depth explanation of each reason or source of evidence
- Knowledge of writing mechanics (e.g. capitalization, punctuation, spelling, indentation, grammatical correctness
- Neatness
- Relationship with family
- Attitudes about homework

After reexamining the essay with these characteristics in mind, they compare their analysis with that of an expert and consider how they might use the essay for each of the three purposes of assessment identified in Part I.

Part III: General discussion of assessment. Students are asked to reflect on five general principles of assessment:

1. To effectively assess students' work, you yourself must have mastered the content being assessed.
2. Your judgments about a student's performance should depend of what children at different ages can reasonably be expected to do.
3. Classroom assessments must be related to instructional goals.
4. Any single assessment can simultaneously yield information about students' learning and achievement in several different areas.
5. The more relevant information an assessment yields, the better able teachers are to identify an appropriate course for future instruction.

Discussion Questions (See the boxed feature in Chapter 14)